CREATION CARE AND THE GOSPEL

RECONSIDERING THE MISSION OF THE CHURCH

Lausanne Library

CREATION CARE AND THE GOSPEL

RECONSIDERING THE MISSION OF THE CHURCH

EDITED BY COLIN BELL AND ROBERT S WHITE

FOREWORD BY LASCELLES G NEWMAN
INTRODUCTION BY EDWARD R BROWN

Creation Care and the Gospel: Reconsidering the Mission of the Church

Hendrickson Publishers Marketing, LLC
P. O. Box 3473
Peabody, Massachusetts 01961-3473
www.hendrickson.com

ISBN 978-1-61970-725-2

Printed in the United States of America

First Printing—May 2016

Printed on paper that contains post-consumer recycled fiber, using soy-based inks.

MIX
Paper from responsible sources
FSC
www.fsc.org   FSC® C005010

Library of Congress Cataloging-in-Publication Data

Names: Bell, Colin (Colin Roy), editor.
Title: Creation care and the gospel : reconsidering the mission of the church / edited by Colin Bell and Robert S. White.
Description: Peabody, MA : Hendrickson Publishers, 2016. | Includes bibliographical references.
Identifiers: LCCN 2015049444 | ISBN 9781619707252 (alk. paper)
Subjects: LCSH: Creation. | Ecotheology. | Human ecology--Religious aspects--Christianity. | Mission of the church.
Classification: LCC BT695.5 .C747 2016 | DDC 261.8/8--dc23
LC record available at http://lccn.loc.gov/2015049444

Contents

Acknowledgements   viii

Foreword—*Las G Newman*   ix

Introduction—*Colin Bell, Robert S White, and Edward R Brown*   1

Call to Action and Exposition
     Jonathan A Moo, Dave Bookless, and Lowell Bliss   7

PART 1—GOD'S WORD

Chapter 1   Ruling God's World God's Way: Dominion in Psalm 8
     Edward R Brown   17

Chapter 2   The Biblical Basis for Creation Care
     Jonathan A Moo   28

Chapter 3   Ecological Hope in Crisis?
     Richard Bauckham   43

Chapter 4   Environmental Missions: An Introduction
     Lowell Bliss   53

Chapter 5   Creation Care and the Great Commission
     Craig Sorley   71

Chapter 6   How Does Creation Care Belong within an
Evangelical Understanding of Mission?
     Dave Bookless   86

Chapter 7   Creation Care: A Brief Overview of
Christian Involvement
     R J (Sam) Berry   103

PART 2—GOD'S WORLD

Chapter 8   Global Warming, Climate Change, and
Sustainability: Challenges to Scientists,
Policymakers, and Christians
     John Houghton   119

Chapter 9   Poverty and Climate Change
     Dorothy Boorse   146

Chapter 10   Is the Weather Going Crazy? Impacts of Climate
              Change in the Cusco Region of Peru
              Juliana Morillo Horne   159

Chapter 11   Population and Ecological Sustainability
              John P McKeown   175

Chapter 12   Unnatural Disasters
              Robert S White   192

Chapter 13   Biodiversity Loss: A Christian Concern?
              Martin J Hodson   208

Chapter 14   Creation Care of the Other 71%
              Meric Srokosz and Robert D Sluka   225

Chapter 15   Planetary Boundaries and the Green Economy
              Paul Cook   237

PART 3—GOD'S WORK

Chapter 16   Holistic Environmental Stewardship in East Africa
              Serah Wambua   249

Chapter 17   The Church and Sustainable Cities in East Asia
              David Gould   263

Chapter 18   Creation Care as a Ministry of Reconciliation:
              A Framework for Environmental Missions
              Susan D Emmerich   275

CONCLUSION

Conclusion   Towards a Robust Theology of the Environment
              Ken Gnanakan   289

CASE STUDIES

Case study 1   Improvisational Drama, Australian Church
                 Youth, and Climate Change: An Educational
                 Tool for Bringing about Positive Changes
                 Sally Shaw   68

Case study 2   The Work of A Rocha Ghana
                 Seth Appiah-Kubi   84

Case study 3   Caring for Creation Down Under: Friends
                 of A Rocha Australia
                 Mick Pope   101

Case study 4   Drought and Flooding in Bangladesh
                James Pender   144

Case study 5   ECHO, a Community Development and
                Agriculture Organization
                Stan Doerr   157

Case study 6   Can the Desert Be Green? Asian Journeys'
                Green Desert Project in Inner Mongolia
                Lawrence Ko   206

Case study 7   Restoring a Mountain, Reconciling
                Communities: A Rocha in Aotearoa
                New Zealand
                Andrew Shepherd   221

Case study 8   Evolving Church Action on Deforestation
                in Argentina
                Andrew Leake   245

Case study 9   A Case Study from Uganda
                Sara Kaweesa   261

Case study 10   A Rocha Living Waterways
                Dave Bookless   273

Appendix   Living Out Our Care for Creation   301

Author Profiles   311

Lausanne Movement   320

Notes   321

Acknowledgements

We are grateful to the organizers of the Jamaica Consultation on which this book is based, to the authors who worked hard at putting their thoughts down in writing, and especially to Las Newman and Ed Brown for all their work in making the conference a success. Mary Davis brought considerable copy-editing skills to the task of melding the diverse manuscripts into a coherent whole, and Julia Cameron from the Lausanne Movement oversaw its publication. Funding which made possible the preparation of the book came from The Faraday Institute for Science and Religion, the John Ray Initiative, and the Hinchley Charitable Trust.

Associated titles from the Lausanne Library

- *The Cape Town Commitment: A Confession of Faith and a Call to Action*

- *The Cape Town Commitment Study Edition* by Rose Dowsett

- *The Cape Town Call: A Call to Action* (book/DVD for small groups) by Sara Singleton and Matt Ristuccia

- *The Cape Town Commitment: Bibliographic Resources* ed Darrell Bock

- *Christ our Reconciler: Gospel/Church/World* ed J E M Cameron (formal published record of The Third Lausanne Congress on World Evangelization)

Foreword

Las G Newman

After the historic Third Lausanne Congress on World Evangelization in Cape Town, South Africa, in October 2010, each of the Lausanne global regions was invited to host a Global Consultation on one of the major issues arising from the Congress. I immediately signed up my region, the Caribbean, to host a consultation on Creation Care.

The Global Consultation on Creation Care and the Gospel took place in Jamaica from 29 October–2 November 2012, the first such Global Consultation following the Congress. And what an amazing experience it was! We had over 50 participants from 23 countries as diverse as Argentina, Bangladesh, Benin, and Canada gathering for five days to pray, talk, and reflect on the state of the planet, the home in which we live, and on the role and ministry of the church in caring for God's creation.

As if to underscore the importance and the urgency of what we had gathered to discuss, a ferocious hurricane arrived exactly a week before the consultation, and threatened to derail it. Hurricane Sandy was one of the deadliest and most destructive hurricanes in the Atlantic region for a long time. Sandy killed at least 285 people in seven countries, destroyed 305,000 homes, and cost some $75 billion in damage. Sandy travelled all the way from the Caribbean, up the Atlantic coast to Canada. It was a brutal reminder that all over the world we are witnessing extreme weather conditions that are causing havoc to many lives, especially among the poor and disempowered. Climate change is a reality.

We had some remarkable presentations, demonstrating how God's people around the world are being moved by their faith in Christ to undertake big and small projects to conserve, steward, and nurture the environment in ways that enhance the sustainability of life on earth. One of these presentations was the green desert project in Mongolia (see Case Study 6) led by Lawrence Ko. With a remarkable team of young Singaporeans across church denominations, they are engaged in a concerted anti-desertification project in the Mongolian desert that could have a major impact on China. This is an exciting project, and captures the vision and energetic imagination of youth in the creative responses needed to address ecological crises.

Caribbean perspective

My own contribution to the consultation was a plenary response from a Caribbean perspective to the presentations of Sir John Houghton and Prof Bob White. Both spoke about the human impact on the environment and made the case for human agency in the changes to the Earth's atmosphere, land surface, marine environment and climate over time. Both presenters emphasized human responsibility to mitigate the effects of disasters that occur as a consequence. For Small Island Developing States (SIDS), such as those in the Caribbean, this is an urgent issue. Even as visitors and locals delight in the breath-taking beauty and magnificence of the Caribbean, this region is known for its vulnerability to catastrophic disasters. They range from tropical storms, hurricanes, volcanic eruptions, droughts, floods, earthquakes, and extreme weather effects, to the rampant poverty and violence which have impacted natural, physical, marine, and social environments.

Christian spirituality

The emphasis on prayer and Christian fellowship at the Jamaica Consultation was a great reminder of the integral place of worship of our creator God—it added the important ingredient of Christian spirituality, based on God's self-revelation in word and deed. This helped tremendously in the reflective exercises on the state of God's creation as we find it in the world today.

In a spirit of prayer and fellowship, participants worked hard and left with a strong *Call to Action* (see page xx). This is an important statement for the global church. Among other things, it calls particular attention to the need for leadership from the church in the Global South to help set the agenda for the advance of the gospel and the care of creation. It also highlights the need to mobilize the whole church and all of society in the task. We need to utilize the gifts of men, women, children, youth, and indigenous people as well as professionals and others who possess experience and expertise; we also need to engage with responsible leadership in government, business, civil society, and academia. It is the Global South—the countries of Africa, Asia, Latin America, and the Caribbean—that bears the brunt and the burden of the ecological crisis. Thankfully, the church of the Global South has begun to embrace this call to action.

Ecological responsibility

As the Jamaica Consultation passionately affirmed: 'urgent and prophetic ecological responsibility' is needed by the whole church.[1] It is the whole church, the united body of Christ, which is called upon and commissioned by our Lord to proclaim the whole gospel to the whole world. The Christian gospel is a gospel of hope for the life of *the world to come*—a hope that should inform our present reality. The brokenness of our world is set against the background of the truth of God's sovereignty over it and his ultimate plans for redeeming it.

I urge everyone to wake up to the challenge. I pray that you will be inspired and enabled by this book to communicate the urgency of the global task of caring for God's creation.

Introduction

Colin Bell, Robert S White, and Edward R Brown

'Creation care is thus a gospel issue within the Lordship of Christ.'

Cape Town Commitment

These words from the *Cape Town Commitment* sum up the motivation behind this book. They are why 31 authors from 6 continents, coming from a variety of academic perspectives and different kinds of personal experience, are able to write with such a similar passion and unity of voice. And they are the reason you need to read this book.

There have been dozens of 'statements' about creation care in the last 20 years, but few that are as important as the creation care affirmations found in the *Cape Town Commitment*. It is a deceptively simple conclusion: What could be more obvious than that 'creation care is a gospel issue'? But it is one that echoes with implications and ramifications for the global evangelical community. This is not an environmental agency, like Care of Creation or A Rocha, saying to the church, 'This is what you *should* believe.' This is the church saying to itself, 'This is what we *do* believe.'

Saying we believe something, and living out that belief with appropriate action, are two different things. The writer of Ecclesiastes famously noted that 'of the writing of books there is no end'; we could say the same for conferences and consultations in our day. Which is why, when the leaders of the Lausanne Movement decided to sponsor a series of Global Consultations to explore themes in the *Cape Town Commitment*, one of the first topics chosen was creation care, a consultation which could produce tangible and meaningful results. And it has.

The first product of our work was the *Jamaica Call to Action*, a document that you will find referred to frequently in the chapters that follow. The second outcome is this book, containing some of the best evangelical thinking on the issues. It is divided into the following sections:

- God's Word—what do the Bible and biblical theology have to say?

- God's World—what does scientific reseach have to tell us about what is happening in God's creation?

- God's Work—which is really *our work* in response to these two: 'What shall we then do?'

The third outcome from the Jamaica Consultation is a Global Campaign for Creation Care and the Gospel that has been running since 2014.

The *Call to Action* document contains a remarkably comprehensive list of action points, beginning with 'simple lifestyle' and ending with 'prophetic advocacy and healing reconciliation.' Its most important features, however, are its two simple convictions near the beginning and an eloquent call to prayer at the end.

A gospel issue

The first conviction is a restatement of the phrase from the *Cape Town Commitment*: 'Creation care is indeed "a gospel issue within the Lordship of Christ".'[1] We wanted to affirm for ourselves and for our evangelical sisters and brothers around the world that our exploration of this topic has made us even more convinced that creation care is central to our faith. It is 'an integral part of our mission and an expression of our worship of God.' And, importantly, this is 'a matter of great joy and hope, and we would care for creation *even if it were not in crisis.*'

We emphasize that last phrase, for here we have one of the most important things that Christians can bring to the wider (secular) environmental movement. Our motivation is not guilt, though there is enough of that to go around. It is not born out of panic, though those who study these things are the first to admit that there are plenty of reasons to panic. And it is not self-interest, enlightened or otherwise. No—we care for God's creation because it is something we ought to be doing in joy and in obedience.

This first conviction undergirds Part 1 of this book, and we trust you can feel some of that hope and joy in these chapters.

David Bookless, Jonathan Moo, and Lowell Bliss open with an exploration of the startling statement cited above, explaining how the gospel connects with creation care, and importantly, why creation care finds a home within the Lausanne Movement. Edward Brown's chapter is a study of Psalm 8 and confronts head-on the question of human dominion over creation. Often blamed as part of the problem, what if it turns out to be the solution? In Chapter 2, Jonathan Moo takes us deep into creation care theology, helping us to discover 'what sort of orientation towards the world is expected of us if we take seriously both what science reveals to us about the state of the planet, and what Scripture reveals about God, ourselves, and the world of his creation.' Richard Bauckham discusses a word desperately needed when we confront the state of God's creation—*hope*—and he makes a vital distinction between 'proximate' and 'ultimate' hope.

In the following three chapters, Lowell Bliss, Craig Sorley and Dave Bookless make connections between creation care and missions. The mission of the church has been commonly understood to be the evangelization of the world; how does creation care fit into, and inform, that understanding? Bliss introduces environmental missions as a new category 'akin to medical missions.' Sorley shows from personal experience how creation care can be a vehicle for discipleship and can transform lives, landscapes, and society itself. And Bookless explains how an evangelical missiology can not only invigorate missionary efforts but also has the potential to transform the wider secular environmental movement.

Finally, Sam Berry brings an important summary of how God's people have viewed and wrestled throughout history with some of the same questions we are facing today. Moving from Origen in the second century to Lynn White, Joseph Sittler and the *Earth Charter*, Berry provides an historical framework for all of these discussions. Of particular importance is his review of Pope Francis' encyclical *Laudato Si,* noting how that document, critical for Roman Catholic thinking, also contains common themes for the evangelical community.

An urgent crisis

Alas, creation is, in fact, in crisis—a fact that informs the *Call to Action*'s second conviction: 'We are faced with a crisis that is pressing, urgent, and that must be resolved in our generation.' It is important to understand the connection between these two affirmations: if we had fulfilled our obligations under the first conviction, we would not even have to state the second one. But we did not heed the first and, because of that, we now have to deal with the devastating consequences that are at work in the world: 'Many of the world's poorest people, ecosystems, and species of flora and fauna are being devastated by violence against the environment in multiple ways.'

One of the mysteries we wrestle with is how this crisis could become so serious without anyone noticing. Those of us who work in the field of creation care or environmental science or even international development have no doubts about the urgency of the task ahead—this is one area where the more you know, the more fearful you are about the future. Many of the rest of us have blithely gone about our business, like cars on a highway driving into a fog bank at top speed, unaware or unconvinced that there are hazards ahead, and that they should have been slowing down long before.

Part 2, 'God's World,' should be read like a set of flashing warning signs on that fogbound highway. Like road workers who know what lies ahead, these authors have spent their lives studying what is happening to God's creation, and we need to heed what they have to tell us.

Climate change is not our only challenge, but it is a big one, so it is appropriate that Sir John Houghton, formerly of the Intergovernmental Panel on Climate Change, leads off this section with a summary of the basic science behind climate change headlines. This will be important reading for those new to this area. Dorothy Boorse begins where Houghton leaves off, exploring the human effects of climate change on the poor. 'As Christians, we are called to care for the poor and promote justice,' and we cannot do that without tackling the climate change problem. Getting even closer to those who are affected, Juliana Morillo Horne reports from the highlands of Peru, showing that climate change is not a future possibility but a present reality among her people. 'The high Andean populations of Cusco are telling us in a silent and long-suffering way that we are following a terrible path of creation abuse—and they challenge us, as believers, to be part of the solution rather than the problem.'

John McKeown takes a subject not often addressed directly, even in secular environmental circles: human population. The mathematics of our present mismatch between birth and death rates (at this time we have twice the number of births as deaths every year) mean that the increasing numbers of people are jeopardizing all our efforts to respond to the environmental crisis. It is a controversial discussion, but one we must have.

Robert White has a different perspective on disasters. What we often call disasters (hurricanes, floods, volcanoes, earthquakes) are in fact natural processes in God's world that are necessary and beneficial. These 'disasters' make life possible; the fact that they so often result in human tragedy is not 'God's fault': 'it is when humans interact badly with them that an otherwise beneficial natural process can turn into a disaster.'

The chapters by Martin Hodson and by Meric Srokosz and Bob Sluka discuss biodiversity loss and the crisis in 'the other 71% of God's creation,' the oceans. Hodson shows us that God's creatures are being lost at an alarming rate—and that an appropriate, God-centred view of non-human creation is needed. Srokosz and Sluka show how many biblical references there are to the seas, and also remind us that 'the ocean is . . . a shadow of its former self. Research suggests that fish are less abundant, waters polluted, ecosystems lost or changed beyond recognition; that seas of trash float around, and physical and chemical changes threaten some species' survival.'

Concluding this section, Paul Cook introduces the concept of planetary boundaries—a relatively new area of research suggesting that earth's capacity to support life can be measured in a number of specific *boundar-*

ies, and that when we violate those boundaries, we threaten the collapse of the entire system that supports us and all other living things. Cook concludes with an appeal to the church, which provides a beautiful transition to the final section: 'The church is probably the world's largest civic society organization—present in virtually every nation and every community, and having an immense impact on how people think. If the church can harness this influence to inspire people to care more for creation and to act upon this care, then the world will be a very different place.'

The task ahead

Part 3, 'God's Work,' is a reminder to us that what God wants to do in the world, he usually chooses to do through his people. Thus, *God's* work is *our* work—in this case, our response both to the call to obedience in Part 1 and to the urgency of our crisis in Part 2. This section also could be viewed in the light of the specific 'action calls', showing ways in which God's people all over the world are already caring for creation creatively and practically.

We begin with East Africa and Serah Wambua's case study of two communities and a church-driven, 'holistic environmental stewardship model.' Coming from a different part of the world, and very different society, David Gould examines the challenges of working in some of the world's largest cities, showing the practical application of Richard Bauckham's proximate and future hope concept (see Chapter 3, 'Ecological Hope in Crisis?').

One of the effects of environmental challenges is how groups of people can be torn apart by anger and hostility when they face the social and economic consequences caused by ecological damage. We learn of Susan Emmerich's pioneering work in the Chesapeake Bay region of the United States to bring the reconciliation of the gospel to communities of crab fishermen who faced the loss of a way of life that had sustained them for generations. This is a beautiful example of how the reconciliation of the gospel can heal human relationships, and heal a community's relationship with that part of creation that sustains it.

Throughout the book, you will find a number of case studies—encouraging and diverse examples of creation care in action—from Argentina to Inner Mongolia, from supporting those at risk of flooding to educating and inspiring the next generation.

Conclusion

Ken Gnanakan as much as anyone helped to shape the original programme of the Jamaica Consultation, so it is appropriate that his thoughts conclude the book. Ken is known as the consummate integrative thinker, and he brings us full-circle, back to the question of theology, reminding us that just as God's created world is an integrated whole, our theological framework needs to be equally integrated: 'what we need to be driving towards is not just holistic mission, but a holistic theology . . . This will lead us to becoming better stewards, caring for creation, "having tasted of the grace and mercies of God in Christ Jesus and through the Holy Spirit, and with hope in the fullness of our redemption" and serving responsibly.'

And with these words, Ken also points us to the final piece of the *Call to Action*, which is a beautiful call to prayer. The final message of that document and of this book should be that it is not enough to understand the biblical command and theological principles, or to be passionate about the urgency of our mission. It is not even enough to devote our lives, our talents and our wealth to this cause sacrificially. The task is too big for us. Rather, 'each of our calls to action rest on an even more urgent call to prayer, intentional and fervent, soberly aware that this is a spiritual struggle.' We dare not forget that the destruction and devastation we see all over God's good creation today is not only the fruit of our sin, but is also evidence of the active work of God's enemy in the world. That this enemy will ultimately be defeated, and in fact has already been defeated by Jesus on the cross, is not a reason to rest, but rather to redouble our efforts in prayer as well as in practical ways.

In the final words of the *Call to Action*, then 'having tasted of the grace and mercies of God in Christ Jesus and through the Holy Spirit, and with hope in the fullness of our redemption, we pray with confidence that the Triune God can and will heal our land and all who dwell in it, for the glory of his matchless name.'

May it be so.

Call to Action and Exposition

We include the text of the *Jamaica Call to Action* below, followed by a theological exposition of the claim 'creation care is . . . a gospel issue within the Lordship of Christ.'[1] This exposition was written by Jonathan Moo, Dave Bookless, and Lowell Bliss at the request of the Consultation. As well as backing up the *Call to Action*, it also acts as a summary of the theology in this book.

Jamaica Call to Action

Introduction

The *Lausanne Global Consultation on Creation Care and the Gospel* met from 29 Oct—2 Nov 2012 in St. Ann, Jamaica to build on the creation care components of the *Cape Town Commitment*. We were a gathering of theologians, church leaders, scientists and creation care practitioners, fifty-seven men and women from twenty-six countries from the Caribbean, Africa, Asia, Latin America, Oceania, North America and Europe. We met under the auspices of the Lausanne Movement in collaboration with the World Evangelical Alliance, hosted by a country and region of outstanding natural beauty, where we enjoyed, celebrated and reflected on the wonder of God's good creation. Many biblical passages, including reflections on Genesis 1–3, Psalm 8 and Romans 8, informed our prayers, discussions and deliberations on the themes of God's World, God's Word and God's Work. Our consultation immediately followed Hurricane Sandy's devastation of the Caribbean and coincided with that storm's arrival in North America; the destruction and loss of life was a startling reminder as to the urgency, timeliness and importance of this Consultation.

Two major convictions

Our discussion, study, and prayer together led us to two primary conclusions:

Creation Care is indeed a "gospel issue within the Lordship of Christ" (*CTC* I.7.A). Informed and inspired by our study of the Scripture—the original intent, plan and command to care for creation, the resurrection narratives and the profound truth that in Christ all things have been reconciled to God—we reaffirm that creation care is an issue that must be included in our response to the gospel, proclaiming and acting upon the good news of what God has done and will complete for the salvation of the world. This is not only biblically justified, but an integral part of our mission and an expression of our worship to God for his wonderful plan of redemption through Jesus Christ. Therefore, our ministry of reconciliation is a matter of great joy and hope and we would care for creation even if it were not in crisis.

We are faced with a crisis that is pressing, urgent, and that must be resolved in our generation. Many of the world's poorest people, ecosystems, and species of flora and fauna are being devastated by violence against the environment in multiple ways, of which global climate change, deforestation, biodiversity loss, water stress, and pollution are but a part. We can no longer afford complacency and endless debate. Love for God, our neighbours and the wider creation, as well as our passion for justice, compel us to "urgent and prophetic ecological responsibility" (*CTC* I.7.A).

Our call to action

Based on these two convictions, we therefore call the whole church, in dependence on the Holy Spirit, to respond radically and faithfully to care for God's creation, demonstrating our belief and hope in the transforming power of Christ. We call on the Lausanne Movement, evangelical leaders, national evangelical organizations, and all local churches to respond urgently at the personal, community, national and international levels.

Specifically, we call for:

1. **A new commitment to a simple lifestyle.** Recognizing that much of our crisis is due to billions of lives lived carelessly, we reaffirm the Lausanne Commitment to simple lifestyle (*Lausanne Occasional Paper* 20), and call on the global evangelical community to take steps, personally and collectively, to live within the proper boundaries of God's good gift in creation, to engage further in its restoration and conservation, and to equitably share its bounty with each other.

2. **New and robust theological work**. In particular, we need guidance in four areas:

An integrated theology of creation care that can engage seminaries, Bible colleges and others to equip pastors to disciple their congregations.

A theology that examines humanity's identity as both embedded in creation and yet possessing a special role toward creation.

A theology that challenges current prevailing economic ideologies in relation to our biblical stewardship of creation.

A theology of hope in Christ and his Second Coming that properly informs and inspires creation care.

3. **Leadership from the church in the Global South.** As the Global South represents those most affected in the current ecological crisis, it possesses a particular need to speak up, engage issues of creation care, and act upon them. We the members of the Consultation further request that the church of the Global South exercise leadership among us, helping to set the agenda for the advance of the gospel and the care of creation.

4. **Mobilization of the whole church and engagement of all of society.** Mobilization must occur at the congregational level and include those who are often overlooked, utilizing the gifts of women, children, youth, and indigenous people as well as professionals and other resource people who possess experience and expertise. Engagement must be equally widespread, including formal, urgent and creative conversations with responsible leaders in government, business, civil society, and academia.

5. **Environmental missions among unreached people groups.** We participate in Lausanne's historic call to world evangelization, and believe that environmental issues represent one of the greatest opportunities to demonstrate the love of Christ and plant churches among unreached and unengaged people groups in our generation (*CTC* II.D.1.B). We encourage the church to promote "environmental missions" as a new category within mission work (akin in function to medical missions).

6. **Radical action to confront climate change.** Affirming the *Cape Town Commitment*'s declaration of the "serious and urgent challenge of climate change" which will "disproportionately affect those in poorer countries" (*CTC* II.B.6), we call for action in radically reducing greenhouse gas emissions and building resilient communities. We understand these actions to be an application of the command to deny ourselves, take up the cross and follow Christ.

7. **Sustainable principles in food production.** In gratitude to God who provides sustenance, and flowing from our conviction to become excellent stewards of creation, we urge the application of environmentally and generationally sustainable principles in agriculture (field crops and livestock, fisheries and all other forms of food production), with particular attention to the use of methodologies such as conservation agriculture.

8. **An economy that works in harmony with God's creation.** We call for an approach to economic well-being and development, energy production, natural resource management (including mining and forestry), water management and use, transportation, health care, rural and urban design and living, and personal and corporate consumption patterns that maintain the ecological integrity of creation.

9. **Local expressions of creation care,** which preserve and enhance biodiversity. We commend such projects, along with any action that might

be characterized as the "small step" or the "symbolic act," to the worldwide church as ways to powerfully witness to Christ's Lordship over all creation.

10. **Prophetic advocacy and healing reconciliation.** We call for individual Christians and the church as a whole to prophetically "speak the truth to power" through advocacy and legal action so that public policies and private practice may change to better promote the care of creation and better support devastated communities and habitats. Additionally, we call on the church to "speak the peace of Christ" into communities torn apart by environmental disputes, mobilizing those who are skilled at conflict resolution, and maintaining our own convictions with humility.

Our call to prayer

Each of our calls to action rest on an even more urgent call to prayer, intentional and fervent, soberly aware that this is a spiritual struggle. Many of us must begin our praying with lamentation and repentance for our failure to care for creation, and for our failure to lead in transformation at a personal and corporate level. And then, having tasted of the grace and mercies of God in Christ Jesus and through the Holy Spirit, and with hope in the fullness of our redemption, we pray with confidence that the Triune God can and will heal our land and all who dwell in it, for the glory of his matchless name.

We, the participants of the 2012 Jamaica Creation Care Consultation, invite Christians and Christian organizations everywhere to signify your agreement with and commitment to this Call to Action by signing this document *as an individual or on behalf of your organization, institution or other church body.* Individuals may sign by going to http://www.lausanne .org/creationcare and following the directions given to add their names. Organizational signatories should send a letter or email signed by their leader, board chair, or authorized representative to creationcare@lausanne .org (Questions about this procedure may be sent to the same address.)

Agreed together by the participants of the Lausanne Global Consultation on Creation Care and the Gospel, St. Ann, Jamaica, 9 November 2012.[2]

Exposition

The first major conclusion of the Global Consultation reaffirms one of the key claims of the *Cape Town Commitment*—that 'Creation care is . . . a gospel issue within the Lordship of Christ' (*CTC* 1-7-A). In the following exposition, we aim to explain briefly the theology underlying this conviction.

The gospel message may take many forms across cultures and circumstances, but the gospel itself is located in the person of the Lord Jesus Christ.

We believe that creation care is included in the gospel because the gospel is the gospel of Jesus, whom the *Cape Town Commitment* calls 'the creator, owner, sustainer, redeemer and heir of all creation' (*CTC* II-B-6). On behalf of the participants of the Global Consultation on Creation Care and the Gospel, we propose the following explanation for creation care being a 'gospel issue.'

The gospel is the gospel of Jesus, the creator and Lord

'The Son is the image of the invisible God, the firstborn over all creation. For in him all things were created: things in heaven and on earth, visible and invisible, whether thrones or powers or rulers or authorities; all things have been created through him and for him' (Col 1:15–16). We affirm that creation is good, and that creation exists firstly for God in Christ (Ps 24:1), and is only ours to enjoy, to care for, and to rule within under the Lordship of Christ, its true owner and sustainer. The Lordship of Christ is also the context for creation care in the *Cape Town Commitment*: 'If Jesus is Lord of all the Earth, we cannot separate our relationship to Christ from how we act in relation to the Earth. For to proclaim the gospel that says "Jesus is Lord" is to proclaim the gospel that includes the Earth, since Christ's Lordship is over all creation. Creation care is thus a gospel issue within the Lordship of Christ' (*CTC* I-7-A-24).

The gospel of Jesus addresses the problem of evil and sin

The effects of sin and evil have caused incalculable misery for humanity and led to the groaning of God's creation (Rom 8; *CTC* 1-8-A). In many cases, creation's suffering is caused directly by human evil and injustice. There are sins which should rightly be called *environmental sins*, because they are sins against our stewardship of the earth, violations of love for our creator and our neighbours. We call upon Christians to join with us in repentance for our carelessness, greed, and selfishness that contribute to the destruction of the earth and are rightly deserving of God's judgement (Rev 11:18).

The gospel is the gospel of the incarnate Christ Jesus

'In Jesus, conceived by the Holy Spirit and born of the Virgin Mary, God took our human flesh and lived among us, fully God and fully human' (*CTC* I-4-1). The incarnation of God's only Son provides an affirmation of the value of this material creation to God, and a challenge to any dualism that would denigrate material creation, since God in human flesh reveals what it is to be truly human.

The gospel is the gospel of Jesus, who inaugurates the kingdom of God

Jesus brings in the restored rule of God over his creation as its king. In proclaiming the kingdom of God, Jesus announces that his *gospel* (good news) is for the poor (Luke 4). Within the kingdom of God, preferential treatment is due to the poor. In today's world, the poor more than any suffer the consequences of resource depletion, deforestation, unsustainable agricultural practices, and, as the *Cape Town Commitment* affirms, 'Probably the most serious and urgent challenge faced by the physical world now is the threat of climate change' (*CTC* II-II-5). Issues of environmental degradation and issues of social justice cannot be separated. Neither do we believe one can separate Christ's love and his justice. And so we pray, 'for God's kingdom to come, that God's will may be done on earth as in heaven, in the establishment of justice, the stewardship and care of creation, and the blessing of God's peace in our communities' (*CTC* II-D-6–4).

The gospel is the gospel of Jesus, the saviour

'In his death on the cross, Jesus took our sin upon himself in our place, bearing its full cost, penalty and shame, defeated death and the powers of evil, and accomplished the reconciliation and redemption of all creation' (*CTC* I-4–4). The gospel of Jesus is good news both for humanity and for the whole of creation, because creation is set free from its bondage to decay and shares in the glory of the freedom of God's children (Rom 8). 'The Bible declares God's redemptive purpose for *creation* itself', bringing hope for the earth that is rooted in God's grace rather than dependent on human activity (*CTC* I-7-A).

The gospel is the gospel of Jesus, the risen and ascended one

The resurrection of Christ is proof that Jesus came to redeem us as whole persons including our physical bodies, and is also the key to understanding the continuity and discontinuity that applies to the relationship between this creation and the new heavens and new earth. 'In his bodily resurrection, Jesus was vindicated and exalted by God, completed and demonstrated the full victory of the cross, and became the forerunner of redeemed humanity and restored creation' (*CTC* I-4–5).

The gospel is the gospel of Jesus, who is coming again

Jesus is reigning as Lord over history and creation, and will come again, restoring all things, and we will dwell with him, not in some disembodied existence, but in an imperishable new creation. Hope in the restoration of all things in and through Christ Jesus is one of the most important, and distinctly Christian, contributions that the church can give to environmental movements. This ultimate hope sheds light back into our current context, so often characterized by disappointment, apathy and despair, and sustains us in perseverance and faithful action.

The gospel of Jesus drives us to mission

The Great Commission tells us that making disciples of all nations includes teaching them to obey all that Jesus commanded. The summary that Jesus himself offers of the Law and the Prophets is to love God with all our heart, soul, mind, and strength and our neighbour as ourselves. It is abundantly clear today that we cannot love and care for our neighbours without caring for the creation of which they and we are a part. If we love God, we will value what he values, which, as the whole of the Scriptures from Genesis to Revelation reveal to us, includes his entire good creation. Christ also shows us what it is to rule as God's 'image bearers' within creation (Heb 2 and Col 3). He did not grasp what was his, but humbled himself as a servant (Phil 2), revealing in his life and death the sacrificial rule on behalf of others to which we too are called. We have discovered that creation care is a *ministry of reconciliation*, requiring not only the restoration of right relationships between God and humanity, but also between each other, and between us and the rest of creation. 'Integral mission means discerning, proclaiming, and living out, the biblical truth that the gospel is God's good news, through the cross and resurrection of Jesus Christ, for individual persons, *and* for society, *and* for creation. All three are broken and suffering because of sin; all three are included in the redeeming love and mission of God; all three must be part of the comprehensive mission of God's people' (*CTC* I-7-A).

In addition to these theological convictions, we offer the following observations about the place of creation care within the Lausanne Movement:

- Creation care has a home in the Lausanne Movement, which is historically a movement of *world evangelization*. The first direct mention of creation care is in fact in the *Manila Manifesto* (A-1).[3]

- Creation care has a home in the *whole gospel* framework of the Lausanne Movement—what the *Cape Town Commitment* calls 'integral mission' (*CTC* I-10-B).

- Creation care has a home in Lausanne's historic call to make disciples among all peoples, especially among the least-reached. In fact, we believe that environmental issues represent one of the greatest opportunities to demonstrate the love of Christ and to plant churches among least-reached people groups in our generation. We encourage the church to promote *environmental missions* as a new category within mission work (akin in function to medical missions). We pursue this, not only for its intrinsic value, but also because of the opportunity it provides for gospel proclamation.

- The Lausanne Creation Care Consultation wholeheartedly affirms the centrality of evangelism and disciple-making. Along with other Lausanne Consultations, 'we are united by our experience of the grace of God in the gospel and by our motivation to make that gospel of grace known to the ends of the earth by every possible means' (*CTC* I-8).

- We have discovered that we could not talk about creation care without also talking about many other worthy topics concerned with the gospel and mission. We ask all others involved in Christian mission in its many forms, in turn, to consider seriously how the backdrop of ecological crisis affects the fulfilment of their particular callings in Christ Jesus.

In summary, we join with all the Lausanne Movement in declaring, 'we share God's passion for his world, loving all that God has made, rejoicing in God's providence and justice throughout his creation, proclaiming the good news [gospel] to all creation and all nations, and longing for the day when the earth will be filled with the knowledge of the glory of God as the waters cover the sea' (*CTC* I-7).

PART 1—GOD'S WORD

CHAPTER 1

Ruling God's World God's Way:
Dominion in Psalm 8

Edward R Brown

'Some people, in order to discover God, read books. But there is a great book: the very appearance of created things. Look above you! Look below you! Read it. God, whom you want to discover, never wrote that book with ink. Instead, He set before your eyes the things that He had made. Can you ask for a louder voice than that?'

St Augustine of Hippo, City of God *Book 16*

Anyone who wants to explore creation care or the environmental crisis will have to come to grips with the fundamental question of where we human beings fit in the overall scheme of things. Are we just one of many thousands of species who happen to have hit an evolutionary jackpot in intelligence, with no more *rights* than any other creature? Or are we divinely appointed dictators, having ability and divine right to determine the fate of anything that is not us? Or something in between? It is a question that cannot be avoided. We human beings are the single biggest force in nature at this time in history, and our own future depends, humanly speaking at least, on how we answer this question.

So who and what are we? From a biblical perspective, we find ourselves immediately wrestling with *dominion*—the concept that God has given us authority over the rest of his world. Dominion suggests that we have the right, the power—and, with that, the ability—to *rule over* God's creation.

Man's supremacy over creation is explicitly seen in Genesis 1:26–28 and Psalm 8—but it is woven throughout Scripture. For example, God's covenant with Noah ('The fear of you and the dread of you shall be upon every beast of the earth', Gen 9:2 ESV) and Psalm 115:16 ('The heavens are the LORD's heavens, but the earth he has given to the children of man' ESV).

Dominion can be and has been the excuse for all kinds of selfishness, arrogance, and general abuse of God's world. Scholar Lynn White famously suggested that Christianity itself is to blame for the modern environmental crisis. Disturbingly, a number of Christians have inadvertently given Lynn White's conclusion support by using dominion as an excuse for their own environmental exploitation and neglect. I am not the only creation care teacher who has had people confront me with 'but the Bible says we can do whatever we want with the world, doesn't it?'

For all these reasons, dominion makes some of us uncomfortable. Given a choice, we would prefer to promote *stewardship* rather than defend such an apparently pernicious doctrine. Genesis 2:15 ('The LORD God took the man and put him in the Garden of Eden to work it and keep it' ESV) feels like a nicer, dare I say, a *greener* concept. Genesis 1 seems to open the door to rulership and seems to sanction actual abuse of creation—but Genesis 2 suggests cooperation, cultivation, and stewardship. Given a choice between them, most would rather build a case for creation care on the latter.

The solution, not the problem

A misunderstanding of dominion is dangerous; understanding it properly is actually the key to figuring out where we as human beings fit in God's creation and how we can correct our many missteps. The authority and power of dominion in Genesis 1 does not contradict the stewardship of Genesis 2; in fact, it is necessary to it.

Another passage that explores dominion is Psalm 8. This poem's affirmation of human dominion over creation is unavoidable: God has given human beings authority over all of his creation. However, the implications of that message may be different from what we were expecting.

Here is the psalm as a whole:

O LORD, our Lord,
   how majestic is your name in all the earth!
You have set your glory
   above the heavens.
Out of the mouth of babies and infants,
   you have established strength because of your foes,
   to still the enemy and the avenger.
When I look at your heavens,
   the work of your fingers,
the moon and the stars,
   which you have set in place,
what is man that you are mindful of him,
   and the son of man that you care for him?
Yet you have made him a little lower than the heavenly beings
   and crowned him with glory and honour.

You have given him dominion over the works of your hands;
    you have put all things under his feet,
all sheep and oxen,
    and also the beasts of the field,
the birds of the heavens,
    and the fish of the sea,
        whatever passes along the paths of the seas.
O LORD, our Lord,
    how majestic is your name in all the earth! (ESV)

Divine bookends

The missing pieces of the dominion puzzle are at the beginning and end of the poem—an identical pair of bookends, framing the rest of the psalm:

O LORD, our Lord, how majestic is your name in all the earth! (ESV)

Our poet says a great deal about human beings in the middle, but we can only go there after we understand that he begins and ends with God. More specifically, he begins and ends with *God's name*.

One can miss the significance of the phrase 'O LORD, our Lord' in English. If reading in French or many other languages, you can more easily get the true meaning. In English the repetition of 'Lord' sounds like poetic repetition, but it is not. There are actually two Hebrew words in play here. The first, capitalised, LORD translates the Hebrew *YHWH* or *Yahweh*, the name God gives to himself in the burning bush encounter with Moses (Exod 3:15):

God also said to Moses, 'Say this to the people of Israel, "The LORD [Yahweh], the God of your fathers, the God of Abraham, the God of Isaac, and the God of Jacob, has sent me to you." This is my name forever, and thus I am to be remembered throughout all generations.' (ESV)

There is much theology wrapped up in this name. But what is important for us to note here is the simple, astounding fact that God wants Moses, and later David and all of his people, to know his name—and, knowing it, to proclaim it in various ways.

The second occurrence of 'Lord' translates the Hebrew word *Adonai*. This is a functional term, a job title. It can be used for anyone who has authority or control over someone else—a master over his slaves; a foreman on a construction crew. David is acknowledging that his God, Yahweh, is in a position of authority over him.

Thus the beginning and end of Psalm 8 affirm God's control and sovereignty over us, his people. It could be paraphrased like this:

O Yahweh, you who are our absolute master and sovereign, how majestic is your name in all the earth.

These bookends are critical to how we read the rest of the psalm: the central message of Psalm 8 may be that God has given human beings authority over his creation, but its message begins and ends with God's authority over us. Whatever human dominion over creation may turn out to mean, it is bookended—limited, constrained, guided, confined—by God's dominion over us.

A cosmic golden rule

We can go further here. Our dominion is *constrained* by God's authority over us. Therefore, the way we exercise dominion should be guided by the way God exercises his authority over us. We should rule creation as God rules us. We might also consider whether we should rule creation the way God rules creation. In fact, there are some excellent examples of efforts to do just that, as in the Africa-based Farming God's Way program, which my own organization promotes in Kenya and Tanzania (see Chapter 5, 'Creation Care and the Great Commission').

For our purposes, however, the point of interest here in Psalm 8 is the parallel between God's sovereignty over us and our dominion over creation. God's sovereignty is marked by mercy and compassion and love. Our dominion should mirror God's—our dominion should be modeled on his sovereignty. When God exercises his dominion over us, he does so not harshly, vindictively or arbitrarily, but with a goal-driven purpose that rises out of his love for us:

> And we know that in all things God works for the good of those who love him, who have been called according to his purpose. (Rom 8:28)

God rules us in love, always seeking our best. And we should—no, we *must*—do the same in our care of God's creation. As stewards, we must seek his goals for his creation, not our own. We can best do that by looking at the goals God has as he cares for us. We can think of it like a creation-wide version of the golden rule: not just that we should 'do unto others as we want them to do unto us' but that we should care for all of creation as we would want God to care for us—which, in fact, is exactly how he does care for us.

This line of reasoning is actually reinforced by the Christological aspects of Psalm 8. The writer of Hebrews, for example, uses Psalm 8:4–6 in his own argument that Jesus has been given supreme authority over the entire cosmos: 'Now in putting everything in subjection to him, he left nothing outside his control' (Heb 2:8 ESV). Jesus, having that supreme authority, used it not for his own purposes but chose instead to go to the cross:

> But we see him who for a little while was made lower than the angels, namely Jesus, crowned with glory and honour because of the suffering of death, so that by the grace of God he might taste death for everyone. (Heb 2:9 ESV)

Jesus, exercising his supreme authority by giving himself up to death, is thereby both our saviour, having died for our sins, and our model for how we can and should exercise our own authority in creation.

Two things follow from this discussion.

First, an observation—God's care for us is marked by tenderness, compassion, mercy, and ultimately sacrifice. He is a loving father, a gentle guide, a forgiving saviour. His approach to us is that of the shepherd who searches long for a lost sheep and brings it home rejoicing (Luke 15:3–7). It is that of the lost son's father, waiting by the gate daily to welcome us home (Luke 15:11–32). God's care for us is, in almost every case, the opposite of how we act toward his creation. God gives; we take. God seeks our best, and those God cares for blossom and flourish under his care; we, by contrast, seek from creation what is best for ourselves, while creation withers and dies under our hands. This is not godly dominion.

Second, a question—if we were to apply this principle as a test, how much of the present human enterprise (society, economy, business, government, and everything else) would pass that test? We have a society built on an economic system fuelled by greed, where benefits accrue to those who destroy God's creation more than to those who seek to preserve it. How much of what we do as human beings comes even close to meeting such a standard? If we are honest, not very much.

What God wants us to want

God's sovereignty over us is goal-driven and guided by his love for us. How can we follow that model with regard to our dominion over creation? We might start by trying to understand what God's goals for us are—we could then translate his goals for *us* into goals for his creation. One place to look is the prayer known as the Lord's Prayer, in which Jesus taught his disciples how to pray. The disciples want to know how to pray, and so they ask Jesus to show them. 'Pray then like this', Jesus says:

> Our Father in heaven, hallowed be your name.
> Your kingdom come, your will be done,
> on earth as it is in heaven.

Give us this day our daily bread, and forgive us our debts,
  as we also have forgiven our debtors.
And lead us not into temptation,
  but deliver us from evil. (Matt 6:9–13 ESV)

Keep in mind that Jesus *is* God. In his dictation of this prayer, we have God telling us what we should ask God for. It is a list of what God wants us to want, a summary of God's goals and desires for us.

Some time ago, I was living as a foreigner in Pakistan and I needed an extension to my visa. Granting the extension required the authorities to make an exception for me, something that would not normally be approved. I went to discuss my case with the officer in charge of visa applications. We had a good relationship and he was considerate and sympathetic; he wanted to help me, but he also had rules he had to follow. He explained what I needed to do—in detail—to get my case approved: I needed to write a covering letter explaining why I should be granted this exception. This should be addressed to him as he was the one who would approve it. And then he told me exactly what I should say in the letter I was going to write to him.

The officer who *would* approve my request was telling me how to state my case so that he *could* approve it. I wrote the letter, exactly as I had been told—and my visa was granted. That is what is happening in the Lord's Prayer: God wants to answer prayers which conform to his own goals for us—and he is telling us what to ask for and how to ask, so he can give us our requests.

Based on this prayer, what are God's goals for us? What does God want *for* us and *from* us?

First, *God wants us to know him and to proclaim his name:* 'Our Father in heaven, hallowed be your name'. God wants his name to be revered, respected, known, proclaimed. God wants to be known as God. This is a knowing that is more than simply acknowledging that God exists. Proclaiming God's name in this way implies having a relationship with him, which is, of course, implied in the term 'Father' and is the greatest benefit any of us can have in life. Recognizing the 'hallowedness' of God's name takes us a step further. This God whose name we proclaim is worthy of worship and praise, for he is not only Father, but also king. This leads us to the next phrase:

God wants his kingdom to be established: 'Your kingdom come, your will be done'. The parallel phrasing is important. God's kingdom 'comes' when his will is done. What is reality in heaven is God's goal for us on earth. He desires that we desire for his will to be done. This is the essence of God's kingdom—a life and a society that operates according to what we might call *kingdom values*.

And finally, *God wants to provide for people:* 'Give us this day our daily bread . . . forgive us our debts . . . lead us not into temptation'. God wants us to be fed, clothed, forgiven—all of the things we normally have on our minds when we think about praying. We would do well, however, to note that this goal comes last in the sequence of requests. The order is important. God desires that we have a relationship with him; that our lives separately and together conform to the values that mark his kingdom; and then that our needs are met.

Looking again at Psalm 8, a close reading shows the same three principles at work.

In verses 1 and 9 (the bookends we looked at earlier), we see *God's name being proclaimed*: 'how majestic is your name in all the earth! You have set your glory above the heavens' (ESV). This is a statement of fact about God's name in creation, that the name is already being proclaimed, even above the heavens, rather than a prayer that God's name would be proclaimed, as in the Lord's Prayer. Even so, the argument remains the same: God is proclaiming his name throughout creation and, by implication, wants us to proclaim it, too.

In verse 2, God's enemies, those who would oppose his rule or his kingdom, will be defeated: 'Out of the mouths of babies and infants, you have established strength . . . to still the enemy and the avenger' (ESV). The corollary of enemies being defeated is that *his kingdom will be established.*

And in verses 3–8, we see how *God is providing for us, his people*: he has created us 'a little lower than the heavenly beings', 'crowned (us) with glory and honour' and 'put all things under (our) feet' (ESV).

These three goals—name, kingdom, people—offer us a framework on which to build a dominion based on God's goals for us and his creation, rather than on our own goals for ourselves.

Proclaiming God's name has implications for how we practise our faith. Evangelism, worship, prayer all have to do with proclaiming God's name. But God reveals himself through creation as well as through the Bible, and there are implications for how we care for creation.

Establishing God's kingdom follows directly from proclaiming his name: God's kingdom is established where his influence—his values—are visible and operative. Establishing God's kingdom means creating a society that is based on what we have already called *kingdom values*. Today's social justice movement fits into this category, and it is wise to remember that no matter how much we want God's kingdom, we cannot achieve it without God himself. We proclaim his name; *then* we can establish his kingdom.

Providing for people is, humanly speaking at least, where we want to end up, in a world in which our needs are taken care of. It is not selfish to admit this—after all, Jesus himself told us we could bring our (self-interested) needs to him in prayer. But we would do well to remember that he also told us to 'seek first the kingdom of God . . . and all these things will be added to you' (Matt 6:33 ESV). If God's name is proclaimed, if his kingdom is established, it will follow quite naturally that people will be provided for.

Each of these deserves much more attention than these brief paragraphs allow. Here our focus is on proclaiming God's name through caring for his creation.

Proclamation on two channels

One of the great themes of history as seen through the perspective of the Bible is that God has been, from day one, proclaiming his name. While this proclamation is self-evident through Scripture, it is also true with regard to his creation:

> The heavens declare the glory of God,
> and the sky above proclaims his handiwork.
> Day to day pours out speech,
> and night to night reveals knowledge.
> There is no speech, nor are there words,
> whose voice is not heard.
> Their voice goes out through all the earth,
> and their words to the end of the world. (Ps 19:1–4 ESV)

The phrasing of this passage, with creation itself doing the proclaiming, does not contradict our premise that it is God who is actively proclaiming his name through nature. We might think of creation as a loudspeaker, which is transforming electrical impulses into sound waves so an audience can hear a speech. The speaker system produces the sound, but the content comes from the person behind the microphone. In this psalm, all creation transmits the message of God's glory and his name, as we read it in Psalm 8—but God himself is the source of that message.

Using the loudspeaker analogy to explore a further dimension of this proclamation-through-creation process, imagine the speakers in a television set. This device gives us information on two synchronized channels: audio and video. Both of these channels carry information; both are telling the same story. As the image of a person's lips move on the screen, the voice comes through the speakers. Each gives us part of the story; only when they function together do we get a complete experience and better understanding.

Say the audio channel is equivalent to God's written word, the Bible. The video screen is analogous to God's created word. Both are faithfully proclaiming God's name and glory, and together they give us a more complete understanding of God than either would alone. This is beautifully illustrated in Psalm 19, where we see God using both of these channels to proclaim his name. In the first part (19:1–6), creation is doing the talking;

in the second half (19:7–14), God's Law (Torah) or the Bible is the means by which God speaks:

> The law of the LORD is perfect,
> reviving the soul;
> the testimony of the LORD is sure,
> making wise the simple;
> the precepts of the LORD are right,
> rejoicing the heart. (Ps 19:7–8 ESV)

Two channels, creation and Scripture, the world and the word, join in one psalm. The two are not equivalent—Scripture contains more explicit content about God than creation does—but both are essential to a complete experience of God's proclamation. This is confirmed in Paul's appeal to creation as a source of revelation in Romans 1:

> For what can be known about God is plain to them [*ie* sinful mankind], be-cause God has shown it to them. For his invisible attributes, namely, his eternal power and divine nature, have been clearly perceived, ever since the creation of the world, in the things that have been made. So they are without excuse. (Rom 1:19–20 ESV)

If God uses two channels to proclaim his name, who are we to prefer just one? Our proclamation of his name solely with the written word does not fulfil what the written word itself declares.

Biospherical proclamation

What does proclaiming his name through the world mean? What does it look like?

I would like to introduce a new term—*biospherical proclamation*—the proclamation of God's name through the care and nurturing of his creation, particularly the biosphere (the term used by biologists and ecologists to refer to the world of living creatures). Though there is plenty of wonder and beauty in the non-living world, it is the world of DNA-based life that is of particular interest to these scientists—and to us as well.

If verbal proclamation is the communication of God's name by use of human language, biospherical proclamation is the communication of that name through the vocabulary of the created world, and in particular the *living* created world. Where that world flourishes, God's name is loudly proclaimed. Where it suffers or declines, the sound of God's name fades. All gardeners are proclaimers of God's name, whether or not they recognize it. Every person walking in a forest is immersed in a flood of praise and wor-ship that no human choir can hope to equal.

Seen in this light, the oft-repeated idea that God wants us to *tend the garden* becomes far more than a horticultural task. It is part of our worship, our discipleship, even our evangelism. Biospherical proclamation requires the preservation and flourishing of creation as a central part of the proclamation task, and makes creation care a task for God's people that is a key part of the gospel itself.

We don't know our own strength

Through most of history, proclaiming God's name in creation was a passive concept. It required no effort. Creation was just there, and the creator's name flowed from every corner. It was written across the skies for all to see (Psalms 8 and 19), and was evident in every tree and flower and the great beasts described in the latter chapters of the book of Job. The idea that struggling humanity could wipe out portions of God's creation would have been ludicrous.

Not so today. The stars are still there, but we have to make an effort to see them. (Could David, our psalmist, have even imagined human structures so bright and air so foul that the stars themselves would disappear?) Many of us are not often outside at night anyway, and, when we are, streetlights and shopping malls often obscure our vision. There are still mountains and sunsets, but many of us spend our days in cocoons of artificial light and artificial air, staring at computer screens. When we do glimpse nature, even in worship, it is probably in the form of electronic pixels. When we venture outside and open our eyes, we more often see smog and streetlights than the splendour of God's name splashed across the heavens.

And worse, we are actively destroying large parts of that revelation. Rather than proclaiming God's name in the biosphere, we are busy erasing it. Fields become parking lots. Mountains are reduced to rubble to get at the coal underneath them. Coral reefs are bleached and dying. The list of endangered and extinct species, every one of which proclaims God's name, grows longer and longer.

Can we really say that we are proclaiming God's name in creation when the things we build and the way we live diminish and destroy it?

Why this matters

We started with the doctrine of *dominion*, arguing that it is a biblical concept, but that, to be legitimate, it must be modeled on God's dominion over us. Our goals for God's creation should mirror God's goals for our part in it. And one of God's goals is that his name should be proclaimed in his creation.

Does our current practice of dominion enhance God's proclamation of his name? In a word: no. Measured in this way, human dominion over creation is an abysmal failure, as is demonstrated throughout this book. This failure is not an accident nor due to incompetence. It is because of disobedience, and an indictment against us.

Our failure to obey is not something hypothetical or theoretical—it has important, immediate consequences. God's world was created to operate in harmony with God's purposes. When we ignore those purposes, we can expect to have big problems.

We have economies that do not work; paralyzed political systems; environmental nightmares; corruption and crime on every level in all of our countries. Should we be surprised at what they cause? It is surely what we should expect from a world built around the pursuit of our own goals rather than God's. All of humanity's problems today—political, economic, societal and environmental—are due to human failure to choose God's goals.

We *ought* to proclaim God's name because he wants us to. More, we *must* do this, if we are to survive and flourish in God's creation. This is apparent in the *Call to Action* which leads with two convictions: (i) 'Creation Care is indeed a "gospel issue"' and 'we would care for creation even if it were not in crisis', and (ii) we are 'faced with a crisis that is pressing, urgent, and that must be resolved in our generation'.

These two convictions are linked theologically and scientifically. If we had heeded the first, we would not be in our current situation. This linkage may point to a new kind of approach. Perhaps we should not focus on 'solving' the environmental crisis as such; rather, we should commit ourselves to proclaiming God's name verbally, through prayer, worship and evangelism; and biospherically, by working toward a flourishing biosphere with all the tools that science can give us. That would fulfil what the environmental scientists, ecologists and climatologists all urge be done: we will be rebuilding the biological foundation which humanity must have to flourish.

It is almost as if that verse from Matthew's gospel were coming true: 'seek first the kingdom of God and his righteousness, and all these things will be added to you' (Matt 6:33 ESV).

CHAPTER 2

The Biblical Basis for Creation Care

Jonathan A Moo

'Be joyful though you have considered all the facts.'
Wendell Berry[1]

Considering the facts

The Bible was not written to address contemporary 'environmental issues'.
Nonetheless, faithful witness to the God revealed in the Christian Scriptures
demands that the church adopt a robust and distinctive ethos of creation
care as integral to its mission. In Scripture, we learn what it is to be truly
human; we learn the value of non-human creation; we learn something
of God's purposes for creation; and above all we are confronted with the
creator and redeemer God himself. In Christ, God reconciles all things to
himself, invites us into his kingdom and calls us to his mission of spreading
the gospel to the ends of the earth. Those who become disciples of Jesus are
charged to 'make disciples of all nations', 'teaching them to obey' everything
that Jesus commanded (Matt 28:19–20). The 'obedience that accompanies
[our] confession of the gospel of Christ' (2 Cor 9:13), or what Paul elsewhere
calls the 'obedience that comes from faith' (Rom 1:5), must therefore include
keeping Jesus' commands to love God with all our heart, soul and mind
and to love our neighbours as ourselves (Mark 12:30–31; Matt 22:37–39;
Luke 10:27; *cf* James 2:8). As has become abundantly clear, we cannot love
and care for our human neighbours without caring for the environment in
which they live—and indeed for the whole earth. Nor can we love God with
all of our being if we do not value what he values, if we do not care for all
he has made, the creation that belongs to him.

It is with sadness, then, that we acknowledge that we as a species, and
we as God's people, have not cared well for his creation. We must not ignore
such things as the ongoing catastrophe of biodiversity loss, the destruction
of the world's tropical forests, the acidification of the oceans, the degradation and loss of topsoil, the pollution of the atmosphere, the changing of the
earth's climate, and the human suffering that so often attends these 'envi-

ronmental crises'. Our century is likely to be defined by how we address—or fail to address—human-caused environmental challenges that are unprecedented in their scope and magnitude. They are unprecedented not because the world has never faced severe human-caused crises before, but because we have never faced them on such a planetary scale. By any measure, our collective impact on the earth is out of all proportion to anything seen before, and it continues to increase exponentially. History has much to teach us, but sometimes it also leaves us unprepared for the unprecedented, for situations that are genuinely new. Martin Rees, formerly President of the Royal Society in the UK, captured the significance of this in his book *Our Final Century*, in which he claimed that 'even in a cosmic or a geological time-perspective, there's something unique about our century'.[2]

It is no wonder that many in the so-called developed world are increasingly prone to despair or apathy in the face of what seem such immense challenges and the predictions of worse to come. Meanwhile, for many in the majority world the degradation and collapse of ecosystems and the effects of an increasingly warm and erratic climate have already begun to threaten survival itself. In times like ours, we need to recapture the hope and joy that lie at the centre of a biblical ethos of creation care, but this is a hope and joy that exists alongside—and even in and through—lament and groaning. The gospel ought to drive us to support and join in the work of caring for God's creation. As the worldwide body of Christ, we must seek to reflect, in all we do, God's intention that creation be liberated from the ruin that it so often suffers at our hands and come to share in the 'freedom and glory of the children of God' (Rom 8:21).

A biblical understanding of the world as God's good creation demands that we use the gifts of science and technology and all the knowledge, wisdom, and ingenuity that God gives us to understand and make sense of the world in which we live. We must, to borrow the words of the poem by Wendell Berry cited at the beginning of this chapter, 'consider all the facts', however uncomfortable they are for us and however awkward they may prove to be for business as usual. A biblical vision of creation care also reminds us, however, that our ultimate hope is for a future that is finally given only by the grace of God, a future that does not depend on us and yet towards which we are called to work with all that we have. In the light of such a transformative hope, we are called to persevere no matter what the circumstances, to go on working towards a world that more nearly reflects God's purposes of peace and justice, a world where we care well for our human and non-human neighbours, and where we allow space for the flourishing of all of life. When we turn to Scripture for a biblical basis for creation care, we do not find answers to all of our contemporary questions. But we do discover what sort of orientation towards the world is expected of us if we take seriously both what science reveals to us about the state of the planet, and what Scripture reveals about God, ourselves, and the world of his creation.

A picture

In his book *The Mission of God*, Chris Wright provides a simple picture that illustrates well the role of non-human creation within the biblical narrative.[4] Wright suggests that Acts 17 and the Bible as a whole portrays the relationship between God, humanity, and the rest of creation as something like a triangle of relationships—with God, us, and non-human creation at each corner of the triangle. While God is wholly transcendent and so set apart from all else, the triangle model usefully illustrates that God freely and graciously chooses not only to create but also to enter into relationship with all he has created. Some argue that human beings belong to the rest of creation and so should not be distinguished from *nature*; but we are indeed set apart as God's image-bearers, as those uniquely granted particular responsibility within and for the rest of creation. We relate to God in a way that is different from salmon, fir trees, grizzly bears, butterflies, elephants and tree frogs. The rest of creation glorifies and praises God merely by being itself; we, on the other hand, are able to respond to God in obedience. We are given the privilege and responsibility to rule over other creatures, and we are called to work and to keep the earth, participating by God's grace even in bringing about his purposes for creation.

The biblical story is one of our rejecting God's purposes, of turning away from him as our source of life and light and being, of becoming a law unto ourselves and so suffering the inevitable brokenness, death and destruction that results. In rejecting God, our relationship with him is broken; and broken too are our relationships with each other, with ourselves and with the rest of creation. All of creation suffers the results of this rejection. Its intended subjection to humankind as its rulers and keepers becomes, as Paul puts it in Romans 8, a subjection to futility.

But the biblical story does not end in rejection. For it is also the story of what God does to reverse this state of affairs, to save and redeem and restore. Christ, as the *cosmic* redeemer, reconciles us with God, healing the brokenness that otherwise must separate us from our creator. Just as our rebellion against God means brokenness in all our relationships, so Christ's reconciliation means the healing of all our relationships: with each other and with the rest of creation. Creation, as Paul says in Romans 8, now shares in the hope to be liberated from ruin and to reach the purposes for which God always intended it. As those who have been adopted as children of God, we strain towards a godly orientation to each other and to all of creation, to reflect God's purposes of wholeness, restoration and healing.

A good earth

Now we consider more precisely some specific things we learn about God, creation, and ourselves in the Bible. From the beginning, we learn that this world is indeed a *creation*. It is neither a random accident nor itself divine. It is the gift of God, the result of his free decision to create something that is distinct from himself and yet which reflects his glory and goodness and serves his creative purpose. Most importantly for our theme, in the very first chapter of the Bible we find a seven-fold affirmation of the fundamental goodness of creation (Gen 1:4, 10, 12, 18, 21, 25, 31), concluding with the affirmation, 'God saw all that he had made, and it was very good' (Gen 1:31). If we want a biblical perspective on creation, this is where we have to start. God values everything that he has created; so must we.

Notice that the subsequent events of Genesis do *not* overturn God's assessment of the goodness of creation. Even beyond humankind's rebellion against God and the disasters that result, we find a God who remains committed to his earth and its creatures. The 'everlasting covenant' that God makes after the Flood encompasses not just God's promise to Noah and his descendants but also 'all living creatures of every kind on the earth' (Gen 9:16; *cf* vv 10, 15, 17). We are reminded over and over again, especially in the psalms, that the earth and the sky, the entire created order, goes on testifying to the glory of God (Ps 19:1). These celebrations of creation reach their pinnacle in Psalm 104, which eloquently describes God's care for a marvellously diverse creation. The wonderfully fruitful world described here includes those parts of creation that provide for human sustenance and well-being—'plants for people to cultivate' (v 14), 'wine that gladdens human hearts, oil to make their faces shine, and bread that sustains their hearts' (v 15)—and also those parts of creation that thrive far apart from human civilization: the stork that makes its home in the junipers (v 17), the wild goats and hyraxes of the high mountains (v 18), and even those creatures that most represent a threat to human safety and well-being: the lions roaring for their prey (v 21) and the terrifying Leviathan (v 26). The Leviathan can be linked in other contexts to the threat of chaos itself, but the psalmist claims that God formed it simply so that it might 'frolic' in the sea (v 26). 'How many are your works, LORD! In wisdom you made them all; the earth is full of your creatures' (v 24). The joy that the psalmist expresses in the diversity of all of God's creatures ought to be a stimulus for our own praise of God and also for our work to care for all that he has made.

The book of Job similarly confronts us with a God who creates, cares for, and delights in lions (38:39–40); in ravens (38:41); in mountain goats (39:1); in wild donkeys that roam the hills and laugh at the world of human beings (39:5–8); in ostriches (39:13–18); in hawks and eagles that feast on blood (39:26–30); and in Behemoth (40:15–24) and Leviathan (41:1–34), creatures that again represent, as nothing else can, the threat that a wild creation poses to the settled world of humankind. There are some non-canonical Jewish texts and later Christian ones that claim that creation was made for human beings (for example, 4 Ezra 6:55; 7:11). But, as Job and the Psalms attest, that is not the biblical picture. Hebrews 2:10 tells us that it is God 'for whom . . . everything exists'. In Colossians 1:16, we learn that Christ, as the image of the invisible God, is the one through whom all things have been created and *for whom* all things exist. Creation does not exist for us. It exists for God's glory.

The Bible challenges us to recognize value in non-human creation, value that is not ours to assign or to take away. Ethicists sometimes debate whether nature or other creatures have intrinsic value. Within a biblical worldview, *intrinsic* may be a misleading term, since non-human creation depends, from moment to moment, entirely upon God, its creator and sustainer. Yet Scripture suggests that non-human creation does indeed have value given it by God, a value that is not finally dependent on us.

Non-human creation is portrayed throughout Scripture as glorifying and praising God, even apart from the participation of human worshippers. This is most striking perhaps in Psalm 148, where the psalmist issues a call to praise to the sun and moon, mountains and hills, sea creatures and all ocean depths, fruit trees and cedars, wild animals and all cattle, small creatures and flying birds, finally addressing human beings too, inviting us to join in the praise that all of creation offers to God. The *Benedicite* has preserved a similar canticle (derived from the Greek text of Daniel) in the church's liturgy, calling Christians through the centuries to add their voices to the cosmic praise offered to the creator. The book of Revelation paints just such a magnificent picture in John's vision of the heavenly throne room in chapters 4 and 5, where all of creation gives God and Christ the glory for what has been accomplished in the creation and redemption of all things.

In texts such as these, we are forcefully reminded that the biblical tradition is not, as it is so often portrayed, all about humanity's dominance over nature. Even in the Genesis account, which has sometimes been read as supportive of exploitative human rule over creation, we should not miss the fact that human beings are created with all the other land animals on day six. Nor are we the only ones told to 'be fruitful and multiply'; so too are all the creatures of the sea, the waters and the sky (Gen 1:22 NRSV). Nor does the creation story end with the making of human beings but rather with God's rest on the seventh day, when he sits enthroned over all he has made. It is worth noting that the insights of contemporary biology into our essential creatureliness, and of astronomy and physics into the vastness of our universe, serve to recall us to a more truly biblical picture of our humble place in the cosmos.

A role for humankind

A biblical text like Psalm 8 anticipates modern questions about the significance of humankind in the light of the vastness of the universe: 'what is mankind that you are mindful of them, human beings that you care for them?' (Ps 8:4). Yet this same psalm provides dramatic affirmation that God has given human beings an exalted role within creation. 'Crowned . . . with glory and honour' and made 'rulers over the works' of God's hands, with all things placed under our feet (vv 5–6), humanity is described by the psalmist in terms that echo the Genesis creation account itself, where human beings are told to 'fill the earth and subdue it. Rule over the fish in the sea and the birds in the sky and over every living creature that moves on the ground' (Gen 1:28). The strong language of Psalm 8 and Genesis 1 leaves no doubt that human beings are granted an active and powerful role within creation, an authority that is distinct from that of other creatures. As uniquely the bearers of God's image, we are given the privilege and responsibility of ruling over other creatures.

Genesis 2 immediately reminds us, however, that this subduing and ruling involves above all the humble working of the land and taking care of it. The author uses the language of *service* and *protection* to describe God's purposes in putting the man in the garden (Gen 2:15). Israel would later be reminded of this responsibility as it applied in their relationship to the promised land; their faithful obedience to God would be seen among other things in its effects on the land, revealed in its health and fruitfulness, in its ability to sustain life. Care for the land was thus woven into Israel's law, exemplified most obviously perhaps in the provision of Sabbath days and years, a weekly rest for people and their animals and an every-seventh-year opportunity for the land to lie fallow. Israel's law reveals God's concern for land and suggests for Christians something of God's purpose for how we live in his earth.

Ultimately, however, we only discover what our God-ordained rule within creation looks like in the person of Christ. The author of Hebrews, for example, recognizes that there is a tremendous gap between the exalted role assigned to humanity in Psalm 8 and what we actually observe. He discerns, therefore, that the role of human beings (the 'son of man' described in

Psalm 8) could ultimately be fulfilled only in Christ (Heb 2:5–9). It is Christ who defines for us the image of God. And if we look to Christ to understand what it is to *image* God and to rule in his creation, what do we find? We discover one who was in the very form of God and yet did not take advantage of what was rightfully his, humbling himself in the form of a servant and going to death on a cross; we see the Son of God demonstrating God's love for us by dying on our behalf, buying back a broken world for himself; we find a Lamb who conquers by being slain. Our rule as God's image bearers, then, finds its model in the self-sacrificial love of God displayed in Christ. To suggest that our Genesis-ordained role as subduers of the earth justifies exploiting creation, merely to satisfy our greed, is utterly to reject God's purposes for us and for his creation in Christ.

Brokenness

Such a rejection of God is just what Genesis 3 describes, what the rest of the Old Testament details in the story of Israel, and what the prophets lament time and time again. Because the fate of the earth is linked to God's image bearers, and because the health of Israel's land is tied to the righteousness of the nation, the land and all of creation is necessarily caught up in and affected by the lives of the people to whom it has been made subject. Thus, when there is evil and injustice in the land, the prophets tell us that creation itself suffers, that even the earth mourns. In Isaiah 24, we read, 'The earth dries up and withers, the world languishes and withers, the heavens languish with the earth. The earth is defiled by its people; they have disobeyed the laws, violated the statutes and broken the everlasting covenant. Therefore a curse consumes the earth; its people must bear their guilt' (Isa 24:4–6). Hosea 4 similarly describes a time when there is no knowledge of God in the land and 'because of this the land dries up, and all who live in it waste away; the beasts of the field, the birds in the sky and the fish in the sea are swept away' (Hosea 4:3).

The apostle Paul universalizes this theme, perceiving that such groaning is the ongoing state of an entire creation that has been subjected to fallen human beings. The created world has become subjected to futility, Paul says in Romans 8, enslaved to decay and ruin (Rom 8:20–21). Paul, like the prophets before him, sees a creation that groans under the weight of human sin. When human beings reject God and his purposes, when they become empty through their idolatrous worship of all that is not God, the creation itself becomes subject to emptiness and futility, and it groans in longing to reach the ends for which God originally intended it.

In their day, Isaiah and Hosea saw signs of a fundamental cosmic disorder in the fall of cities and devastation of the land, in drought, and in crop failure. No doubt Paul too saw the 'natural disasters' in his day as evidence of the ways in which all of creation continues to suffer and to groan. First-century residents of the Roman Empire were as well acquainted as people of any era with natural disasters, many caused by forces beyond their control but others more obviously linked—even then—to human over-exploitation of the local environment. When we read Romans 8 today, we cannot help but see—and indeed *ought* to see—creation's groaning reflected above all in our current ecological crises, especially now that the truly global consequences of our actions have become so evident.[5] If the biblical picture of humankind's role within creation once appeared naive for assigning such profound responsibility for the earth to one species, it no longer appears so—not in an age when human beings are having such widespread effects on the earth that some scientists have begun to call it the *Anthropocene*, or *age of man*. The need for us to take seriously our responsibility within creation has never been greater, and the potential consequences of the failure to exercise our responsibility well have never been so cataclysmic.

Gospel

The good news is that despite our unfaithfulness, God is faithful. This is why Paul can say in Romans 8 that the subjection of creation was done 'in hope' (v 20). It was God's intention that all of creation should share not only in the results of the fall of humankind but also in our redemption. Creation, Paul says, will one day be freed from its slavery to ruin and enter into the glory that accompanies the redemption of the children of God (Rom 8:21). In Christ, the new Adam and true image of God, the future full healing of all of creation is secured.[6]

Paul does not give any details about what creation's freedom will look like apart from suggesting that it means the undoing of its present futility. It will reach the purpose for which God always intended it. It will be liberated from corruption and ruin, because the children of God will finally fulfil the role in Christ for which they were created. The brokenness that marks life in this age—brokenness in the relationship between humankind and God, and between humankind and the rest of creation—is healed in Christ. In Christ, God's *shalom*, peace and wholeness, and the flourishing of life, is secured. More expansive pictures of what this looks like are found in other biblical texts, where this hope is described as the reconciliation or renewal of all things (Matt 19:28; Acts 3:21; Col 1:20); a new heaven and new earth (Isa 65:17; 66:22; 2 Pet 3:13; Rev 21:1); or the kingdom of this world becoming the kingdom of God and of his Messiah (Rev 11:15). In all such texts, the glorious future of creation so exceeds human imagination that only symbol and metaphor can begin to describe it. What Romans 8 makes unmistakably clear is that this very same creation that is now groaning has a future in God's purposes. Whatever else we might conclude about the details of biblical hope, we must affirm in the light of Romans 8 that this creation, this very earth, will not be left behind.

It has sometimes been suggested that other biblical texts—notably the book of Revelation and 2 Peter 3—teach that this earth will be left behind or destroyed and discarded in the end. If this world is going to be tossed aside, so the argument goes, then perhaps we ought not to spend time and effort in caring for the present creation; it would be as futile as polishing the railings of a ship that is destined to sink. But in the light of the whole of the biblical story of God's faithfulness to creation, the *Titanic* analogy is simply wrong. Such a negative conception of the earth's future is most obviously contradicted by Paul's portrayal of an entire creation that anticipates sharing in the freedom and glory that attends our resurrection, the 'the children of God to be revealed' and the 'redemption of our bodies' (Rom 8:19–23). Whatever discontinuity there may be between the present age and the age to come, this same creation finds the creator's intentions for it fulfilled, its future secured, and its healing accomplished in the new creation. Yet even if Scripture did suggest that there was no continuity between this world and the next, the command to love God and neighbour would still compel us to care well for the world as it has been entrusted to us now, for the sake of future generations.

Consider 2 Peter 3, a text that more than any other emphasizes discontinuity, the break between this age and the age to come. The 'day of the Lord' is described in this passage as coming at an unknowable and unpredictable time, 'like a thief' (2 Pet 3:10), and it will involve God's fiery judgement of 'the present heavens and earth' (v 7), the disappearance of the 'heavens' and the destruction by fire of the 'elements' (v 10). Due to some textual confusion among original manuscripts, some readers might think that 2 Peter 3:10 also describes the burning up and destruction of the earth itself. The King James Version, for example, renders the end of the verse as 'the earth also and the works that are therein shall be burned up'. But, as recent commentators have recognized, and as is reflected in most contemporary translations, the best Greek manuscripts attest to a reading that has the earth and the works done being 'found' or 'laid bare' before God.[7] The emphasis of 3:10 is on the impossibility of anything being hidden from God's final judgement and on the concomitant importance of how life is lived now. This serves as a direct challenge to the false teachers, dealt with throughout 2 Peter, who deny the coming of the Lord and encourage the heedless pursuit of greed and pleasure without regard for the priorities of God's kingdom.

The 'elements' which 2 Peter 3:10 says are 'destroyed by fire' may well refer to the heavenly elements, the *stoichea* that later texts associate with the stars, sun, and moon. The scenario described in 2 Peter 3:10 would then best be understood as a picture of God coming to his creation, the heavens that symbolically separate his throne-room from the earth disappearing with a roar, the elements in between dissolving before his fiery presence, and the earth and all the works of humanity being 'found' before him, laid bare and discovered for what they really are. This is a cosmic picture of what 1 Peter describes as the testing of our faith by fire, which will be 'found [the same Greek verb as is used for 'laid bare' in 2 Peter 3:10] to result in praise and glory and honour when Jesus Christ is revealed' (1 Pet 1:7; *cf* 1 Cor 3:13). The emphasis of 2 Peter 3 is thus on the enduring value and significance of present life, and perhaps even of the earth itself, which is finally 'laid bare' or 'found' on the day of the Lord in the midst of the fire of his 'judgement and destruction of the ungodly' (2 Pet 3:7).

The analogy that 2 Peter uses in the immediate context is telling: the future judgement by fire is compared to the Flood of Noah's day, when 'the world of that time was deluged and destroyed' (3:6). The reference to the Flood narrative reminds readers of God's 'everlasting covenant' with all the creatures of the earth (Gen 9), of his faithfulness and commitment to his creation, of the promise anticipated in his call of Noah to save all non-human life through the waters of judgement. The waters of the Flood, like the fire of final judgement, certainly mean 'destruction' for a world corrupted by injustice and polluted by evil. But it is not a destruction into nothingness, a rubbishing of this earth and a starting over with something else (all anachronistic ideas for first-century readers).[8] The earth that Noah and his family discovered after the waters receded was the same earth they had stood upon before the Flood, yet it was also a new world, cleansed of the human evil and violence that had been corrupting and destroying it (*cf* Gen 6:11–12). The 'new' world that emerges on the other side of judgement is quite clearly *this* world made new, a world purified and reclaimed: 'a new heaven and a new earth, where righteousness dwells' (2 Pet 3:13). The challenge to Peter's readers is to live now as those who belong to this coming earthly realization of God's kingdom, to embody the godly ways of living that pertain to new creation life and to be 'found' to be at 'peace with him' (v 14) on the day of the Lord's visitation. The comfort of 2 Peter 3 is found in the reminder that God's purposes will prevail no matter what. In the end, the new heavens and new earth is granted by the grace of God, and does not finally depend on us. God, by his grace, enables and ennobles our efforts, even using them to speed on the day of the Lord (v 12), yet the transcendent hope presented us in this text both humbles and frees us from the burden and despair of thinking that the future ultimately depends only on our own successes or failures. As Paul reminds readers at the end of his magnificent description of resurrection hope in 1 Corinthians 15, the certainty of the future resurrection means that our labour is not in vain (1 Cor 15:58), for the results are finally in God's hands.

Romans 8 and 2 Peter 3 provide tantalizing hints of God's purposes for this earth, of a creation liberated from futility and ruin, where evil is vanquished and righteousness makes its home. But it is especially in the cosmic visions of John's Apocalypse that we find a canvas large enough to begin to glimpse the beauty and wonder of the new heaven and new earth. Revelation reminds us from the beginning that the hope of God's people is not finally to escape to heaven but to 'reign on the earth' (5:10), and this reign is not confined to a temporary millennial period but encompasses the 'for ever and ever' of the new creation (22:5) when the New Jerusalem will have come down from heaven to earth (21:2). This reign is only possible because of the redemption and victory obtained through the blood of the lamb (5:9), in whose reign we are made able to share: 'the kingdom of the world has become the kingdom of our Lord and of his Messiah, and he will reign for ever and ever' (11:15). Read in the context of the rest of Scripture (as Revelation demands to be read), we find here the restoration of the image of God (*cf* Col 1:15; 3:10) and of the role originally intended for us as 'kings and priests' (Rev 1:6 KJV) within creation. This renewal begins now for all of those in Christ, yet the last chapters of Revelation point beyond merely present realities to the future hope of 'a new heaven and a new earth' (21:1) when all things are made new (21:5). This is not a making of *all new things,* but a restoration and renewal of everything; a bringing to fulfilment of God's purposes for creation from the beginning. God dwells intimately with his people (21:3) as he did in the garden, and the tree of life is restored, now serving to heal the nations of the world.

The new creation to come is not merely a return to Genesis, however. Christ's resurrected body yet bears the wounds of his crucifixion and, though transformed, it is recognizably continuous with his body before the resurrection. In the same way, the new creation entails the gathering up and the renewal of all of the first creation and its history. The new heaven and new earth is thus described as both the Garden of Eden and the city of the New Jerusalem, and the kings and the nations enter it with their splendour. The glory they contribute is perhaps a sign of the endurance of all that is best of human culture and civilization—with art, science, and all human striving now freed from captivity to sin, evil, and injustice. The new creation is a place where all of the results of humankind's rebellion are no more—death, mourning, crying, pain (21:4), the curse (22:3)—but it is not merely a resetting of the clock to day one, but rather the fulfilment of God's original intentions for this creation. The latent threat symbolized by the sea (21:1) and night (22:5), the 'waters' and 'darkness' of Genesis 1:2, are not even present in the new creation, as the world has been taken beyond all threat, with God's purposes for humanity and all of creation brought to fruition.[9]

A biblical environmental ethos finds its driving vision here, in this hope for the liberation and renewal of creation itself. This cosmic hope reaffirms the value of all of creation in God's ultimate purposes. It calls upon those who claim to be in Christ to begin to live like it—to begin to live as those who have been adopted as God's children, in whom the image of the creator is being renewed, and whose lives now reflect the priorities of God's new creation.

To return to Romans 8, Paul implies in this passage that the revelation of the children of God awaits the future resurrection (v 23), but he also affirms in the very same chapter that we have *already* been adopted as God's children and already are expected to live like it (vv 14–17). If the entire creation longs to see us become who we are—to have our status as God's children revealed—then our lives even now ought to begin to be orientated towards creation in a way that is in keeping with God's ultimate purposes. We ought to live in a way that is consistent with creation's eventual freedom from futility and ruin when all things are made new. God's new creation breaks into the present in Christ and in all of those who have been made God's children in Christ. Our work is not to *save* the planet, or to bring about the kingdom of God by our own efforts. We are rather called to live as instantiations of the kingdom of God, members of a resistance movement against all that would destroy God's creation, trusting in his grace for the future.

When we take seriously the cosmic breadth of Christian hope and our call to live as God's children now, we find that the scope of our love and of our ethics extends beyond our fellow human creatures to embrace all of God's creation. Our casual selfishness in how we use the earth's resources, in how we treat our global neighbours, and in how we treat creation itself is seen in this light to be an affront to God, an abrogation of our responsibility, and a rejection of our identity as his children in Christ.

We may be tempted to avoid the radical implications of a biblical theology of creation care. We might claim that our calling is to care for our human neighbours and not to get caught up in misanthropic *green* concerns. Or we might plead ignorance, claiming that we cannot know precisely how to reflect God's love in the way we relate to non-human creation. If there are difficult ethical questions for Christians about interpersonal ethics, it may be all the more difficult to agree on what it means to live ethically in relation to non-human creation. Where are we to go for guidance in weighing trade-offs, and in making detailed, difficult decisions as individuals, communities, churches, and missions agencies?

Scripture is not a manual to give us all the answers. But we *are* given an ethos, a set of principles. We have seen that these include the recognition of the value that all of creation has before God; of the particular and distinctive value of human beings as members of the community of creation; and of the call to reflect the sacrificial love of Christ in all of our relations. We must use the abilities God has given us to study creation, and to make the best decisions we can in caring for it and for its human inhabitants; indeed, as has become clear, it is impossible to care for our human brothers and sisters without caring for the environment in which they, and we, live. We must be wary, however, of our predilection to find answers that fit comfortably within our societies and cultures; of our temptation to evade the challenges of radical discipleship.[10] We must be wary, for example, of the language of *prioritization* of human welfare versus the environment. Such language, especially as it is used in wealthier parts of the world, is too often rooted in false trade-offs that ignore longer-term consequences or reflect unexamined commitments to conducting business as usual. It too often represents assimilation to a world where money and Western notions of development and success reign unchallenged. In short, it represents a failure of the imagination. We must also remember, based on the testimony of Scripture, that non-human creation, in all its wonderful diversity, has value before God. Wherever possible, we are therefore compelled to work towards solutions that enhance the health of both human and non-human communities.[11]

We must also be wary of the language of prioritization of gospel proclamation versus care for the poor and care for the earth, as if one did not enrich the other. It is obviously possible to care for the needy and to care for the environment without proclaiming the gospel. Plenty of non-Christian organizations and even many Christian organizations and churches attest to that. But is it possible to proclaim the gospel, to be faithful witnesses to the God who reveals himself to us through the Spirit in the incarnate Christ and in his written word without caring for the poor and caring for his earth? The *good news* revealed to us in the New Testament is that in Jesus, the Son of God and Messiah of Israel, God has defeated the powers of sin and death and inaugurated his restored rule over all of his creation. He has made provision through the incarnation, death, resurrection, and ascension of Jesus for all people to receive forgiveness of sins and new life in the Spirit, enabling them to live forever as his children under the Lordship of Christ. This good news is for the whole of the earth, because it reveals the way in which God's purposes for all of creation are accomplished in Christ—the means by which a world wracked by sin and corruption is renewed and restored to its creator. Thus, as the *Cape Town Commitment* expresses it, 'to proclaim the gospel that says Jesus is Lord is to proclaim the gospel that includes the earth, since Christ's Lordship is over all creation. Creation care is thus a gospel issue within the Lordship of Christ.'[12]

Hope and joy

Caring for creation in the midst of a world facing the sorts of challenges outlined in other chapters of this book is not easy. One of the penalties of an ecological education, Aldo Leopold once said, is to 'live alone in a world of wounds'.[13] At least the basics of an ecological education is demanded of us all today if we are to live faithfully as God's people in caring for creation. So we groan alongside the rest of creation as we long for the return of Christ our king, for the making of all things new (Rev 21:5). Often, in fact, it may be only in lament and groaning alongside all of creation, in concert with the Holy Spirit, that we are enabled to persevere and keep from giving up.[14]

God has not left us alone. He is present with us by his Spirit, granting us—as Peter says—'times of refreshing . . . from the Lord' as we await the renewal of all things (Acts 3:19–21). We have our hope in Christ as an anchor for our soul (Heb 6:19). So we are also hopeful and joyful as we plant trees, as we restore wetlands, as we grow food more sustainably, as we teach and we research, as we support and get involved with those who are working on the front lines to transform our communities and our world, as we seek to reshape the priorities of our societies and to live as signposts to God's kingdom, as we engage in all of the hard work of caring well for creation, and also as we celebrate and enjoy the world of God's creation, glorifying our creator and redeemer.

In the biblical hope of new creation, we are given the gift of seeing this world with new eyes. We are freed to love and find joy in *nature* as God's good creation—just as the psalmists did; and we are enabled to join alongside all of creation in its praise of God in Christ. Indeed, in the light of what Scripture promises about our future and the future of the earth, we might rephrase the line from Wendell Berry's poem at the beginning of this chapter as, 'Be joyful *because* you have considered all the facts'.

I conclude with the story of Jeremiah. When Jerusalem was under siege by the king of Babylon and the prophet was imprisoned by his own king for predicting that the Babylonians would destroy the city, that the world as the king of Judah knew was about to come to an end, Jeremiah did an odd thing. He bought a field and ensured the deed for the field would be stored for a long time to come (Jer 32). Why? Because Jeremiah had a confident hope in God's promise that one day in the future, houses, fields, and vineyards would once again be bought and sold in the land. One day, the Lord would gather his people back from exile, make an everlasting covenant with them and plant them securely in the land. So Jeremiah invested in God's future. He expected the end of the world as he knew it; but he was joyful because he has considered *all* the facts. For us too, in the face of what sometimes seems like the end of the world as we know it, we can go on joyfully caring for creation and engaging in all of the gospel work that God calls us to, because we know all the facts—or at least as many facts as we need. We know the challenges that are facing God's creation; we know what God demands of us; and we know that he is faithful.

CHAPTER 3

Ecological Hope in Crisis?

Richard Bauckham

'It [love] bears all things, believes all things, hopes all things, endures all things' (NRSV)

1 Corinthians 13:7

Christian hope in our context

The church has frequently had to think afresh about Christian hope in changing contexts. It is not that the essence of Christian hope—the great hope, founded on Jesus Christ, for God's redemptive and fulfilling renewal of all his creation—changes. But if Christian hope is to retain its power to be the engine of the church's engagement with the world, if it is to be more than an ineffective private dream, hope itself needs renewal as the world changes. From the infinite riches of God's future for the world we must draw those that can be transformative for our time. That way we can re-envision the world in the light of hope.

That is what happened when John the prophet, in the book of Revelation, was taken up to heaven in order to see how the critical moment of history in which his first readers were living looked from God's perspective—from the perspective of God's purpose to actualize his kingdom on earth as it already is in heaven. John had to be abstracted in vision from the world of the beast, the world as projected by the imperial propaganda, in order, not simply to see the future goal of God's purposes, but also to see how that goal shed light on the present, how God's people there and then were to live towards the coming kingdom of God and the coming renewal of all creation. A great deal of misunderstanding of Revelation arises from missing the fact that it contextualizes the Christian hope in the realities of the late first-century Roman Empire. It inspires and models the kind of contextualizing we need to do, but it cannot do that for us. We need, if not the revelatory vision with which John was privileged, at least the discernment of Christian wisdom to read the world aright in the light of the Christian hope and to enable us here and now to live towards the new creation.

Part of that contextualizing of Christian hope has to be engagement of some kind with the secular hopes of our time. The book of Revelation engages with Rome's pretensions to universal and eternal rule. In our own time we are still living amid the fading glory of modern progressivism, that pervasive ideology of the modern world that seduced everyone into thinking that tomorrow will—or at, least, should—be better than today. Its major surviving versions are economic neoliberalism and globalization, with their myth of never-ending economic growth, and technological optimism, with its ignorant confidence that human ingenuity will solve all our problems and put us back on track, still headed for the technological utopia in which nature will be finally mastered, all its unruly potential harnessed to our needs and desires. Both economic growth and technological optimism—natural allies, of course—are versions of the delusion that there are no limits to what we can have and do. The dawning ecological catastrophe should surely have dispelled those dreams, but such is the power of progressivism, especially in the USA, that they live on. Climate change denial is one version of their delusive power.

Another feature of the contemporary context of Christian hope—if I may use 'contemporary' to mean the last three or four decades—is that for the first time in human history humans themselves have acquired the power to annihilate human life and much of the rest of creation on this planet. Humans in the past have often faced the prospect—real or imagined—of world-destroying catastrophe. And many civilizations have collapsed through overexploitation of their natural resources, as Jared Diamond's book *Collapse* demonstrated so compellingly.[1] But only with the development of nuclear weapons capable of annihilating the human world did humans face the prospect of an entirely human-caused (anthropogenic) terminal catastrophe. In the period of the Cold War it hung like a sword of Damocles over all our lives. We have displaced that threat for the time being, though it will never go away. The ecological catastrophe that is now underway is much more complex in its causes and challenges, as well as in its foreseeable results. Moreover, while the nuclear threat, since Nagasaki and Hiroshima, has remained no more than a threat, ecological catastrophe is under way. It is engulfing us. Although, like nuclear bombs, it was created by humans, we have now, like the sorcerer's apprentice, lost control of it. It has its own momentum, which, even if humans stopped all carbon emissions worldwide tomorrow (an impossible hope), would still keep going, with some foreseeable consequences that are very alarming and doubtless others we cannot guess. If there is, for concerned Christians, a crisis of hope, I guess that is the main factor. All the books that have taught us that care of creation is a Christian responsibility, that there are all sorts of things we can do—from recycling to lobbying at climate change summits—all seemed to assume we had time to stop anything really bad happening. They exuded hope of a fairly uncomplicated kind. Now we are realizing that, although, of course, we can stop things getting even worse than they will anyway, quite a lot is going wrong unstoppably. And if we haven't managed to stop what is happening—and if neither the politicians in power in China and the USA nor the Christians in the pews are taking the situation seriously—how can we go on hoping?

Ultimate hope and proximate hopes

The relation between ultimate hope and proximate hopes is crucial to our topic. By ultimate hope I mean the final achievement of all God's purposes for his creation when he brings this temporal history to its end and takes the whole creation, redeemed and renewed, into his own eternal life. If we believe in the God of Jesus Christ, that is an unconditional hope that rests on God's faithfulness to his creation and the promise made in the resurrection of Jesus Christ from the dead. Christians have by no means always thought that this hope includes the non-human creation, but happily we have been recovering that full hope. The new heaven and the new earth are not a replacement for this creation, but its renewal, when God will take it beyond the reach of evil, death and transience. Not only is that clear in Romans 8:19–21, for example, but also it is coherent with our own destiny as resurrection to renewed bodily life.

Our bodies are our solidarity with the rest of creation. We are Adam's children, earthy, made of the stuff of this earth like the mammals, the birds, the clouds, the rivers and all the creatures of this earth. So is Jesus Christ, who by rising bodily from death maintained his solidarity with all the creatures of earth through death into new creation. Since new creation is a radical renewal of creation, a transposition of the created world into the conditions of eternity, our ability to conceive of it is necessarily very limited. In my view, we should think of God taking into his new creation the whole chronological extent of this creation's history, everything that has value for eternity. Extinct creatures and lost landscapes—all that God has found good in his creation—will be there. Nothing will be lost except evil and the damage it has done. Of course, we can't imagine it. Ultimate hope ought to be mind-blowing.

Proximate hopes are all the hopes we have for the temporal future. If they are fully formed Christian hopes, they, like ultimate hope, will be based on what God has done for us in Jesus Christ and on the images we are given of the goal that God is going ultimately to realise for his world. Our proximate hopes are for what we can desire and envisage that reflects, within this world, the ultimate hope of new creation. They are on the way to ultimate hope, but must always, of course, fall short of it. It is very important in our contemporary context that we distinguish this vision from modern progressivism and modern utopianism. We are not engaged in a step-by-step progress towards utopia. What we are able to do in realizing our hopes does not, as it were, accumulate, as though we were building the New Jerusalem brick by brick. Sometimes good follows good in a process of improvement, sometimes it doesn't. But the value is not dependent on progression. We have all been brainwashed by progressivism. For things to be worth doing and worth having, they do not have to lead on to even better things. They have value in themselves, and nothing will be lost in the end. When Paul says that our labour will not be in vain (1 Cor 15:58) he does not mean that it will contribute to a historical process of improvement but that it will have effects that will be preserved in the new creation.

One key difference between ultimate hope and proximate hope is that ultimate hope is unconditional. It depends only on God's transcendent act of re-creation. So Paul can call it a hope that does not disappoint (Rom 5:5). But proximate hopes depend partly on what humans do. God's providence is constantly at work engaging with human evil, limiting its effects, bringing good out of it, but he does not abolish it in this world. This world will always be the ambiguous sphere in which evil can frustrate our most reasonable hopes. Proximate hopes can be disappointed. If you have been to Jerusalem, you have probably been to the modern church of Dominus Flevit on the Mount of Olives. It has a fine view over the whole of the old city of Jerusalem, and it is shaped like a tear because it commemorates Jesus' tears of disappointment, when he lamented: 'Jerusalem, Jerusalem . . . How often have I desired to gather your children together, as a hen gathers her brood under her wings, and you were not willing' (Matt 23:37). There was nothing wrong or inadequate about Jesus' hopes for the people of Jerusalem. They flowed from his love for them, which was God's love for them. His hopes were disappointed because love can be rejected.

Getting the relationship between ultimate hope and proximate hopes right has been continually problematic for Christians in the modern period. On the one hand, modern progressivism merged the two in a vision of improvement that would issue in utopia. Utopia became a goal we might achieve—with the catastrophic results we saw in Stalin's Russia and Mao's China. Utopianism is dangerous partly because it cannot content itself with what is pragmatically possible in given circumstances. It overreaches the real limits of the human situation in a massive effort to wrest history towards its utopian goals, usually involving violent suppression of dissent. When it comes to the non-human creation, modern utopianism was usually wedded to the technological exploitation of nature, with the sad ecological consequences we saw in the Soviet Union and Eastern Europe.

On the other hand, in the modern period traditional Christianity has been accused of the opposite error: setting its hopes on an other-worldly goal in order to keep the masses happy with their unfortunate lot here and now. Hope for another world to compensate for the ills of this one incurred the Marxist critique of being the opium of the people. I think the charge has been exaggerated, and we should not devalue the role that ultimate hope has played for people in hopeless circumstances, helping people to go on living when any hope for improvement in this world was entirely unrealistic.

But how can ultimate hope and proximate hopes relate in a way that empowers hopeful activity without falling into the trap of unrealistic utopianism? I think we need to see it like this: Ultimate hope can fund proximate hopes. It enables us to work in the direction of God's purpose, knowing that we are working with God's purpose, working with the grain of the universe. But distinguishing ultimate hope and proximate hopes enables us to be appropriately modest and realistic about what we can hope for here and now in particular contexts. We have to seek out those concrete possibilities for movement in the direction of the kingdom that we can actually identify and work with here and now. We do not hold the tiller of history. We must simply do what we can, more or less, this or that, as the case may be.

Faith, hope and love

If we need to sustain, to refresh, or to renew our hope, one good approach is to reflect on the way it is connected with faith and love in that New Testament trio of Christian virtues that Paul expounds with poetic eloquence in 1 Corinthians 13. The three belong together. I am tempted to say that, like the persons of God the Trinity, they are perichoretic. In other words, they are formed through their mutual relations. Faith, hope, and love are mutually engaging, mutually sustaining, mutually enhancing, and each is necessary for the flourishing of the others. Among other things he says about love, Paul says that it believes all things (faith) and that it hopes all things (hope).

When Paul writes about faith, hope and love, he is speaking about Christian virtues, the work of the Holy Spirit in Christian lives, but it is important to note that there are, as it were, natural versions of each. Without faith, hope, and love, human beings cannot live at all. Although it may be entirely below the level of conscious reflection, all human beings live by a kind of basic trust in reality. We assume that all the ordinary things we do will have the kind of effects they usually have. Hope is natural to human beings and necessary to human life, and similarly care and concern for others, even if only a select group, are indispensable to the life of the social animals we are. In all three of these natural virtues the individual is directed outwards, if not explicitly to God, at least to the world and to other humans. Sin is what impedes that positive, outward directedness of human life, and turns people in on themselves in despair and self-centredness.

What the Holy Spirit does is to renew and to revitalize these good aspects of what it is to be human in the world. Christian redemption is the renewal of human nature, not its replacement. What the Spirit especially does is to re-source these virtues in God and to refocus them on God as their primary object. We live not by some merely implicit trust in reality, vaguely defined, but by faith in the living God. We do not just hope for the best, as they say, but place our hope in God. We love because he first loved us and by loving God we learn to love all that God loves.

The fact that these Christian virtues are the renewal of natural virtues means that it should be natural and not problematic for Christians to work with non-Christian people who care about the planet and share many of our hopes and fears for it. We have Christian distinctives, important to us, but they need not cancel out what we have in common with others. I shall now reflect briefly on each of the three virtues and the way it relates to the others.

Love

I take this first because Paul says that love is the greatest of the three (1 Cor 13:13). The reason may be partly that love is mutual between God and us. Preachers sometimes say that God has faith in us or that God is pinning his hopes on us. No doubt that makes a point in its own way. But Scripture does not speak that way. In the Bible God does not have faith or hope, but God does love. God loves us and we return God's love. Moreover, this is not just a closed circle. It expands as we learn to love what God loves. We come to value other people in something of the way God does and we come to value the rest of creation in something of the way God does. This is not a case of loving only because God tells us to. It is a matter of really sharing in the movement of God's love that encompasses his whole creation and returns to him in reciprocal love. God's love for the rest of creation empowers ours.

Some time ago I was thinking about the first chapter of Genesis when I had one of those breakthrough moments when you see something significant in Scripture that you have not noticed before, even though the passage is familiar. If you read through the creation narrative in Genesis 1, you read that at the end of each day God looks at what he has created on that day and sees that it is good. In other words, he is delighted with it. He appreciates its value. I think the narrative is inviting us to share God's delight in his creation. Whenever it says, 'God saw that it was good,' we are prompted to agree. Knowing the created world as we do, we can enter into God's appreciation of it. So when we get to the creation of humans late on the sixth day and we read God's command to us to have dominion over the creatures, we already know that what God is entrusting to our care is something of great value. It's the world we have begun to delight in as God does. We can only exercise dominion—that is, care responsibly for other creatures—if we have learned to appreciate them, to love them as God does.

'[Love] . . . hopes all things' (NRSV), Paul says in 1 Corinthians 13:7. Love empowers hope. Actually, when we love, we simply cannot help hoping. No one who loves their children can fail to have hopes for them. No one who loves the lovely products of human art and culture can fail to hope that they survive to inspire others for all time. No one who loves the wild places of the world can fail to hope that they will be preserved. No one who loves red squirrels or starlings or snow leopards or rare orchids or coral reefs or tigers can fail to hope that they survive in the habitats they belong to. No one who loves and appreciates the astounding diversity of life in every nook and cranny of this diverse world can fail to hope that it can be preserved and that even the species as yet unknown to us may live for the value they have in themselves. Love inspires hope and energizes hope.

Faith

Faith is what makes Christian hope something much more than optimism about human capabilities. Faith means we do not expect to achieve what we hope for all by ourselves. It means we have to believe in providence.

Providence is a difficult doctrine, but, I think, essential. One way of putting it is this: God can make of what we do much more than we can make of it ourselves. What is actually happening when some human effort for the good is successful? Often it is not just a human person's act or a group of people's act that gets the result, but a collocation of unplanned circumstances that accompany the act. In other circumstances it would not have been successful. Things had to come together in just the way they did. A great deal of human achievement depends on what a secular person would have to say is just coincidence. Maybe we think too much of ourselves to think too much about that, but it doesn't undermine the importance of human achievement. What the human person is intentionally doing to get the result is essential, but it is not all that is going on. God honours what we do by making of it more than we can make of it ourselves.

An interesting biblical illustration of this is the story of the book of Esther. This is a book that never mentions God. It is rather extraordinary that the Bible contains a book that never mentions God. There is one point in the text where we really cannot help thinking of God: when Mordecai says to Queen Esther, 'Who knows? Perhaps you have come to royal dignity for just such a time as this' (4:14 NRSV). But even here the writer scrupulously does no more than suggest that God may be at work behind the scenes. Why this curious absence of God from this narrative of a great deliverance of God's people from threatened genocide? In some ways, the story of Esther is a new exodus narrative, with Esther as the new Moses. But in the original Exodus narrative God is very explicitly present—in manifest and miraculous power. Perhaps the author of Esther thought, as we are also inclined to think when we read of the pillar of fire and cloud and the parting of the Red Sea, that God doesn't seem to do that sort of thing nowadays. So is God not at work in this apparently secular world? Well, Esther does the right and rather courageous thing, and it works—but only because other events, coincidences, conspire to ensure its success. This is the anonymous work of God in a world where he is not evident in manifest interventions. He takes what Esther so resourcefully and courageously does, and he makes more of it than she could have made of it herself.

Faith is another form of protection from hubris and utopianism. What we can do is important but we must let God make of it what he will.

Hope

'Love,' says Paul, 'hopes all things' (1 Cor 13:7). Love, as we have seen, is what empowers and energizes hope, but for 'all things'? Of course, this is elevated poetic style. It surely doesn't endorse indulging utterly fanciful fantasies of hope. But it raises the issue of hope and realism, which is near the heart of our concerns in the crisis of ecological hope.

The first point to make is that proximate hopes must be moderated and directed by realism about the real possibilities of the here and now. Let climate change denial be a warning to us. People who deny climate change are devoted to the American dream of limitless economic growth. They see all the evidence for climate change as a kind of left-wing conspiracy to imperil America's great future. They refuse to face reality because they cannot surrender their very unrealistic hope.

I have learned quite a lot from Bill McKibben's most recent book, *Eaarth: Making a Life on a Tough New Planet*.[2] He spells *Eaarth* with an extra 'a' in it, because, he says, we need a new name for a planet that climate change has already made a different world from the one that humans have lived in for the rest of human history. He writes to address precisely the situation that poses for us the question, 'How can we go on hoping?': the situation in which climate change is not only already under way, but actually has its own momentum that is now unstoppable. We can limit the damage if we act soon, but a lot of damage is inevitable, especially because climate change is bound to trigger other processes, like the release of the vast quantities of methane under the arctic tundra. We are already living in a different and tougher world, and it is bound to get tougher.

But McKibben insists that this is not an excuse to give up. Rather, we need the opposite: increased engagement. We must keep up the fight to prevent climate change getting even more out of control, but also

> we need now to understand the world we've created, and consider—urgently— how to live in it. We can't simply keep stacking boulders against the change that's coming on every front: we need to figure out what parts of our lives and our ideologies we must abandon so that we can protect the core of our societies and civilizations.[3]

(I would want to add: so that we can protect what we can of the rest of creation too.) This doesn't mean giving up hope, but it requires being mature and realistic about where we have got to and need to be going; 'Maturity is not the opposite of hope; it's what makes hope possible.'[4] What, he argues, we must do has a lot in common with what the Transition movement is envisaging and working towards.[5] It means scaling down. It means getting more local than global. In comparison with modern so-called progress and its dreams of limitless growth of many kinds, it means decline. We will need, he says, 'to focus not on growth but on maintenance, on a controlled decline from the perilous heights to which we've climbed.'[6] If we are wise, we need not experience the sort of collapse that Jared Diamond's book documents for societies of the past. We can decline, McKibben says, 'lightly, carefully, gracefully.'[7] And it will bring some benefits of its own, such as the recovery of local community.

But then, what is the role of hope in such a scenario? I would suggest that hope's role will be to be *discerning* and *imaginative*. Discernment is partly about seeking out, spotting and choosing the real possibilities for hope. Remember that hope is empowered by love and remember also the old saying that love will find a way. The truth in the saying is that love may see what merely dispassionate surveys and calculations may miss. Love may be undeterred by the false realism that pours cold water on all our hopes. Love may find the real possibilities for hope—not unrealistic ones, but the ones that need some spotting and some work.

Another Old Testament story can make my point: David and Goliath (1 Sam 17). Of all the unlikely things, the shepherd boy with his sling and his five stones from the brook brings down the giant no one else dares to confront. He refuses Saul's offer of weapons and armour, which would only weigh him down. He just uses his sling and it proves to be precisely the way Goliath can be defeated. With a sling David is able to attack before he comes within range of Goliath's weapons, and with it he reaches the one exposed bit of Goliath's body: his forehead. So David's remarkable success is not a miracle in the ordinary sense. What is remarkable is that David did just the thing that was needed but that no one else thinks of doing. David, confident that God is with him, does the only thing he knows how to do and the one thing likely to succeed. That's what discerning real possibilities for hope might be like.

Hope should be discerning and it can also be *imaginative*. I don't mean fantasizing. Imagination has a much more serious role in human thinking than that. It opens up real possibilities. It suggests how we might do something quite differently. Giving up modern progressivism does not mean giving up human ingenuity and inventiveness. It does not mean giving up technology but adopting and developing appropriate technology. Not the big technological dreams for getting nature back under control. They are just moving on in the same direction that got us here in the fix we're in. We need technologies that suit our properly human place within a creation for which we should care, not enslave. There are a lot of other things to think about. What are the priorities for conserving the non-human creatures when we cannot do everything? How can we scale down to a more localised life without abandoning global relationships and responsibilities in a world where the poorer countries are going to suffer most from what the rich nations have caused, and in a world where there are going to be climate refugees on a scale it is not easy to imagine the world coping with? And among all the manifold good things that we all busy ourselves with, what is really going to matter most? Must we focus more and prioritize?

In conclusion

In a situation of disappointed and uncertain hope, it is the virtuous trio of faith, hope and love that must keep us going. In the New Testament, faith and hope are often linked with endurance.[8] We may need to be prepared for a lot of just keeping going, sticking it out, not giving up when it would be easy to. But faith, hope and love, working, of course, with all the resources of knowledge and expertise that we can muster, must also lead us into new visions of the possible even within a sorely damaged world.

CHAPTER 4

Environmental Missions: An Introduction

Lowell Bliss

'If I am content to heal a hurt slightly,
saying "Peace, peace," where is
no peace;
if I forget the poignant word "Let
love be without dissimulation"
and blunt the edge of truth,
speaking not right things but
smooth things,
then I know nothing of Calvary love.

Amy Carmichael (1867–1951), missionary to India[1]

How should the church respond to the global ecological crisis facing our world? The purpose of this chapter is to introduce a new category within the mission work of the church—environmental missions—an integration of creation care and traditional evangelism, discipleship, and church planting.

If one has the money, the desire, and the suitable substrata topography, it is not difficult to build a wall down into the aquifer below your property. These underground dams impede the flow of water away from your land and can raise the water table below your thirsty crops. As a water storage method, underground dams have advantages: they avoid high evaporation, siltation, and most pollution. The technological know-how for this is not new. The Central Ground Water Board of India built a 160-metre dam across a narrow valley in Kerala State in 1979. It was a brick wall with some tarred felt and plastic sheeting and resulted in an estimated storage of 15,000 cubic metres.[2] God has made *Homo sapiens* an ingenious species and given us the gifts to address ecological issues with skill and creativity.

However, there are political and spiritual dynamics at play. Consider, for example, the first underground dam in India—it was a private dam constructed in Ottapalam, Kerala, and completed in 1964. Whenever you hear the word *private* in relation to Kerala—a state which popularly elected to power its first communist government in 1957—you can know that no construction project is ever as easy as brickwork and tarred felt.

The private Ottapalam underground dam reminds me of a dam project near Hyderabad in India that is over a kilometre in length and effectively seals off the aquifer for use by wealthier *forward caste* landowners.[3] The Dalit (formerly known as *untouchable caste*) villages located on the other side of the dam are denied access to the aquifer. The level of the ground water below their fields has dropped. This poses an intriguing dilemma for Indian Christians and for a global missionary church who, for centuries, have loved the Dalit people in Jesus' name. Whenever we hear of a Dalit village that lacks access to drinking water or to irrigation, it is an easy enough thing to raise some money, form a short-term team, and go dig them a well. But now, any number of wells on the Dalit side of this underground dam will not help. The issue in this case is not *sustainable* water usage, but rather *selfish* water usage. This region of India does not need more ingenious creation care technology. It needs the gospel of reconciliation: the message of Jesus Christ crucified and risen again, in whom there is one baptism in one Spirit, the forgiveness of sins.

What percentage of ecological problems is the direct result of sin? Leaving aside the issue of whether all evil and sin originate in Adam's rebellion in the Garden of Eden, what percentage of the ecological crises mentioned in the headlines is traceable to individual or collective acts of injustice and disobedience to a holy and righteous God? The *Cape Town Commitment* states that a love for God's creation 'demands that we *repent* of our part in the destruction, waste and pollution of the earth's resources and our collusion in the toxic *idolatry* of consumerism' (italics added).[4] Stuart K Hine, the British missionary who translated into English the great nature hymn *How Great Thou Art*, wrote additional verses for it in 1949, including this stanza:

> O when I see ungrateful man defiling
> This bounteous earth, God's gifts so good and great;
> In foolish pride, God's holy Name reviling,
> And yet, in grace, His wrath and judgement wait.[5]

As Hine's verse points out, despite God's generous and gracious provision, our foolish pride and ingratitude lead us to defile his earth and revile his name and mistreat his people whom he has created on that earth, as our neighbours. I know this is sin because I have been guilty of it. Additionally, having tasted of the mercies of God in Christ Jesus, I know that the only remedy for sin is the blood of Christ shed on the cross. I know also that the only hope for a changed lifestyle is the indwelling of the Holy Spirit. What this means, as Jonathan Moo demonstrates in Chapter 2 of this book, is that the cross of Christ is the supreme act of creation care. It also means that even when we bring the best of our scientific or engineering skill to bear, there is no more potent tool in a Christian environmentalist's labour than proclamation evangelism.

Item 5 in the *Call to Action* reads:

> Environmental missions among unreached people groups. We participate in Lausanne's historic call to world evangelization, and believe that environmental issues represent one of the greatest opportunities to demonstrate the love of Christ and plant churches among unreached and unengaged people groups in our generation (*CTC* II.D.1.B). We encourage the church to promote 'environmental missions' as a new category within mission work (akin in function to medical missions).[6]

The rest of this chapter will 1) define environmental missions; 2) develop its analogy to medical missions; and 3) provide three reasons why promoting environmental missions is crucial for the success of creation care efforts worldwide.

William Carey and environmental missions

William Carey is often referred to as the 'father of Protestant missions' or the 'father of modern missions'. He had been sent to India by the London Missionary Society and sailed to Calcutta in 1793. Carey is certainly the archetype of the cross-cultural evangelist and disciple maker, obedient to the Great Commission (Matt 28:18–20). He responded to the same call that the Lausanne Movement has taken up—world evangelization, demonstrating Christ's love and establishing churches 'among unreached and unengaged people groups'. This type of mission work is largely characterized by proclamation evangelism and Christian teaching and training. It has been a familiar activity of the Protestant church since Carey's time.

Many Christians are unaware that William Carey was also a world-class botanist. He had 108 scientific journals tucked away in his baggage. He discovered three species of plants which now bear his name. He introduced the *Linnaean* system of classification, edited Roxburgh's *Florica Indica*, and almost singlehandedly founded the Agricultural Society of India.[7] He had a genuine wonder about the beauty and diversity of God's creation, and his own personal garden grew to become the second largest botanical collection in India. But it is how his passions for ministry and botany converged that is so intriguing. After only a year in India, he sent back to supporters in England a shopping list of farm implements and seeds. He wrote: 'Apply to London seedsmen and others, as it will be a lasting advantage to this country; I shall have it in my power to do this for what I now call my own country.'[8] Employing a sentiment easily applicable to underground dams which exclude the Dalit, one of Carey's earliest biographers wrote: 'It appeared to Carey that if an Agricultural Society could be formed for India, it would show the proprietors of the soil that their interest lay not in rack-renting the peasantry, but in developing the resources of the country, and might besides be a preparation for the time when men should beat their swords into ploughshares and their spears into pruning hooks.[9] Environmental missions thus may be 'a *new* category within mission work', but William Carey effectively integrated creation care with evangelism, discipleship, and church planting over 200 years ago!

In 2010, a small group of missions and creation care leaders met together in order to devise a definition under which to operate: environmental missionaries, they concluded, are 'those sent cross-culturally to labour with Christ—the creator, sustainer and redeemer of all creation—in caring for the environment and making disciples among all peoples.'[10] This is not a difficult definition to unpack.

- 'To be sent' is inherent in the etymology of the words *missionary* and *apostle*, whose Latin or Greek roots mean simply 'sent one'. A missionary is called by the Holy Spirit and, in some way, commissioned by his or her local church, as per the model presented in Acts 13 of Barnabas and Saul sent out from the church at Antioch.

- To be sent 'cross-culturally' is to honour the insistence of Scripture that the good news is intended to be preached to 'all peoples' (Matt 28:19).

- This mandate to go into 'all' the world applies to the new sending churches of the Global South as well. The mentality that believes the missionary enterprise is 'from the West to the Rest' may have held sway for much of the time since Carey, but it has now been largely abandoned by the church.

- As for the theological underpinnings of environmental missions, environmental missionaries embrace the theology (articulated by Moo in Chapter 2) that Jesus is 'the creator, sustainer, and redeemer of all creation'. In the words of theologian Chris Wright, the gospel that environmental missionaries preach is 'good news for the whole creation'.[11]

- Finally, environmental missionaries engage in two types of 'labour'— in caring for the environment, and in making disciples of all nations. Both of these activities can be traditionally understood. Making disciples involves evangelism, teaching and training, and the establishment of local indigenous churches. Examples of creation care are reforestation, sustainable agriculture, waste management, renewable energy, wildlife conservation, toxic mitigation, etc. For many people, what is innovative is that both mandates might exist on the same missionary team and that both activities might be synergistically integrated into a single ministry. As I have written elsewhere: 'Churches planted without trees planted, who is to lament that except the environmental missionary? Souls saved without soils saved is considered a job half done, if only to the heart and calling of an environmental missionary.'[12]

Of course, the story of William Carey is proof that it is not altogether accurate to claim that environmental missions is 'a *new* category within mission work.' Generations of faithful missionaries have followed in Carey's wake, labouring as in his words for a 'lasting advantage' for the ecosystems of their adopted homelands, serving the inhabitants of those ecosystems—human or otherwise—with a Bible in one hand and a shovel in the other. One should read the late Dr Paul Brand's classic essay, 'A Handful of Mud', about soil erosion in the Nilgiri Hills of South India.[13] Or to narrate a different story:

> In 2005 Sister Dorothy Stang, a Catholic nun from Ohio, was found murdered in Pará, Brazil. She was age seventy-three, and she died with a Bible in her hand. Sr Dorothy was a defender of a trans-Amazon development project that was designed to generate jobs for the Anapu people through creation of a fruit processing industry, construction of two small five-hundred-kilowatt hydroelectric power plants, and reforestation in degraded areas. However, 'according to Reuters [news agency], loggers, ranchers, and large farmers have been strong opponents of the project and of Stang.'[14] One of these opponents has since been convicted of hiring the two assassins who murdered her. People call Sr Dorothy a 'rainforest martyr.' Is that silly? But what if we said she was a martyr for the Anapu people? What if we said she was a martyr for the Bible she held in her hand when she died?[15]

Admittedly, Carey and his successors would never have identified themselves as environmental missionaries. The terminology is new. None of them served their people during a period of such severe global crisis. In the end though, it is the commitment to integrate creation care (*bona fide* and scientifically-informed) with evangelism (crucicentric and conversionist) which suggests that environmental missions is a valid new category. Carey was passionate about his horticultural studies but feared that if the church back in England found out about his research, it would—as he wrote in an early letter to a confidant—'mock the expectations of our numerous friends, who are waiting to hear of the conversion of the heathen and overthrow of Satan's kingdom.'[16] It is possible that creation care is fated to be no more than an ancillary avocation on the mission field, but this strikes me as unlikely when I witness the new generation of evangelists who are determined to proclaim the 'whole gospel' and engage in integral mission. The late Ralph Winter, famous missiologist and founder of the US Center for World Mission, told the Korean World Missions Conference in 2009: 'The biggest trend in world mission is the polarization occurring among mission agencies that either focus exclusively on personal salvation or, in contrast, physical needs when they should be doing both.' Or the 'polarization of some doing good things and some saying good things when the two need to be put together.'[17] That polarization is being breached, and the anachronistic language of the 'conversion of the heathen', and the 'West to the Rest' missions model superseded.

Figure 1: Bible translator David Price included frogs, fish, and his natural surroundings as part of his study of the Ambai language. (Photograph: David Price, used with permission)

Scottish evangelist Stuart McAllister writes, 'John Calvin reminded the world that God has given his creatures two books: the book of nature and the word of God. For the Christian, they are not equal in authority or revelatory power, and yet it is a serious neglect to focus on one at the exclusion of the other.'[18] New Zealander David Price is both a Bible translator and a naturalist and so has embraced these 'two books' in a unique way. His life and work is thus helpful in visualizing a definition of an environmental missionary. David and his wife worked on a remote island in southeast Asia. Rejecting classroom walls, he went into the bush with a language helper for his language study—pointing at the birds and twigs which are so significant for this people group's ecology, and also their worldview. By the time they were finished, this passionate naturalist had not only helped translate the Scriptures into the Ambai language, but had combined this with his passion for God's creation: he collected a number of undescribed frog species; he has two species of fish named after him—the saltwater damsel *Chrysiptera pricei* and a freshwater rainbowfish *Chilatherina pricei*. One of David's recent interests is the promulgation of vetiver grass—a non-invasive species whose planting helps prevent erosion while simultaneously enabling restoration of native hillside vegetation. David is now senior environmental consultant for Lead Asia and the John Croumbie Brown ecologist for Eden Vigil—he assists teams of Bible translators and traditional church-planting missionaries in caring for the local ecosystems to which God has called them.

Akin in function to medical missions

The *Call to Action* explains that the work of environmental missions is 'akin in function to medical missions'. This has been a helpful analogy to explain environmental missions since most Christians are familiar with medical missions—and generally uphold the value of caring for 'body and soul'. We can imagine a medical missionary with a Bible in one hand, a stethoscope in the other. Interestingly, there is little explicit sanction for the medical role in Scripture. We find few references to medical practice— many are unflattering, or generally incidental to the main context.[19] Luke, the 'beloved physician' who accompanied the apostle Paul on a portion of his missionary journeys, is not shown as practising his profession, although this probably formed part of the care he gave Paul. In other words, there was a period when biblical scholars undertook a scriptural inquiry of medicine and medical missions, resulting in a legitimization that the church takes for granted today. That same work is currently being done for creation care and environmental missions (see Chapter 3, 'Ecological Hope in Crisis?'), and I fully expect the same legitimizing result.

One of William Carey's first teammates was in a fact a physician and had preceded Carey to India by a handful of years. The story of Dr John Thomas describes a journey with which many environmental missionaries can identify. In the past few years, I have met many Christian university students who ask, first with incredulity and then with great joy, 'Do you really mean I can combine my passion for environmental studies with my heart for missions?' At the time of his own conversion, John Thomas was practising surgery and midwifery in London. The reason for his first trip to India was decidedly financial; having amassed some debt, he took employment as a surgeon, sailing on an East India Company ship to Calcutta. There he eventually stumbled upon some Christians, including one devout soul, presumably Charles Grant, who 'wished me to stay in the country, learn the language, and preach the Gospel to the Hindoos', in other words, to engage India as a *missionary*, not as a surgeon.[20] Thomas writes that, initially, he 'could not accede to the proposal; yet it would often return to my mind, and after a few weeks I became greatly concerned at heart for the condition of these perishing multitudes of Pagans, in utter darkness; and was inflamed with fervent desires to go and declare the glory of Christ among them.'[21] He finally declares that he 'gave [him]self up to this work'—apparently implying the sacrifice of his medical practice in favour of proclaiming the gospel. Indeed, much is written about his preaching and Scripture translation, but nothing is said of surgery and midwifery. The sole appeal made by him and his colleagues, capitalized by them for emphasis, is: 'SEND PREACHERS INTO THIS COUNTRY, AND THEM THAT WILL HELP FORWARD THE TRANSLATION.'[22]

Upon returning to India with Carey in 1793, one of the first things that Thomas did was resume medical practice while Carey went searching for land to procure for their ministry. Thomas' practice was, however, just a temporary measure to help fill the mission's coffers. In the same way, an environmental studies student today who joins a church-planting missionary team, might practise his or her trade simply to provide a visa platform to get the team into a closed country where they can then do their 'real work'. Once Thomas and Carey's team settled in Serampore, the 'former' surgeon was finally able to write to his father and say,

> I act part of the day as a servant, part as a master, doctor, missionary, merchant, justice of the peace, and can even make bread occasionally. I like the part of a strolling missionary best of all; and, next to that, it is a pleasure to heal the poor and relieve them from any of their pains and diseases. I have patients from all parts, all poor and costly, but some of my sweetest moments are spent in giving them relief.[23]

It is a telling comment by Thomas because, as I mentioned earlier, around this same period his colleague William Carey was finding some of his 'sweetest moments' not in the pulpit, but out in his garden, embarking on a career which would advance the horticultural health of Bengal. Both Carey and Thomas rejoiced in the integration of their environmental/medical work with that of taking the gospel to the 'perishing multitudes'.

Finally, there came a climactic moment, whose narration I quote here for the sake of all future environmental missionaries:

> On the 26th of November, [Dr Thomas] set the broken arm of a Hindoo, Krishna Pal by name, and afterwards preached to him the plain gospel in a very effective manner. The man had heard the message before this, but not savingly. 'When his arm was set right,' says Thomas, 'he complained still of pain, but more of himself, as a sinner; and with many tears, cried out: "I am a great sinner! A great sinner am I! Save me, Sahib! save me!" Then with unusual light and enlargement of soul, I renounced all power to save him myself, and

referred him to Jesus, my Saviour, of whose mission and power to save all those who come unto God by Him I spoke many things.'[24]

Figure 2: John Thomas and Krishna Pal[25]

Carey subsequently baptized Krishna Pal in the Ganges. Surely here, could Dr John Thomas be characterized as anything other than a 'medical missionary'—in other words, not merely a surgeon, nor exclusively a proclamation evangelist, but rather as an integrated minister who saw Krishna Pal in all aspects of his humanity and brought good news to both Pal's body and soul? After Thomas' death shortly thereafter, Joshua Ward (another famous member of that first missionary band) said, 'Never shall I forget the time after setting Krishna's arm, he talked to him with such earnestness about his soul's salvation that Krishna wept like a child. Thus Thomas led the way to India, and was the means of the planting of the church by the conversion of the first native.'[26]

Medical missions thus 'led the way to India'. Today, in analogous fashion, environmental missionaries—whether from North or South India, or from overseas—can lead the way to modern India, a country troubled by deforestation, flooding, food insecurity, environmental injustice and biodiversity loss, a country which also hosts the largest number of unreached people groups within her borders. The *Cape Town Commitment* defines *unreached* peoples as those where 'there are no known believers and no churches among them'; and *unengaged* peoples as those where 'we currently know of no churches or agencies that are even trying to share the gospel with them'.[27] The *Call to Action* believes 'that environmental issues represent one of the greatest opportunities to demonstrate the love of Christ and plant churches among unreached and unengaged people groups in our generation'. Of course, this will depend in large part on whether creation care is treated as a value in its own right, not simply as a 'means to an end'—in other words, as a platform for evangelism.

Encourage the church to promote environmental missions

As the director of Eden Vigil, an environmental missions organization, I often have one foot in the creation care world and one in the world of traditional church planting missions. When I talk to a traditionally missions-minded audience, my approach is to appeal to the strategic nature of environmental missions, as stated in the paragraph above: a loving environmental touch can open closed hearts and closed national borders to the preaching of the gospel. Mostly, I echo what all the chapters in this book propound: that the Creation mandate to 'bless, flourish, subdue, rule, till, and keep' (Genesis 1:28; 2:15) applies to all Christians, and that the Creation mandate and the Great Commission are combined in the greatest commandment: to love God and our neighbours.

The audience for this book however has likely come from the creation care world, and so my encouragement to you to promote environmental missions in your own church and organization is three-fold—based on 1) the nature of effective mobilization for the sake of creation, 2) the nature of the global ecological crisis, and 3) the nature of the gospel message itself. To speak more clearly, if you want to make a contribution to creation care in this world, you are well advised to 'promote environmental missions as a new category within mission work'. Here are three reasons why.

The church knows (missionary) compassion and mobilization

Bill McKibben, founder and president of 350.org, is one of the most influential climate change activists in the world and the author of the first popular book on global warming, *The End of Nature*.[28] As he recounted before an audience at Wheaton College, his most personal epiphany on climate change was during a visit to Dhaka, Bangladesh, when he contracted dengue fever. (An increased range of mosquitoes and other disease vectors is a projected effect of warmer temperatures.) McKibben narrates,

> Down at the hospital, in a huge ward, there's just beds as far as you can see, cots you know, and there's somebody in every one of them shivering, and there's people shivering on the floor in between every one of them because there's not enough cots to go around, and in between shivers myself, I remember standing there, and my main thought was 'these people have done nothing to deserve

this.' . . . When the UN tries to calculate how much carbon each country in the world emits, in the hope that we'll someday have some kind of agreement about how to control it, you can't really even get a number for Bangladesh.[29]

McKibben often describes himself as 'just a Methodist Sunday School teacher'.[30] As he told his Wheaton audience, 'In very deep ways, my work all along on this topic of global warming has been informed by my faith and my faith background.'[31] My point in this story is that there are any number of settings where McKibben's faith background and climate change activism could have been integrated—in his Methodist church in Vermont, in a lecture hall at Wheaton, even in his offices at the time at *The New Yorker* magazine. Instead, it was in a *missionary* setting—a hospital room in Bangladesh—where McKibben found compassion, the *heart* knowledge about climate change to accompany the head knowledge.

My mother-in-law was also influenced by an experience connected with Bangladesh. Having heard one of my climate change presentations, she commented afterwards, 'I don't know about this global warming stuff, but if it's affecting Bangladeshis, we should do something about it.' Missions, I am convinced, is an open door for evangelicals into climate action. My mother-in-law understands missions, having been a missionary herself for 26 years in Pakistan. In some ways, these stories are similar to the many occurrences of white Christians in the American South during the Civil Rights years who suddenly stopped and thought, 'My church sends missionaries over to Africa to love black people; why aren't we loving them here at home too? And how do we stop being part of the problem, and start being part of the solution?' Missions provided a recognizable framework in which they could access 'God's love [which] has been poured out into our hearts through the Holy Spirit, who has been given to us' (Rom 5:5).

More than just fuelling compassion, missions provides a framework and an already deployed infrastructure for acting on that compassion—what we would call *mobilization*. Mobilization is at the core of missions. Paul (Saul at the time) experienced that mobilization in Acts 13 when the Holy Spirit ordered the elders at Antioch that he and Barnabas be set apart. Later, Paul would write that there is a bottom line for missions: 'And how can anyone preach unless they are sent?' (Rom 10:15). If the mobilization message of creation care is merely 'Go Green!' then we are promulgating a message that is recent, ill-defined, and met with scepticism. However, the message of 'Go Ye!', as in the words of the Great Commission—'Go and make disciples of all nations'—has the weight of the centuries, the saints, the martyrs, and the promises from God of his authority and presence. It has a deployed infrastructure (agencies, networks, publishing houses, etc) that already extends to the uttermost parts of the earth. Traditional church-planting missions agencies like OMF, Christar, TEAM, and others have all recently appointed environmental strategists. What can evangelicals offer the climate crisis? Nothing less than the missionary enterprise of upwards of 3.7 million sending churches.

Gospel proclamation strikes at the roots of the environmental crisis

The second reason to promote environmental missions as a new category within mission work concerns the nature of our global ecological crisis, namely that there always seems to be 'one more root cause' behind the problems we are trying to analyze and solve. Missions gets to the heart of the matter. For an example which again involves climate change, consider the villager on one of the Maldives' inhabited islands who looks at the coastline eroding around him and asks: why is this happening? The answer, the root cause, is sea level rise, but then that leads to the next question: why are ocean levels increasing? You then can launch upon a chain of inquiry which looks something like this: sea level rise *because* of thermal expansion of the oceans and glacial melt *because* of rising average global temperatures *because* of increased infrared re-radiation toward the planet's surface *because* of an increased percentage of greenhouse gases (especially CO_2) in the atmosphere *because* of the prolonged and increased burning of fossil fuels. And so, as a result of this string of inquiry, many conscientious Christians around the world—motivated by love—have embarked on a colossal undertaking: to first stabilize and then reverse the trend of humanity's emissions from fossil fuels.

But this enterprise will ultimately fail if it does not ask at least one more root cause question: why are human beings burning all that carbon? Henry David Thoreau, the nineteenth century prophet of a simple lifestyle, once observed: 'There are a thousand hacking at the branches of evil to one who is striking at the root.'[32] To strike against carbon emissions—action which has come to be called 'climate change mitigation'—is certainly to strike at root causes, but the *Cape Town Commitment* goes on to identify the primary taproot: we burn so much fossil energy because humanity is enslaved to the idolatry of consumerism. To quote the *Commitment* again: 'Such love for God's creation demands that we repent of our part in the destruction, waste and pollution of the earth's resources and our collusion in the toxic idolatry of consumerism.'[33] Later, it encourages Christians worldwide to 'adopt lifestyles that renounce habits of consumption that are destructive or polluting.'[34] *Anthropogenic global climate change* is a helpful phrase for describing the phenomenon of global warming and for ascribing causation. However, it is a woefully reductionist phrase if we fail to account for all that is *anthropos*—the species created in the image of God, yet who 'exchanged the truth about God for a lie, and worshipped and served created things rather than the Creator—who is forever praised' (Romans 1:25). Consumerism is the ascendant idolatry of the era of cheap energy.

Lest we who are Christ's disciples today be tempted to relegate idolatry to ancient Israel, Canaan, Babylon, Greece, or Rome, consider where Paul tells us (twice) that *greed* amounts to idolatry (Ephesians 5:5, Colossians 3:5). Immediately after calling Christians to repent of 'our collusion in the toxic idolatry of consumerism', the *Cape Town Commitment* declares, 'Instead, we commit ourselves to urgent and prophetic ecological responsibility.'[35] What does it mean to be a responsible prophet in the age of climate change? The way of God's kingdom means that we will not overpower evil by multiplying chariots, gold and alliances (Deut 17:14–17). God is not like 'all the nations around us' (Deut 17:14). Our chief and most effective activity is proclamation. We proclaim repentance of sin and the renunciation of evil. We proclaim the glories of the true and living God. We proclaim the gospel. As the *Commitment* states,

> The gospel challenges the idolatry of rampant consumerism. We are called, as those who serve God and not mammon, to recognize that greed perpetuates poverty, and to renounce it. At the same time, we rejoice that the gospel includes the rich in its call to repentance, and invites them to join the fellowship of those transformed by forgiving grace.[36]

Environmental missions, as a creation care activity, insists on the integration of proclamation evangelism with compassionate creation care—good words to accompany good works.

Our true environmental message is 'Feed on Jesus'

Finally, the nature of the gospel message itself encourages the promotion of environmental missions. The Lausanne Movement is very specific when it declares, 'To evangelize is to spread the good news that Jesus Christ died for our sins and was raised from the dead according to the Scriptures, and that as the reigning Lord he now offers the forgiveness of sins and the liberating gifts of the Spirit to all who repent and believe.'[37] The gospel is not the message of 'emit less carbon!' nor 'consume less!' nor 'reduce; reuse; recycle!' The message of the gospel is rather 'feed instead on the person of the Lord Jesus Christ.' 'I am the bread of life,' Jesus says (John 6:35), and 'I am the living bread that came down from heaven. Whoever eats this bread will live forever. This bread is my flesh, which I will give for the life of the world' (John 6:51). For the hunger in the empty places of our souls, we twenty-first century humans feed on everything *except* Jesus. We consume oil-based plastic objects; we eat petroleum-fertilized processed luxuries; we feed on high-octane purchased experiences. Only the Bread of Life satisfies. Come, find peace in Christ alone.

The gospel subsequently presents us with a model for living as new creatures in Christ. When the sons of Zebedee encountered some recalcitrant Samaritans, they asked Jesus, 'Lord, do You want us to command fire to come down from heaven and consume them?' Some manuscripts record Jesus' rebuke of them as, 'You do not know what kind of spirit you are of; for the Son of Man did not come to destroy men's lives, but to save them' (Luke 9:54–56 NASB). Indeed, just as the Son of Man came not to be served, but to serve, so he came not to consume (in fiery judgement), but to be consumed (in self-sacrifice), and thus to purchase our salvation. 'As the Father has sent me, I am sending you', Jesus says (John 20:21). We are consumed when we offer ourselves to the world in gospel proclamation and gospel compassion.

I understand that scientists and governments around the world are scrambling for what is often called a 'solution to the climate crisis'. A pragmatist may object that my promotion of Christian evangelism as part of that solution is naïve, particularly if a climate solution is dependent on the death of consumerism, which, in turn, is dependent on the conversion of a significant majority of the world's seven billion people. Additionally, a cynic may object that evangelism is a surrender tactic, a giving up on the world. Those objections may well be true for the ways we Christians have formerly understood evangelism. 'As you sent me into the world, I have sent them into the world,' Jesus prays to his Father (John 17:18) and by this we now know that we are called to share in the world's afflictions and compassionately strive alongside our species to seek solutions. But Jesus also says of us, 'They are not of the world, even as I am not of it'—this, despite him being the creator of the world and its incarnate Lord (John 17:16). By this we understand that the church's greatest contribution to any solution for any of the world's problems—including climate change—will invariably be one which falls from the Father's hands, proceeds out of the mouth of God. Many Christians who are working on environmental problems are surely doing so *in* the name of Christ—that is, the compassion of Jesus is their motivation. Environmental missions encourages us also to do this work *with* the name of Christ. This is more than just a subtle distinction between prepositions. Proclaiming the name of Jesus Christ is our privilege, and also our hope of progress in particularly intractable problems. The apostle Peter spoke about the lame beggar now healed:

> Rulers and elders of the people! If we are being called to account today for an act of kindness shown to a man who was lame and are being asked how he was healed, then know this, you and all the people of Israel: It is by the name of Jesus Christ of Nazareth, whom you crucified but whom God raised from the dead, that this man stands before you healed. Jesus is "the stone you builders rejected, which has become the cornerstone." Salvation is found in no one else,

for there is no other name under heaven given to mankind by which we must be saved (Acts 4:8–12).

In a time of drought, an underground dam like the ones constructed in South India can be a tribute to human ingenuity, a fulfilment of the Creation mandate, a good solution. When its benefit is shared with all neighbouring villages, including among 'the least of these', an underground dam can be a monument to the Greatest Commandment. In the end though, an underground dam is simply a one-sided cistern. God's lament, during the time of Jeremiah the prophet, was that 'my people have exchanged their glorious God for worthless idols' (Jer 2:11). Therein is the true drought. 'My people have committed two sins', God goes on to declare—two sins for which the Son of God would one day die in atonement, two sins for which environmental missionaries with a Bible in one hand and a shovel in the other will preach a gospel of hope: 'They have forsaken me, the spring of living water, and have dug their own cisterns, broken cisterns that cannot hold water' (Jer 2:13). The environmental missionary says, 'Feed on the Bread of Life, drink of the Living Water.' Then also, since we do live in parched times, we roll up our sleeves and help dig together the type of unbroken cisterns which are characterized by Christ's life and love.

IMPROVISATIONAL DRAMA, AUSTRALIAN CHURCH YOUTH, AND CLIMATE CHANGE: AN EDUCATIONAL TOOL FOR BRINGING ABOUT POSITIVE CHANGES

We can no longer afford to be complacent and simply engage in endless debate about caring for God's creation. Love for God, our neighbours, and the wider creation, as well as our passion for justice, compels us to 'urgent and prophetic ecological responsibility'.[1] But how do we encourage the church to heed this important responsibility—especially in Australia, a country with government policies that encourage the opposite?

I have been researching the response of Australian young people to climate change—the future generation who will need to cope with its consequences. Perhaps rather surprisingly, given the extreme weather events that are now affecting Australia, both the Australian government and the evangelical church still hold an apathetic view regarding climate change. The former is influenced by the multi-million dollar coal export business (thought to be the only way to boost Australia's economy) and the latter is influenced by poor theology that believes in prioritizing the saving of souls who will then go to heaven at the expense of other concerns including care for God's creation.

I set out to assess whether an improvisational drama workshop could be an effective educational tool for communicating positive initiatives and lifestyle changes, in response to climate change, among Australian church youth. This involved three workshops, of three hours' duration each, combined with pre- and post-workshop questionnaires and a post-workshop focus group discussion. A total of 31 young people from three different evangelical church youth groups participated in separate workshops.

Following a pre-workshop questionnaire, the workshop involved a number of introductory improvisational drama exercises, followed by a future vision exercise. The young people were given three scenarios. To imagine:

- what their life (home and environment) would look like in 20 years' time if no action was taken to reduce the impacts of climate change

- what their life would look like if action was taken
- what action they could take personally to help reduce the impacts of climate change

From each scenario they were asked to create a still image with a sound. The sound was to express the feeling of their selected image.

In the first scenario, one participant felt her image of being 'an increased temperature' to be very unpleasant. She expressed this with the word 'yuck!' She said this activity helped her realize the seriousness of temperatures becoming extremely hot. Another said, 'I liked acting out the feelings—got me into the character of trees being destroyed and helped bring out how I was feeling; it made it all more real.' Other participants expressed a wide variety of images and noises: a number were miserable as their health deteriorated; another cried because she was unable to find enough food to eat; one despaired seeing the forest destroyed by bush fires and a home disappearing under rising sea levels. An unhappy noise occurred from a person feeling hot and sweaty all the time; another was a distressed child who could not play outside due to the intense heat; another was frustrated over escalating electricity costs; and one person was depressed seeing animals and plants dying from the heat.

The images in the second scenario were much more positive as the participants expressed some of the following images and noises: happy driving an electric car; humming while wearing environmentally-friendly clothing; excitement from receiving electricity from solar panels; happy while riding a bike to school; enjoyment while using recycled materials; deep breathing noise because the air was not polluted; singing while picking homegrown fruit and vegetables; sighs of relief at having low electricity bills, having regularly turned off power points; laughter re-designing clothing or furniture; and contentment living in a well-insulated house.

The combined quantitative and qualitative results demonstrated a developing openness among most of the young people to take personal action to reduce the effects of climate change. Most said that they found the improvisational drama to be a non-threatening and entertaining way to think about climate change—a controversial issue among many in Australia.

Based on the results, and in the light of both Liberal (Conservative) and Labour Governments' apathy to climate change and our recent heatwaves, I believe improvisational drama could be an effective educational tool to explore and challenge young and older people on issues related to climate change. It is my hope that this research project will help the Christian community discover that media—such as improvisational drama—can be used to facilitate a genuine and sustainable global creation care movement, within and outside the church.

Sally Shaw, steering group, A Rocha Australia

CHAPTER 5

Creation Care and the Great Commission

Craig Sorley

'The custody of the garden was given in charge to Adam, to show
that we possess the things which God has committed to our
hands, on the condition, that being content with a frugal and
moderate use of them, we should take care of what shall remain.
Let him who possesses a field, so partake of its yearly fruits, that
he may not suffer the ground to be injured by his negligence; but
let him endeavour to hand it down to posterity as he received it . . .
that he neither dissipates it by luxury, nor permits it to be marred
or ruined by neglect . . . let everyone regard himself as the steward
of God in all things which he possesses.'

John Calvin[1]

Little regard for the work of his hands

Several years ago I was leading a *God and Creation* workshop for a group
of Kikuyu people who live on the escarpment of Kenya's famous Rift Valley.
The topic focused on the acute problem of deforestation, and how Christians should respond to such a problem. Once carpeted by a lush cedar and
African olive forest, feeding streams into the valley, most of this escarpment
now lies completely denuded of all forest cover. Many streams have dried
up, firewood is in short supply, and crop yields have dwindled due to soil
erosion. As I spoke about the biblical foundations for creation stewardship,
and how we can honour Christ by caring properly for the land that he created, an older man raised his hand. It was the first time he had heard such a
teaching—he had a question which he asked with a sense of urgency. 'Why
is it that for all these decades the missionaries right here have never told us
that God was concerned about how we managed the forests? Why have they
just watched this destruction taking place all this time?'

This question is one that we as Christians and as evangelical missionaries cannot ignore. It points to the fact that something has been missing in
our efforts to advance the gospel. We have often shown little regard for what

God has made, and most of us have overlooked the wonderful truth that caring for creation is an excellent means of loving both God and people. By mission standards, the area described above is a *reached* community. Thousands have accepted Christ and churches of several denominations were planted decades ago. A majority of the population attends church, but the destruction of the forest has continued unabated. The critical supplies of wood and water that the forest provides are running out, and opportunities to harvest sustainable income from activities like bee-keeping are lost across large swathes of this escarpment.

Fortunately, there is hope, and a consensus is growing among this community. The truth that we should glorify God in all things, that we should respect and care for the work of his hands, is a message that is being planted. More people are showing interest in planting trees and are learning to give proper care to those trees. A program called Farming God's Way is helping to cast a new vision for agriculture, demonstrating that soils and crop yields can be restored when a farmer commits himself to becoming an excellent steward of his fields. Farmers are starting to learn that beehives in the forest can provide an income year after year, as long as the forest remains intact. And many are learning to use fireless cookers—insulated baskets that dramatically reduce the amount of fuel required to cook a meal, providing savings in time, money, and firewood.[2]

This illustration highlights the unfortunate reality that Christians have often failed to embrace creation care as an integral part of living for Christ—but it also points to a very promising and hopeful solution. When God is put back into the centre of our perspective, and when we come to understand the significance of our responsibility to care for creation, transformation can take place, both in the hearts of people and on the land which sustains them.

Christ's creation groans

As Great Commission Christians enter fully into the twenty-first century, this dwindling forest in Kenya is just a microcosm of growing realities that are impacting the whole world. Across the globe, communities are facing unprecedented environmental challenges. According to Colossians 1:16, Christ is the author and creator of all things. Close inspection of the facts reveal that almost every dimension of his creation is under assault. In East Africa, this assault is mournfully obvious in terms of what is happening to the forests, grasslands, water resources, rainfall and climatic patterns, wildlife and bird populations, and soils. The situation is urgent if not critical. These problems converge to cause greater hardship for people. They perpetuate poverty, hunger, heightened competition among ethnic groups, civil unrest, disease, and even death. The Bible speaks clearly about this kind of decay in Romans 8:22, 'We know that the whole creation has been groaning as in the pains of childbirth right up to the present time.'

One of the most disturbing facts about these trends is the speed at which they are taking place. About 10 years ago, the Kenyan Government reported that in just half a generation, the country had lost roughly half of its woodland and forest cover.[3] While tree-planting efforts have increased since that report, the quality of care given to newly planted trees has remained low, and the demand for wood in the form of timber, building poles, and cooking fuel has risen sharply due to a rapidly growing population. As a result deforestation continues to be a major problem.

When we turn to agriculture, the consequences that various environmental problems bring to the human side of this picture are equally, if not more, significant. Deforestation and farming on steep slopes has led to significant soil erosion and a loss of precious water resources. Intensive use of the arable land over several decades has left the land exhausted and worn out. Many leading agriculturalists, such as Roland Bunch, now acknowledge that Africa as a whole is facing a soil fertility crisis.[4]

Over the past eight years, Care of Creation Kenya (CCK) has been conducting informal crop yield surveys with older farmers from various locations across the country. The results have been startling. For primary food crops like maize and beans, farmers consistently report that over 25 to 30 years, their yields have dropped substantially—in many areas harvests today are only 30 percent of what they had been before. A 70 percent loss in per acre productivity is clear evidence that the agricultural landscapes of Kenya are groaning. This figure has been consistently confirmed by groups of farmers who have visited CCK from different parts of Kenya since 2010.

As coaxing food from the ground becomes more difficult, this leads to significant social consequences. Farmers watching their yields decline have become discouraged, and they openly admit that farming is no longer a profitable livelihood. As a result the younger generation has a pessimistic view of farming. Youth across Kenya are generally abandoning agriculture as a viable option for supporting their own families. When we combine this trend with the fact that the average age of the Kenyan farmer is 55, and the life expectancy for the average Kenyan is 60, the urgent nature of this dilemma becomes clear.[5] It raises a rather disturbing question: who will be growing our food in the future? Are we going to sit back and watch millions abandon their land and migrate to urban areas, where the accountability structures of rural life break down, where employment opportunities are few, and where many end up living in slums? Or can we offer something better, something that will bring healing to a groaning creation, a solution that would allow agrarian communities across the world to live productively on their own farms, in his creation, as originally intended by God when he placed man into the Garden of Eden?

The heart of the problem

Agriculture is not only central to Kenyans, it is central to countless millions across the world, especially in developing nations. In Africa, small-scale agriculture is the single most common vocation providing a livelihood for the greatest proportion of its people. The foundation of entire cultures and people groups are built upon farming. Why then have Great Commission Christians, eager to spread the gospel, all but ignored this reality? We plant churches, we train pastors, we translate the Scriptures, we teach theology, we run medical clinics, but we pay little attention to farming, forestry, or other creation care topics. This is where the heart of the problems lies.

While agriculture is the economic mainstay for communities all across Africa, most African farmers who confess Christ as Lord have little or no meaningful connection between their faith in Christ and their primary vocation in life. What they learn at church on Sunday often has no bearing on the daily outworking of life on their farms. Spiritual things are put into one box, and agricultural things into another box. There is little if any relationship between the two.

The root of this problem goes much deeper. It lies in the ultimate truth that communities and societies are corrupted by sin, and the hearts, perspectives, and minds of people are not oriented toward our mandate for creation care. The majority of Christian farmers in Kenya have little or no vision for restoring degraded landscapes. There is little or no passion to honour God in every step of the agricultural process, from planting to harvest. There is no commitment to discover and implement the most sustainable practices at all times. As Christians, we must humbly admit that something has been missing in our own understanding and presentation of the gospel. Most of us have never studied, seriously discussed, heard sermons on, or been discipled in creation care, and as a result it is usually a blank page in our ministry or discipleship programs. Our greatest need is to be transformed by the renewing of our hearts and minds, in accordance with Romans 12:2. If Christ's creation is groaning, we should do something about it, because when creation groans, people groan. Our worldview on environmental matters has often been shaped more by science, politics, or by secular economic thinking than by Scripture. When farmers in Kenya have heard no biblically-based teaching in church related to agriculture, we must recognize that as a tragedy. It is equally a tragedy for Christians in the West.

But God is moving to bring about an exciting and refreshing change to the evangelical church, a change that will mature and brighten its testimony. As we consider what we should be doing as Christians, let us reflect on what Joseph Sittler once said:

> When we turn the attention of the church to a definition of the Christian relationship with the natural world, we are not stepping away from grave and proper theological ideas; we are stepping right into the middle of them. There is a deeply rooted, genuinely Christian motivation for attention to God's creation, despite the fact that many church people consider ecology to be a secular concern. 'What does environmental preservation have to do with Jesus Christ and his church?' they ask. They could not be more shallow or more wrong.[6]

Creation care and the Great Commission: a field ripe for the harvest

Joseph Sittler urges that we adopt something new into our traditional mode of advancing the gospel. There is a new tool we need in our toolbox, one which can bring countless benefits to people around the world in a way that glorifies God, and particularly helps the poor.

As environmental concerns gain more attention; as drought, deforestation, water scarcity, and other issues scar landscapes and bring greater suffering to many; how seriously has the evangelical church considered the beauty of integrating two things into one cohesive whole? What if we combined efforts to fulfil the Great Commission with efforts to bring healing to creation as well? In my own thinking, this concept bursts forth with beauty.

Let us recall the words of Christ in Matthew 28:19–20: 'Therefore go and make disciples of all nations, baptizing them in the name of the Father and of the Son and of the Holy Spirit, and teaching them to obey everything I have commanded you.'

Jesus did not command that we go out and make mere converts. He called us to make *disciples* whose lives would change the world. Discipleship transforms people, communities, and entire nations—and, in a world that changes over time, that discipleship will need to be applied in fresh new ways to new circumstances.

A passion for Christ must include a commitment to care for everything he has made. The time has come for a *theology of creation* to be incorporated into discipleship training. We often lack the biblical foundations and conviction to preach, to articulate, to develop Bible studies, or to provide leadership in this area, so it will not be easy to initiate this.

Imagine a world where churches and ministries of all kinds were able to provide sound biblical guidance on this issue, guidance which would stimulate the application of sound scientific and practical solutions, and the ability to lead the world by example. Imagine mission agencies committed to discipling others towards a Christ-honouring creation care ethic, agencies which refused to be content with simply handing out relief supplies when famine strikes. Imagine these agencies committed to a much larger vision where they worked hand in hand with local communities to restore watersheds, to rebuild degraded landscapes, and to prevent hunger or famine from afflicting people in the first place. Paul Brand, the famous medical missionary to India, once said, 'I would gladly give up medicine and surgery tomorrow if by so doing I could have some influence on policy with regard to mud and soil. The world will die from lack of soil and pure water long before it will die from lack of antibiotics or surgical skill and knowledge.'[7]

Here are some questions to consider in the context of designing missions strategies to spread the gospel:

- If Christ desires to change people into his likeness, how should that transformation be lived out in terms of environmental and agricultural stewardship? How would it be demonstrated in the life of a farmer or pastoralist, a fisherman, or in the life of a businessman who uses natural resources to sustain his business?

- In a community where wood is collected from a dwindling forest, or where farmland is losing productivity due to erosion, how should a local pastor be trained, and what role should he play in leading his community to address these problems? How can missionaries, seminaries, and Bible schools best prepare a pastor for this kind of role?

- For the indigenous or foreign missionary who is called to serve an unreached people group struggling with chronic hunger, what type of education would best prepare that missionary for this kind of situation? What priorities should be emphasized by the sending church or the mission agency to reflect a holistic gospel that brings both spiritual healing to the people and physical healing to their land?

As we think of the opportunities that exist by integrating creation care as a meaningful component of our Great Commission endeavours, here are a few examples that fuel my own enthusiasm.

Potential for discipling millions of believers

Around the world countless Christians are poorly equipped to apply their faith in a way that provides meaningful solutions to environmental concerns. Discipling these believers with the biblical foundations of creation care will lead to a transformation of perspective and behaviour. When God convicts the hearts of people, widespread change can take place. Imagine the beauty of restored landscapes and the testimonies of Christian farmers who put faith into action on the ground, because God has convicted them to become excellent stewards of their land.

Potential for stemming the tide of poverty and for saving lives

When the land becomes impoverished, people become impoverished. As Christians, God has called us to bring mercy and justice to the poor. When we integrate creation care as a long-term component of our efforts to show mercy to the poor, to restore the productivity of farms, and to replant lost forest cover, the impact will be felt for generations to come. Isaiah 58:9–11 gives us ample reason to move in this direction: 'If you do away with the yoke of oppression . . . and if you spend yourselves in behalf of the hungry and satisfy the needs of the oppressed, then your light will rise in the darkness . . . You will be like a well-watered garden, like a spring whose waters never fail.'

Potential for opening doors to unreached people groups

There are countless communities around the world where little or no presence of the church exists. These communities are on the front line of serious environmental decline. A mission strategy designed to bring healing to the creation—where wood, water, and food supplies are restored—is a strategy that will be met with open arms. Christ's love demonstrated practically, on the ground, could break down barriers, cultivating opportunities to share the gospel.

Potential for drawing in people who shun the church

Thousands of people who are part of the environmental movement have rejected the gospel simply because the church has been so silent on this topic. When we begin providing a thoughtful response to the issues in our churches, our witness to these potentially energetic allies will be strengthened. This is not to minimise the spiritual aspect of evangelism, for it is only the Holy Spirit who can convict of sin, and of the need for salvation. A biblically-based creation care ethic would provide a powerful foundation which supports the passions they already possess. By thoughtfully engaging with them, cooperating with their endeavours, and sharing our own convictions, many such people, through the power of the Holy Spirit, might be brought to saving faith in Christ. The discipleship that would ensue would then equip them to express their passions in a way that glorifies the creator.

Potential for enlisting young people into holistic ministry

Christian young people around the world are far more concerned about environmental matters than their parents' generation. This groundswell of interest holds tremendous promise, and the critical task before us is to channel that energy effectively. Combining Christian ministry or discipleship with caring for creation opens up huge possibilities. Young people who are being trained in Christ-centred churches or institutions in Africa, Asia, North America or elsewhere, and who never thought of themselves as being eligible for missions or Christian ministry in the traditional sense, can play a strategic role in advancing the cause of Christ.

The frontier is wide open. It is a field ripe for the harvest. Embracing our neglected role to care for creation not only will help strengthen the testimony of the church, not only will bring hope to the hungry—but will also provide one of the most promising answers to one of the most pressing issues of our time.

So as we consider this new frontier, it is clear that new approaches to ministry and a new type of missionary should be added to the team. For decades we have seen wonderful work accomplished by the hands of medical doctors, by those who train pastors, plant churches, or who translate Scripture into a native tongue. It is time to add to those collective efforts and broaden the vision. Integrating creation care into Christian outreach and missions can help us rediscover the beauty of holistic ministry that does not separate the spiritual from the physical.

Our world needs missionaries with expertise in forestry, fisheries, and sustainable agriculture. It needs godly people who are trained in appropriate technology, wildlife conservation, water resource management, environmental education, and other similar fields. And since God is the author of both science and the Bible, these missionaries should receive sound training theologically, scientifically, and socially, so they can effectively demonstrate the fullness of Christ's love to a hurting world, and disciple those who find faith in him.

Discipleship integrated with creation-care works

Elsewhere in this book we have sound reasoning for embracing a creation care ethic because of multiple truths found in Scripture. Do we have evidence that a creation care ministry actually works in the context of missions? Can a biblical worldview on creation change both the perspectives and behaviour of people? Can we fulfil the Great Commission while also working to heal broken landscapes in a way that brings hope to the hungry? At Care of Creation Kenya (CCK) we would answer these questions with a resounding 'yes'. Discipleship integrated with creation care really works.

Evidence of transformation

CCK training and discipleship program

As part of our strategy to spread a biblical vision for creation care in East Africa, CCK has engaged in ongoing efforts to organize and host a wide range of training workshops and conferences. They have revolved primarily around work with professing Christians. In this sense, our ministry is one of discipleship rather than evangelism. Some events have been international; more commonly, they have taken place on a regional or local level, attended by denominational leaders, community leaders, leaders from Christian organizations, or local farmers and pastors. In brief, and as general practice, most training courses are between one and four days in length and incorporate the following elements:

1. Training begins with a thorough review of the pressing environmental or agricultural concerns common to East Africa. Emphasizing the urgent nature of these issues sets the stage for why people from all walks of life must consider an appropriate response.

2. Next, a focused emphasis on biblical principles is presented, including concepts taken from both the Old and New Testaments. This teaching clearly underscores the biblical mandate to care properly for God's creation and serves as the central and most critical discipleship piece leading to a change in worldview and attitude.

3. The third portion of the training is practical, highlighting ways to take action. Topics include tree planting and tree nursery management, Farming God's Way (see below), beekeeping, the use of fireless cookers, spreading the vision through biblically-based education in churches and communities, and so on. The emphasis given to a particular topic will vary depending on available time and the particular interests of the audience. A considerable portion of this element includes hands-on outdoor training at our tree nursery and Farming God's Way demonstration site.

One of the most important aspects of training, however, occurs during the discipleship process, continuing over a period of several years, through CCK's extension outreach program. Follow-up visits by CCK staff are conducted with farmers, pastors, women's groups, or community leaders, where both the biblical and practical aspects of the initial training are reviewed and reinforced. While consistent follow-up with those living further afield is difficult, many choose to participate in subsequent training courses to improve their knowledge and skills.

Change of attitude and worldview

At CCK, we are convinced that believers from across the country must be mobilized to action if we are to restore the broken landscapes of Kenya. Behaviours will not change if attitudes are not changed. Therefore, the first and most critical step in mobilizing such action is the transformation of the people's mindsets and attitudes towards creation. CCK routinely conducts post-conference evaluations to help measure the impact of training. The following quotations show how God can use events like this to transform the hearts and minds of people.

- 'I was deeply challenged because I realized that I had the lowest level of knowledge about environmental concerns. I have been the best tree cutter and have never replanted anything. My sermons only focused on spiritual needs and never touched on the physical things which God has created.' *Pastor Festus Kamunde*

- 'I was challenged to hear that God is coming to reconcile the whole creation to himself and I feel the need to repent before God as I have neglected his creation. I have never thought about environmental stewardship—but now I have a whole new perspective.' *John Mwangi Kerugoya*

- 'I am committed to go back to Kitui and train my people there. This training has transformed my life.' *Reverend Nelson*

- 'This is a refreshing aspect of the gospel that can truly transform our future both spiritually and physically. It should be taught everywhere.' *Ibrahim Chemunay, Nairobi Great Commission School*

- 'I now see how caring for God's creation can be a very powerful way to disciple our fellow Christians. This was the most significant realization for me as a result of this training. When can we do a Training of Trainers course on this issue?' *Rev Patrick Mureithi Maina, Presbyterian Church of East Africa*

- 'This training has really changed my mindset and I am ready to go and become an example to the rest of my flock.' *Pastor Alex Mwaura Kimani, First Baptist Church, Matathia*

Change of behaviour and action

Such quotations are encouraging and show a change of attitude as a result of training events. However, the real evidence of transformation is only seen through action. Several years ago, a thorough post-conference evaluation helped measure and document behaviour change six months after an international CCK conference. One hundred delegates participated and the results were very encouraging: 15 new tree nurseries had been established and 16,000 trees were reported to have been planted. A third of respondents had conducted educational outreach activities on creation care through speaking, preaching or holding local workshops. Others indicated they had made specific changes in lifestyle; some had adopted the practice of Farming God's Way—others had used proceedings from the conference to develop teaching materials on creation care.

There is further evidence of change. Over the past eight years, leaders from several evangelical denominations have attended CCK training, some attending two or more courses. There are currently four mainline denominations making deliberate efforts to embrace a creation care ethic and to develop long-term action plans: the Presbyterian Church of East Africa (PCEA), the Methodist Church of Kenya (MCK), the Full Gospel Church of Kenya (FGCK), and the Anglican Church of Kenya (ACK). Similar efforts have been made in individual churches—for example, Membley Baptist Church, which serves middle- to upper-income people in a suburb of Nairobi. In July 2013, Rev Benson Irungu and his elders formally endorsed creation care as a strategic ministry they will develop and pursue as a congregation.

Farming God's Way (FGW): Changed behaviour and improved harvests

The lives of small-scale farmers are being blessed and transformed by the ministry of FGW.[8] The beauty of this movement, now sweeping across Africa, is that it is far more than a new system of growing crops. It is a holistic ministry that disciples farmers, stimulating them towards a commitment to restore their soils and become excellent stewards of their land. As such, FGW does not separate the spiritual from the physical, effectively addressing the roots of the declines that are taking place. Biblical principles are deliberately integrated and taught along with practical and sustainable hands-on techniques. Compared with conventional agricultural practice seen across much of Africa, FGW is a distinct and discipleship-oriented version of what is known as *conservation agriculture*. FGW has a proven track record in healing degraded land and improving crop productivity at the same time. In many cases, three- to five-fold increases in crop yields have been realized. The following quotations illustrate how FGW training can transform farmers' hearts and minds.

In terms of actual harvests, FGW is breathing life and hope back into agrarian communities. Trials in the Rift Valley using FGW methods, conducted by farmers and at local schools and churches, have produced corn

- 'I have now learned that we have completely left God out of our farms. Your teaching has opened my heart to realize that we have strayed from God's will and I know God is calling us back to the garden. We claim to have faith but have not been practising it.' *Henry Njoroge Munjuga*

- 'These teachings on Farming God's Way are a big revelation and the best thing to have happened in our lives as farmers, particularly because we have realized that farming is ordained by the First Farmer—God, himself.' *Representative of a Farmers Group from Ndeiya*

- 'Since I attended the Farming God's Way course, I have changed my perspective of farming. I used to hate farming but now I love it and I dream about it every day.' *Hannah Wanjiku*

and bean harvests between two and four times larger than adjacent fields farmed in the conventional manner. Similar results have been reported from other parts of the country. In 2011, the corn yield from a farmer named Simon Njoroge was almost six times greater than his neighbour's plot, which held the exact same number of corn plants.

CCK has also documented conclusive results on the campus of Moffat Bible College, where our FGW demonstration site is located. Over the past five years forty trials have been conducted with five different crops—corn, beans, potatoes, onions, and cabbage. FGW fields have consistently produced yields two to three times larger than fields managed in the conventional manner, where all factors between the FGW and conventional plots were equivalent. (That is, both plots were equivalent in size, planted on the same day, using the same crop variety, same spacing, same amount of external inputs such as manure or fertilizer, and receiving the same amount of rainfall.)

The results and success of FGW speak for themselves. Imagine the joy experienced by a farmer who realizes that he can honour God in how he farms, that he can restore his soil and double or triple his yields without the costly input of chemical fertilizers. Imagine a young person who realizes that farming is not a gruelling and hopeless means of making a living, but a potentially profitable vocation. Imagine communities across Africa, living productively in the garden of God's creation. While poverty and chronic hunger still plague millions, Farming God's Way is one example of a promising creation care solution that points us in the right direction and brings glory to God.

Summing up: Our glorious opportunity

Something significant has been missing from our understanding and presentation of the gospel. We have often shown little regard for what God has made and have overlooked the truth that creation care should be an integral part of living fully for Christ. His creation groans. There are serious and urgent issues affecting people and communities across the globe. Our world cries out for Christ-centred leadership in this field.

A glorious opportunity stands before us in discipling believers and non-believers alike—discipleship which can transform hearts and mind-sets, can change behaviour, and can bring healing to broken landscapes. By learning how to embrace, articulate, and implement a biblical worldview on this topic, we can develop a response offering hope to the poor, a healthier future for the next generation, and a hope that vividly demonstrates the all-encompassing nature of Christ's love. By integrating creation care into the cause of evangelical ministry, we will bring good news to a world that strives to wrestle with this problem in its own strength—a world that normally leaves God entirely out of the environmental picture. Caring for creation can be a wonderful way to love God and to meet the needs of others.

CASE STUDY 2

THE WORK OF A ROCHA GHANA

A Rocha Ghana (ARG) has a mission 'to effectively manage the resources of the earth given to us by God through sustainable actions' of local communities.

One group of projects is concerned with community-based conservation. The work of ARG has helped to ensure that key areas of Ghana are now being protected and managed sustainably by local communities. Since 2005, for instance, 1,300 square kilometers of community land has been allocated to Community Resource Management Areas. Communities have benefited from working together, and are ready to receive Payment for Ecosystem Services through REDD+ (Reducing Emissions from Deforestation and Forest Degradation). ARG is also working with UNESCO to create a Biosphere Reserve at Lake Bosomtwe—Ghana's only natural lake and a unique ecosystem—which local communities are learning to manage.

Another area being protected is the Atewa Range Forest Reserve, home to an exceptional number of plant species not found elsewhere in Ghana, and the source of three rivers supplying water to much of Ghana. This area has been under threat from illegal logging, hunting, and mining. ARG is working to raise the global profile of this area, and to promote it as a destination for ecotourism to provide alternative livelihoods for local people.

Various tree-planting initiatives are also in place across Ghana in partnership with schools and farmers. In five years, 63,000 trees have been planted—all of local species, such as Odum (*Chlorophora excelsa*), Kusia (*Nauclea diderrichii*), Mahogany (*Khaya senegalensis* and *Khaya ivorensis*) and Dawadawa (*Parkia clappertoniana*).

A second group of projects is based around education. ARG helps run numerous eco-clubs in universities and second-cycle schools (14–17 year olds), focused on conservation education and the Climate Stewards project. It has also started to work with churches and Christian groups to help them understand how creation care is part of their faith as Christians, and how to apply it.

ARG also works in Muslim areas. In Ghana, Christians and Muslims co-exist peacefully and take national actions together. Through the Inter-faith Alliance for Management of Natural Resources, leaders from both faiths are helped to become more aware of creation care and to prepare creation care messages and sermons.

A final group of ARG's projects involves research, to find out how best conservation should be carried out, particularly when it comes to *flagship mammals*.

One example of this is to survey elephants and chimpanzees in various national parks, with the aim of helping to create a corridor between western Ghana and eastern Cote d'Ivoire. This facilitates the migration of these animals and helps alleviate the problems of their habitats being under severe strain.

A second example is working out how to deal with elephant-human conflict. Elephants raiding agricultural crops is a problem in many parts of Africa, including the Bia Conservation Area in western Ghana. Here it has resulted in the death of several elephants and widespread hostilities by fringe communities towards park staff. Following research, ARG now educates and supports farmers in using safe deterrents such as *hot pepper grease* to discourage elephants from coming into crop areas.

A Rocha Ghana aims to carry out its mandate, showing through its work that it is Christian, and that it seeks the cooperation of all people across cultures in communicating the need for the conservation of God's creation.

Seth Appiah-Kubi, National Director, A Rocha Ghana

CHAPTER 6

How Does Creation Care Belong within an Evangelical Understanding of Mission?

Dave Bookless

'If Jesus is Lord of all the earth, we cannot separate our relationship to Christ from how we act in relation to the earth. For to proclaim the gospel that says "Jesus is Lord" is to proclaim the gospel that includes the earth, since Christ's Lordship is over all creation. Creation care is thus a gospel issue within the Lordship of Christ.'

Cape Town Commitment[1]

Evangelical Christians concerned about the care of God's creation have been on a long journey. Francis Schaeffer's *Pollution and the Death of Man* was published as early as 1970, offering a biblically-based response both to the growth of environmental consciousness and to those who sought to blame environmental destruction on Christianity.[2] Through the 1970s and 1980s, the Au Sable Institute in the USA and the A Rocha movement—first in Portugal and from the 1990s spreading across nearly 20 countries—explored the theology and practice of evangelical environmental concern.[3] Since the 1990s there has been a surge of initiatives, statements, and books from evangelicals addressing issues as diverse as biblical foundations, climate change, biodiversity loss, and sustainable agriculture. Yet, for many, the notion of creation care as an expression of Christian mission has continued to appear exotic, eccentric or even erroneous. Those few evangelicals who have been on the journey of creation care for many years have become familiar with being ignored, marginalised or regarded with bemusement by their fellows.

In this context, the *Cape Town Commitment* marks a significant milestone. It illustrates, as quoted above, how environmental concerns have moved from the margins of mission concern to the centre of a mission theology. Mission agencies are now becoming aware both of their own environmental impact and of how a changing global environment is hurting people in developing countries first and hitting them hardest. Among many responses, some mission agencies are implementing travel policies minimizing unnecessary flights and offsetting the harmful emissions from those they still have to make; others are changing their work in disaster relief and poverty alleviation to mitigate and adapt to the consequences of a changing climate. In my 20 years with A Rocha, I have seen us move from being an oddity on the fringes of mission to having partnerships with a range of major European and global mission agencies.

All of this could simply illustrate that evangelicals are seeking to be relevant to today's context. However, it appears that there is something much deeper going on. Caring for creation raises theological issues for evangelicals that could potentially lead to a seismic shift in evangelical missional theology. Mission itself is beginning to be understood as not just about people but also about the non-human creation, not merely preparing for heaven but also caring for earth. To comprehend this shift, it is important to offer working definitions of the key terms *evangelical* and *mission*.

Defining *evangelical* is a potentially dangerous exercise, as it is a term that has been fought over verbally on many occasions. Some definitions are effectively negative (neither Catholic nor Orthodox nor mainstream Protestant), and others somewhat tribal, identified with specific issues, institutions or key leaders. However, evangelicalism is a global movement, now strongest in the Global South, yet with its roots in eighteenth and nineteenth century Europe and North America. Perhaps the best definition, and the one followed here, is left to an historian rather than a theologian. In his authoritative history of British evangelicalism, Professor David Bebbington defines evangelicalism as characterised by four fundamental positive qualities:[4]

- Biblicism: a particular regard for the Bible as the source of all spiritual truth

- Crucicentrism: a focus on the atoning work of Christ on the cross

- Conversionism: the belief that individual humans need to be converted to Christ

- Activism: the belief that the gospel needs to be expressed in practical outcomes

This chapter will trace how these core values are shaping the evangelical response to today's environmental crisis. It will be suggested that evangelical missiology has largely failed to be fully biblical, cross-centred, conversionist and activist in engaging with non-human creation. However, where these core values are rediscovered and applied to the environmental crisis, an evangelical approach to mission offers a distinctive and vital contribution to an environmental context often paralysed by lethargy or fear.

In terms of defining *mission*, John Stott, writing in 1975 and effectively expounding the 1974 Lausanne Covenant, helpfully distinguished God's mission (*Missio Dei*) from the church's mission, which is necessarily more limited but includes 'everything the church is sent into the world to do'.[5] He made it clear that this not only includes evangelism but that, as in the ministry of Jesus, Christians are called both to proclaim and demonstrate the good news, to evangelize and to be involved in acts of mercy and justice. In his later writings, Stott specifically emphasised that creation care should be an integral part of the Christian life. His final book, *The Radical Disciple*, focused on eight areas of Christian discipleship often neglected by contemporary evangelicals, with a chapter explicitly on creation care, where he wrote, 'God intends our care of the creation to reflect our love for the Creator.'[6]

An evangelical understanding of mission should always be based on an overview of the great themes of Scripture. Professor N T (Tom) Wright, the evangelical New Testament scholar, helpfully summarizes these in the following way:

> The early church saw history as a five-act play, with creation, fall and the story of Israel as the first three acts, and the drama reaching its climax in the fourth act, the events concerning Jesus of Nazareth. The early church itself was living in the fifth act, where the actors are charged with the task and responsibility of improvising the final scenes of the play on the basis of all that has gone before.[7]

In my book *Planetwise*, these five biblical acts—creation, fall, Israel, Jesus, the present and future age—are each examined through the lens of God's purposes for the whole creation.[8] What became abundantly clear in researching the book is that no Christian who takes Scripture seriously and reads it with an open mind can honestly ignore the implication that we have got it wrong in terms of our definition of mission. From Genesis to Revelation, God's purposes are far wider than human salvation or human welfare—although the place of humanity within those purposes is critical.

The rest of this chapter will seek to examine an evangelical understanding of mission through a matrix combining Bebbington's four-point definition of evangelicalism with N T Wright's five-act summary of the biblical narrative.

- Creation and Israel (Act 1 and Act 3) will be examined in looking at *biblicism*

- The Fall (Act 2) will be covered in exploring *conversionism*

- Jesus (Act 4) under *crucicentrism*

- Present and future age (Act 5) under *activism* and *biblicism*

Another valuable way of approaching the place of environment within mission is *The Five Marks of Mission*. These derive from an Anglican or

Episcopal source—rather than an explicitly evangelical one—but they outline the dimensions of mission in a way that is consonant with the biblical witness. The *Five Marks* are:

1. To proclaim the good news of the kingdom

2. To teach, baptize and nurture new believers

3. To respond to human need by loving service

4. To seek to transform unjust structures of society, to challenge violence of every kind and to pursue peace and reconciliation

5. To strive to safeguard the integrity of creation and sustain and renew the life of the earth[9]

Biblicism

The gospel is sometimes described as an eternal, unchanging message expressed afresh in changing contexts. Today's context of increasing resource depletion, climate uncertainty, massive migration, biodiversity loss, and unjust sharing of resources has led Bible-based Christians in one of two directions.

To some, all these are signs that Jesus must be coming back soon. Climate change simply means we need to evangelize the world more quickly. At the risk of over-simplifying, mission is all about soul-winning. This earth doesn't matter . . . we're going to get a new heavens and new earth anyway, aren't we? The American Christian writer Cal Thomas comes close to this in saying that 'Jesus' teaching has nothing to do with global warming or the environment' and that the task of Christians is simply to 'prepare themselves and others for the world to come'.[10]

However, an increasing number question this. Good evangelical theology always returns to Scripture in the light of a changing context, and the biggest biblical questions provoked by today's context are surely: what is God's mission in his world, and consequently what is ours? Just as Wilberforce, Shaftesbury, and others went back to the Bible when faced with massive social injustice in the form of slavery or prison reform, so today we can trace the beginnings of a radically biblical rediscovery of God's heart for the whole creation.

There is a parallel to what happened after the biblical foundations laid by the Lausanne Covenant in the 1970s, which led on to books such as Ronald Sider's *Rich Christians in an Age of Hunger*, and the growth of movements like World Vision, Compassion and Tearfund.[11] All of these were inspired by a renewed evangelical conviction that, in order to be fully biblical, mission must combine both evangelism and social action. Just as God spoke through Old Testament prophets to condemn injustice and the exploitation of the poor, so must we. Just as Jesus cared for body, mind, and soul, so must we heal the sick, visit the prisoner and relieve poverty—not simply as an aid to evangelism, but as an expression of mission in their own right. The Lausanne Movement, and more recently the Micah Network, have both strongly supported this *holistic* or *integral* understanding of mission.

All of this is well and good but, so far, definitions of integral mission have been overwhelmingly anthropocentric. Mission is seen in entirely human terms. Even the most holistic and integral evangelical definitions of mission imply that the rest of the planet matters only in relation to how it affects human well-being materially or spiritually. Human-induced climate change is seen as the largest driver of poverty, and the biggest obstacle to human development. Environmental issues are a legitimate expression of biblically-based mission, but only insofar as they improve conditions for human flourishing.

Today, however, just as the 1974 Lausanne Covenant widened evangelical understandings of mission to embrace social action, the 2010 *Cape Town Commitment* has opened evangelical eyes to creation care as a further dimension of mission that is profoundly biblical:

> Integral mission means discerning, proclaiming, and living out, the biblical truth that the gospel is God's good news, through the cross and resurrection of Jesus Christ, for individual persons, and for society, and for creation. All three are broken and suffering because of sin; all three are included in the redeeming love and mission of God; all three must be part of the comprehensive mission of God's people.[12]

The *Cape Town Commitment* did not appear from nowhere. Since the 1970s, there has been a gradual process of evangelical rediscovery that creation care is essentially biblical. Theologians and missiologists from across the globe including Richard Bauckham,[13] N T Wright,[14] Vinoth Ramachandra, Howard Peskett,[15] Chris Wright,[16] Ken Gnanakan,[17] Loren Wilkinson,[18] Bishop Zac Niringiye,[19] Bishop James Jones,[20] Jonathan Moo,[21] Steven Bouma-Prediger,[22] and Ruth Padilla DeBorst[23] have all written important works in this area. They have been joined by evangelical scientists—from fields as diverse as genetics, biology, and climatology—who have also made important contributions to the literature, including Professor R J Berry, Sir Ghillean Prance and Sir John Houghton. The field is growing all the time, and important works and authors have inevitably been omitted in this short indicative list.

What these authors and others have demonstrated is that a biblical understanding of mission begins not with the Great Commission of Matthew

28:19–20 but with the creation accounts of Genesis 1–3. A biblical theology of creation immediately gives a broader focus to our calling and mission. The whole creation exists not for us, but for God. It is God's by creation (called into being *ex nihilo*) and by ownership. Psalm 24:1 is clear that 'the earth is the LORD's, and everything in it'. While it is true that the Psalms also state that 'the highest heavens belong to the LORD, but the earth he has given to mankind' (Ps 115:16), it is clear that this *giving* is only in a secondary sense. God is owner, and we are leaseholders—tenants within God's world.

Understanding that creation is not our plaything or playground—and that creation has intrinsic value to God—has immediate missiological implications. We should use natural resources with restraint and respect. If this is God's world, it is not a neutral stage for our human dramas. It is holy ground.

Looking at the Bible's creation accounts also puts us in our place. We are used to seeing ourselves as the image of God (Gen 1:26)—different from the rest of creation. However, the language of *image* is only half the story. Genesis 2:7 speaks of God making us 'from the dust of the ground' and the name of the first man is related to *adamah* meaning earth or soil. We are both earthy creatures made from the same stuff as all other life-forms, and at the same time set apart by God to bear his image. Psalm 8 holds these two sides of the coin together magnificently, in seeing us both as cosmically insignificant ('What is man that you are mindful of him?' ESV) and yet also given a privileged role within creation ('a little lower than the angels').

The crucial missiological implication comes when we explore what it *means* to be the image of God. Genesis 1:26–28 is about God calling one part of creation (humanity), to fulfil a specific job description within creation. It is a commissioning—the very first great commission—for the task of reflecting God's just and gentle rule towards the rest of creation. To put it simply, to be in God's image is to care for creation in a godly way. Image-bearing is a missiological task. And when humanity fails to reflect God's character in how we care for the earth, we fail to reflect the image of God.

Biblically, therefore, our primary mission as a species is an ecological one. In the New Testament, our mission as the redeemed people of God still contains this creation ordinance. In Mark's gospel Jesus' Great Commission is worded somewhat differently from the more familiar 'make disciples of all nations' of Matthew 28:19. Mark 16:15 reads 'preach the gospel to all creation', a message that is preached in our lifestyles, our attitudes, and our relationships with creation as well as in our words. While some of the oldest biblical manuscripts do not contain this passage, it remains part of the biblical canon and thus should be read alongside the versions contained in the other gospels.

The other major biblical theme to explore at this point is that of *Israel*. Many missiologists give least attention to this, the third act of the biblical drama, although it occupies the majority of the Bible's pages. If we approach it from the context of God's purposes for all creation, the story of Israel is less about middle-eastern politics, and more about the three-way relationship between God, people, and place. As Walter Brueggemann in his important book, *The Land*, has argued so persuasively, land is a severely neglected biblical theme; the story of Israel is centrally about how God's purposes always take place within a specific geographical and ecological context.[24] Chris Wright builds on this in looking at the ethical consequences of being a people rooted in a particular place, stating: 'Nothing that you can do in, on or with the land is outside the sphere of God's moral inspection.'[25]

Israel's mission in Old Testament times was primarily to model God's purposes in a particular place of God's choosing—a land of promise. This mission encompassed their life of worship (including many creation-linked festivals), a moral and legal framework for living together as human community (including attitudes to the stranger or foreigner), and a framework for interaction with the earth and the other creatures with which they shared it. The Torah contains numerous injunctions about farming practice and animal welfare. Sabbath and Jubilee are about land and animals as well as about people and God. The prophets frequently lament Israel's failure to fulfil its mission in the land of promise. Hosea 4:3 is a vivid example of this, illustrating how moral failure and idolatrous worship are interlinked with failed harvests and ecological disaster:

> Because of this the land dries up,
> and all who live in it waste away;
> the beasts of the field, the birds in the sky
> and the fish in the sea are swept away.

The words seem to echo the command of Genesis 1, where humans are to reflect God's image in ruling considerately over the beasts of the field, the birds of the air, and the fish of the sea, but here it is human failure to reflect God's image that brings ecological disaster. If Israel's mission was ultimately to be a light to the nations, then that light was to shine not only through words but in all their relationships: with God, each other, and with the whole creation.

We can thus see that the twin themes of *Creation* and *Israel* both provide strong biblical foundations for a theology of mission which sees the natural environment not simply as the stage on which we act out our mission but also as the object of God's mission and of ours.

Crucicentrism

The second evangelical hallmark—crucicentrism—goes to the heart of God's mission: the atoning, reconciling work of Christ on the cross, the fourth and pivotal act of the great biblical drama. Evangelicals, amazed by God's grace to fallen sinners, have traditionally focused on the cross in relation to individual human beings. However, the cross of Christ is the place where *all* the relationships broken and damaged by the Fall are—at least in potential— restored. Not only is our spiritual communion restored through forgiveness of sins, and our broken relationships in a fallen society made new—but also the fractured state of a fallen world can find renewal and restoration.

Bishop James Jones, in *Jesus and the Earth*, has pointed out how the earth itself reacts in eclipse and earthquake to the death and resurrection of the one 'by whom and for whom all things were made' (Col 1:16).[26] Just as God has made all of creation and sustains it in love, so also he plans re- demption for the whole creation. Jones goes on to demonstrate the parallels between the damage brought about by the first Adam (whose name can be translated as 'son of the soil' or '*adamah*'), and the redemption brought about through Christ as the second Adam, stating, 'Jesus . . . undoes the earth-damaging work of Adam.'[27]

This is a major shift in thinking for many evangelicals—to extend the work of the cross from individuals to a cosmic scale—yet it is entirely bibli- cal. Paul's words in Colossians about God reconciling 'all things . . . on earth [and] . . . in heaven' to himself through the cross (Col 1:20), and the vision in Romans of the whole creation longing to be set free from its bondage to decay (Rom 8:18–22), are key passages in this respect—yet it is a theme that can be traced throughout Scripture. The story of Noah is a key Old Testa- ment precursor of Christ's saving work, and demonstrates a God whose saving actions incorporate all living things.

Ultimately, the cross provides the possibility of hope in a time of en- vironmental despair. God is committed to creation. However desperate the environmental situation, God honours his commitment. While some evangelicals have seen an evangelistic opportunity in climate change ('turn before you burn'), the full biblical gospel goes further and proclaims good news not just for sinful humanity but for a groaning creation. When we re- alise that the cross includes hope for all creation, then our message and our mission are rather different. The evangelistic message becomes: 'Don't lose hope—God can transform the situation, and God can transform you.' Our mission is both to proclaim this and also to demonstrate it through practical mission action that restores and serves the whole creation, not just people.

Conversionism

To speak of transformed individuals in a transformed creation moves us to the third evangelical hallmark—conversionism—the belief that individuals need to be born anew in Christ. Key to this is an understanding of what N T Wright would call 'act two'—the Fall. Conversionism takes seriously the notion that every human being is alienated from God and responsible for their own downfall. It is the antithesis of the evolutionary view of human progress, championed by secular humanism, which holds that rational human beings provided with good science and good education should make good choices. The evidence over the past 20 years has been the opposite. Despite growing scientific certainty, overwhelming evidence, and clear advice regarding environmental depletion and a changing climate, people in Western democracies have not changed their behaviour.

Conversionism takes the Fall seriously and thus humanity's desperate need for redemption—we cannot get ourselves out of the mess we are in. Rather, we need to respond to God's initiative in Christ. Translating this to the environmental crisis, the evangelical analysis of what is needed is very different from the secular one. The secular environmentalist believes more science, more technology, more political will, more education might save us. Some Christian responses have paralleled this track, relying on campaigning and education alone. However, a genuinely biblical response recognises that people need transforming *inside out*. Only a redeemed humanity can tackle the environmental crisis. Creation, according to Romans 8, is 'waiting for the sons and daughters of God' to be revealed. Creation is waiting for the church—the redeemed community of those who know their need of God, and who can share his hope for all creation.

What this means is that while creation care is a missional issue, it is also a matter of worship and discipleship. If we are to be authentic followers of Jesus Christ, and if our lives are to demonstrate that he is Lord, then we must love and care for the creation that has been made by and for him, and for which he suffered and died. Choosing to live more sustainably, to recycle, reduce consumption, and rebuild the fabric of our fragile world, is not a pharisaical duty but a joyful act of worship for the living Lord Jesus. Conversion, therefore, is not simply the moment when individuals choose to turn to Christ. It is an ongoing lifelong process of living sacrifice (Rom 12:1), as our attitudes, our relationships, our choices and our lifestyles are conformed to the likeness of Christ.

Activism

Once evangelicals are convinced of a matter theologically, they tend to do something about it. As Bebbington argues, evangelicalism is an essentially activist religion. History is full of examples of those evangelicals who have read and understood the Bible and have thereby become committed to tackling slavery, prison reform, education, literacy, health-care, global poverty, the AIDS epidemic, and many more areas. Writing as a social scientist, Robert D Woodberry has demonstrated convincingly that today's most stable liberal democracies are underpinned by institutions set up by 'conversionary Protestants'—a term well-suited to describe evangelicals. He states:

> In particular, conversionary Protestants were a crucial catalyst initiating the development and spread of religious liberty, mass education, mass printing, newspapers, voluntary organizations, most major colonial reforms, and the codification of legal protections for nonwhites in the nineteenth and early twentieth centuries.[28]

Woodberry's thesis reflects the theology-and-action dynamic at the heart of evangelical spirituality. With the exception of the most extreme pietists, evangelicals have historically believed that prayer, Bible study, and practical action go hand-in-hand; that God should be taken at his word and biblical principles should be applied to the real world. This reflection-action cycle can operate in both directions. Sometimes theological reflection takes place as a result of the questions raised by engagement in practical mission. Today, it is often as evangelical development agencies reflect on the environmental causes of poverty that they are now asking theological questions about our responsibility to care for creation, and beginning to become engaged in creation care.

Once evangelical missions catch a vision for creation care there is great potential. Whereas some Christian traditions may turn every issue into a subject for endless papers and conferences, evangelicals are often impatient to see a practical outcome. In terms of the urgent need to tackle global climate change this is a real advantage, as long as evangelicals resist the activist temptation of inadequate reflection and theological shallowness.

Returning to Tom Wright's 'five acts', activism relates most to the fifth and final act: the present and future kingdom. Our mission is in the context of the kingdom of God, inaugurated by Jesus Christ yet still only here in part. Our missiological task is to be agents of God's kingdom rule—transforming not just individuals but society and also seeking the renewal and healing of creation, praying and working for God's kingdom *on earth* as in heaven.

Theologians such as N T Wright[29] and Richard Bauckham[30] have laid powerful foundations for a renewed evangelical eschatology, taking the future of the earth seriously, as Bauckham also writes in Chapter 3 of this book. N T Wright's work emphasizes the resurrected body of Christ as the most complete biblical template of new creation, combining both continuity and discontinuity. Just as the risen Jesus was the same flesh and blood, bearing the nail marks, and yet different in being able to walk through locked doors, and often not recognised at first even by close followers, so the new creation will be physical and tangible, a radical recreation rather than a replacement of this current earth and heavens. Mission therefore is not simply about peopling heaven but about transforming earth—seeking signs of the kingdom which point to the coming rule of the king.

It is difficult to emphasise how profound a paradigm shift this is for evangelical missiology. For two centuries, the prime motivation in mission has been to save people out of a condemned world before it is too late. Now evangelicals are increasingly appreciating that God has good purposes for the whole creation, and (as with Noah) calls us to be his agents of transformation. As we care for creation in Christ's name, we find that Jesus, 'the image of the invisible God' in whom 'all things hold together' (Colossians 1:15–17), is exalted and revealed ever more clearly.

Conclusions: Evangelical motivations for environmental mission

This brief overview interweaving Bebbington's four marks of evangelicalism with N T Wright's biblical five acts has hopefully illustrated that, despite a generally poor track record, evangelical mission agencies have the greatest possible reason to engage with environmental mission. It is the author's experience, in 20 years of speaking and writing about creation care and mission across the world, that evangelical mission agencies and churches are undergoing a major shift in this area. Within A Rocha, we have seen a single small project in Portugal grow into a global movement—by 2014 in 20 countries and with conversations about future projects in further nations which could double that number. We have also seen rapid growth in partnerships with national and international mission agencies, and in requests for teaching materials from Bible colleges and mission-training colleges.

The final section of this chapter consists of five points that have proved helpful in communicating the missional importance of creation care to evangelical Christians and organizations.

1. The biblical imperative

The full biblical gospel is not only about individual salvation but about God's saving love for all creation. Christian mission can therefore be summarised thus:

> Our being sent in the name of Jesus Christ to bring (preach, live and teach) the good news of the kingdom of God (forgiveness, healing, and restored relation-

ships between God, people, and creation) to a world in need (not just individuals but communities, cultures, and ultimately the whole created order).

A detailed treatment of the missiological implications of each of the five great biblical themes of creation, fall, Israel, Jesus, and the present and future age can be found in my book *Planetwise*.

2. The Spirit's leading around the world

God appears to be calling forth practical expressions of *missionary earthkeeping* around the world in ways that are spontaneous and independent of each other.[31] Within A Rocha we have often heard Christians saying, in effect, 'This is exactly what God has been putting on my heart, but I didn't know there were other Christians who felt the same!' One such is Rev Pavel Svetlik, a Brethren minister and ornithologist, who persuaded his church to release him to become the founder of A Rocha Czech Republic and combine his two callings—caring for creation through scientific study, and sharing his love of Jesus, particularly through Bible-based environmental education. Another example, from outside A Rocha, is on the coast of Andhra Pradesh in eastern India. Here, a Pentecostal mission had been working in evangelism and church planting but had encountered major environmental problems linked to the destruction of coastal mangroves, leading to erosion, infertile land, health problems and endemic poverty. Motivated by compassion, the mission set up a Christian Coastal Development Programme which grew into a major mangrove regeneration project. When I was privileged to visit, I was told, 'The Holy Spirit has led us into this work. Now we need a theology to tell us why.' The result was a two-day seminar, translated into Telegu, explaining the biblical concept of integral mission, where involvement in the spiritual, social, and ecological aspects are all dimensions of the kingdom of God.

3. The missiological opportunity in local evangelism

People respond when they see the gospel lived out in all its dimensions; when care for spiritual, social, and material well-being is interwoven with care for the natural world. In post-modern cultures, people do not like to be preached at, but they are attracted by models of integrated lifestyle and relationship that demonstrate the good news of Jesus Christ. The late Rev Dr Rob Frost, a leading British Methodist evangelist, once said, 'When Christians take the earth seriously, people take the gospel seriously.'[32]

We see examples of this kind of unplanned, non-programmatic, but entirely natural evangelism in books written about A Rocha's work, including Peter Harris' *Under the Bright Wings* and *Kingfisher's Fire*,[33] Leah Kostamo's *Planted*,[34] Chris Naylor's *Postcards from the Middle East*,[35] and my book,

God Doesn't Do Waste.[36] My own experience of establishing an urban conservation project in London gave me many more opportunities to talk with non-Christians about faith at a personal level than I ever had as minister of a local church! On one occasion, a visitor from a secular environmental organization visited A Rocha UK's headquarters, initially appearing suspicious and defensive but gradually warming through the day. Afterwards, she wrote on her blog, 'As an Anglo-Welsh, practising Pagan, I felt really welcomed by the staff and many diverse volunteers at their UK office. I joined the group for lunch—everybody eats together once a day—and was inspired by experiencing a profound depth of dialogue and debate about pressing issues of spirituality and sustainability.'[37]

Local churches—in Canada, the UK, Netherlands, the USA and elsewhere—are taking on practical environmental projects and, through them, building links into their communities that are having a gradual but significant evangelistic impact. The Vineyard Christian Fellowship of Boise, Idaho, is just one congregation that found adding *creation care ministries* to its mission activities led to a substantial increase in attendance.[38] More research is needed in this area, and the temptation must be resisted to see creation care as merely a means to an evangelistic end, but it is clear that the demonstration of genuinely integrated mission is a key factor in people's response to Christian action.

4. The missiological opportunity in influencing the environmental community

In a survey by the UK Government's Environment Agency, twenty-five leading British environmentalists were asked about their 'top tips' for tackling climate change. Among obvious responses about energy conservation, transport, and food, the second most significant suggestion was for religious leaders to make the planet their priority. The report states, 'It is time the world's faith groups reminded us that we have a duty to restore and maintain the ecological balance of the planet.'[39]

We should not be surprised at this. There is a growing awareness among secular environmentalists that technology and education are not enough to solve a crisis that is moral and ultimately spiritual. The UK's Sustainable Development Commission has published a report (jointly written with WWF UK) entitled *Sustainable Development & UK Faith Groups: Two Sides of the Same Coin?*[40]

Environmental issues now provide one of the few areas where an increasingly secular Western worldview is open to spiritual and religious insights. A Rocha representatives often find themselves invited to give a faith perspective at otherwise secular events—varying from the World Conservation Union (IUCN) and the European Union, to invitations in the UK to participate in events for Friends of the Earth and the British Ecological Society.

There is an enormous missiological opportunity in this. Globally, environmentalism is in search of its soul. In an influential paper entitled *The Death of Environmentalism*, Michael Schellenberger and Ted Nordhaus have argued, 'Environmentalists need to tap into the creative worlds of myth-making, even religion, not to better sell narrow and technical policy proposals but rather to figure out who we are and who we need to be.'[41] A theocentric biblical understanding of the world is the best way of solving many of the interminable dilemmas faced by a polarization between anthropocentric and ecocentric views. Where Christians have sometimes lost their confidence in addressing today's big questions, here is an extraordinary opportunity for mission—an open invitation from the environmental community for a faith-based contribution.

5. The missiological task of challenging the materialistic captivity of the Western church

Finally, the reshaping of mission to take account of creation offers an opportunity for the church itself—particularly in the West—to rethink its relationship with the material world. A Rocha's founder Peter Harris speaks of 'The genetically modified church, where the DNA of our societies has been patched in, such that the Gospel we preach is no longer biblical.'[42] A growing number of evangelicals, following in the tradition of Sider and the Lausanne commitment to a simple lifestyle, are questioning the Western church's accommodation to a cultural obsession with material comfort and economic growth.[43]

Nearly a century ago, Gandhi complained of 'Western nations groaning under the heel of the monster god of materialism' and in later life he attributed his rejection of Christianity to the failure of Christians to live up to Christ's teaching.[44] The so-called Christian West's obscene overconsumption of resources can only have negative missiological repercussions, both in its impact on the world's poor and in the image it portrays of Christianity.

Today, many evangelicals are rediscovering simpler lifestyles as they re-read Christ's teaching on money and possessions, and as evidence grows of the impact of Western over-consumption on the poor and the planet—and often on the mental and physical health of the rich. In the UK there has been a recent growth of simpler lifestyle initiatives including the Year of Living Generously, the Breathe Network, and A Rocha UK's Living Lightly campaign.[45] Time will tell if these remain a small counter-current to evangelical consumerism—or if the tide is beginning to turn.

Summary

The past contribution of evangelical mission agencies to creation care has been fairly peripheral. However, both biblical theology and evangelical culture provide solid foundations and good reasons why evangelicalism should engage with creation care as mission—as well as evidence that it is beginning to do so. Some significant thinkers and mission agencies have begun asking the right questions about God's mission, and our mission, towards the whole creation. The next few years will be critical as to whether the world's 600 million evangelicals accept the challenge to rethink and rework mission to take God's creation seriously, and to take God's word seriously when it states that 'The creation waits in eager expectation for the children of God to be revealed' (Rom 8:19).[46]

CARING FOR CREATION DOWN UNDER: FRIENDS OF A ROCHA AUSTRALIA

There is an old expression taken from the title of a book by Geoffrey Blainey: The Tyranny of Distance. Not only is Australia far from anywhere else, the distance between the major cities is huge. This has presented something of a challenge for the establishing of A Rocha: Christians in Conservation in Australia.

Over almost a decade, there has been a discussion about what constitutes distinctly Christian conservation in Australia. Australia has a long tradition of conservation organizations—from the Australian Conservation to the World Wildlife Fund for Nature onwards. Christians from a variety of denominations could see the value in Christians having a distinct voice in conservation—not so much as a way of preaching the gospel, but as a way of embodying the gospel and acknowledging the rich biblical material on the transformation of the whole of creation. The inclusion of creation care into the gospel mission of the church is known as eco-missiology.

Eco-missiology sees mission in terms of reconciliation at all levels. The gospel is broader than *me and Jesus* because God is involved with the whole of creation, not just human beings. Eco-missiology has a concern for creation because God saves us *with* and not *from* creation. Eco-missiology is also a matter of eco-justice, since it is the global poor who face the worst effects of environmental degradation. Finally, it includes eco-spirituality, which represents a new way of seeing creation, because it views caring for creation *in its own right* as a form of mission.

A Rocha represents an eco-missiological community established in twenty countries, deeply engaged in the practice of creation care based around five Cs—Christian, Conservation, Community-based, Cross-cultural and Cooperative. Australia is looking at working through the process of establishing an A Rocha here as well. The process is complicated by the need to establish levels of organization and fundraising—and, all the while dealing with the tyranny of distance, the fact that those who are interested in being involved are already busy with other projects, and the need to find viable projects.

In Australia, we have decided to prioritise the last of these, so the focus of Friends of A Rocha Australia will be in encouraging local projects, and building the infrastructure from the ground up. While this is a pragmatic decision, it is also more in line with an incarnational view of mission that is locally-focused and locally driven. A national level of oversight and reflection is enabled via video-conferencing.

The first project concerns the restoration of farmland known as Watchbox Valley—a 1,160-acre conservation-focused farm 90 kilometers north of Melbourne. It represents a variety of remnant ecosystems and underlying geology. It is ideal for restoration because of this variety, its proximity to a major city, and the enthusiasm and expertise of the property owner. There are already funded projects underway, and Friends of A Rocha Australia will provide expertise and labour for weeding, fencing, and planting.

In line with A Rocha's practice, conservation weekends will be structured around conservation, Christian reflection, and community, as well as the science of the property.

Another project involves Tahlee Ministries, whose mission is to 'honour the God and Father of our Lord Jesus Christ by being a kingdom-building ministry, embracing the Christian church and community with God's love and truth.' Tahlee Ministries has a history of gospel ministry in rural Australia, and has a large property, rich in local wildlife, north of Newcastle in the Hunter Valley region of New South Wales. Tahlee works with church and school groups, and in teaching English as a second language.

Tahlee is looking to establish itself as an ecological study centre associated with A Rocha. Already blessed with natural resources, Tahlee is also developing skills in permaculture (ecologically sustainable cultivation methods), which is not only ecologically sound, but a useful tool for missionaries to develop. Tahlee hopes also to work with the national school curriculum in developing materials that present a Christian worldview as well as practical creation care skills. Theological training in creation care will also be developed for online presentation—again a recognition of the problems of distance.

In a warming climate, with an ever-urbanizing population, and an increasingly marginalised church, any opportunity to demonstrate the holistic nature of the gospel should be seized. It is hoped that Friends of A Rocha Australia, drawing on this gospel and the technical expertise of various volunteers, will become a credible witness in this country.

Mick Pope, Friends of A Rocha Australia

CHAPTER 7

Creation Care: A Brief Overview of Christian Involvement

R J (Sam) Berry

'Creation care is neither a selfish interest of the developed North, nor a minority enthusiasm peculiar to bird-watchers or flower-lovers, but an increasingly mainline Christian concern ... Christians have been slow to respond to the imperatives of creation care, and we evangelical believers in particular have been even more laggardly.'

John Stott[1]

Our understanding of the environment has changed significantly through human history as we have moved towards an assumed (albeit illusory) independence from it. Now we are recognising the impact we make on our surroundings, and the finiteness of the world. As we grow in our knowledge of interlocked scientific processes, we have had to learn that our *local* concerns cannot be separated from *global* problems. We are having to learn humility while rejoicing in the missional opportunities of sharing these understandings with our non-Christian brethren.

Early attitudes to the natural world

In the second century after Christ, Irenaeus derived a theology of nature from his understanding of the cosmic significance of the incarnation, death and resurrection of Jesus. Irenaeus was concerned with refuting two ideas—1) the Hellenistic assumption of human superiority; 2) the sub-Christian Gnostic notion which treated the material creation as merely a shadow of the divine light from which the enlightened soul needs liberating.

Unfortunately, Irenaeus's teaching was quickly clouded by the emerging Neoplatonism of Origen and Plotinus. Their world was dominated by a pyramid of being, with God at its apex. Origen saw the Fall as an inevitable consequence of creation. His thinking permeated the early church with the effect that attention shifted from God's redemption of the universe to

the salvation of the individual sinner. This was significant as it introduced
a distinction between creation and God's saving work. This split persisted
and deepened through the Renaissance, Reformation and Enlightenment,
encouraged by Augustine's emphasis on original sin transmitted from generation to generation by individual heredity.[2] Richard Bauckham comments,

> A series of ideas about the human relationship to the rest of creation, which
> were not of biblical but of Greek philosophical origin, came to be associated
> with the Genesis text [that humanity should subdue the earth and have do-
> minion over other living creatures] . . . The rest of creation was held to have
> been made by God for humanity. This highly anthropocentric (human centred)
> view of the world derives not from the biblical tradition but from Aristotle
> and the Stoics.[3]

This anthropocentric assumption was compounded by the influence of
William Harvey, Isaac Newton, and other early scientists and bolstered by the
philosophy of René Descartes, all conceiving the natural world as a machine.[4]
Their ideas reinforced the perception of a dualism between human-ness and
God's creation. In the century before Christ, Cicero had speculated about
human dominion having the potential of 'fashioning another nature within
the bounds and precinct of the one we have'.[5] This suggested that the effects
of the Fall might be reversed through an increasing ability to control and
manipulate the natural world.[6] This vision is usually associated with Francis
Bacon, who called for 'a spring of a progeny of inventions, which shall overcome and to some extent, subdue our needs and miseries'.[7] Bacon recognized
three limitations to his optimism: 'The first, that we do not so place our felicity
in knowledge as we forget our mortality; the second, that we make application
of knowledge to give ourselves repose and contentment; the third, that we do
not presume by the contemplations of nature to attain the mysteries of God'.[8]

Such assumption of human dominion was not unconditional. John Calvin
was a contemporary of Bacon. He wrote in his commentary on Genesis 2:15,

> The earth was given to man with this condition, that he should occupy himself
> in its cultivation . . . the custody of the garden was given in charge to Adam
> to show that we possess the things that God has committed to our hands, on
> the condition, that being content with a frugal and moderate use of them, we
> should take care of what shall remain . . . let everyone regard himself as the
> steward of God in all things which he possesses.[9]

A century later, in 1677, Matthew Hale emphasized the responsibility of
humans to God for the earth. In the introduction to *The Primitive Origination of Mankind*, he wrote,

> In relation to this inferior world of Brutes and Vegetables, the end of Man's
> Creation was that he should be the Vice-Roy of the great God of Heaven and

Earth—his Steward, Villicus, Bailiff or Farmer of this inferior world . . . Man
was invested with power, authority, right, dominion, trust and care to correct
and abridge protection to the mansuete [domesticated] and useful, to preserve
the species of divers vegetables, to improve them and others, to correct the re-
dundance of unprofitable vegetables, to preserve the face of the Earth in beauty,
usefulness and fruitfulness . . . [We] conclude . . . even without Revelation,
this was one end of the creation of Man to be the Vice-gerent [the delegated
representative] of Almighty God in the subordinated Regiment especially of
the Animal and Vegetable Provinces.[10]

We are God-appointed stewards, acting in God's place.

Three other books were published at the end of the seventeenth century
which shaped attitudes to the natural world for at least the next one hundred years. The most eccentric was Thomas Burnet's *Sacred Theory of the
Earth*, published in the 1680s. It was the most popular geology of the eighteenth century. Burnet (1635–1715), Fellow of Christ's College, Cambridge,
and then Master of Charterhouse, believed that the original creation had
been disastrously damaged by a global flood, with—his calculation—eight
times the volume of water in the contemporary oceans bursting from hith-
erto unsuspected subterranean caverns and carving out the mountains and
hills of our present world from the perfect sphere God had created. Joseph
Addison took his idea of the sublime from Burnet; Isaac Newton wrote
congratulating Burnet for his work.

Then in 1687, Newton (1643–1727) produced his *Philosophiæ Naturalis
Principia Mathematica*. It postulated universal gravitation, and laid out a
new science of dynamics, linking Kepler's laws of planetary orbits to Gali-
leo's conclusions about terrestrial motion. More than anything else, Newton's *Principia* set the agenda for Enlightenment science.

The third of the books was John Ray's *Wisdom Manifested in the Works
of Creation*, which appeared four years after Newton's *Principia*. Ray was
the most orthodox of the three. All three books were concerned with God,
but they reflected very different ways of understanding how divine activity relates to the natural world. Something they had in common, however,
was that they all reflected an ushering in of a discussion of the relationship
between science and religion.

Like Charles Darwin two centuries later, Ray was essentially a naturalist. His biological writings were firmly based on observation, and he
extended a similar discipline into his theology. *Wisdom* makes two important and lasting generalizations. Ray captured the growing acceptance that
God had concerns other than humankind. In an often repeated sentence,
Ray stated, 'It is a generally received opinion that all this visible world was
created for Man [and] that Man is the end of creation, as if there were no
end of any creature but some way or other to be serviceable to man . . . But

though this be vulgarly received, yet wise men nowadays think otherwise.'[11] This was certainly not the end of anthropocentrism, but it was a clear indication that there were other valid ways of looking at the world.

Ray's other generalization was expressed in the preface to his student Francis Willughby's *Ornithology*; he and Willughby 'wholly omitted what we find in other Authors concerning *Homonymous* and *Synonymous* words, or the divers names of *Birds, Hieroglyphics, Emblems, Morals, Fables, Presages* or ought else pertaining to *Divinity, Ethics, Grammar*, or any sort of Humane Learning.'[12] In other words, Ray wanted to distance himself from the view that living things are symbols with an underlying meaning, and chose to concentrate instead on 'only with what properly relates to their Natural History'—an attitude in line with the re-evaluation of the Bible and its interpretation which led to and flowed from the Reformation.[13]

The approach to the natural world and to the Bible inculcated by Ray persisted. The Rev Gilbert White (1720–93), author of the *Natural History of Selborne*, regarded Ray as his mentor, both scientifically and theologically.[14] John Wesley drew up and revised a *Survey of the Wisdom of God in the Creation* over a period of 15 years or so. He acknowledged Ray's contributions and expressed his own attitude in words which Ray himself might have used:

> [God] does not impart to us the knowledge of himself immediately; that is not the plan he has chosen; but he has commanded the heavens and the earth to proclaim his existence, to make him known to us. He has endued us with faculties susceptible of this divine language, and has risen up men who explore their beauties and become their interpreters.[15]

More recent commentators have argued similarly. In his masterly survey, Clarence Glacken concluded that stewardship is a theological necessity: 'Man was made in God's image. He was not a part of nature in the way that plants and animals were; he was more a steward of God, and if he partook of the lowliness of nature, he also partook of the Godhead from which his stewardship came.'[16] Robin Attfield agrees: 'the Old Testament cannot be reconciled with either the anthropocentric view that everything was made for mankind or the despotic view that people are free to treat nature and non-human creatures as they please.'[17] Prince Charles has developed a parallel thesis, seeming to suggest that stewardship is part of natural law, believing

> there is a sacred trust between mankind and our Creator under which we accept a duty of stewardship for the earth, [which] has been an important feature of most religions and spiritual thought throughout the ages. Even those whose beliefs have not included the existence of a Creator have, nevertheless, adopted a similar position on moral and ethical grounds. It is only recently that this guiding principle has become smothered by almost impenetrable layers of scientific rationalism.[18]

Modern times

> [A] disastrous dualism still exists in many Christians between the sacred and the secular, the spiritual and the material, the soul and the body, as if God were interested only in the former, in the 'religious' bits of our lives, and as if only they deserve to be called 'Christian'. But the living God of the Bible is the God of both creation and redemption, and is concerned for the totality of our well-being. Put another way, the older theologians used to say that God had written two books, one called 'nature' and the other called 'Scripture', through which he has revealed himself. Moreover, he has given us these books to study. The study of the natural order is 'science', and of the biblical revelation 'theology'. And as we engage in these twin disciplines, we are (in the words of the seventeenth-century astronomer Johann Kepler) 'thinking God's thoughts after him'.[19]

The beginning of modern theological interest in environmental morality is commonly attributed to a 1954 essay by an American Lutheran, Joseph Sittler, on *A Theology for Earth*. Unfortunately Sittler's prose is very opaque, and his work went largely unnoticed. It was certainly ignored in reactions to the publication in 1967 of Lynn White's American Association for the Advancement of Science lecture, *The Historical Roots of Our Ecologic Crisis*. White declared that

> In its Western form, Christianity is the most anthropocentric religion the world has seen . . . Christianity, in absolute contrast to ancient paganism and Asia's religions (except, perhaps Zoroastrianism) not only established a dualism between man and nature but also insisted that it is God's will that man exploit nature for his proper ends.[20]

Notwithstanding, he concluded 'what people do about their ecology depends on what they think about themselves in relation to things about them. Human ecology is deeply conditioned by beliefs about our nature and destiny—that is, by religion.'

White's essay has been strongly criticized by both theologians and historians, but has remained influential, particularly in encouraging antagonism to Christianity among environmentalists.[21] Somewhat unfortunately, it was lauded by the pastor and philosopher Francis Schaeffer in the first significant contribution to the environmental debate by an evangelical. Schaeffer's welcome to White's thesis was based on his view that creation was so damaged by the Fall that we have to use our God-given dominion to protect and care for it.[22] A different and more perspicacious understanding has been that of historian Max Oeslchlaeger:

For most of my adult life I believed, as many environmentalists do, that religion was the primary cause of ecological crisis. I also assumed that various
experts had solutions to environmental malaise. I was a true believer: if only
people would listen to the ecologists, economists and others who made claims
that they could manage planet Earth, we would all be saved. I lost that faith
by bits and pieces, especially through the demystification of two ecological
problems—climate heating [climate change] and the extinction of species—
and by discovering the roots of my prejudice against religion. That bias grew
out of my reading of Lynn White's famous essay blaming Judeo-Christianity
for the environmental crisis.[23]

Notwithstanding, White was certainly correct in his identification of a
widespread apathy to the natural world and creation care. He quoted Ronald
Reagan as allegedly saying during his 1966 campaign to become Governor of
California 'when you've seen one redwood tree, you've seen them all'. James
Watt, Reagan's Secretary for the Interior and an avowed evangelical, notori-
ously approved the opening up of large tracts of land for mining and deforestation; he testified to the US Congress, 'I do not know how many future
generations we can count on before the Lord returns, whatever it is we have
to manage with a skill to leave the resources needed for future generations.'
Watt was a convinced dispensationalist, confident that we are living in the
last days and eager to hasten the coming of a thousand-year reign of Christ
on earth before the Final Judgement. Such pre-millennialism remains common among evangelicals (particularly in the US) and undoubtedly contributes to the all-too-prevalent lack of interest in the environment.[24]

However, this indifference is complicated and deepened by active
antagonism to environmental care. In 1994, an *Evangelical Declaration
for the Care of Creation* was issued in the United States by the Evangelical Environmental Network. This precipitated a number of reactions, the
most prominent of which was the *Cornwall Declaration on Environmental
Stewardship* which set out a call to control and improve the human condition by 'exercising . . . dominion', the very activity condemned by Lynn
White.[25] The *Cornwall Declaration* has received considerable support from
conservative politicians in North America, and gives apparent backing to
climate change scepticism—a perspective backed both by some industrial
leaders and libertarian politicians.[26] A biblical justification for the *Cornwall
Declaration* has been claimed by its spokesman, historian Calvin Beisner,
who regards the modern environment movement as 'the greatest threat to
Western civilization [because it combines] the utopian vision of Marxism,
the scientific façade of secular humanism, and the religious fanaticism of
jihad.'[27] Beisner's condemnation is typical of anti-environmentalists in many
parts of the world.

The widespread debate which followed the publication of White's thesis overshadowed Glacken's massive review which appeared in the same year. They were followed in 1969 by two significant publications: 1) a Church of England Report—*Man in His Living Environment*[28]—which was prepared for the 1970 European Year of the Environment, and 2) by a book by Bishop Hugh Montefiore querying the sustainability of our way of life.[29] Three years later, John Cobb's *Is It Too Late?* appeared, beginning a stream of theological writing on the environment developed from process thought and panentheism.[30] This theme has been particularly influential among North American liberal theologians (for example, Charles Birch, William Eakin, Jay McDaniel, and Philip Clayton).[31] These pioneering studies stimulated a flood of other publications of varying quality, but certainly helped to advance an interest in the theology of the environment. The 1960s, however, were marked not by theological concern but by increasingly secular unease. This was sparked by Rachel Carson's *Silent Spring* in 1962 and, in western Europe, by the saga of the oil tanker *Torrey Canyon* which was wrecked off Land's End in 1967 and leaked oil onto many of the holiday beaches of Devon and Cornwall.[32] In 1968, the image called "Earth-rise" of the Earth seen from the orbiting Apollo 8 capsule showing the finiteness of our planet was widely seen and is frequently credited as consolidating the environmental conscience of many of those previously unconcerned.

In the same year as the "Earth-rise" image appeared (1968), an *ad hoc* group met in Rome and initiated a project 'to examine the complex of problems troubling men of all nations: poverty in the midst of plenty, degradation of the environment, loss of faith in institutions; uncontrolled urban spread'.[33] The first product of this *Club of Rome* was a simulation study (carried out at the Massachusetts Institute of Technology and published in 1972) showing how population growth, agricultural practices, resource use, industry, and pollution interacted with each other, resulting in inevitable 'limits to growth' with potential consequences to the quality of life.[34] This conclusion was unpalatable to economists who denied the concept of any 'limit to growth' on the grounds that a scarce resource does not become unavailable, its cost merely increases. However, the concept was intuitive for the public at large. It was widely promoted in *A Blueprint for Survival*, a manifesto for restraint and the reordering of our demands upon the environment, drawn up by the editorial team of a recently founded journal, *The Ecologist*.[35] Many leading UK ecologists formally endorsed the *Blueprint*, asserting 'there is now no escape from the necessity of a fundamental rethinking of all our working assumptions about human development in relation to the world we live in'.[36] The first leader in the London *Times* on the day it was published was headed 'The prophets may be right'.

The first international conference on the environment—the United Nations Conference on the Human Environment—also took place in 1972, in Stockholm. An underlying theme was 'development without destruction'.[37] A lasting result was the establishment of the UN Environmental Programme (UNEP). The *Declaration* issued at the conclusion of the Conference introduced the key concept of sustainability into general discourse:

> A point has been reached in history when we must shape our actions throughout the world with a more prudent care for their environmental consequences. Through ignorance or indifference we can do massive and irreversible harm to the earthly environment on which our life and well-being depend.[38]

An unintended consequence of the Stockholm Conference was an apparent distinction between social and economic development on one hand, and environmental conservation on the other. Alleviation of poverty was seen as an overriding concern, producing an imperative to concentrate on development at the expense of conservation. Conservation came to be regarded as an indulgence for developed nations, acceptable only when the basic needs of poverty alleviation and adequate housing and sanitation were achieved.

To counteract this, UNEP in association with the International Union for the Conservation of Nature (IUCN) and the World-Wide Fund for Nature (WWF) drew up a *World Conservation Strategy* to insist that 'For development to be sustainable it must take account of social and ecological factors, as well as economic ones; of the living and non-living resource base; and of the long-term as well as the short-term advantages of alternative actions'.[39] The *Strategy* has been described as

> the first major international policy statement to affirm the *human* importance of nature conservation . . . it is vital that we recognize that deliberately intervening or refraining from intervening, or adopting any conscious positive strategy towards the natural world is a human *choice*, whether it is for reasons of economic self-interest, scientific inquisitiveness, faith or pure sentimentality.[40]

The attitudes and commitment needed to respond to the *Strategy* were more fully recognized in 1986 with an IUCN review of its impact. The review established an Ethics Working Group, and a revised *Strategy* containing a chapter on ethics was produced in 1991.[41] It formed the base document for the UN Conference on Environment and Development (the Earth Summit) held in Rio de Janeiro in 1992. A parallel initiative stemming directly from the UN General Assembly was a World Commission on Environment and Development, chaired by Gro Harlem Brundtland. This reported in 1987, concluding that 'human success and well-being could depend on elevating sustainable development to a global ethic'.[42] The Brundtland Commission produced the often-quoted definition of sustainable development as 'that which meets the needs of the present without compromising the ability of future generations to meet their own needs'. This has been much criticized on the grounds of vagueness and its emphasis on 'needs'. The revised *World Conservation Strategy* suggested that sustainable development could better be described as that which 'improves the quality of human life while living within the carrying capacities of supporting ecosystems'.[43]

Convergence

There is a clear and apparently growing convergence between the attitudes of responsible secular bodies and of Christians. The UK Government's submission to the Earth Summit verged on theology. It stated

> The starting point for this Government is the ethical imperative of stewardship which must underlie all environmental policies. Mankind has always been capable of great good and great evil. This is certainly true of our role as custodians of our planet . . . We have a moral duty to look after our planet and to hand it on in good order to future generations. That is what experts mean when they talk of 'sustainable development': not sacrificing tomorrow's prospects for a largely illusory and narrowly enjoyed gain today. We must put a proper value on the natural world: it would be odd to cherish a painting by Constable but not the landscape he depicted.[44]

The Anglican Consultative Council produced its own submission to the Earth Summit, summed up as, 'All creation is of God and as part of creation we are given the specific task of responsible and faithful stewardship of all that is.'[45] The Church of England General Synod issued a report setting out the biblical basis for this understanding.[46] The World Council of Churches has also given its own assessment of the challenge of the outcomes of the Earth Summit.[47]

The Earth Summit agreed on a *Framework Convention on Climate Change* and a *Convention on Biological Diversity*.[48] Uncertainties about how to implement the latter led to UNEP and the World Bank seeking 'a more integrative assessment process for selected scientific issues, a process that can highlight the linkages between questions relevant to climate, biodiversity, desertification, and forest issues'.[49] This in turn led to a *Millennium Ecosystem Assessment* (MA) by a worldwide group of ecologists to assess the consequences of ecosystem change for human well-being; and to produce a scientific basis for action needed to conserve those systems and use them sustainably. The MA provided a state-of-the-art scientific appraisal of the condition and trends in the world's ecosystems and the services they provide

(such as clean water, food, forest products, flood control, and natural resources) and the options to restore, conserve or enhance the sustainable
use of ecosystems.[50] It complemented eight *Millennium Development Goals*
(MDGs) adopted by the United Nations, the seventh of which was 'to ensure
environmental sustainability'. The MDGs were supposed to realize their
aims by 2015. They have been partially successful, but have now been superseded by *Sustainable Development Goals* (SDGs), which include continuing
commitments 'urgently' to combat climate change and its impacts; conserve
and sustainably use the oceans, seas and marine resources for sustainable
development; and protect, restore and promote sustainable use of terrestrial
ecosystems, sustainably manage forests, combat desertification, and halt
and reverse land degradation and diversity loss.[51]

The need for a global or universal ethic has been reiterated on a number
of occasions.[52] Hans Küng has argued strongly for 'global responsibility'
based on a world ethic.[53] However, the greatest impact has been Jürgen
Moltmann's convincing of the World Council of Churches (WCC) at its
1983 Assembly that the traditional Christian call for 'peace with justice' was
futile unless it took place within a *whole* creation, a creation with 'integrity'.
Moltmann's advocacy led to the replacement of the notion of seeking a 'Just,
Participatory and Sustainable Society' which had dominated WCC policy in
the 1970s with a more inclusive 'Justice, Peace and the Integrity of Creation'
(JPIC) Programme. It was welcomed by developing countries, which had
(rightly or wrongly) associated other proposals for sustainability with the
maintenance of colonial injustice. In contrast, JPIC implied regional associations, with environmental concern being seen as integral to *justice and
peace*. The concept of the *integrity of creation* was intended to convey the
dependence of creation on its creator and the worth and dignity of creation
in its own right.

The JPIC process culminated in a global consultation in Seoul in 1990,
which revealed more discord than harmony. Sectional and marginal interests dominated and blunted the conclusions. Reacting to this, the World
Evangelical Fellowship[54] Unit on Ethics and Society convened a consultation
at the Au Sable Institute in northern Michigan, USA. This in turn led to the
setting up of an Evangelical Environmental Network and the drafting of an
Evangelical Declaration on the Care of Creation.[55] The *Evangelical Declaration* has been endorsed by a wide spectrum of evangelical leaders[56] but, as
noted earlier, has also been attacked by some conservative theologians bas-
ing themselves on the *dominion* assumptions condemned by Lynn White.[57]

Meanwhile, representatives of the main world religions met with the
leaders of the international conservation movement in Assisi in 1986 as
part of the twenty-fifth anniversary of the World-Wide Fund for Nature and
shared their beliefs regarding the moral imperative to care for the environ-

ment. These were published as a set of *Assisi Declarations*. The initiative has continued as an Alliance of Religions and Conservation, one of whose projects is a Seven Year Plan for Generational Change, launched in association with the UN Development Programme. Then, in the early 1990s, a number of independent factors led to the establishment in the United States of a National Partnership for the Environment—these factors were:

- an *Open Letter to the American Religious Community*, spearheaded by Carl Sagan and signed by 32 Nobel laureates[58]

- a statement by Pope John Paul II on *The Ecological Crisis, a Common Responsibility*[59]

- a pastoral statement 'Renewing the Earth', from the US Roman Catholic bishops[60]

- a consultation on 'environment and Jewish life' in Washington DC in 1992, leading to the formation of the Coalition on the Environment and Jewish Life (COEJL)

- the publicity and momentum surrounding the 1992 Earth Summit

The National Partnership for the Environment in 1993 brought together the US Council of Catholic Bishops, the National Council of Christian Churches, the Coalition of the Environment and Jewish Life, and the Evangelical Environmental Network.

Meanwhile in Europe, in 1989 the Ecumenical Patriarch dedicated the first day of September as a day of protection for the environment. His successor, Bartholomew I of Constantinople has enthusiastically developed this concept and has hosted a series of international and interdisciplinary symposia to force the pace of religious debate on the environment. He has called on all Orthodox Christians to repent of the sinfulness of failing to protect the planet. For him, biodiversity is the 'work of divine wisdom'; it is not granted to humanity to abuse it.[61]

At the same time (1990), the UN Secretary-General, Kofi Annan called for a *Covenant on Environment and Development*. In his Annual Report to the UN he wrote, 'The Charter of the United Nations governs relations between States. The Universal Declaration of Human Rights pertains to relationships between the State and the individual. The time has come to devise a covenant regulating relations between humankind and nature'. The International Environmental Law Commission responded by drawing up an *International Covenant on Environment and Development* (ICED) to codify into hard law, the large amount of soft law on the environment contained in a range of agreements and treaties (such as the Stockholm Conference, the

World Charter for Nature, the Law of the Sea, and the *Rio Declaration* of the Earth Summit of 1992).[62] The draft Covenant has been through various revisions, most recently at the Rio+20 conference in 2012.

Another UN-inspired environmental document is the *Earth Charter*, finalised in 2000 'to promote the transition to sustainable ways of living and a global society founded on a shared ethical framework that includes respect and care for the community of life, ecological integrity, universal human rights, respect for diversity, economic justice, democracy, and a culture of peace'. It sets out its principles under four headings:

- respect and care for the community of life
- ecological integrity
- social and economic justice
- democracy, nonviolence and peace

These are not arbitrary elements; rather, they represent a distillation of the debates and conclusions about environmental responsibility over the past half-century. But, intriguingly and importantly, the content of the *Earth Charter* and the 'fundamental principles' which preface the ICED give essentially the same message as the creation care paragraphs of the *Cape Town Commitment* and the conclusions of the Jamaica Consultation (see *Call to Action* on page 7 of this book).

Such initiatives and collaborations have been given support and impetus by Pope Francis, notably in a 2015 encyclical *Laudato Si'*[63] in which he develops and expands traditional Roman Catholic thinking as well as complementing statements from other religious leaders (such as the Ecumenical Patriarch and the Dalai Lama) and successive Lambeth Conferences.[64] The main theme of the encyclical is the moral imperative to care for our planet. Francis focuses on climate which he describes as 'a common good, belonging to all, and meant for all', while climate change is real, urgent and must be tackled. He accepts that technology has improved our lives in very many ways, but condemns our treatment of it as more an idol than a tool. In words that could almost be part of the Cape Town Commitment, Pope Francis concludes that 'a true ecological approach always becomes a social approach; it must integrate questions of justice in debates on the environment, so as to hear both the cry of the earth and the cry of the poor'. His solution for true progress is a new 'integral ecology' involving 'serene harmony with creation'. This is not the romantic idealism which some have criticised,[65] but a recognition that purely technical solutions to both environmental and social problems have thus far failed, and a set of new ways of thinking is required.

It could be that we are reaching an understanding of creation care which is based on the workings of creation itself and not merely worldly consensus. Perhaps we are beginning to read God's 'Book of Works' as the author intended.[66] This gives enormous grounds of hope. It also provides encouragement to work with secular agencies, while proclaiming the theology which underpins the *Earth Charter* and similar endeavours.

PART 2—GOD'S WORLD

Global Warming, Climate Change, and Sustainability: Challenges to Scientists, Policymakers, and Christians

John Houghton

'Where there is no vision, the people perish.'

Proverbs 29:18 (KJV)

In this chapter, we look at some of the growing threats to the environment, and the important concept of sustainability; we then examine the threat arising from human-induced climate change, summarizing its scientific basis and most significant impacts. Following this, we explore the action that is necessary to halt climate change. Finally, we face the moral imperative for action, and suggest how Christians in particular should respond to the challenge.

Why care for the environment?

It has always been important to look after our local environment—if only so that we can pass on to our children and grandchildren an environment at least as good as we have enjoyed. Today it is not just the local environment that is at risk, but the global environment. The small amounts of pollution for which each of us is responsible are affecting everyone in the world. For instance, very small quantities of chlorofluorocarbons (CFCs) emitted to the atmosphere from leaking refrigerators or some industrial processes have resulted in degradation of the ozone layer that shields the earth from dangerous ultraviolet radiation from the sun. Of greater importance is the carbon dioxide that enters the atmosphere from the burning of fossil fuels, coal, oil, and gas, which is leading to damaging climate change. Pressures from rapidly increasing world population and from overuse of the earth's resources are making such problems much more acute and exacerbating the damage both to the natural world and to human communities. The perils of human induced climate change are now widely recognized.

It is often described by responsible scientists and politicians as probably the greatest problem the world faces. Global pollution demands global solutions.

To arrive at global solutions, it is necessary to address human attitudes very broadly, for instance those concerned with resource use, lifestyle, wealth, and poverty. They must also involve human society at all levels of aggregation—international organizations, nations with their national and local governments, large and small industry and businesses, non-governmental organizations (for example, churches), and individuals. A modern term to describe such breadth of environmental care is *sustainability*.

What is sustainability?

Imagine you are a member of the crew of a large spaceship on a voyage to visit a distant planet. Your journey there and back will take many years. An adequate, high quality source of energy is readily available in the radiation from the sun. Otherwise, resources for the journey are limited. The crew on the spacecraft is engaged for much of the time in managing the resources as carefully as possible. A local biosphere is created in the spacecraft where plants are grown for food and everything is recycled. Careful accounts are kept of all resources, with special emphasis on non-replaceable components. That the resources be sustainable at least for the duration of the voyage—both there and back—is clearly essential.

Planet Earth is enormously larger than the spaceship I have described. The crew of Spaceship Earth—at over seven billion and rising—is also enormously larger, but the principle of sustainability should be applied to Spaceship Earth as rigorously as it has to be applied to the much smaller vehicle on its interplanetary journey. In a publication in 1966, Professor Kenneth Boulding, a distinguished American economist, employed the image of Spaceship Earth. He contrasted an *open* or *cowboy* economy (as he called an unconstrained economy) with a *spaceship* economy in which sustainability is paramount.[1]

Sustainability is an idea that can be applied to activities and communities, as well as to physical resources. Environmental sustainability is strongly linked to social sustainability—creating sustainable communities—and sustainable economics. *Sustainable development* provides an all-embracing term. The Brundtland Report, *Our Common Future*, of 1987 provides a milestone review of sustainable development issues.[2]

There have been many definitions of sustainability. The simplest I know is 'not cheating on our children'; to that may be added 'not cheating on our neighbours' and 'not cheating on the rest of creation'. In other words, not passing on to our children, or any future generation, an earth that is degraded compared to the one we inherited, and also sharing common resources as necessary with our neighbours in the rest of the world and caring properly for the non-human creation.

Crisis of sustainability

The human activities of an increasing world population, together with the accompanying rapid industrial development, are leading to degradation of the environment on a very large scale. Notwithstanding, some deny that degradation is happening; others deny that degradation matters. Scientists have an important role in ensuring the availability of accurate information about degradation—and also in pointing to how humans can begin to solve the problems.

Many things are happening in our modern world that are just not sustainable. In fact, we are all guilty of cheating in the three respects I have mentioned. Five of the most important causes of unsustainability are:

- human induced climate change
- deforestation and land use change
- over-consumption of resources
- overgeneration of waste
- overfishing

These are increasingly impacting human communities and ecosystems—in particular, leading to large-scale loss of biodiversity and loss of soil as well as threatening food supplies.

These issues present enormous challenges. For much of the rest of this chapter, I will address in some detail the world's most serious environmental and sustainability issue—one with which I have been particularly concerned—that of global warming and climate change, explaining the essential roles of both science and faith in getting to grips with it.

Global warming and climate change: the basic science

I begin with a quick summary of the basic science. The earth's surface is kept warm by absorbing radiation from the sun to which the atmosphere, in the absence of clouds, is largely transparent. This incoming energy is balanced by the emission of infra-red or heat radiation from the earth's surface. Some of this outgoing radiation is absorbed by greenhouse gases present in the atmosphere, such as water vapour and carbon dioxide, that act as *blankets* over the earth's surface, keeping it on average 20 or 30°C warmer than it would otherwise be (Figure 1). The name *greenhouse* comes from the fact that glass in a greenhouse possesses similar optical properties: it is transparent to solar radiation and opaque to infrared. The existence of this natural *greenhouse effect* has been known for nearly 200 years; it is essential to the provision of our current climate to which ecosystems and we humans have adapted.

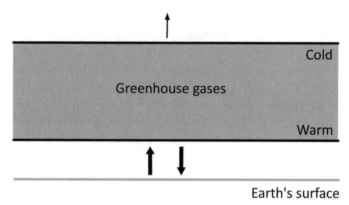

Figure 1: The blanketing effect of greenhouse gases, illustrating the greenhouse effect for a planetary atmosphere that is largely transparent to radiation from the sun.

A record of past climate and atmospheric composition is provided from analyses of the composition of the ice and air bubbles trapped in the ice obtained from cores drilled out of the Antarctic or Greenland ice caps (Figure 2). Temperature changes can be deduced from variations in the ratio of oxygen isotopes incorporated in the ice and CO_2 concentrations from inspection of bubbles of air trapped in the ice. The main triggers for ice ages have been small regular variations in the geometry of the earth's orbit about the sun. The next ice age is predicted to begin to occur in about 50,000 years' time.

From such records we find that since the beginning of the industrial revolution around 1750, one of the greenhouse gases—carbon dioxide— has increased by over 40 percent and is now at a higher concentration in the atmosphere than it has been probably for millions of years. Chemical analysis demonstrates that this increase is due largely to the burning of fossil fuels—coal, oil, and gas. If no action is taken to curb these emissions, the carbon dioxide concentration will rise during the twenty-first century to

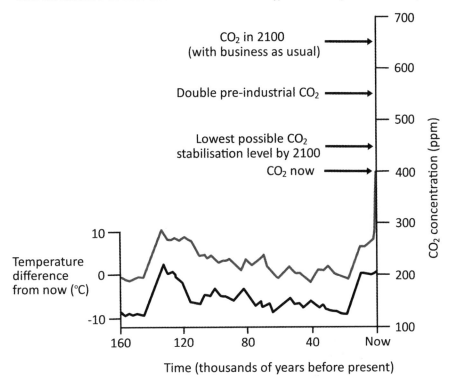

Figure 2: Changes of atmospheric temperature (black line) and carbon dioxide concentration (grey line) in the atmosphere during the last ice age as shown from the 'Vostok' ice core drilled from Antarctica.[3]

The climate record over the last one thousand years shows a lot of natural variability—including, for instance, the *medieval warm period* and the *little ice age*. There are also variations that occur because of small changes in the radiation received from the sun—or the effect of volcanic eruptions that emit large quantities of dust and other particles into the stratosphere, where they remain for a few years tending to cool the climate. However, the rise in global average temperature (and its rate of rise) during the twentieth century is well outside the range of known natural variability. Careful comparisons have been carried out between the observed global average temperature from the beginning of the twentieth century to the present and the global average temperature for the same period, simulated by computer models that take into account not only natural variations but also human induced influences. Agreement between the observed and simulated temperatures can only be achieved if the influence of increased greenhouse gases is included (Figure

3). The evidence is very strong that most of the warming over the last 50 years is due to the increase of greenhouse gases, especially carbon dioxide.

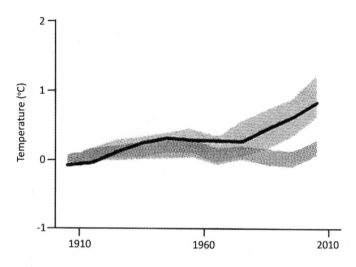

Figure 3: Atmospheric global average temperatures 1910–2010. The black line shows the temperature as observed relative to 1900 (year to year fluctuations smoothed). The shaded areas show the range of calculations of the temperature simulated by computer models of the climate; the upper area includes the effect of increased greenhouse gases (especially CO_2); the lower area does not include the increased greenhouse gases.[4]

Greenhouse gases other than CO_2 that are increasing because of human activities—for instance, methane (for example, from belching cattle) and nitrous oxide—also contribute to global warming. Their total effect at the moment is approximately equivalent to half that of the added carbon dioxide since the industrial revolution—an increase from about 270 ppm (parts per million) to over 400 ppm today. Further, in addition to greenhouse gases, small particles in the atmosphere called *aerosols* also contribute to the atmosphere's radiation budget. Sulphate particles formed from the sulphur dioxide released from coal burning power stations reflect solar radiation back to space and tend to cool the atmosphere. Other particles, such as black carbon from burning forests, absorb solar radiation and tend to warm the atmosphere. At the moment, the reflecting particles are dominant and the net effect of aerosols is a cooling that approaches in magnitude the warming effect of greenhouse gases other than CO_2.

The average warming of the land surfaces of the world since 1950 has been a little over 1°C and of the ocean surfaces about 0.25°C. That the oceans are also warming below the surface provides further confirmation of the global average temperature increase. Over the last decade or more, measurements have been made of the ocean temperature down to about 2,000 metre depth using accurate thermometers programmed to move up and down throughout the oceans. Significant temperature increases have been observed at all levels that are consistent with the warming seen in the atmosphere above. Because the thermal capacity of the oceans is about 100 times larger than that of the atmosphere, the average rate of warming in the oceans is much smaller, even though about 90 percent of the energy increase that has occurred in the whole climate system has been in the oceans. The warming of the oceans will continue for many decades into the future until it approaches the level of the atmospheric increase. This warming is essentially irreversible and would continue even if all new carbon emissions were stopped immediately.

During the last decade, the rate of increase of global atmospheric temperature appears to have slowed. This seems to be connected with events in the Pacific Ocean: a strong El Niño event in 1998 brought about an unusually warm year, followed by a succession of cooler years.[5] There is no suggestion, however, that long-term warming of the climate system has changed in any permanent way, as is confirmed by observations of ocean temperatures mentioned above.

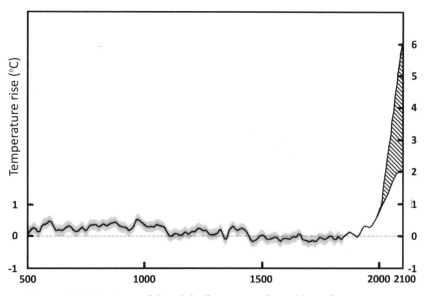

Figure 4: Variations of the globally averaged earth's surface temperature relative to the period 1850–1900. Historical data has been smoothed by taking averages over 10-year periods. Future data shows a range of forecasts with different assumptions about future greenhouse gas emissions.

Over the twenty-first century, the global average temperature is projected to rise by between 2 and 6°C (3.5 to 11°F) from its preindustrial level;

the range represents different assumptions about emissions of greenhouse gases and the sensitivity of the climate model used in making the estimate (Figure 4). For global average temperature, a rise of this amount is large. Its difference between the middle of an ice age and the warm periods in between is only about 5 or 6°C. So, associated with likely warming in the twenty-first century will be a rate of change of climate equivalent to, say, half an ice age in less than 100 years—a larger rate of change than for at least 10,000 years. Adapting to this will be difficult for both humans and many ecosystems.

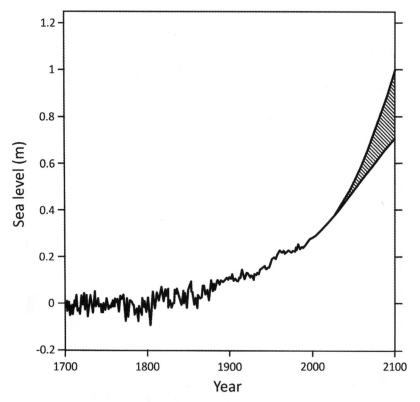

Figure 5: Global mean sea level rise as observed from 1700 to 2010 and with a range of projections to 2100.[6]

The impacts of climate change

Rise in sea level

Talking in terms of changes of global average temperature tells us rather little about the impacts of global warming on human communities. Some of the most obvious impacts will be due to the rise in sea level that occurs mainly because ocean water expands as it is heated. Melting of ice on glaciers and polar ice caps adds to the rise. The projected total rise is estimated to be from half a metre up to one metre this century and the rise will continue for many centuries—to warm the deep oceans as well as the surface waters takes a long time. This will cause large problems for human communities living in low-lying regions. Many of the world's cities are close to the sea or the ocean and will have to improve their sea defences at very substantial cost. However, there are also many areas in the world, for instance in Bangladesh (where about 10 million live within the one metre contour, the darkest-shaded area in Figure 6), southern China, islands in the Indian and Pacific oceans, and similar places elsewhere that will be impossible to protect, and many tens of millions will be displaced.

Extreme heat waves

There will also be impacts from extreme heat waves. The extremely unusual high temperatures in central Europe during the summer of 2003 led to the premature deaths of over thirty thousand people. Careful analysis leads to the projection that such summers are likely to be average by the middle of the twenty-first century and cool by the year 2100. Extreme heat waves sometimes coupled with severe forest fires are occurring more frequently in many areas of the world.

Water

As world population rises, water is becoming an increasingly important resource. A warmer world will lead to more evaporation of water from the surface, more water vapour in the atmosphere, and more precipitation on average. This increase in average rainfall worldwide has already been observed. There are also likely to be significant changes in the distribution of precipitation. For instance, some parts of the world are likely to become substantially drier—for example, the Mediterranean, the Caribbean, and southern Africa—while some tropical regions and higher northern and southern latitudes can expect substantially more precipitation. Of particular importance is the fact that condensation of water vapour as clouds form causes latent heat to be released into the atmosphere. Since this latent heat release is the largest single source of energy driving the atmosphere's circulation, more latent heat release implies a more intense hydrological cycle. This means a strong likelihood of more intense rainfall events—hence more floods. Also, in some semi-arid areas, there could be a tendency to less rainfall—hence the likelihood of more and longer-lasting droughts. Furthermore, farmers—especially in parts of Africa—have noticed in recent years that rainfall as well as being sometimes more intense, has also tended to become much less reliable and spasmodic in terms of its timing.

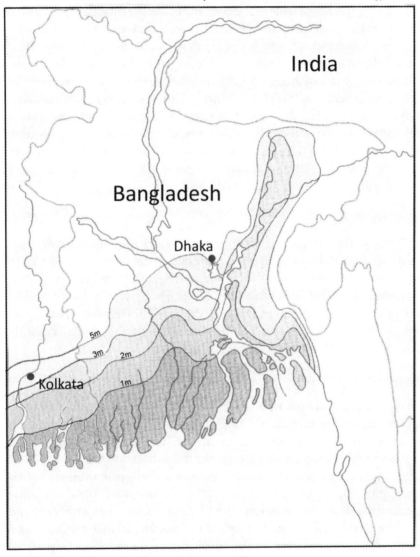

Figure 6: Land affected in Bangladesh by various amounts of sea level rise. Shaded areas are those below the 1, 2, 3 and 5 metre contour lines.[7]

On average, floods and droughts are the most damaging of the world's disasters. For instance, between 1975 and 2002, due to flooding from rainfall over 200,000 lives were lost and 2.2 billion affected, and due to drought over half a million lives were lost and 1.3 billion affected.[9] Their greater frequency and intensity is bad news for most human communities—and especially for those regions such as southeast Asia and sub-Saharan Africa, where such events already occur only too frequently.

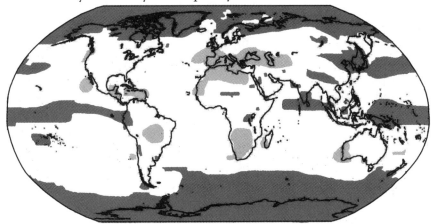

Figure 7: Projected relative changes in June, July, and August precipitation (rain, hail or snow) for period 2090–2100, relative to 1980–99 under 'business as usual' global CO$_2$ emissions (ie no action taken to reduce emissions) estimated by global climate models. The darker shading indicates a rise in precipitation of 20% or more; the lighter shading a decline by 20% or more.[8]

On average, floods and droughts are the most damaging of the world's disasters. For instance, between 1975 and 2002, due to flooding from rainfall over 200,000 lives were lost and 2.2 billion affected, and due to drought over half a million lives were lost and 1.3 billion affected.[9] Their greater frequency and intensity is bad news for most human communities—and especially for those regions such as southeast Asia and sub-Saharan Africa, where such events already occur only too frequently.

Extreme weather events

Regarding tropical cyclones (hurricanes or typhoons), there is no evidence that they will increase in number with increased greenhouse gases. However, the intensity of storms is connected with the ocean surface temperature in the region where the storms develop, not surprisingly so, because the main energy source for such storms comes from the latent heat released as water vapour condenses. In recent years, there is evidence of a connection between warmer ocean surface temperatures and a rising trend in the proportion of the most intense cyclones—a trend that is expected to continue as ocean surface temperatures rise further. An example is provided by Typhoon Haiyan—the most intense such storm ever recorded to make landfall—that did enormous damage as it hit the Philippines on 8 November 2013.

Sea level rise, changes in water availability, and extreme events will lead to increasing pressure from environmental refugees. Conservative estimates[10] suggest that, due to climate change, there could be many more than 100 million extra refugees by 2050.[11] Where can these refugees go in our increasingly crowded world?

In addition to the direct impact on human communities are the impacts on ecosystems with an estimated 15 to 40 percent of species potentially facing extinction after only 2°C of warming. A further worrying concern is that the increased levels of carbon dioxide in the atmosphere mean that more carbon dioxide dissolves in the ocean causing it to move to levels of acidity that the ocean has not seen for millions of years. It has only recently been appreciated that this could cause large problems. The increased acidity is already seriously affecting coral reefs and shellfish of all kinds.

Can we believe the evidence?

Many people ask how certain is the scientific story I have just presented. Let me explain that it is based largely on the very thorough work of the Intergovernmental Panel on Climate Change (IPCC). Formed in 1987 jointly by the World Meteorological Organization (WMO) and the United Nations Environment Programme (UNEP), it has produced five assessments—in 1990, 1995, 2001, 2007, and 2014—covering science, impacts and analyses of policy options.[12]

Thousands of scientists drawn from many countries have been involved as contributors and reviewers in these assessments. Our task was honestly and objectively to distinguish what is well known and understood from those areas with large uncertainty and to present balanced conclusions to the world's policy makers. Summaries of the assessments prepared by the scientists were reviewed sentence by sentence, and agreed to at formal intergovernmental meetings involving delegates typically from around 100 countries and with simultaneous translation into six languages. These were strictly scientific, not political, meetings. Text could only be changed on the bases of clarity or scientific accuracy. No assessments on any other scientific topic have been so thoroughly researched and reviewed. I had the privilege of being chairman or co-chairman of the scientific assessments from 1988 to 2002. I have described some of the challenge involved in my work with the IPCC in my recently published autobiography, *In the Eye of the Storm*.[13]

In June 2005, just before the G8 Summit in Scotland, the Academies of Science of eleven of the world's developed countries (the G8 plus India, China, and Brazil) issued a statement endorsing the conclusions of the IPCC and urging world governments to take urgent action to address climate change. The world's top scientists could not have spoken more strongly.

Unfortunately, there are strong vested interests that have spent tens of millions of dollars on spreading misinformation about the climate change issue.[14] First, they tried to deny the existence of any scientific evidence for rapid climate change due to human activities. More recently, they have largely accepted the fact of anthropogenic climate change but argue that its impacts will not be great, that we can *wait and see* and in any case we can always *fix* the problem if it turns out to be substantial. I have already pointed out how completely inappropriate such arguments are. The scientific evidence shows very clearly the commitment that already exists to far more average warming than we have yet seen—warming that is essentially irreversible. Even if carbon emissions stopped tomorrow, the oceans would continue to warm for many decades into the future as they catch up with warming at the surface that has already occurred. Continuing to *wait and see* will ensure that damaging changes in the future become much greater.

Further impacts

In addition to the main impacts summarized above are changes which are further in the future and less certain, but which if they occurred would be highly damaging and possibly irreversible. For instance, large changes are being observed in polar regions. With the rising temperatures over Greenland, substantial melting of the ice cap is occurring. Complete meltdown of the ice cap is likely to take very many centuries but if it occurred, 7 metres (23 feet) would be added worldwide to the sea level. Rising temperatures in polar regions are also likely to result in the release of methane, a powerful greenhouse gas trapped in large quantities in the permafrost under the surface. This could become a more serious and imminent threat if global average temperatures were allowed to rise above 3 or 4°C.

A further concern is regarding the thermo-haline circulation (THC)—a circulation in the deep oceans, partially sourced from water that has moved in the Gulf Stream from the tropics to the region between Greenland and Scandinavia. Because of evaporation on the way, the water is not only cold but salty, hence of higher density than the surrounding water. It therefore tends to sink and provides the source for a slow circulation at low levels that connects all the oceans together. This sinking assists in maintaining the Gulf Stream itself. In a globally warmed world, increased precipitation together with fresh water from melting ice will decrease the water's salinity, making it less likely to sink. The circulation could therefore weaken and possibly even cut off, leading to large regional changes of climate. Evidence from paleoclimate history shows that such a cut-off has occurred at times in the past. It is such an event that is behind the highly speculative happenings in the film *The Day After Tomorrow*.

I have written so far about adverse impacts. You will ask: are none of the impacts positive? There are some positive impacts. For instance, in Siberia and other areas at high northern latitudes, winters will be less cold and growing seasons will be longer. Also, increased concentrations of carbon dioxide have a fertilizing effect on some plants and crops which, providing there are adequate supplies of water and nutrients, will lead to increased crop yields in some places, probably most notably in northern midlatitudes. However, careful studies demonstrate that adverse impacts will far outweigh positive effects, the more so as temperatures rise more than 1 or 2°C (2 to 3.5°F) above preindustrial levels (Figure 4).

Around 2005, Lord Stern was asked by the UK Government to review the likely damage due to Climate Change and to estimate its cost. I quote from his report:

> In summary, analyses that take into account the full range of both impacts and possible outcomes—that is, that employ the basic economics of risk—suggest that 'business-as-usual climate change will reduce welfare by an amount equivalent to a reduction in consumption per head of between 5 and 20%. Taking account of the increasing scientific evidence of greater risks, of aversion to the possibilities of catastrophe, and of a broader approach to the consequences than implied by narrow output measures, the appropriate estimate is likely to be in the upper part of this range.[15]

These estimates in economic terms are large yet they take no account of the human cost in terms of deaths, dislocation, misery, lack of security and all the rest that would also accompany large-scale climate change. Nor do they emphasize sufficiently the predominance of impacts in poor countries.

International action

Because of the work of the IPCC and its first report in 1990, the Earth Summit at Rio de Janeiro in 1992 could address the climate change issue and the action that needed to be taken. The Framework Convention on Climate Change (FCCC)—agreed to by over 160 countries, signed by President George Bush Sr for the USA, and subsequently ratified unanimously by the US Senate—agreed that parties to the Convention should take 'precautionary measures to anticipate, prevent or minimize the causes of climate change and mitigate its adverse effects. Where there are threats of irreversible damage, lack of full scientific certainty should not be used as a reason for postponing such measures.'[16]

In combating climate change, action has to be of two kinds, *adaptation* and *mitigation*. Because of the time lag in the global climate, a substantial amount of climate change is now inevitable due to greenhouse gases already emitted. So attention needs to be given to means of adapting to it so as to limit the damage—for instance, from sea level rise or extreme events. Because of large changes in water availability in many areas, issues such as management of water resources and development of new crop strains possessing heat and drought resistance must be thoroughly addressed.

Equally urgent is the mitigation of climate change through reductions in greenhouse gas emissions, in order to slow climate change and eventually to halt it. The Objective of the FCCC in its Article 2 is 'to stabilize greenhouse gas concentrations in the atmosphere at a level that does not cause dangerous interference with the climate system' and that is consistent with sustainable development. Such stabilization would also eventually stop further climate change. However, because of the long time that carbon dioxide resides in the atmosphere, the lag in the response of the climate to changes in greenhouse gases (largely because of the time taken for the ocean to warm), and the time taken for appropriate human action to be agreed upon, the achievement of such stabilization will take at least the best part of a century.

Global emissions of carbon dioxide to the atmosphere from fossil fuel burning are currently over 30 billion tonnes of CO_2 containing about eight billion tonnes of carbon per annum and rising rapidly (Figure 8). Unless strong measures are taken they will reach two or even three times their present levels during the twenty-first century and stabilization of greenhouse gas concentrations or of climate will be nowhere in sight. To stabilize carbon dioxide concentrations, emissions during the twenty-first century must reduce to well below their present levels by 2050 and to close to zero emissions before the century's end.

The reductions in emissions must be made globally; all nations must take part. However, there are very large differences between greenhouse gas emissions in different countries. Expressed in tonnes of CO_2 *per capita* per annum, they vary from about 18 for the USA, eight for Europe and China and less than two for India and Africa. Further, as global population increases, the global average *per capita*, currently about six tonnes per annum, must fall substantially during the twenty-first century. The challenge is to find ways to achieve reductions that are both realistic and equitable. I return to this issue later.

The FCCC recognized that developed countries have already benefited over many generations from abundant fossil fuel energy; that has been the major source of our growth in wealth. There is therefore a strong moral imperative that developed countries should be the first to take action. First, developed countries were urged by 2000 to return to 1990 emission levels—something achieved by very few countries. Secondly, in 1997, the Kyoto Protocol was agreed to as a beginning for the process of reduction, averaging about 5 percent below 1990 levels by 2012 by those developed countries which ratified the protocol.[18] However, it could not come into force until enough countries had ratified it—this did not occur until 2005. Since then, progress has been very disappointing. Global carbon dioxide emissions have continued to rise even more sharply than before—at about 3 percent per annum—and despite high expectations, no further international agreements have been achieved.

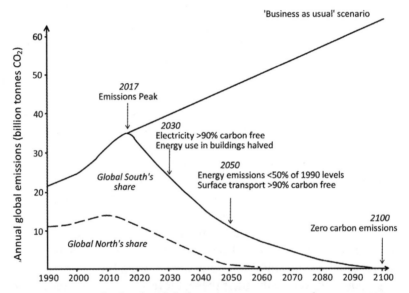

Figure 8: Waymarks for the global energy emissions road map to 2100 showing International Energy Agency (IEA) Reference Scenario (upper line); and also a profile (lower line) aimed at targets of <2°C temperature rise from pre-industrial. The division between developed and developing countries from today until 2100 is a construction based on the developed countries' share, compared with that of developing countries, peaking earlier and reducing further—for example, by at least 80% by 2050.[17]

Much discussion has taken place, however, regarding the target level that should be the aim for stabilization of greenhouse gases. At the meeting of the world's countries under FCCC auspices in Copenhagen in December 2009, there was wide acceptance of a target consistent with keeping the rise of global average temperature below 2°C from its preindustrial value—a target first put forward by the Council of the European Union in 1996. However, no formal action regarding how to achieve it was agreed in Copenhagen.

The meeting of the FCCC that took place in Paris in December 2015 saw the largest-ever gathering of Heads of State in one place on a single day, and included representatives from 195 countries. It resulted in much more positive action and, once ratified by most of the 195 countries, it commits the nations to reducing the maximum temperature rise to less than 2°C—aiming at 1.5°C—from preindustrial levels. That 1.5°C should be included was particularly urged by a group of small countries with a lot of land very close to sea level. Since the rise in temperature has already passed 1°C, this is a very challenging target to meet and demands urgent action by all nations.

The diagram of waymarks on the energy *road map*—Figure 8—shows that to have a good chance of keeping the rise in global average temperature below the target of 2°C would require global emissions of carbon dioxide to peak before 2020 and then decline at an average of about 4 percent per annum until 2050, by when emissions should be less than 50 percent of their 1990 levels. Failure to achieve the peak in the global emissions curve before 2020 and this level of decline afterwards would mean a serious increase in the likelihood of the actual rise being as high as 4°C for which the damaging impacts would be very large indeed—much greater than those described in the earlier sections of this paper. The urgency of action required cannot be stressed too strongly.

What actions can be taken?

In order to allow some growth in emissions by developing countries as they grow economically, it is necessary for much larger reductions than the global average to be made by developed countries (Figure 8). For instance, the UK Government has taken a lead on this issue and in the Climate Change Bill that became law in 2008, a target is set for the UK of a reduction in its greenhouse gas emissions (but not including those from aviation and shipping) from 1990 levels of 80 percent by 2050. However, substantially greater reductions will be necessary in developed countries than are currently envisaged. One reason for this is the growing influx of manufactured goods imported into developed countries such as the USA and Europe from developing countries such as China and India. For instance, about 25 percent of China's emissions arise from exports that have generated large carbon emissions in the manufacturing process. For those imported into the UK, if these emissions were attributed to the UK rather than to China, they would add about an additional 20 percent to UK emissions—approximately wiping out all UK's emissions reductions since 1990. We in the developed world often point a finger at China for their rapidly growing emissions but fail to recognize that it might be fairer if some of that growth were allocated to us. If it were, it would substantially increase the pressure for us to take on greater reductions.

Some leading climate scientists led by Professor James Hansen of the USA are arguing that the targets of 2°C and 450 ppm CO_2 stabilization are insufficient to prevent serious risk of large unacceptable climate change and that a target of 350 ppm CO_2 should be the aim.[19] Since 350 ppm is below the present level of atmospheric CO_2, such a target would be very difficult to reach this century. However, Hansen and others are beginning to look into how large amounts of CO_2 can be drawn down from the atmosphere and sequestered in trees, soils or in other reservoirs. It is important that preparations of this kind are begun as it may well turn out that this more drastic action is required.

I now address actions that need to be taken if the reductions required are to be achieved. Three sorts of actions are required. First, there is *energy efficiency*. Very approximately, one third of energy is employed in buildings (domestic and commercial), one third in transport, and one third in industry. Large savings can be made in all three sectors, many with significant savings in cost. But to achieve these savings in practice will require appropriate encouragement and incentives from central and local government— and a great deal of determination from all of us.

Take buildings for example. All new buildings need to include energy sources that are carbon-free. Existing buildings need to be modified for much greater energy efficiency. In the transport sector, large efficiency savings are also possible. For cars, for instance, petrol/electric hybrids or all-electric vehicles, with electricity generated from non-fossil-fuel sources, are beginning to become available. Within the industrial sector, a serious drive for energy savings is already occurring. A number of the world's largest companies have already achieved savings in energy that have translated into money savings of billions of dollars.

Secondly, there are possibilities for *sequestration of carbon underground*— for instance, in spent oil and gas fields, or in suitable rock formations. Because of the large number of coal fired plants being built, especially in China, India, and even in the USA, rapid development, demonstration, and implementation of *carbon capture and storage* (CCS) in all new plants must be a very high priority.

Thirdly, *global deforestation*, especially in the tropics, that today accounts for about 20 percent of carbon dioxide emissions needs to be very rapidly reduced and eventually halted.

Fourthly, a wide variety of *non-fossil-fuel sources of energy* are available for development and exploitation—for instance, biomass (see box on next page), solar power, hydro, wind, wave, tidal, geothermal, and nuclear energy. The potential of solar power—both photovoltaic and *concentrated solar power* (known as CSP, in which solar energy is used to drive heat engines)—is especially large, particularly in developing countries and near desert areas with high levels of sunshine. For instance, large solar projects are envisaged that couple electricity and hydrogen generation with desalination in desert regions, where water is a scarce resource. The opportunities within industry for innovation, development, and investment in all these areas are large.

Energy from biomass and waste

It is important to realize that biomass—biological material from living or recently alive organisms—is a renewable resource. The carbon dioxide that is emitted when biomass is burnt or digested is *fixed* in the next crop as it is grown. When fossil fuels are burnt no such replacement occurs.

The disposal of waste and the generation of energy can frequently go together and waste is gaining increasing recognition as an important energy source. It has been estimated that the potential energy value in agricultural and forestry wastes and residues could, if realized, meet at least 10 percent of the world's total requirement for energy—a very significant contribution.

Biomass crops can be employed either as fuel for power stations for electricity and hot water or for the production of liquid biofuels. In Brazil, for instance, sugar cane has been successfully grown to produce ethanol for many years. A strong focus of recent work is commercial scale production of what are called *second generation biofuels* from lignocellulose, extracted from grasses, woody material, or from the residue from cereal or other crops. Decisions regarding large-scale biofuel production need to be guided by comprehensive assessments that address not just their effectiveness in reducing carbon emissions but also their use of land that may be competing with food crops or adding to deforestation.

Because biomass is bulky, transport costs can be large. Biomass is best used, therefore, to provide local energy or relatively small additional feed to large power stations. There are substantial advantages in local biomass energy schemes. For instance, they can easily include *combined heat and power* (CHP) so achieving nearly double the efficiency of schemes providing power alone. They also bring employment to rural areas and a feeling of ownership to local communities. Further, they are also more secure not being liable to political interference.

The potential is large for modern biomass sources together with solar energy sources to provide reliable energy for rural areas especially in the developing world. Such provision is vital to the improvement of local quality of life and to the development of small- and medium-sized industries within rural communities. It would maintain the sustainability of rural communities and help to stem the growing migration to large cities that is happening in many countries.

How about the cost of the action we have been talking about? World leaders meeting at that G8 summit in Scotland in 2005 asked the International Energy Agency (IEA) to study what changes would be required in the world's energy production and use for the 2°C target mentioned above to be achieved; we have already shown the emissions reductions that would be required by 2050. The IEA based in Paris is a body set up and managed by the OECD countries to provide expert advice on energy matters. The IEA first published its *Energy Technology Perspectives* in 2008—this describes in detail the technologies and investment required by the world's energy industries to reduce global fossil fuel emissions to the extent required by 2050 to have some chance of meeting the 2°C target (Figure 8). They clearly demonstrated that the required technology is available. But can the world afford to do what is necessary?

Subsequent volumes from the IEA each year since that date have confirmed their message regarding the availability of technology between now and 2050. They have also addressed the cost of such programmes of action over the next 40 years or so, and demonstrated that 'the cost of creating low-carbon systems now will be outweighed by the potential fuel savings enjoyed by future generations.'[20] In other words, we cannot afford not to make the changes required.

In addition to the mitigation of climate change, many beneficial moves towards other aspects of sustainability can be identified, associated with the revolution in energy generation and use that I have presented. In particular, the new sources of energy would be less polluting and more secure. The overall net cost of this action, often quoted as a main concern, would appear to be small, even possibly negative, and certainly far less than the costs of taking no action that were mentioned earlier.

At the end of this section on action, we are bound to ask: can it be done? Figure 8 summarizes elements of the road map that will have to be fulfilled for a 50 percent chance of success in achieving the 2°C target. It represents an extremely ambitious timetable that can only be fulfilled if the programme of energy transformation is raised to a much higher level of urgency—action that could also provide positive assistance in addressing the current financial crisis. Figure 8 illustrates that if steeply falling global carbon emissions—rather than rising emissions as now—are not achieved by 2020, the necessary target of 2°C will rapidly vanish beyond reach.

Can we wait and see?

I now address those who argue that we can *wait and see* before action is necessary. That is not a responsible position. The need for action is urgent for three reasons. The first is scientific. Because the oceans take time to warm, there is a lag in the response of climate to increasing greenhouse gases. Because of greenhouse gas emissions to date, a commitment to substantial change already exists, much of which will not be realized for 30 to 50 years. Further emissions just add to that commitment. As I have already mentioned, even if all carbon dioxide emissions were terminated tomorrow, the atmosphere and oceans would continue to warm for many decades into the future, a warming that would be virtually impossible to reverse.

The second reason is economic. Energy infrastructure—for instance, in power stations—lasts typically for 30 to 50 years. It is much more cost effective to begin now to phase in the required infrastructure changes rather than having to make them much more rapidly later.

The third reason is political. Countries like China and India are industrializing very rapidly and their carbon emissions are increasing. Nevertheless, these countries alongside their clear commitment to grow their economies are also actively pursuing renewable energy sources and greater energy efficiencies. Chinese leaders have often said that although they realize the potential damage of climate change, it is not up to them to take the lead in emissions reductions. As the International Climate Change Convention clearly states, it is the developed nations that have the clear responsibility to take the lead so far as action is concerned—they have mainly caused the problem and have already benefited much from fossil fuel energy. Until developed countries—especially the United States—show some real leadership and a much greater degree of commitment to effective action, it is unrealistic to expect from countries like China and India more than they are already doing. Since late 2014 there have been some signs that the world's superpowers—the United States and China—have finally begun seriously to work together on this most important world issue. If this continues, there is some chance of meeting the essential target of no more than 2°C of warming.

Many of us reading this—whether from the developed or the developing world—need to recognize that we are a part of the problem the world faces. With that recognition we need also to grasp the challenge of being part of the solution.

Stewards of creation: an ethical and Christian challenge

People often say to me that I am wasting my time talking about global warming. 'The world', they say, 'will never agree to take the necessary action.' I reply that I am optimistic for three reasons. First, I have experienced the commitment of the world scientific community (including scientists from many different nations, backgrounds, and cultures) in painstakingly and honestly working together to understand the problems and assessing what needs to be done. Secondly, I believe the necessary technology is available for achieving satisfactory solutions. My third reason is that I believe we have a God-given task of being good stewards of creation.

What does stewardship of creation mean? In the early part of Genesis, we learn that humans, made in God's image, are given the mandate to exercise stewardship/management care over the earth and its creatures (Gen 1:26, 28 and 2:15). We therefore have a responsibility first to God to look after creation—not as we please, but as God requires—and, secondly, to the rest of creation as ones who stand in the place of God. To expand on what this means, I quote from an unpublished document, *A Biblical Vision for Creation Care*, developed following a meeting of Christian leaders at Sandy Cove, Maryland, USA held in June 2004.

> According to Scripture, only human beings were made in the divine image (Gen 1:26–27). This has sometimes been taken to mean that we are superior—and are thus free to lord it over all other creatures. What it should be taken to mean is that we resemble God in some unique ways—such as our rational, moral, relational, and creative capacity. It also points to our unique ability to image God's loving care for the world and to relate intimately to God. And it certainly points to our unique planetary responsibility. The same pattern holds true in all positions of high status or relationships of power—whether in family life, education, the church, or the state. Unique capacity and unique power and unique access create unique responsibility. Being made in God's image is primarily a mandate to serve the rest of creation.

> Only in recent decades have human beings developed the technological capacity to assess the ecological health of creation as a whole. Because we can understand the global environmental situation more thoroughly than ever before, we are in a sense better positioned to fulfil the stewardship mandate of Genesis 1 and 2 than ever before. Tragically, however, this capacity arrives several centuries after we developed the power to do great damage to the creation. We are making progress in healing some aspects of the degraded creation—but are dealing with decades of damage, and the prospect of long-lasting effects even under best-case scenarios.

We are only too aware of the strong temptations we experience—both personally and nationally—to use the world's resources to gratify our own selfishness and greed. Not a new problem, in fact a very old one. In the Genesis story of the garden, we are introduced to human sin with its tragic consequences (Gen 3)—humans disobeyed God and did not want him around anymore. That broken relationship with God led to broken relationships elsewhere too. The disasters we find in the environment speak eloquently of the consequences of that broken relationship.

We in the developed countries have already benefited over many generations from abundant fossil fuel energy. The demands on our stewardship take on a special poignancy as we realize that the adverse impacts of climate change will fall disproportionately on poorer nations, and will tend to exacerbate the increasingly large divide between rich and poor. Our failure to be good stewards is a failure to love God and a failure to love our neighbours—especially our poorer neighbours in Africa and Asia. The moral imperative for the rich countries is inescapable.

Some Christians tend to hide behind an earth that they think has no future. But Jesus has promised to return to earth—earth redeemed and transformed.[21] In the meantime, earth awaits, subject to frustration, that final redemption (Rom 8:20–22). Our task is to obey the clear injunction of Jesus to be responsible and just stewards until his return (Luke 12:41–48). Acting in obedience to this instruction provides an important part of our fulfilment as humans. In our modern world we concentrate so much on economic goals—getting rich and powerful. Recent events have illustrated the fragility, even the unreality, of many such goals.

Stewardship or long-term care for our planet and its resources brings to the fore moral and spiritual goals. Reaching out for such goals could lead to nations and peoples working together more effectively and closely than is possible with many of the other goals on offer.

New attitudes: sharing

Another example of a new attitude to be taken on board—again, at all levels from the international to the individual—is that of *sharing*. At the individual level, a lot of sharing often occurs; at the international level, it occurs much less. Perhaps the most condemning of world statistics is that the rich are getting richer while the poor get poorer—the flow of wealth in the world is from the poor to the rich. Considering aid and trade added together, the overwhelming balance of benefit is to rich nations rather than poor ones. Nations need to learn to share on a very much larger scale.

We often talk of the *global commons* meaning, for example, air, oceans, or Antarctica—by definition these are *commons* to be shared. But more *commons* need to be identified. For instance, there are respects in which land should be treated as a resource to be shared, as should fish and other marine resources. One of the biggest *sharing* challenges faced by the international community is how emissions of carbon dioxide can be shared fairly between nations. Imagine being in a United Nations meeting with all nations present attempting to address this issue. I mentioned earlier some national emissions expressed in *per capita* terms that showed variations of more than a factor of 10 between poor countries and rich ones. The Framework Convention on Climate Change (FCCC) has now started negotiations including all countries regarding emissions allocations. One proposal is that the starting point is current emissions, so that it is reduction levels from the present that are negotiated. That is called *grandfathering* and tends to perpetuate current inequities. A proposal by the Global Commons Institute is that emissions should first be allocated to everybody in the world equally *per capita*, and then via trading between nations these allocations could be transferred.[22] The logic and the basic equity of this proposal is, in principle, quite compelling—but is it achievable?

Sustainability will never be achieved without a great deal more sharing. Sharing is an important Christian principle that needs to be worked out in practice. John the Baptist preached about sharing (Luke 3:11), Jesus talked about sharing (Luke 12:33), the early church were prepared to share everything (Acts 4:32) and Paul advocated it (2 Cor 8:13–15). The opposite of sharing—greed and covetousness—is condemned throughout Scripture. The sharing of knowledge and skills with those in the Global South is also an important responsibility.

These new attitudes are not just to provide guidance to policy makers in government or elsewhere. They need to be espoused by the public at large. Otherwise government will not possess the confidence to act. For the public to take them on board, the public have to understand them. To understand, they have to be informed. There is a great need for accurate and understandable information to be propagated about all aspects of sustainability. Christian churches could play a significant role in this.

You may ask: but what can I as an individual do? There are some actions that all of us can take. For instance, we can become better informed about the issues and support leaders in government, industry, and in our locality who are advocating or organizing the necessary solutions. We can also ensure our homes, the appliances we use, and our means of transportation are as energy efficient as possible. We can buy *green electricity*, shop responsibly, create as little waste as possible, and recycle as much as possible. Further, we should learn about the needs of those much poorer than ourselves and the challenges they face—whether in our own country or in the world's poorer countries—and do all we can to help to supply their needs or face their particular challenges. To quote from Edmund Burke, a British parliamentarian of 200 years ago, 'No one made a greater mistake than he who did nothing because he could do so little.'

Partnership with God

We may feel daunted as we face the seemingly impossible challenge posed by care for the earth and its peoples and the need for sustainability. But an essential Christian message is that we do not have to carry the responsibility alone. Our partner is none other than God himself. The Genesis stories of the garden contain a beautiful description of this partnership when they speak of God 'walking in the garden in the cool of the day' (Gen 3:8)—God, no doubt, asking Adam and Eve how they were getting on with learning about and caring for the garden.

Just before he died Jesus said to his disciples, 'Apart from me you can do nothing' (John 15:5). He went on to explain that he was not calling them servants but friends (v 15). Servants are given instructions without explanation; as friends, we are brought into the confidence of the Lord. We are not given precise prescriptions for action but are called to use the gifts we have been given in a genuine partnership. Within the creation itself there is enormous potential to assist us in the task; the pursuit of scientific knowledge and the application of technology are an essential part of our stewardship. Both need to be approached and used with appropriate humility. I often speak of three qualities that should guide our stewardship—honesty, holism (in other words, taking a balanced and integrated view), and humility. The alliteration of the three Hs assists in keeping them in mind.

An unmistakable challenge is presented to the worldwide Christian church to take on the God-given responsibilities for caring for creation and caring for the poor. It provides an unprecedented mission opportunity for Christians to take a lead and demonstrate love for God the world's creator and redeemer and love for our neighbours wherever they may be—remembering the words of Jesus, 'From everyone who has been given much, much will be demanded' (Luke 12:48).

DROUGHT AND FLOODING IN BANGLADESH

Jobarpar village in Barisal District in the southern part of Bangladesh is very picturesque with verdant green rice paddies, a small river, ponds, a large stylish Hindu temple, and an attractive Church of Bangladesh compound with church, school, hostel, and sisterhood with its indigenous order of nuns. However, being located in the heart of the vast floodplain of the Ganges-Brahmaputra-Megna delta, this area has always been disaster-prone, particularly from floods, so homesteads, roads, and paths are all raised on stilts or mounds of earth. This means that in the dry winter, there is a great vista looking down over the farmland. In the summer monsoon season, these homesteads become little islands in a vast inland lake which stretches as far as the eye can see.

To some degree, the local inhabitants have become accustomed to disasters—with periodic floods, and more occasional cyclones, pest outbreaks, and severe hailstorms. Nevertheless, these disasters regularly destroy crops and other assets and kill both people and livestock—as a result, residents struggle to escape the vicious cycle of poverty and vulnerability. Due to the impacts of climate change, this situation is changing from bad to worse; worldwide there has been a measurable increase in climate-related disasters as they increase in severity, frequency, or both. Local people from Jobarpar and other villages in this remote corner of Barisal District tell a similar story—despite being unaware of the science of climate change and worldwide trends.

However, there are also some surprises: farmers talk about not only floods but also droughts affecting their farms in this normally marshy floodplain area of Bangladesh. At a workshop held in Jobarpar for a cross-section of society from this and nearby villages, people drew up seasonal calendars (looking at the crops grown, weather patterns, and other variables—comparing the situation now with 10 years ago). It was clear that there had been significant changes. Spring rains were now coming later, and farmers had shifted their planting dates for a wide variety of crops one to two months later. (However, as the weather is increasingly unpredictable and the monsoon/wet season also seems to be getting shorter, it remains to be seen whether shifting planting dates alone will be sufficient to maintain good harvests.)

Through partnership with Tearfund and Christian Aid, the Church of Bangladesh Social Development Programme is trying to help communities in the Jobarpar area improve their disaster preparedness and implement climate change adaptation measures. For example, vegetables or rice seedlings can be grown on floating gardens planted on rafts made from water hyacinth; alternatively, hanging gardens on bamboo trellises can also raise seedlings above seasonal floodwaters. However, even these measures will eventually become ineffective as sea levels rise and land use changes, resulting in salinity intruding inland up rivers, canals, and within groundwater aquifers; as disasters increase; and as weather patterns become increasingly unpredictable.

A Christian man—Sudir from Jobarpar—has two daughters who he has named *Bristi* which means 'rain' and *Bonna* which means 'flood.' Of course, in the poetic tradition of Bengal, these are considered beautiful names, but they also seem somehow prophetic. The name 'Methuselah' in Genesis 5:21 predicted the forthcoming threat of the biblical flood. In the same way, the names of Sudir's daughters highlight the future climate-related challenges they and their descendants will face—increased disasters such as floods, and unwelcome changes in rainfall patterns: reductions in rainfall when it is needed in the dry season, heavier rainstorms that destroy crops, and a shorter monsoon.

James Pender, Programmes and Advocacy Officer/Environmental Advisor for The Leprosy Mission England and Wales

CHAPTER 9

Poverty and Climate Change

Dorothy Boorse

'We need to be especially aware of how those who have
contributed least to the climate change will be impacted the most.
In addition, those who are the most vulnerable, who have the
least resources and capability to cope, will often face the greatest
threats and experience the greatest hardship'.

Most Rev William Skylstad[1]

In December 2012, a member of the Philippine Climate Change
Commission—Naderev (Yeb) Saño—spoke to the UN as a delegate to a climate change meeting held in Doha, Qatar. As his country reeled from the
recent Typhoon Bopha, the senior diplomat broke down in the middle of his
speech, saying:

> I appeal to the whole world, I appeal to leaders from all over the world, to open
> our eyes to the stark reality that we face. I appeal to ministers. The outcome
> of our work is not about what our political masters want. It is about what is
> demanded of us by seven billion people. . . . I appeal to all, please, no more
> delays, no more excuses . . . Please, let 2012 be remembered as the year the
> world found the courage to find the will to take responsibility for the future
> we want. I ask of all of us here: if not us, then who? If not now, then when? If
> not here, then where?[2]

Later, Saño explained in an interview, 'Each destructive typhoon season
costs us 2% of our GDP, and the reconstruction costs a further 2%, which
means we lose nearly 5% of our economy every year to storms. We have
received no climate finance to adapt or to prepare ourselves for typhoons
and other extreme weather we are now experiencing'.[3]

A year later, in November 2013, the Philippines was still shaking from
Typhoon Haiyan. Saño was again in deliberations with the UN over climate
change—this time, in Warsaw, Poland. Again, he pleaded with world leaders
to pay attention to the costs of climate change on the everyday people of
the world. Saño declared a hunger strike to demand climate progress.[4] The
hunger strike caught on around the world—people joined together, fasting
for international climate agreement.[5]

Saño is only one of many world leaders making a link between the suffering of their people and global greenhouse gas emissions. Here we will look at why we should care about the impact of climate change on poverty, what major effects climate change will have on humans, how those effects interact with poverty, and a few of the actions being taken to merge poverty alleviation and climate change solutions.

Why care about poverty and climate change?

God calls us to care for the poor, the vulnerable, and future generations as part of the gospel message. Thus, we care because of our faith.

We live in a world where the seemingly innocuous choices of people in distant lands can cause a change in the atmosphere that produces wide-ranging effects around the globe. The Bible does not tell us anything directly about climate change, but in it we see several principles that might help us to form a response.[6] These include loving your neighbour, care of the poor and oppressed, doing justice, stewardship of creation, and living out the gospel message. Other chapters in this book more thoroughly address stewardship of creation generally, and how climate change relates to the gospel. Here we will look more closely at the relationship between care of the poor and vulnerable, justice, and future generations.

Care of the poor

In Matthew 22:39, Jesus gave us a command: 'Love your neighbour as yourself.' In Luke's account of the same incident (10:25–37), a bystander asks, 'Who is my neighbour?' Jesus answers with the story of the Good Samaritan. According to the parable, loving my neighbour includes responding to the needs of someone who has been hurt or is in need. Our neighbour—like the neighbour in the parable—needs food, clothing, shelter, and healing. In a world in which 2.7 billion people live on less than $2 a day, 114 million children lack basic education, 2.6 billion people need basic sanitation, and 800 million experience daily hunger—there are many needs.[7] The church, both rich and poor, is a part of meeting those needs.

Care of the poor and oppressed is a resounding theme in both the Old and New Testaments, as, for example, in Deuteronomy 15:10–11:

> Give generously to them and do so without a grudging heart; then because of this the LORD your God will bless you in all your work and in everything you put your hand to. There will always be poor people in the land. Therefore I command you to be open-handed toward your fellow Israelites who are poor and needy in your land.

In Matthew 25:34–46, Jesus tells his disciples that we will stand before God on Judgement Day and answer for the way we treated those who were hungry, naked, and sick, and those who were strangers and prisoners, saying, 'Truly I tell you, whatever you did for one of the least of these brothers and sisters of mine, you did for me' (25:40).

To do justice

While the Bible tells us to care for others as an outgrowth of our love for God and our neighbour, doing so is not exactly the same as doing *justice*. Micah 6:8 says, 'He has shown you, O mortal, what is good. And what does the Lord require of you? To act justly and to love mercy and to walk humbly with your God.' And Proverbs 21:3 says, 'To do what is right and just is more acceptable to the Lord than sacrifice.'

Pursuing justice is not simply doing kind or charitable actions, but is pursuing that which is *right*. In the case of climate change, the key justice issue is that those who have contributed the most to climate change are not the ones who will most feel its negative effects.[8] If we all contributed *equally* to environmental degradation, it would still be appropriate to help each other survive the struggles that ensue—through charitable acts. That would still be part of loving our neighbour. However, when some people have disproportionately benefited and others been disproportionately harmed by the activities that change our environment, we have a different reason to try to change the outcome—to right an injustice.

Bangladesh, for example, contributes very little to greenhouse gas emissions but is extremely vulnerable to their effects.[9] Similarly, the Pacific island nation Kiribati—one of the world's poorest countries—lies two metres above the sea at its highest point. Its land is overwhelmed by rising seas that threaten its small freshwater supply, and possibly the land itself.[10] Even though some research shows that reef islands change shape as sea level rises, and may not sink, this effect may only be short term.[11] Yet in 2008, Kiribati produced 0.3 metric tons of CO_2 emissions per person—compared with the United States' 17.96 metric tons.[12] The highest emitters, however, are not all in the wealthiest countries.[13]

This disparity in outcomes is true for other environmental ills as well. For example, minority and poor communities are more likely to be sites of toxic waste facilities, highly polluting industries, and power plants.[14] The costs of mitigation (lowering greenhouse gas emissions) and adaptation (promoting resilience through ways of surviving changes already occurring) are also uneven. The disproportionate effect of climate change on those in poverty—a part of the larger issue of environmental injustice—is expressed in the term the *climate gap*.[15]

Stewardship for future generations

Those alive today in poor regions are not the only stakeholders being harmed unjustly by environmental degradation. Another group harmed by the *status quo* are the future generations who will follow after us. Questions of how much we should sacrifice today to protect options for our children and grandchildren are thorny ethical and practical dilemmas.[16] Nonetheless, avoiding the costs of mitigation and adaptation now further jeopardize the future welfare of those not yet able to advocate for themselves.[17]

The term *stewardship* is often used to describe how we ought to think of our relationship to God's creation. We are like the servants in the parable of the talents (Matt 25:14–30). We hold the natural world in trust for God. John Calvin understood the concept of stewardship, saying in his commentary on Genesis 2:15:

> Let him who possesses a field, so partake of its yearly fruits, that he may not suffer the ground to be injured by his negligence; but let him endeavour to hand it down to posterity as he received it, or even better cultivated. Let him so feed on its fruits that he neither dissipates it by luxury, nor permits it to be marred by neglect. Moreover, let everyone regard himself as the steward of God in all things which he possesses.[18]

Stewardship does not mean that the world can never change. We live in a dynamic environment with a climate that has been both warmer and colder at times in geological history. The change today is so rapid, and comes on top of so many other stressors, that its effects are difficult for humans to cope with.

Main effects of climate change on people

Rising greenhouse gases warm the world, causing an array of indirect effects as the water cycle and heat dispersal mechanisms of the globe change, and as carbon dioxide increases acidify the oceans.

Yeb Saño, speaking at the UN climate talks, described the suffering that comes to the Philippines as typhoons hit it. One of the difficulties with understanding the effects of climate change is that it interacts with so many other factors. We cannot ascribe any particular storm to climate change. In fact, the impact of climate change on storms is still a matter of discussion in the scientific community. However, currently, while the trends in extreme rainfall are not clear, the Philippines is already experiencing sea level rise, an increase in mean temperature, an increase in extreme high temperatures, and a decrease in low temperatures.[19] The main projected effects of climate change are described thoroughly in a number of reports and elsewhere in this volume.[20] Here we will just summarize briefly.

Sea level

The experience of the Philippines and Kiribati illustrates some of the changes that face the globe. Sea level rise is one of the effects of climate change that is already well documented.[21] Island nations are particularly vulnerable—as are those with long, low-lying coasts. We know that Bangladesh is considered one of the countries most vulnerable to climate change. It is low-lying, densely populated, and poor—a combination that leaves its populace reeling from every disaster.[22] Bangladesh has extreme weather events, monsoons, and cyclones. Storm surge heights greater than 10 metres are not uncommon, and normal tides can vary by two metres. Coastal and river bank erosion, and *back water effect*—the phenomenon of ocean water flooding a river—are common because some parts of the country are so low and flat. Low-lying coastal areas of Alaska, such as that near the town of Shishmaref, offer an American example of the effects of sea level rise.[23]

Health

A number of global factors—including poverty and climate change—play roles in human health.[24] Health problems that are anticipated to increase in a warming world include the spread of infectious diseases, particularly malaria. Dengue fever and cholera are likely to increase due to a combination of urbanization and warming.[25] Food-borne illnesses are likely to rise. Waterborne illnesses may rise particularly after natural disasters.[26] In addition, climate change makes respiratory distress due to pollution worse.[27] Some other important human health effects result from extreme events, disasters and food insecurity.

Extreme events

Heat waves are already increasing.[28] An enormous 2003 heat wave in Europe left seventy thousand dead and had researchers scrambling to figure out what this means for the future.[29] Events such as droughts and floods are expected to increase in size and/or frequency.[30] Some suggest that water will be available at different times of the year, and that droughts will be more extensive in already drought-prone areas.[31]

Natural disasters have captured the public's imagination. Every time a major storm occurs, someone wonders if this was due to climate change. Indeed, there is still a good deal of uncertainty over what will happen with storms in different parts of the world.[32] Some studies indicate that the largest storms may become more frequent.[33] Extremely high storm surges result not only from large storms but in combination with higher seas, something already documented.[34] Extreme events have a multitude of consequences including loss of property, loss of livelihood, and human health impacts.[35]

Water, agriculture, and hunger

Because global warming speeds up the water cycle, some of its chief effects will be on precipitation patterns and evaporation.[36] While you might expect that higher carbon dioxide will increase plant growth (the *fertilization effect*), in fact, many sectors of agriculture will be hard hit in a warmer world.[37] The loss of glaciers lowers water availability in regions such as the Andes and the Himalayas.[38] Food insecurity is already the norm in a large part of the world.[39] Climate change will exacerbate food security problems already caused by population growth but the effects will be uneven. If food prices rise, some farmers may benefit. Some Himalayan farmers are already experiencing increased vegetable yields.[40] However, yields of wheat, rice and maize, staple crops for billions of the poor, could decline significantly.[41] Urban workers are likely to suffer the most if global food prices rise—because, unlike those who are in the agricultural sector, urban workers only experience the negative effects of food price rise.[42]

Biodiversity

Healthy forests and wetlands slow flood waters, produce oxygen, transfer nutrients from forest to field, and maintain material cycles. Haiti's condition is an example of how important forests and wetlands are. In Haiti, dramatic deforestation has caused massive erosion and loss of soil productivity. Climate change reinforces other environmental degradations and stresses ecosystems.[43]

Loss of biodiversity and natural systems may lower global GDP by 7 percent by 2050. All of us depend on ecosystems for goods and services, but much of this loss would be borne by the world's poorest billion and a half because they are most likely to depend directly on ecosystem products.[44] Marine biodiversity loss is another concern. Warmer oceans and lower pH will exacerbate changes to the ocean due to overfishing, causing a loss of livelihood to the 500 million who depend on these resources for food.[45]

Ocean acidification—the other carbon dioxide problem

One feature of the rise of greenhouse gases is an effect on the ocean that is unrelated to a change in global temperature. Nonetheless, it is ecologically important and is well verified. That change is the fall in pH of ocean waters, called *ocean acidification* or OA.[46] The ocean—like soda—becomes more acidic when carbon dioxide dissolves into it at a higher rate. Carbon dioxide is increasing in the ocean as it is forced there by higher levels in the atmosphere. In fact, the ocean has acted like a giant storage system for CO_2. Unlike soda, however, the actual pH of the ocean is not acidic. It is slightly basic, and organisms have adapted to a narrow pH range. The pH becomes closer to acidic with the increase in CO_2. While some algae and seagrasses may thrive under these conditions, these changes in pH lower the survival of organisms that require calcium carbonate for shells or bones.[47]

How climate change affects the poor

Climate change reinforces other causes of poverty; mechanisms of escaping its effects are not as available as if people had more wealth. The costs of adaptation are higher for those who are poor.

Heat waves, storms, floods, droughts, and mosquitoes can harm anyone—wealthy or poor. Rich people can lose their homes to a raging forest fire, see their comfortable retirement getaway washed into the surf, or mourn the loss of biodiversity. Those harms are real, and are a compelling argument that we *all* need to care about climate change because it is in *all* of our best interests to do so.

Nonetheless, for those interested in loving your neighbour and in promoting justice, it is clear that climate change hits poor people differently from the ways it hits wealthier people. The relationship between poverty and the effects of climate change is striking if you look at a list of the countries most vulnerable to climate change effects. Maplecroft's *Climate Change and Environmental Risk Atlas for 2015* lists the eight countries most vulnerable to climate change: Bangladesh, Sierra Leone, South Sudan, Chad, Haiti, Ethiopia, Central African Republic, and Eritrea—all of which the World Bank classifies as 'low income' economies, with an annual *per capita* income less than $1,035.[48] Nigeria and the Philippines, also on the list, are both classified as 'lower-middle income' economies (with a *per capita* annual income of $1,036 to $4,085).[49] For the years 1992–2011 and 2001 alone, Honduras, Myanmar and Nicaragua, Thailand, Cambodia, Pakistan, El Salvador, and the Philippines were all identified as having been more affected by climate related disasters.[50] Poverty and climate risk are not evenly divided within countries either. The individual cities most at risk are also in underdeveloped or emerging economies—Dhaka, Mumbai, Manila, Kolkata, Bangkok—while cities with the lowest risk (London and Paris) are in wealthy countries.[51]

Climate change acts as a risk multiplier

For people in these poor countries or poorer areas within countries, climate change interacts with other stressors. Several stressors are increasing population, increased urbanization, deforestation, and intensified agriculture. Globalization of economies has benefitted many countries, however—being at the bottom of the economic heap and climate change act together as a global double whammy.[52]

Loss and damage

In the climate negotiations in Warsaw, Poland, in December 2013, there was a mandate to define institutional ways to address costs of loss and damage.[53] Finding such a mechanism is difficult since these costs are neither simply the same as the costs of adaptation, which is coping with the problems of climate change, or those of mitigation, the prevention of further climate change. In one study of sixteen poor nations, researchers found that poor people will become more vulnerable because they have no buffer to help them deal with sudden changes such as crop failures.[54] They are less likely to have flood or other disaster insurance, or to be able to move. This *climate gap* between wealthy and poor exists within wealthy countries as well as between countries. During heat waves, mortality rates were found to be twice as high among African Americans in Los Angeles as other residents. Poor, urban populations and those with medical problems such as asthma are more likely than others to die in a heat wave.[55]

The cost of adaptation

A recent report by CARE International states:

> Climate change is not the sole cause of poverty, but it works with other factors to intensify the vicious circle which traps people in poverty. This makes it harder to help people out of the downward poverty spiral. It is also likely that more people will fall into poverty if climate change undermines their current livelihood strategy.[56]

To avoid loss and damage, people adapt. Even the poorest countries have taken proactive steps to form climate change plans.[57] Although they are resourceful and resilient, it is often difficult for the people of these poorest countries to take the necessary steps to protect themselves from environmental change. Moving house, building safer structures, or erecting water tanks all cost money.[58] Archbishop Desmond Tutu said that we are moving toward a world of 'adaptation apartheid' by which he meant that the world is becoming separated into those who can afford to adapt to climate change effects and those who cannot.[59]

Displacement

The effects of storms, floods, and droughts on individuals are obvious problems. But climate change can also be a serious concern for societies at large, as groups of people migrate to seek more sustainable livelihoods or places to live, producing climate refugees.[60] In 2008 alone, an estimated 36 million people were internally displaced as a result of sudden-onset natural disasters, of which an estimated 20 million were due to climate related disasters.[61] Migration is not always predictable after disasters. One study of families in Bangladesh showed less mobility as a result of flooding than expected, and more from crop failures.[62] Even though we do not know the exact amount of migration, we are confident that climate change has the 'potential to cause substantial population displacement'.[63]

Conflict

Conflicts, both intra-national and international, arise from complex relationships between factors.[64] There is rarely one cause.[65] Water conflicts, for example, are sometimes projected to increase as water availability becomes even more limited in drought-prone areas. However, one group of researchers found that water resource limitation sometimes results in cooperation rather than conflict. Nonetheless, climate change can be a *threat multiplier* when people are already poor and it interacts with other problems that cause vulnerability. In fact, the study concluded:

> Whereas violent conflict is not the result of climatic hazards, we did find that violence does make affected populations more vulnerable to climatic hazards. We also found that large-scale State-led development projects, often pursued in the name of adaptation to climate change, end up reducing the security of some groups, often those who are most marginalized economically and politically.[66]

The United States Department of Defense (DOD) identified climate change as a national security issue. Concerns of the DOD included the costs of sea-level rise to coastal bases, an increase in requested humanitarian response to natural disasters, and increased migration. In a 2010 report, the DOD stated, 'While climate change alone does not cause conflict, it may act as an accelerant of instability or conflict.'[67] In Nigeria, for example, nomadic herders, fishermen, and farmers clash over resources such as land and scarce water. Drought intensifies this conflict.[68] A 2009 study on the estimated effects of climate change on Africa suggested an expected 'roughly 54% increase in armed conflict incidence by 2030', in part because of a link between violence and high temperatures.[69]

Planning poverty alleviation with climate change in mind

Many development agencies are now convinced that poverty alleviation requires us to plan for climate change. This approach contrasts with a previously held notion that care of the environment and development were at odds. As one commentator said,

> There was indeed a time when Environment and Development were not on speaking terms. . . . Those who loved the environment regarded those who championed progress and 'development' as the enemy, and those who wanted to develop the poorest peoples and nations felt that much of the 'environment' would have to be sacrificed in this worthwhile endeavour.[70]

Solving climate change and development problems together will involve some transfer of money, technology, innovations, and changes in the way projects are done.[71] Some argue that there are solutions that are clearly a *win-win*, and those ought to be tried first.

Co-benefits

Rather than producing climate policies that only act on greenhouse gas emissions, some analysts suggest, we should focus on policies that produce *multiple* benefits. Replanting mangroves in Bangladesh and Indonesia, for example, improves the environment and ecosystem health—and also lowers the damage from storm surges. This *co-benefits approach* could especially help urban areas. Climate change mitigation and energy poverty reduction can enjoy a synergism in energy efficiency, especially in buildings.[72]

In one report—*Urban Development with Co-benefits*—the authors describe efforts such as improving public transport systems, improving energy efficiency, and composting, which all provide co-benefits in urban areas.[73] The reduction of organic waste in the Indonesian city of Surabaya is one such example. Rapid growth and poor infrastructure had left the city with environmental pollution. When the city built an organic waste composting facility they both lowered greenhouse emissions and decreased the amount of organic waste going to other facilities. Development of mass transit in Delhi, India, sewage treatment in Surat, India, and the movement and upgrading of elderly industrial facilities in Tiexi Industrial District, China, all represent the same concept. In each case, the same initiative had the impacts of both lowering greenhouse gas emissions and also solving some other problem in the city. So, one way to help communities act on greenhouse gas emissions is to solve other problems in ways that also lower greenhouse gas emissions.

Climate change effects as an opportunity

While conventional wisdom is that climate change harms the poorest the most, there are times when a dramatic change—such as an extreme event or natural disaster—opens a window of opportunity for broader institutional change that benefits the poor. This can be seen in the outcome of a disaster among the Tawahka community in Honduras. The advent of Hurricane Mitch, which wrought tremendous destruction in this community, catalyzed their adaptive abilities and allowed systemic improvement. The indigenous group members changed their land tenure system, developed increased income equality, and benefited the poorest among them in a bottom-up change.[74] Some of these changes were supported not by traditional food aid or replacement of infrastructure, but by aid that supported the efforts of the community in other ways—such as through diversification of income. Poorer communities may be very vulnerable, but are also innovative and creative in problem-solving and may be able to develop many of the solutions we all need. A successful approach to lowering vulnerability to climate change will focus not only on adaptation and mitigation (preventing the loss and damage), but also on furthering community *resilience*.[75]

We need research on what the effects of climate change will be regionally; on how to prepare better for them; and, in some cases, how to avoid those effects. For instance, should the inhabitants of Kiribati migrate to Fiji, as some suggest? We need international meetings and cooperation that take into account the needs of the poorest, and we need our international development agencies to include climate change as they plan development efforts. Development agencies have seen that poverty alleviation requires attention to the climate. World Vision, Oxfam International, CARE International, and others have statements, initiatives, special staff, and activities related to incorporating climate change into relief and development.

Yeb Saño passionately asked the world to see the suffering of his people. As Christians, we are called to care for the poor and promote justice. The evidence that climate change harms people who did little to cause it makes climate change a pressing moral issue. It is the job of all of us—wealthy, middle income, and poor—to work together creatively to make a better, more equitable, and safer world for our neighbours and for the next generation.

ECHO, A COMMUNITY DEVELOPMENT AND AGRICULTURE ORGANIZATION

For the past 30 years, ECHO has been a global extension agent for those working with small-scale farmers. ECHO provides technical training, technical documents in various languages, and seeds for numerous tropical trees and crops, along with networking opportunities at various international locations.

Recent UN Food and Agriculture Organization surveys indicate that 85 percent of global farmers are classified as small-scale farmers working on less than two hectares. Many of these farmers are net consumers and face overwhelming obstacles in attempting to produce food. Many of the current cropping systems are very capital intensive and require considerably more infrastructure and training than is available in many parts of the world.

However, there are growing systems that are less capital intensive, have the capacity to sustainably build the soil ecology, and can significantly increase crop production. ECHO's role is to be a repository of the research and cropping system advances that have proven to work. Through its extensive global network, which encompasses 177 counties, ECHO is able to make technical information, seeds, appropriate technologies, and training available to those who otherwise would not have access to this type of information or resource. The ECHO network also helps those who have developed new growing systems or crops to get that information into the hands of people around the world. The vision is to provide the technical support for small-scale farmers around the world to increase production of health crops in an economically viable and environmentally sustainable way.

There have been some amazing success stories in this challenge of significantly increasing production. SRI (system of rice intensification) in Cambodia is resulting in an increase in yield of between 50 percent and 150 percent, with 90 percent less seed and a significant reduction in water for irrigation. In Burkina Faso, a small-scale farmer attended the ECHO Networking Forum in 2010 and learned about Conservation Farming. Follow-up visits in 2012 found that this farmer had radically increased his maize yield in a year that had 10 inches (250 mm) less rain, and the grain was of such a high quality that his crop was chosen as a maize seed source which more than doubled the price he got for his crop.

God has put in place everything we need to produce enough food to feed ourselves and our communities in an environmentally responsible way. As a Christian organization, ECHO is committed to providing the agricultural and intellectual resources needed to enable small-scale farmers to be net producers while still being good stewards of the land that God has entrusted into our care.

Stan Doerr, President/CEO of ECHO, http://www.echocommunity.org/

CHAPTER 10

Is the Weather Going Crazy? Impacts of Climate Change in the Cusco Region of Peru

Juliana Morillo Horne

'Now . . . it rains at any moment, during any month. Before . . . we knew when it was to start and when it was to end . . . this helped us in our farming. But that's no longer so. The climate has changed.'

Cusco campesina[1]

As I sit at my desk at home in San Jerónimo, Cusco, preparing to write about the effects of climate change in this region of southern Peru, I am interrupted by the sound of a furious and heavy hailstorm on our rooftop. At times, the bullet-like hailstones are as large as ice cubes, breaking through glass, destroying gardens, and threatening anyone who has not taken cover! The neighbours say they have never seen hail like this before. They promptly join forces to bail out water and ice and to repair the damages caused, while children have the unexpected joy of making *hailmen*, decorating them in the best Cusco style.

I ask myself: how did folk in neighbouring rural communities, whose maize and potato fields are still in the early stages of development, survive? For them, an event like this could ruin their entire investment in one blow.

My mind also turns to the more remote highland Quechua people of this Cusco region, descendants of the ancient Inca peoples who impressed the world with their expert management of the rugged Andean topography and hostile climate, their impressive structures such as Machu Picchu, and their command of water storage and irrigation techniques. Yet these people now live in situations of considerable marginalization and poverty, often having been isolated to the highest regions where they have to cope with the most extreme climatic conditions.

All over the planet, the media and scientific literature confirm that there are profound climatic changes affecting the entire globe. Nevertheless, some areas of the world experience these changes with a much greater intensity. The United Nations Framework Convention on Climate Change (UNFCCC) classified the high Andean region as 'one of the most vulnerable to and one most severely affected by climatic variability and extreme events.'[2]

The Cusco region experiences the effects of climate change at least twice as strongly as that experienced at sea level—most markedly in its upper highlands, over 4,000 metres above sea level.[3] The fact that climate is now less predictable, particularly when it comes to levels of rainfall, increases the uncertainty of the livelihoods of the high Andean population. And climate change does not come to a context of prosperity—but precisely to one of the most poverty-stricken areas of Peru.[4] Although the Cusco region as a whole has recently experienced significant levels of economic growth due to mining and tourism, the benefits are restricted mainly to the larger urban centres and mining areas, rather than the remote rural and upland areas.[5] About 70 percent of Quechua in Cusco live above 3,000 metres.

Following a short review of the scientific evidence for climate change in the Andean highlands of Cusco, this chapter focuses on *listening to the voices* of the local population—how do marginalized Quechua communities perceive the effects of climate change? We also analyse some factors that make Andean populations particularly vulnerable to climate change, and look at adaptation strategies historically used by these peoples. Finally, we examine briefly the explanations that different people—particularly those from the widespread highland churches—give for climate change in the Cusco region, and then suggest some proposals for action.

The Cusco region

The department of Cusco, in southern Peru, is a region crossed by the Andes mountain range, and characterised by abrupt changes in landscape and ecosystems, with a rich biodiversity. At heights over 4,000 metres above sea level, we find snow-capped mountains, such as the Ausangate (6,370 metres); between 3,000 and 4,000 metres, mountains, plateaus, and deep valleys; these are followed by steep inclines between 1,000 metres and 3,000 metres; and lead eventually into vast plains or tropical forests. Given its varied topography, the region possesses good water reserves in its snow-capped mountains, rivers, lakes, and wetlands. Water retained in these systems is slowly released, providing a wonderful means of water regulation especially in times of drought.

Evidence of climatic variability in Cusco

The Cusco region has from age-old times been characterized by its harsh weather conditions. Temperatures in the highest regions can fall as low as -20°C. Extreme climatic events such as frost, hail, and drought have always threatened the livelihoods of the Andean people. However, in the last two decades, the Cusco region has experienced even more extreme and unpredictable climatic conditions. The most visible impacts are registered in mountainous areas above 4,000 metres.

In the Cusco region, the main direct evidence of climate change can be summarized in terms of two phenomena.

Figure 1: A typical Cusco upland scene with glaciers behind.[6]

An increase in the average temperature

Temperature monitoring over the last 48 years in the Cusco region indicates a tendency towards an increase, with values of up to 0.5°C per decade in some weather stations in the Cusco region.[7] This corresponds to about four times the global trend of 0.12°C over a similar period.[8] The majority of weather stations in this region reveal an increased trend in the maximum daily temperature (days getting hotter), as well as an increase in the minimum daily temperature (nights becoming less cold).[9]

Scientifically, it appears that this increased temperature is causing the melting of glaciers, a decreased availability of water in dry seasons, and an increase in the severity and frequency of forest fires. Studies show that farmers are being forced to grow crops at higher altitudes to find the ideal temperature, and also that the native *queuña* forests and other valuable plant and animal species are under threat.[10]

Unpredictable changes in rainfall patterns

During the last decade (2000–09), there has been a decrease in annual precipitation levels compared with the 1990s. Hydrological studies performed in the higher-altitude Cusco provinces confirm a decrease in rainfall quantity and intensity; changes in the rain cycle; the frequent occurrence of frosts, hailstorms and heavy rains out of season; and the increased presence of *Indian summers* during periods that should be rainy. In the last seven years, the number of emergencies due to floods, avalanches, landslides, droughts. and frosts has doubled.[11]

Likewise, the lack of predictable rainfall patterns leads to delayed planting, to changes in crop productivity, or even to complete crop loss (when frosts or hailstorms occur out of season). New plagues also appear, such as the potato blight that can decimate crops. With the reduced productivity of subsistence crops, there is less availability of these agricultural products for household use or for bartering in local markets, and the purchase and consumption of foods with lower nutritional value is accentuated—all of which contributes to reducing food security. Frosts can also cause increased health risk or even death as a result of respiratory diseases (pneumonia), particularly in children and the elderly. They can also put livestock at risk, harming other household economic activities.

Local perceptions of climate change and its effects

Let us now listen to the voices of the people who are living in these Andean highlands. Their testimonies about how climate change affects their livelihood and activities—taken from recent studies on climate change in the Cusco region—clearly support the scientific data presented above, regarding changes in rainfall patterns and increased temperatures in recent years.[12] Perceptions fall into three main categories—the unpredictability of rains and frosts; the effects on production; and the impact on the hydrological system.

First, local perceptions about the unpredictability of rains and frosts. As one Cusco *campesina* put it, 'Now . . . it rains at any moment, during any month. Before . . . we knew when it was to start and when it was to end . . . this helped us in our farming. But that's no longer so. The climate has changed.'[13] People perceive that climatic events (rain, frost, snow, drought, wind, etc) are now *atemporal* (occurring out of season) and often refer to this by saying: 'the weather is crazy!'

Farmers also report the tendency of delayed onset of seasonal rains compared with previous decades—which in turn delays the sowing period, and reduces production. Two typical comments:

> In the past, it rained, hailed and snowed as it should . . . If we sowed at the right time, potatoes grew well, and maize production was good.[14]

> [Now we are obliged to] reschedule our sowing periods . . . With less time to ripen, crops don't produce as well.[15]

The local population also perceives noticeable changes in the way it rains. Rains have become harsher than before—more intense and longer-lasting. Sometimes torrential rains fall for a few days, and then are followed by long periods of drought. These heavy rains, farmers say, cause landslides and damage agricultural lands and infrastructure.

> Lately, there are torrential rains that the soil isn't able to absorb . . . It rains heavily, and then it all runs off.[16]

> Snowfalls occurring in the wet season, leave us with no choice: pastures rot, animals die in great numbers . . . pneumonia affects babies and elderly . . . We no longer have enough to live on . . . There's too much cold . . . It wasn't like that before.[17]

Regarding the temperature, people perceive a much greater intensity of solar radiation during the day: 'The sun isn't the same as before: it used to warm me; now it burns me. The same happens with animals: the sun seems to scorch and peel their skin. They get rare diseases.'[18]

The second area of concern relates to how production is affected. Peru's Climate Change Adaptation Programme (Programa de Adaptacion al Cambio Climatico, PACC)—a programme with Swiss cooperation, and a multidisciplinary approach, covering Cusco and Apurimac—has explored the climate-related issues that the rural Quechua people consider most threatening to their agricultural production.[19] They identified two particular factors: droughts (the prolonged deficit of rainfall during periods when it should rain); and the unpredictability of frosts and snowfall. Both phenomena can decimate or destroy their crop yields, and livestock. For example, 'When there's little rain, potato crops get infested with worms . . . and there's nothing to eat because everything gets destroyed . . . Grass doesn't grow, cattle have nothing to eat and waste away. Food gets scarce even for people.'[20]

Rural farmers are also concerned that, with increased temperatures and frosts, nutritionally rich native varieties such as bitter potato, *kañiwa*, and other tubers no longer yield as much produce as they used to.[21] The result is loss of diversity in production. 'There was barley, potato, wheat, quinoa,

beans, illaco, añu . . . Now . . . just potato and barley.'[22] The crops most exposed to climatic variability are subsistence crops, which tend to depend on
seasonal rainfall, irrigation being limited in these highland regions. In some
cases, the poor performance and uncertainties of agriculture have caused
farmers to focus on other activities such as livestock raising.

Thirdly, there are concerns about the impact on the hydrological
system—the Qori Kalis glacier, the major outlet from the Quelccaya ice
cap, monitored since 1978 and the largest of all tropical glaciers in the world,
lost twenty feet of glacier per year in the first fifteen-year period, and then
lost two hundred feet per year in the next fifteen-year period, indicating a
tenfold increase in the glacial retreat.[23]

*Figure 2: The Qori Kalis Glacier in 1978 and 2011. The new lake covers 84
acres. (Photographs by kind permission of Dr Lonnie Thompson,
Distinguished Professor at the Ohio State University)*

Glacial retreat deeply concerns farmers, as it will negatively impinge on
the provision of water for agriculture, human consumption, and other activities. Some see in this glacial retreat a premonition of the eventual death
or destruction of human beings. It scares them so much that they say: 'I'd
rather not think about it.'[24]

Many highland water sources are drying up and even disappearing—
not only due to climatic factors, but also to human activities such as deforestation, burning, and the destruction of wetlands. All of these cause alarm
in the population: 'This year, all the people are worried. Whereas before the
Tintaya stream supplied all farms with water for their crops, now we have to
wait for our turn, and sometimes the proper time for planting broad beans,
maize, etc, goes by.'[25]

Local people also report that water scarcity has increased the level of
conflict: 'Those who live upstream don't allow those living downstream
to access water.' Likewise, in order to irrigate the lowlands, people 'drain
highland wetlands, causing watershed headwaters to dry up, and increasing
conflicts.'[26] In the words of another affected farmer:

The water problem in my community is critical. We are presently quarrelling because others are deceitfully channelling our water away. Before, each farmer had a spring in his plot and we had no reason to fight. But today, we do: those springs have dried up.[27]

In some cases, the government has also contributed to these conflicts, by authorizing the use of water for mining, irrigation, hydropower, or other projects that benefit foreign companies or more prosperous neighbouring regions. The agro-pastoral communities of Cusco then react to defend their territorial and environmental rights.

Victor Quispe's words sum up the feelings of local people as they face the current situation:

Before, suffering was different . . . we served on the *hacienda* . . . we finished the day exhausted serving the landowner. That no longer happens . . . But instead, we have another type of suffering that is more painful: these days, seeds don't grow as they did before; the day isn't long enough to finish our work. And then . . . everything is expensive . . . We have freed ourselves from the previous suffering . . . but the suffering is almost the same as it was before.[28]

The vulnerability of highland communities in the rural Andean Cusco

Often, when thinking of climate change, we refer only to *climate* as the main factor or *threat* that puts us at risk. But our susceptibility to climate change depends not only on climate itself, but on a series of physical, social, economic and environmental factors that surround and condition us, enabling us or making it harder for us to cope with climatic threats.

The physical conditions in the Cusco highlands—characterized by low rainfall levels, extreme climatic conditions, rugged topography, and low soil fertility—have always made living conditions difficult, and in particular have made agriculture a high risk activity. While the highland Quechua communities of Cusco have a well-developed knowledge and close relationship with their harsh environment, there is evidence of their increasing vulnerability to climate change.

Human vulnerability

Ever since the Spanish conquest in the sixteenth century, the rural populations of Andean Cusco have suffered discrimination and social, political, and economic exclusion. Wider society ignored their rights, and denigrated their cultural traditions and language. Many aspects of this exclusion persist until today and have contributed to low self-esteem and low levels of empowerment to deal with environmental crises. This situation is compounded by factors such as:

- widespread malnutrition, poor education, and inadequate health provision which reduce resilience
- inadequate road access that isolates these highland communities
- the predominance of poorly-constructed adobe houses that makes families vulnerable to floods and landslides

Highland communities have also increased their own vulnerability to climatic disasters through felling of natural woodland and practices of overexploiting the soil and overgrazing, which have increased soil erosion. A recent study also highlights the predominance in the Cusco region, of irrigation systems that rely on gravity to flood cultivated areas. These are highly inefficient and waste large quantities of precious water resources.[29]

Economic vulnerability

Rural highland families—dedicated to the production of potato, maize, barley, and other subsistence crops—are generally isolated and derive little or no benefit from the economic boom in the Cusco region (currently 8 percent annual growth).[30] Having scarce resources (access to land, water, and agricultural inputs), these families are less likely to achieve a reasonable income, access to a healthy diet, or adequate food storage for times of scarcity.[31] Likewise, they are less likely to be able to deal with and recover from extreme climatic events.

The global market also tends to exclude highland populations: often, the prices of consumable goods (such as sugar and rice) rise, and prices of food products grown in the highlands are on the decrease. With all this, the farmers' profit margin is progressively reduced, forcing them to replace agriculture with more profitable productive activities, and/or to migrate elsewhere, as is mentioned below.

Social and institutional vulnerability

Traditional communities had generally functioned as *ayllus* or extended families, with community leaders and some specialized authorities securing good farming practices. Certain cultural activities sought to optimize production, regulate water use, and mitigate the risk of climatic events.[32] Yet many of these collective work traditions have now been replaced by more individualized farming, small irrigation committees, etc, thus weakening the *social capital* of many communities to face major environmental challenges.

Figure 3: Traditional Cusco highland farmers (Photograph: Thomas Müller/SPDA, used with permission)

What has contributed to this? From 1969, the military government in Peru started making extensive land reforms which gave ownership of big land holdings—*haciendas*—to the Quechua peoples. However, these reforms did not take into account the different Quechua communal or traditional systems of land ownership and management. Large *haciendas* were reorganized into cooperative associations, ignoring the demands for restoring the traditional community structures.

The influence of government programs (and of NGOs within the last thirty years or so) has also contributed to the weakening of many traditional forms of land management, through the imposition of high technology systems, and the introduction of *improved crops and livestock* over the many local varieties, without an integrative or adaptive approach.

The government presently provides little support to Quechua highland farmers: there are few effective technical assistance programs to improve or change their crops, or to stimulate traditional beneficial practices. Some government programs (such as reforestation with eucalyptus) have even contributed to environmental problems like water shortage.

In summary, despite their relative isolation, these Andean peoples are still subject to a context of profound social, economic, and cultural changes. Those factors, coupled with the pressure of climate change, are forcing them to question their very presence in the rural highlands. Climate change makes agricultural activities more risky and less profitable, and is thus a significant contributor to the problem of out-migration. Flores observes: '[Rural indigenous communities] are caught in a dilemma between "migrating" and "staying in their lands", but with low agricultural productivity, extreme poverty, poor nutrition, limited access to health services and education . . . and in a context of climatic change and the effects of economic globalization.'[33] And it is particularly the youth who are prone to migrate elsewhere, seeking greater educational and work opportunities.

Adaptation strategies: some local measures to cope with climate change

Traditionally, the Quechua people have had to maximize the dispersal of risks in their agricultural practices. 'The adversities that indigenous peoples have had to face due to climate and to the sudden unpleasant turn of events in their history, have trained them to be extraordinarily prepared [to resist].'[34] They have done this through cultivating a wide variety of crops, locating crops in different plots and in different ecological zones—so that severe climatic events do not harm the entire investment. They also developed ingenious systems for soil conservation and irrigation, such as:

- artificial terraces that help increase agricultural surface on slopes, while preventing erosion and improving use of water resources

- irrigation channels—a pre-Inca technique for carrying water from lakes and rivers to their land plots and terraces, thus diminishing water wastage

- crop rotation and the system of *laymes* (fallow land) that allowed the land to rest and recover between cultivations

To ensure food provision when crops fail, there is also a long tradition of preserving crops and meat through dehydration, for example, *charki* (dried Alpaca meat) and *chuño* (freeze-dried potatoes)—products that can be stored for up to five years.

However, these traditional cultivation and storage practices have been significantly weakened over recent decades. Perhaps the biggest factor in weakening them is the prevalence of a cash economy. Over the last decades, there has been a tendency to favour commercial crops (for example, a commercial variety of potato) over the many traditional varieties that used to be grown.[35] Such *improved* varieties, normally grown in monocultures, are often more susceptible to climatic changes and pests. And growing such cash crops for commercial purposes, rather than for household consumption, significantly reduces storage practices. Traditional soil conservation and irrigation systems are also labour-intensive, and can be difficult to implement in a context of increasing rural-urban out-migration and other competing economic activities, such as commerce or seasonal construction with the local municipality.

The Climate Change Adaptation Programme (PACC)

In the last five years, valuable research has been carried out by PACC in the Cusco region. The aim of these studies is to contribute to strengthening the capacity of the rural population and institutions to adapt to climate change, providing them with experiences of adaptation that they can replicate when seeking to reduce their vulnerability. Simultaneously, PACC seeks to incorporate these issues in regional and national public policy, and in international climate change negotiations.

The PACC programme—collaborating closely with the regional government and local institutions—has achieved wide participation from local communities, and has managed to put forward a Regional Strategy for Climate Change in Cusco, one of the first in the country.[36] Some of the recommendations from this Regional Strategy are picked up in the concluding section of this article.

Characteristics of the local church in the highlands of Cusco

The Catholic faith arrived with the Spanish conquest of Peru in the sixteenth century; and throughout the years, a form of folk Catholicism (integrating Catholic and indigenous beliefs and practices) has become deeply rooted in the rural highlands of Cusco.[37] Nowadays, Catholic churches tend to be found in larger rural towns, while their presence in more remote areas is much weaker or very sporadic, depending on the availability of priests.

In the early 1900s, faith missions from the United Kingdom helped to found the Peruvian Evangelical Church (IEP). Since the mid 1900s, it has grown considerably, particularly among the rural highland communities of Cusco.[38] Currently, there are over 600 churches scattered throughout high Andean and jungle territories. Subsequently other missions—Swiss and American—have also exercised influence in the region, establishing churches such as the Maranatha denomination which also has a strong rural presence. Most rural evangelical churches are small, averaging 15 to 30 baptized members, with meetings mainly conducted in the Quechua language. Such churches are often weakened or struggling due mainly to lack of trained leadership, and to the out-migration of young people to urban centres.

The theological heritage of the evangelical churches planted by different missions tends to place considerable emphasis on *escapist* views of the *end times* that have found resonance with traditional Quechua beliefs about time being cyclical, with catastrophic events at the end of each cycle. These views do not encourage churches to engage with the needs of their communities. Nonetheless, in some regions there is a growing interest among evangelicals regarding local political participation. There are also positive testimonies of evangelical presence within communities—often associated with reduced alcoholism, which is a severe problem in Quechua communities. Secular researchers on the PACC programme observed that some predominantly evangelical communities had an impressive level of commitment and organization enabling them, for example, to reforest an area.[39]

However, the same researchers also pointed out the deep divisions and rivalries that often exist in the communities between evangelicals and followers of folk Catholicism. Evangelicals sometimes attribute environmental problems to the sin and idolatry of the Catholics, while the latter group may maintain that environmental problems result from the way that evangelical Quechuas have not been keeping up their traditional (non-Christian) practices—for example, they no longer make offerings to appease Mother Earth's wrath, and to increase her productivity.

Evangelicals are also 'accused' of refusing to participate in certain cultural forms of intra-community cooperation. For example, they often refuse to do *Ayni* or collective work with others—because if they associate too much with them or support their families, they might 'get contaminated'.[40] Thus, rather than being a reconciling presence in their communities, the different churches often provoke tensions by rejecting those outside their group.

To summarize, we find a highland Quechua church with numerical presence, but struggling to survive; a church with a certain capacity to act, but which struggles to relate to other groups who think and believe differently; and, in the case of evangelicals, a church that claims to have the *whole truth*, yet is biblically and theologically deficient in some of its interpretations.

How does the Quechua rural farmer understand the causes of climate change?

While the perceptions of the Quechua population regarding the effects of climate change seem to strongly support the scientific evidence, their explanations of the causes of these phenomena can contrast greatly with logical scientific explanations.

In general, we can characterize three main ways in which the local population interprets climate change.[41]

- Traditional Quechua, influenced by folk Catholicism, tend to interpret climatic changes as Mother Earth's (*Pachamama's*) retribution for mistreating her and for failing to carry out the *payments* that are seen as a means of *appeasing her disapproval* and *increasing productivity.*

- Especially among evangelicals, climatic events are often seen as punishment or judgement from God for our sins or moral disobedience—as events foretold in ancient history, that now must simply be accepted with resignation as a sign of the end times.

- *Less isolated* rural people—especially young people with wider urban experience, or in contact with NGOs and the media—tend to repeat what they have heard concerning global climate change, and the issue that 'those who contaminate more are the industrialized nations, [yet] we are the ones who suffer the consequences.'[42]

In reference to the second interpretation, we can see that for many evangelicals in the Cusco region, the current climatic variability is not surprising. It is rather something expected, almost longed-for. The worse climatic conditions become, the closer will be the second coming of the Messiah, and the pre-announced *end times*. In the conditions of great uncertainty, suffering, and hopelessness in which many high Andean people live, this message of the evangelical churches provides a sense of *certainty and hope* of final justice and an *escape* to eternal life. However, an inevitable result of this message is fatalism: why get involved if everything is going to end anyway?

Here we observe a great need to enrich the biblical vision of local Quechua believers to help them understand their Christian responsibility for creation stewardship, to amplify their vision of God (not only as saviour but also as creator, sustainer and restorer of creation), and to develop an *eschatology* that might provide hope and encourage their involvement in creation care.

Proposals for action against climate change in Cusco

'We have to adapt. Sometimes we say it's God's punishment . . . What have we done? Sometimes we say we will go elsewhere . . . but then . . . Where would we go?'[43] The words of this Cusco farmer remind us that, today, adaptation is not something optional for the Andean highland communities. Rather, it is a pressing need. Climate change profoundly threatens the welfare of these people, and requires an urgent response at different levels of society.

Families and communities as key actors

The primary level of response to the local consequences of climate change involves the Quechua families and communities themselves. Any strategies to respond to the effects of climate change must involve reducing vulnerability of these families. At the same time, they must be helped to implement adaptation practices that value their ancestral know-how, incorporate scientific knowledge, and take into account the socio-economic context. It is also important to promote their active participation in planning and implementation—measures must be contextualized and sustainable; they must not be an external imposition. Some key actions at local level include:

- Strengthening capacity for diversifying production, valuing more resistant local crop varieties—thus improving food security

- Improving the protection of water sources and rainwater storage, promoting more efficient irrigation and a fairer, more rational distribution of water for different uses

- Reducing the vulnerability of family homes to extreme climatic events through re-location or improved construction

- Reforestation of high Andean areas with native species to help generate micro-climates that diminish the effects of hard frosts

- Strengthening levels of organization and capacities within communities to deal with climatic threats

Local churches are well placed to be key actors in implementing these local adaptive responses to climate change—through offering their church buildings for meetings, or contributing to community activities. They could also participate in early warning systems for preventing or responding to disasters, thus demonstrating Christian love and solidarity.

Strengthen the capacity of local and regional government

Local governments in high Andean areas are characterized by their low capacity and their focus on road building and large infrastructure projects—rather than on promoting local-level productive, social, or ecological interventions. Here, there is an enormous challenge of helping to build resilience. At the regional level, climate change strategies are weakened by regional government's inability to carry out territorial planning and ecological/economic zoning of their lands, particularly watersheds. Local and regional governments must be helped to form effective alliances with the private sector, civil society, and universities. This will allow interdisciplinary responses to the complex phenomena of climate change. The Cusco Climate Change Regional Strategy highlights the key role that regional governments play in enhancing the water resources in their region, promoting both their protection and rational use.[44]

Communication and training

Communication and education about climate change is vital—highlighting issues of vulnerability, adaptation, and management of risks at the community level. In the state educational system, such issues are virtually absent from the curriculum. With Quechua being better understood than Spanish, and with low levels of literacy and reading comprehension in the highland areas of Cusco, training in Quechua would be most effective at a wider community level. Local churches can have a key role: some have radio stations that can be used to broadcast environmental messages; also they can educate their own members about their own contribution to environmental problems, and their role as responsible stewards. As agronomist Karin Kancha states: 'I think that for a lot of believers . . . what they hear in church . . . is the law! And if the church keeps informing about what is happening and about what can be done . . . I think that they could make a big contribution.'[45]

Promoting environmental and social justice

Adaptation programmes must be accompanied by appropriate social and environmental justice measures. The national government has a key role in ensuring justice for rural populations—for example, in situations where large-scale mining operations might increase the vulnerability of local populations. How can demands be made of high Andean populations to adapt to climate change when nearby mining megaprojects, hydroelectric projects, or large-scale irrigation schemes use water and resources freely and without limit?

The current Peruvian government has approved favourable legal measures like the Prior Consultation Law. This applies to indigenous populations, and it has committed itself to making issues of climate change and sustainable development mainstream within state policies. Nevertheless, on the ground, its response and support of local Andean populations is weak. There is a Global Fund to assist high Andean regions in adaptation programmes. However, it is small compared with the enormity of the problem. There is a need to tap into other sources, such as the considerable revenues from mining royalties and from the booming tourist industry.

Solidarity of the global community

The task of responding to the local effects of climate change in the Cusco region is enormous and complex. It requires the collaboration of many actors at different levels—government, private sector, specialized institutions, wider civil society—and especially the affected communities and families themselves. However, the reality is that responsibility for dealing with this problem is falling disproportionally on the most affected communities. From their situation of marginalization and poverty, they lack the resources, influence, and complex knowledge to respond effectively to difficulties.

One of Jesus' parables reminds us of the need to show solidarity. 'Who is my neighbour?', an expert in the law asked him. Jesus responded with the familiar story of the man travelling from Jerusalem to Jericho who had been beaten, robbed, and left to die. A priest and a Levite had passed by the severely injured man without giving him any attention. 'But a Samaritan . . . when he saw him . . . took pity on him . . . went to him and bandaged his wounds . . . Then . . . he brought him to an inn and took care of him' (Luke 10:33–34).

One of the characteristics of environmental problems is that those who cause the problem can be far removed from those who are most affected—preventing them from seeing their wounded *neighbour*. This familiar parable invites us to see the highland farmers of Cusco as our 'neighbours', who suffer the consequences of climate change and need our urgent support. Those responsible for climate change—you and I—are at a distance and often, without even realizing it, 'beating the wounded' and 'leaving them half dead' through our consumerist and wasteful lifestyles. The high Andean populations of Cusco are telling us in a silent and long-suffering way that we are following a terrible path of creation abuse—and they challenge us, as believers, to be part of the solution rather than the problem.

CHAPTER 11

Population and Ecological Sustainability

John P McKeown

'Overpopulation is more than just an environmental issue; it's also
an issue of social justice. The greater the world's population, the
smaller the share of natural resources available to each person.'

Rob Dietz and Dan O'Neill [1]

Population is an important environmental issue. We have grown in number
from three billion, back in 1960, to more than seven billion. The impact of
our demands on the earth's life support systems is unsustainable, as other
chapters in this book explain. Shrinking our lifestyle is not enough, because even an ecofriendly but comfortable level of per-person consumption
(that we may wish for all) multiplied by our population size would already
approach earth's biocapacity according to one method of calculation.[2] If
the total *ecological footprint* of consumption sustainable by one earth were
shared equally among the global population today, a fair share would be
little more than the level of consumption per-person in Mali.[3] Some people
use more than others—for example, per-person consumption in the European Union is three times larger than in Mali—but everyone adds to
the total. Much of the impact arises from needs and luxuries such as food,
housing, commodities, and travel. The Cape Town Commitment affirms the
Millennium Development Goals.[4] Though future technology and efficiency
can help reduce poverty (and ecological impact), a large population size
makes achieving those goals more difficult.

There is hope: in most developing countries birth rates have decreased
since the 1960s, and the rate of population growth is slowing. There is also a
challenge: the population is expected to rise above nine billion by 2050, and
the future peak of global population is not expected to be earlier than 2100.
But that future is not fixed: in places where young women have cultural
permission to limit their own reproduction and also easy access to modern
family planning technologies, many choose to have smaller families. Faster
progress toward low birth rates could deliver an earlier and lower peak of
global population.

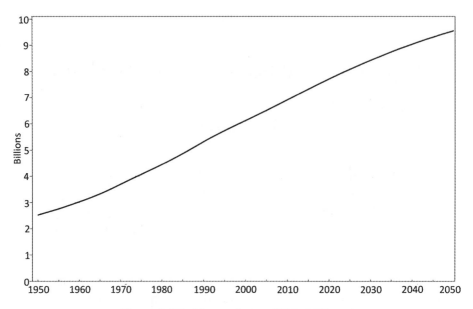

Figure 1: World population 1950–2010 and
United Nations medium projection to 2050.[5]

This chapter looks at the following topics: a consideration of Christian perspectives, past and present; some reasons why efforts to actively encourage lower fertility languished for two decades after demotion to a low priority concern by most politicians, economists, and development NGOs (non-governmental organizations); a description of current trends in population size, birth rates, and ageing; an exploration of reasons why birth rates in many countries have not declined as rapidly as death rates; and finally how a preference for smaller family sizes can be encouraged and facilitated by Christians and others.

Christian ideas about fecundity and population

There are diverse perspectives on reproduction among modern Christians. Some Protestant writers, for example R C Sproul Jr, urge parents to be open to bearing a large number of children, and interpret Old Testament texts such as the 'quiver full' of sons (Ps 127:5) and 'be fruitful and multiply' (Gen 1:28) as reasons for Christians today to avoid family planning.[6] Raising many (genetic) sons was a priority for people in Old Testament times. The rivalry motivating Leah and Rachel to compete at bearing sons for Jacob illustrates the patriarchal and pro-natalist character of ancient Israelite culture (Gen 30:1–24). But raising many genetic sons was *not* a priority in the

New Testament church. This highlights a wider principle: we should not always imitate ancient values and practices, some of which may have been pragmatic in their historical context but are inappropriate now.

For ancient Israelites, the pre-modern reasons that are the basis for a cultural esteem of large family size (described in more detail later in this chapter) prevailed: high infant mortality and a need for agricultural labour. The early Israelites lived in the highlands, on rocky slopes with poor soil that needed much work to clear scrub (Josh 17:18), remove stones, and maintain terraces on sloping land, so the demand for labour and for large families was unusually strong even by ancient standards.[7] That need for prolific reproduction was embedded in Israelite customs.

Sons were highly valued. Daughters were helpful while children, but at maturity most married and went to another household where they worked: the bride-price compensated the father. But married sons still had a duty to help the father—for example, by patching his roof, or supplying *muscle* in disputes with neighbours. Psalm 127 has spiritual and messianic meanings, but builds on ancient popular appreciation of the benefits of a quiverfull of sons born during 'one's youth' (v 4) i.e. grown-up sons. The original refers to sons—but some modern translations change it to gender-neutral 'children', which unfortunately removes a flag that might alert modern readers to cultural distance, and prompt them to discover why parents in the ancient world wanted many sons.[8]

Culturally, a man's identity depended on perpetuating his genealogical line: 'bless the boys; and in them let my name be carried on' (Gen 48:16, ESV). If a man died without a male heir, a custom obliged a brother to marry the widow and donate the first offspring to the dead man to preserve his lineage (Deut 25:5–6). Also, a man would want sons to bury him (Gen 35:29), and archaeology suggests a popular belief that ancestors needed descendants to make offerings and memorials.[9] So there were strong reasons why ancient Israelites desired many sons.

Christian perspectives on reproduction

An important strand in early Christian thought moved away from the old model of an ethnic religion, perpetuated by natural birth, to an emphasis on being *born again* into a new *family* open to anyone regardless of ancestry. Jesus, when told that his mother and brothers waited outside, applies those *kin* words to his followers (Mark 3:33). Joining the church might mean distancing oneself from genetic kin (Mark 13:12, Luke 14:26). Paul, who was celibate, is nevertheless called a 'father' (1 Cor 4:15), and a disciple is called his 'son' (Philem 10). Jesus was celibate—as were many Christian leaders in the church's early centuries. The meaning of *fruitfulness* was spiritually transformed. Eusebius devoted part of *Demonstratio Evangelica* to the question: 'Why a numerous offspring is not as great a concern to us as it was' in the Old Testament. The reasons for 'the ancient men of God begetting children cannot apply to Christians today' because now 'preachers of the word' (including celibates) 'bring up not one or two children but a prodigious number' by spiritual birth. They are 'multiplying daily, according to the divine commandment, "Increase and multiply and fill the earth" which in them is fulfilled more truly and divinely'.[10]

Biological reproduction continues as part of the natural order, as the way humankind and all species are perpetuated. Thankfully, humankind has moved beyond the *natural* death rate and we intervene with medicine. Combining an artificially low death rate with a *natural* birth rate would lead to rapid population growth. A modern couple that marries young, if they do not use any practical methods to limit conceptions, could end up with ten or more offspring. We have a responsibility to subdue our fecundity.[11]

Pope Paul VI's 1968 encyclical *Humanae Vitae* allows contraceptive intention—but the only permissible method is periodic abstinence. Catholicism supports *natural family planning* (NFP) in which conjugal relations are scheduled out from each month's period of fertility. This can work well if done carefully with self-control, a good Christian virtue. NFP enables many couples to limit their family size. However, in some marriages it does not work well, especially in cultures that disempower wives, so a legalistic application is questionable. A survey of Catholic laity in twelve countries found that 78 percent support the use of 'artificial birth control'.[12]

Pythagoreans and some Stoics (ancient Greek philosophers) developed an anti-contraceptive ideology. This had roots in male fears that *wasting seed* could weaken a man's reproductive faculties and result in his producing offspring that were born weak and sickly. It was also rooted in civic concern for elite reproduction. These ideas were adopted by Philo (a Jewish philosopher) and later *Christianized* by Clement of Alexandria.[13]

A biblical text often cited against contraception is Genesis 38:6–10. The patriarch Judah had three adult sons: Er (the eldest), Onan, and Shelah. When Er died with no heir, Onan's potential status rose: the clan headship would pass to Onan when Judah died, and he would only have to share inherited land with Shelah. However, following custom, Judah asked Onan to give a posthumous heir to Er by marrying the widow and producing a son who would be regarded as Er's heir and revive his lineage. Onan pretended to go along with it, but verse 9 tells us that 'Onan knew that the child would not be his; so whenever he slept with his brother's wife, he spilled his semen on the ground to keep from providing offspring for his brother.' Despite this explanation, some interpreters turn to Deuteronomy

25:7–10 (set in a later period). They argue that because in the later custom the penalty for refusing to cooperate is only humiliation it does not explain why God killed Onan—and they claim the real offence was contraception. However, the case here differs: Onan could have simply refused to help and, if he had, the later case would be comparable. But Onan did not refuse openly; instead, he pretended to obey but secretly disobeyed his father and that was a serious offence. A rebellious son might be punished by death (Deut 21:18, 21). Also, if Onan had plainly refused, then perhaps Shelah—the third brother—could have stepped in to provide Er's heir. However, Onan's deceit prevents that possibility and cuts off all hope for his elder brother's posterity. This text has been misused to generate false guilt in people using contraceptive technologies.

Population growth today is not a blessing

The ancient Israelite reasons for having sons are not applicable today, despite the claims of modern cornucopians (advocates of unlimited growth). The biblical phrase 'be fruitful and increase' signifies the reproductive power that is embodied in living creatures and which creates many new lives each year. In the beginning, when diverse aquatic species are called to 'be fruitful and increase in number and fill the water in the seas' (Gen 1:22), and after the Flood when 'every kind of living creature' is to 'multiply on the earth and be fruitful and increase' (Gen 8:17), the picture is an empty world across which animals will spread and multiply.

Later, the world is not empty: 'the earth is full of your creatures' (Ps 104:24). The increase commanded had already occurred. Biblical writers knew that, in their own time, birds and animals were not steadily growing in number year after year. If 'be fruitful and increase' applies today, it signifies births—the annual *increase* that counteracts the regular losses to mortality. Sometimes, the net result is population growth; at other times reproductive increase just preserves a population.

'Be fruitful and increase' (Gen 1:28) is framed as a blessing. In ancient Near Eastern cultures, including Israel, the essence of blessing was *prosperity* and *success*.[14] The word is used with reference to water springs (Josh 15:19), rain (Ezek 34:26), stored food (Mal 3:10), wealth (Prov 10:22), and reproduction (Gen 49:25). Ancient Israelites wanted as many sons as they could get. However, with regard to other blessings, they saw a possibility of imbalance or excess. For example, sleep is a blessing (Ps 127:2)—but too much brings poverty (Prov 6:10). In the lives of individuals and communities, different kinds of blessings should be in balance. Today, population growth is not a blessing: it is detrimental to the ecological foundations of prosperity.

Changing views on population

One of the four key recommendations of the Royal Society's 2012 report on *People and the Planet* is that 'population and the environment should not be considered as two separate issues'.[15] Unfortunately, politicians and NGOs have neglected that link since the 1990s. Before then, many did voice concern about population growth. For example, Norman Borlaug (1914–2009), who was awarded the Nobel Peace Prize in 1970 for his work on high yielding crops which averted famines, warned in his acceptance speech that 'The green revolution has won a temporary success in man's war against hunger and deprivation; it has given man a breathing space . . . But the frightening power of human reproduction must also be curbed; otherwise the success of the green revolution will be ephemeral only.'[16] Back then, politicians also were concerned. For example, George H W Bush in 1973 advised that 'Success in the population field, under United Nations [UN] leadership, may, in turn, determine whether we can resolve successfully the other great questions of peace, prosperity, and individual rights that face the world.'[17]

The sustainable development agenda originally included population. It welcomed a *demographic transition* (demography is the study of population) from regimes of high fertility and high mortality toward lower birth and death rates, and it aimed to accelerate that transition. In 1987, the Brundtland report, *Our Common Future,* by the UN Commission on Environment and Development devoted a chapter to population, and urged that 'governments must work . . . to limit population growth'.[18] In 1994, the United Nations conference on Population and Development agreed 'to facilitate the demographic transition as soon as possible in countries where there is an imbalance between demographic rates and social, economic and environmental goals, while fully respecting human rights. This process will contribute to the stabilization of the world population.'[19] But before the millennium the mood had changed.[20]

One reason for that change is hinted at in the phrase 'human rights' above. In many people's minds, concern about population became associated with draconian policies such as the compulsory sterilization used in India in the 1970s, and China's one-child policy. However, other countries using an entirely voluntary approach also achieved rapid reductions in the *total fertility rate* (TFR).[21] Costa Rica had a TFR of around seven children per woman in the early 1960s, but now it is around two. Sri Lanka, Iran, South Korea, and Thailand have all halved their TFR by investing in efforts to cater to women's needs and wishes to have smaller numbers of children. Coercion is not necessary, but a proactive approach to investment in family planning is needed in all countries. Many women globally experience pronatalist coercion because lack of modern family planning services and lack of cultural permission to limit their own reproduction force them to start bearing offspring in their youth and later to carry on getting pregnant after they already have as many children as they want.

Two paradigms: growth or limits

Another reason why early concerns faded is the *growth* paradigm. Most economists perceive no upper limit to the size of GDP (gross domestic product) or population, but are concerned about relative rates of growth. So they like to see a country's economic growth stay well above its rate of population increase, so that per-person wealth is not eroded. In the mid-twentieth century, rapid population growth in developing countries alarmed them. For example, annual population growth was 2.70 percent in China during the period 1965–70. Later, when population growth slowed, economists' concerns receded. Belatedly—in many countries the only reliable data was a census every 10 years—it became clear that population growth averaged across the *less developed countries* had peaked back in 1965–70 at 2.53 percent.[22] The rate stayed above 2 percent until 1990, and that still caused concern, but then by 2000–05 in those *less developed countries* population growth slowed to 1.46 percent per year. Economists were confident that economic growth could keep ahead of those new lower rates.

According to the growth paradigm, only a few countries still have worryingly high rates of population growth. Another UN category is the 48 *least developed countries* (LDCs), and their annual population growth rate did not peak until 1990–95 when it was 2.75 percent. In the period 2010–15 the annual population growth of the LDCs was 2.38 percent, and it still exceeds 3 percent in a few countries, including Uganda, Tanzania, Zambia, Angola, Congo, Niger, Chad, South Sudan, Iraq, and some smaller countries.

But the growth paradigm is inadequate: population size is a problem beyond those few countries. Total global human impact on many natural systems is already beyond sustainable levels. The growth rate of a population has indirect significance as a portent of its future size, but if we accept the *limits* paradigm we should turn away from the old Malthusian interest in comparing the two rates of growth (economy and population) and instead focus on limits: a ceiling for our ecological impact, and a ceiling for the number of people.

One way to sum impact is the *ecological footprint* method. It converts diverse aspects of consumption into a measure of the land area required, using standard units called global hectares (gha). To use a financial analogy, ecosystems provide an annual *income* called biocapacity, and our consumption footprint is *expenditure*. Overall, the planet has around 12 billion gha of biocapacity. The average footprint per person is around 2.7 gha, which multiplied by the number of people globally means that we overshoot our ecological budget by 50 percent.[23] Now, each year's deficit is not immediately catastrophic but it means that we are forced to liquidate natural capital such as soil depth and aquifers. Cumulatively the ecological debt is unsustainable.

Focusing on consumption only

Many people working in development and environment think that any mention of population distracts from their core message against high consumption. That fear is based on a false dichotomy between consumption and population that associates only poor countries with population-as-problem. Since rich countries are most responsible for ecological impacts, any mention of population is perceived as an attempt by the rich to shift blame unfairly to the poor. But the dichotomy is false: rich countries have big populations that multiply their large per-person consumption footprints into an ecological problem. Many rich countries overshoot their national biocapacity: for example, the UK population of 63 million (in 2012) had a total footprint above 300 million gha, but UK biocapacity is only 82 million gha, and the UK population relies on ecosystem services from overseas, including resources imported from developing countries. Those reluctant to consider population also observe that within each country there is inequality of consumption. For example, in the UK, or in any country, the top ten percent (by spending) have bigger ecological footprints than the bottom ten percent. While that inequality may be suggestive for just policies to shrink a national footprint, it does not alter the fact that a country's total footprint is proportional to its population size.

Also, by analogy with models of emissions *contraction and convergence* that take account of historical pollution, we should remember past population growth. For example, the USA's population in 1800 was 5.3 million, by 1900 it was 76 million, and by 2000 it was 273 million—and, contrary to popular perception, most of the extra people were added by being born in the USA, rather than by immigration.[24] Figure 2 shows that, in the USA, a centuries-long imbalance between the numbers of births and deaths has persisted in recent decades. Rich countries' efforts to become sustainable could include allowing birth rates to fall by removing financial incentives (such as child tax credits), as well as by reducing per-person footprints through better technologies and changed lifestyles.

Some argue that population is a less important factor than per-person consumption. But just as the area of a rectangle is governed by its width and height, both factors multiply impact. For those who insist on comparison, we can ask which has changed most—and we would find differing answers depending on our choice of indicator and time period. For example, globally (different pictures would emerge if we looked at individual countries) in the period 1961 to 2007, the ecological footprint per person rose 14 percent while population grew by 117 percent, suggesting that the latter was the main driver of rising impact. For those who want to focus only on greenhouse gases, between 1900 and 2000 the per-person quantity and population both increased by a similar amount, around 400 percent, suggesting that both were important drivers of the rise in greenhouse emissions during the twentieth century.[26]

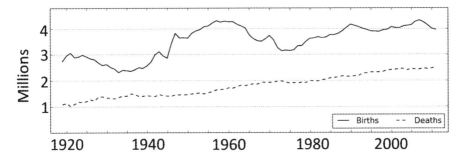

Figure 2: Numbers of births and deaths in the USA from 1919 to 2012.[25]

Reactions to ageing

Many governments want higher birth rates because they are worried about ageing populations. A rising average age is the inevitable result of lower birth rates and longer lives. Life expectancy at birth in the USA has risen steadily for over a century. In the UK, it was 71 years in 1960, and by 2012 it was 81 years. The UN surveys official views and, in 2013, found that in *developed* countries 92 percent of governments consider population ageing a 'major concern', while 65 percent judge that their birth rate is 'too low' and 49 percent have policies designed to increase it.[27] Governments offer citizens financial inducements to additional births—for example, Russia gave a baby bonus to women bearing three or more babies. The UK is not one of those explicitly pro-natalist governments, but some UK policies elevate birth rates. For example, research on the first year of a per-child low-income benefit (Working Families Tax Credit) found that births among recipients increased by 10 percent.[28]

Economists still rely on the *old-age dependency ratio* that arbitrarily uses age 65 as a cut-off to calculate the proportion of people that is (supposedly) unproductive and costly for health services. But, as Adair Turner found, 'health at any given age is increasing rapidly': for example, in the 1990s, French women aged 75 were as fit as women aged 62 were back in 1900.[29] Sarah Harper, of Oxford University's Institute of Ageing, investigated the 'myths of demographic burden' that blame age structure for problems in health services and pensions that also have other causes: the strain on healthcare provision is mostly due to lifestyle and technological possibilities. The major special cost of elderly care is in the final years before death, whenever that happens, rather than across the whole 65+ period, so structural ageing is moving that cost forward in time.[30] Also, if we use *expected years left to live* to define what *elderly* means then the population of England is getting younger![31]

Pension problems are artificial. The retirement age was first set at 65 by Chancellor Bismarck in nineteenth-century Prussia. Since then, our healthy lifespan has extended, and shifting a few (not all) of those added years into work would balance the finances.[32] Many countries have a large older generation, making age-structure diagrams top heavy, and that is a temporary challenge. In a few decades, the bulge will naturally pass away and the age-structure will even out. The transitional period is difficult but must be passed through. If we push for higher birth rates to improve the *dependency ratio*, that would increase the population faster. Given that population size cannot keep rising, at some time in the future the challenge would still have to be negotiated but by then it would have a larger magnitude.

Population size in the future

The global population was two billion in 1927, and doubled by 1974 to four billion. Growth continues, but the percentage rate of growth has slowed as birth rates have decreased since the 1960s. UN forecasts use a *demographic transition theory* that was originally based on European historical experiences and it assumes that birth rates in *developing regions* will continue falling towards a replacement rate. An indicator called the *total fertility rate* (TFR) is used to predict the average number of children per woman. In Figure 3, all the projections (except the constant-fertility curve) assume that TFR in developing countries will decline from today's levels: they differ according to the speed of that change and the TFR reached by 2100.

The medium scenario (the plain line) assumes that the TFR in the *least developed countries* will decline from 4.27 children per woman (the average in 2010–15) down to 2.91 by 2050, and then down to 2.14 children by 2100. Even if that future decline in birth rates is achieved, the world's population would still rise to 9.7 billion by 2050, and then to over 11 billion by 2100. Much of that increase would be concentrated in sub-Saharan Africa (the continent excluding North Africa). An extreme example is Uganda where a population of 6.8 million in 1960 grew to 33 million by 2010. The medium projection for Uganda assumes that its TFR will drop from 5.91 to 3.37 by 2050, and then down to 2.12 by 2100. Even if that reduction in Uganda's birth rate is achieved, the country's population will reach 101 million in 2050, and then 202 million by 2100. Uganda's ecological footprint already exceeds its national biocapacity, so future population growth is locally unsustainable and will eventually lead to a decline in the resources available per person.

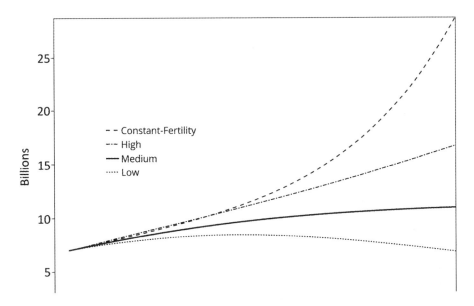

Figure 3: Future population of the world to 2100,
according to UN variant projections.[33]

Small differences in fertility lead to widely diverging outcomes. The UN high and low variants are based on projected national TFRs that are half a child more (high) or less (low) than the medium projection for each year. They serve to illustrate the range of possibilities. All those variants already include anticipated future declines in birth rates, of varying magnitudes. UN demographers warn that if there is 'a slowdown in modern contraceptive method uptake or persistent levels of early marriage and desires for large family sizes, then the fertility projections may be too low'.[34] They emphasize this by including a *constant fertility* scenario, which is what would happen if the birth rate in each country stayed the same as it is now. By 2050, the global population would be 10.8 billion—and, by 2100, it would be 25.9 billion. That is unlikely, but if birth rates are slow to fall, the world will either have to adjust to deeper poverty, or death rates will rise, or both.

One worry is the recent slowness or stalling of reduction in birth rates across much of Africa, excluding the northern and southern African countries. On average, countries such as Kenya, Nigeria, Zimbabwe and Tanzania had a three times slower decrease in birth rate in 1997–2003 than in 1991–1996. In Nigeria, the TFR stalled at around six children per woman during the first decade of the twenty-first century. Some of those countries—notably Zimbabwe, Kenya, and Nigeria—were already overshooting their biocapacity by 2009, and most of the remainder will overshoot soon into ecological deficit if high rates of population growth persist, so a hastening of lower birth rates is needed for local sustainability.

Around the world, birth rates are already low (the lowest they have ever been in human history) and yet to make even the *high* UN projection, birth rates must go even lower. And to achieve the UN *low* projection would require convergence to a world average TFR below two. Ashok Khosla, President of the International Union for Conservation of Nature, suggests that: 'Each country will need country-specific, culturally appropriate ways of making people comfortable with limiting their number of children to one or two.'[35]

Cultural reasons for large families

From ancient times until recent centuries, almost every culture valued numerous offspring for pragmatic reasons. Community survival required it because high rates of mortality stalked all age groups, and especially infants, with half dying by the age of five. On average, a woman had to give birth at least five times just to maintain the population. Afflicted also by plague, war, and famine, local populations went up and down. Growth in world population was slow for most of history.

Subsistence farming families benefitted economically from additional offspring. The infant years were an investment that paid off if the child survived because, by the age of five, a child could help in food preparation, water carrying, wood gathering, gardening, and guarding livestock. As a child grew, the range of tasks and hours worked expanded until they became profitable, producing more than they ate. Parents also relied on their children's help in old age. However, many mothers died as a result of childbirth, so the costs and benefits of their reproduction were not equally shared between men and women.

Sons were especially valued. In many cultures, a man's identity and hopes were invested in continuing his lineage and family name, a proxy *immortality*. Many cultures also believed that ancestors benefit from memorial rituals that only male descendants could perform, often on inherited land where the dead rested. Men's desire for sons was reflected in pre-modern culture: for example, a woman's status was linked to the number of sons she produced. Today *son preference* still inflates birth rates because some parents keep trying until they have a son.[36]

When child mortality is high, parents often seek additional births, as *insurance* against likely (but unpredictable) losses. Further reduction of infant mortality in the least developed countries would help reduce the number of births as parents become more confident that their children will usually survive. In the modern era, improvements in hygiene, nutrition, and medicine have rapidly and drastically reduced mortality rates for infants, children and young adults. While the pragmatic need for numerous births is lessening, often traditional cultures are slow to change and so birth rates remain high. Then a large difference between the numbers of deaths and births opens up and population rises rapidly. That happened in England in the nineteenth century, and is prevalent now in the least developed countries. For example, in Angola, Chad, and Niger the average number of births per woman is still six or more, and the annual population growth rate exceeds 3 percent.

Helping birth rates go lower

The challenge for all countries is to achieve an earlier and lower peak of global population through lower birth rates. One way to achieve that is to enable access everywhere to a wide range of safe contraceptives. The global picture is mixed: in developing countries (excluding China) the proportion of married women of childbearing age using contraception rose from 40.3 percent to 54.1 percent between 1990 and 2010, and in East Africa it advanced from 12.0 percent to 32.6 percent, but in West Africa only from 7.6 percent to 15.1 percent. Contraceptive prevalence is below 10 percent in four countries: Chad, Mali, Sierra Leone, and South Sudan.

One hopeful sign is that many women who do not yet use contraceptives would like access to family planning. Surveys find a gap between wishes and actions. Married women aged 15 to 49 who express a wish to delay or stop their childbearing, but are not using any modern method of family planning, are defined as having *unmet need*. Back in 1994, a UN conference resolved to make family planning accessible to all, but chronic underfunding from rich countries has retarded progress. Between 1990 and 2010, though the global percentage with unmet need for contraception fell from 15.4 percent to 12.3 percent, the absolute number of women with unmet need grew from 99 million to 145 million.[37] Annual funding spread across all developing countries has been $4 billion—but twice that much is needed. The 2012 Summit on Family Planning hosted by the UK Department for International Development (DFID) and the Bill and Melinda Gates Foundation gained many funding pledges that would go some way toward meeting that need.

The essential ingredients for lower fertility are contraceptive access, information, and abolition of the worst aspects of patriarchy: for example, child-brides are a major reason for persistent high fertility in Niger.[38] In

traditional cultures, even adult wives may be reluctant to refuse the expectations of husbands and grandparents. Radio and television *infotainment*
with new ideas about women's roles are making a real difference.[39] Family
planning only becomes a thinkable option when there is cheap and continuous reliable availability of technologies for safe and easy contraception: then
a mass demand emerges.[40] Lower fertility can precede (and enable) other
dimensions of development, which is good news. If we had to wait for everyone to be wealthy before birth rates could fall, we would be in a hopeless
trap, but rapid progress in family planning first is perfectly possible.

Karan Singh reflected in his autobiography:

> In 1974, I led the Indian delegation to the World Population Conference in
> Bucharest, where my statement that "development is the best contraceptive"
> became widely known and oft quoted. I must admit that 20 years later I am
> inclined to reverse this, and my position now is that "contraception is the best
> development."[41]

Lower birth rates ease pressure on national budgets, enabling progress in
other areas of development which themselves encourage lower fertility,
driving a virtuous cycle. In cultures where childbearing has been the main
way for women to gain status, new opportunities for education and employment can help. For example, in Cameroon in 1998, the total fertility rate
(TFR) was 6.6 for women with no education, 5.3 for those who completed
primary school, and 3.6 for those who completed secondary school.[42] A
correlation of longer schooling with a lower birth rate is found in many
developing countries. Investment in increasing the years that girls are in
school is a good way to reduce birth rates.

Helping low birth rates stay low

The previous section focused on the *developing* world. Rich countries
also have a role—not just as funders of global family planning abroad, but
also in resisting the pro-natalist temptation at home. For example, in 1984
the European Parliament resolved to promote higher birth rates, and 'expressed concern about the declining share of Europe's population in the
world total, and ensuing effects on Europe's standing and influence in the
world'.[43] Such nationalism must be rejected; instead the West should humbly
accept that it will not be globally dominant, and embrace opportunities to
be models of how economies can be sustained without the stimulus of an
ever-growing population.

So far, only a few countries are experiencing *natural decrease*, which
means fewer births than deaths. Two big populations pioneering this are

Japan and Germany. Japan achieved a natural decrease in 2009 and is pro-jected, by the end of the century, to shrink in population from 127 to 60 million.[44] If footprint per-person stays around 4 gha, that predicted popula-tion shrinkage would reduce the national footprint below 240 million global hectares (mgha). But the biocapacity of Japan is only 77 mgha, so popula-tion shrinkage alone would only go part of the way toward achieving eco-logical sustainability. The situation is similar for Germany. Looking at the European Union as a whole, in 2012 births and deaths were roughly equal in number, and soon a natural decrease is expected.[45] However, since 2001, birth rates have been rising in many European countries and that could slow future shrinkage, making less contribution to shrinking our footprint.

The United States is unlikely to achieve natural decrease in the near fu-ture. Though the birth rate is low, the death rate is even lower. For example, in 2011 in the USA, there were 3.95 million births compared with 2.51 mil-lion deaths. US birth rates have been at or below the so-called *replacement level* TFR since 1970, but that has not yet delivered true replacement: an equal numbers of births and deaths. That long delay is due to demographic momentum, youthful migration, and lengthening lifespans. The Census Bureau forecasts that US births will continue to outnumber deaths until 2050 and beyond, as shown in Figure 4.

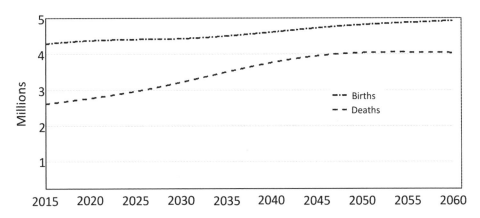

Figure 4: USA births and deaths. Census Bureau,
National Population Projections 2015–2060[46]

Mission, ministry and family planning

The day after the 2012 Summit on Family Planning (mentioned ear-lier), some of the delegates from Christian NGOs stayed on for a faith-based follow-up event. Religion may sometimes be part of the population problem (though usually the underlying obstacle is patriarchy), but many Christians are working hard to make family planning available in developing countries.[47] On the biblical dimension, in the 1990s, medical workers in the Eglise du Christ au Congo produced *Be Fruitful: Bible Studies on Responsible Parenthood* in French, and later an English version was developed in Kenya. With further input from discussion groups in Malawi, Rwanda, Tanzania, the USA, and elsewhere, a set of Bible studies entitled *Love, Children, and Family Planning* was published in 2013.[48] Christian Connections for International Health (CCIH) is a forum for varied ministries, and it provides inspiring case studies of practical efforts—for example, by the Uganda Protestant Medical Bureau.[49] At the 2014 launch of a *Faith and Family Planning* report, Karen Sichinga, Executive Director of the Churches Health Association of Zambia, urged ministries to not be reticent about this dimension of their development work: 'Let's . . . share what we are doing in family planning, so others will know.'[50]

Most agencies—whether Christian or secular—working to facilitate family planning do that simply to improve women's and children's health. However, a more integrated vision and approach that recognizes the ecological benefits of lower birth rates has emerged in the small but growing field of *population, health, and environment* (PHE) development and conservation projects. Examples include:

- Community Health and Sustainable Environment Africa, which works with local NGOs in rural Kenya[51]

- Blue Ventures in Madagascar, which combines marine conservation and family planning with health services[52]

- Health of People & Environment in Lake Victoria Basin (HoPE-LVB)— a project to help biodiversity and family planning[53]

- Other PHE projects—many funded by the United States Agency for International Development (USAID)—work to help local providers of family planning in Ethiopia, Tanzania, Mozambique, Rwanda, Congo, Uganda, Sudan, Guatemala, Papua New Guinea, Nepal, the Philippines, and elsewhere, often in biodiversity hotspots.

Christian perspectives on the links between population and ecological sustainability were pioneered by John Guillebaud (a Professor of Family Planning who was born in Rwanda),[54] and also by Susan Power Bratton,[55] James Martin-Schramm,[56] Jim Ball,[57] Christine Gudorf,[58] and Matthew Sleeth.[59] In the journal of the Oxford Centre for Mission Studies, *A Christian Response to Population Issues* is featured alongside case studies by Olly

Mesach about Indonesia;[60] and Daisy Nwachaku on Nigeria.[61] Elsewhere, attitudes to reproduction among charismatic Christians in Ghana were analyzed by Kwabena Asamoah-Gyadu.[62] The need for rich people to exercise reproductive self-restraint was explored in depth by Bill McKibben.[63] In addition, my book considers attitudes to human fecundity held by some US Protestants today, comparing those with historical Christian ideas through a focus on the writings of Martin Luther and the great African church leader Augustine of Hippo.[64]

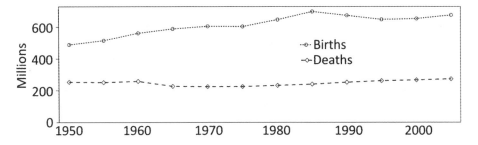

*Figure 5: Births and deaths, all nations, 1950–2005 in
five-year ranges starting at the given year.*[65]

Globally, the birth rate continues to be much higher than the death rate—as Figure 5 shows. At present, there are still many more births than deaths each year, and this generates a large increment added to the global population every year. Population will only stabilize when the gap between numbers of births and deaths disappears. Since it is good to carry on working to further reduce premature mortality, the right way to hasten a peaking of population is through lower birth rates. Happily, this coincides with the wishes of many women to bear fewer offspring. The most hopeful aspect of the population issue is that since 'family planning could bring more benefit to more people at less cost' than any other technology, and because this approach has been comparatively neglected, there is a great potential for small investments to yield significant gains.[66] There are also opportunities for more Christian ministries to help.

CHAPTER 12

Unnatural Disasters

Robert S White

'Sometimes it takes a natural disaster to reveal a social disaster.'

Jim Wallis[1]

'This catastrophe did not result from an act of "God". It resulted from acts of "People".'

Team Louisiana[2]

Background

We live in a world where the same natural processes that make it habitable can also be extremely dangerous. Disasters may kill thousands or even hundreds of thousands of people at a stroke. Natural disasters pull us up sharp and make us face head-on the hard questions of life and death. For atheists and agnostics they challenge humankind's hubris that we can control our environment—or that our cleverness can keep us from suffering. For Christians they raise the hard question of why an all-powerful, all-loving God allows such things to happen. Disasters bring into sharp focus the relationship between the creator God, his creation, and humans made 'in his image'.

The problem of disasters

Thirty seconds was the start of eternity for over 200,000 people caught up in an earthquake in Haiti in 2010. They died as a magnitude 7 earthquake destroyed the capital, Port au Prince, at 4:53 pm local time on Tuesday, 12 January.

Such massive casualties are not unique to the Haiti disaster. In a matter of minutes on Ascension Day 1902 the entire population of 26,000–36,000 people in Saint Pierre, Martinique, died. The culprit was Mont Pelée volcano, which poured a cloud of burning ash and gases across the town. The only survivor in town was a minor criminal, Ludger Sylbaris, who had been thrown into the local prison. The prison happened to be the old explosives store. It therefore had very thick stone walls and a thick door: these protected him and saved his life, although he was badly burned. When his pleas for help were finally heard two days later he was released—and given a pardon!

We could also take an example from the third of the trio of earthquake, fire, and flood. On the single night of 12 November 1970, half a million people drowned when Typhoon Bhola hit the Ganges delta region of East Pakistan (now Bangladesh). There are many other examples of large-scale deaths caused by floods. Although seemingly the most mundane of disasters, because they are not generally as dramatic in their occurrence as earthquakes or volcanic eruptions, floods are actually the world's biggest killers globally.

A single disaster which combined earthquake, fire, and flood occurred on the morning of All Saints Day 1755. A massive earthquake in the North Atlantic shook much of northwest Africa and Iberia. Lisbon, in particular, was badly affected and many of the buildings collapsed. It was a Sunday morning, so there were many candles alight in the churches, and Sunday meals were being cooked in ovens and over open fires. As the densely packed wooden buildings toppled, numerous fires started and soon the whole city was ablaze. Many people rushed to the quayside to escape the firestorm—only to be drowned by a massive tsunami wave which swept in half an hour later and reached 5–15 metres high. Up to one hundred thousand people died in total. To the present day it remains the worst single disaster in Europe, although more recent disasters elsewhere such as the 2010 Haitian earthquake and the 2004 Boxing Day tsunami in Indonesia dwarf it in terms of the numbers of people killed.

It was a major shock to the rational world view of Enlightenment thinkers that such a primeval disaster as the 1755 earthquake could flatten one of the most sophisticated and prosperous cities in Europe without a moment's notice. Religious platitudes were not sufficient to address such a catastrophe; but then again, neither was there a secular answer as to why devastation on this scale occurred.

Despite the explosion over the past century of our scientific understanding of the world in which we live, the numbers of people affected or killed by disasters is increasing with every decade that goes by. Indeed, it is likely that in the not-too-distant future there will be an earthquake that kills over one million people.[4] This is largely a result of the exponential increase in population. The number of people on this planet has more than doubled in the last 50 years. Since 2010, more than half the world's population has lived in cities, where people are more vulnerable to disasters than they are in dispersed rural populations. The percentage of city-dwellers is projected to increase still further over this century as people migrate to urban agglomerations from rural areas.

Figure 1: Lisbon in flames, with tsunami overwhelming ships in foreground, 1755. (Copper engraving, France)[3]

We are accustomed to calling such catastrophes 'natural disasters', as if humans played no part in them. Yet once you scratch beneath the surface it becomes clear that almost always it is the actions, or the inactions or neglect of humans which turn natural processes into disasters. To this extent the term 'natural disasters' is a misnomer and is actually highly misleading.

This fruitful earth

Far from being unwelcome intrusions, in fact earthquakes, volcanoes, and floods are essential to the well-being of this planet. They are what make the earth a fruitful, habitable place where humans and indeed the whole biosphere can live and thrive. Without them earth would be a barren planet without life as we know it. Planet Earth is astonishingly fruitful. Indeed, the term *anthropic principle* has been coined for the observation that the physical structure of the universe and the processes that control how it works are extremely finely tuned for the existence of life on earth.[5] This is a topic of serious academic research and debate by the secular world. For the theist it is a source of awe and wonder, but is entirely consistent with belief in the creator God, as Psalm 104 proclaims.

Many of the processes that give rise to disasters are also what make it possible for humans to live on earth. For example, if there had never been any volcanoes on earth then the main geological source of carbon dioxide in the atmosphere would be missing. The likely result is that the planet would have been frozen for most of its history.[6] Volcanic eruptions also continually cycle to the surface of the earth huge volumes of minerals essential for life. Volcanic islands such as Hawaii support lush growth of plants and animals, and are some of the most biodiverse areas on earth. Yet volcanic eruptions may be explosively fatal to humans caught up in them.

Another example of a normally beneficial natural process is floods. They are a means of distributing fertile soils. For millennia it was the annual flood of the Nile that enabled Egypt to prosper. When the Nile flood failed, as it did for example in 1784, one sixth of the population died.[7]

Lastly, without plate tectonics and the accompanying earthquakes which are produced as the plates move, there would be no mountain ranges. The continual building and erosion of mountains provides a steady supply of nutrient-rich sediments which allows life to thrive on this planet. Mountains also trigger rainfall which in turn makes the surrounding areas fertile and habitable. Without the Himalayan mountain range the annual monsoons which provide water for one billion people in India would not occur.

Although natural processes are beneficial in generating a suitable home for humanity, it is when humans interact badly with them that an otherwise beneficial natural process can turn into a disaster. Unfortunately, it is often the actions of humans that hugely exacerbate the scale of disasters, as I discuss next.

Human factors

Over the past century, millions of people have died in disasters as a result of human failings. For example, an identical earthquake to the one that killed over two hundred thousand people in Haiti occurred twenty years earlier in Loma Prieta, in the San Francisco Bay area of California. Yet the Californian earthquake killed only fifty-seven people. The reason for such a low death toll? California enforced building codes that meant houses did not fall down in the quake. Indeed, most of the casualties were on a collapsed two-level freeway that was in the process of being prepared for earthquake strengthening. In contrast, people died in Haiti when their poorly built concrete slab houses situated on landslide slopes collapsed on top of them. It is no coincidence that 70 percent of Haiti's population lives on less than $2 per day, making it the poorest nation in the western hemisphere. By comparison of the two death tolls from identical earthquakes, you could say that 99.98 percent of the deaths in Haiti were due to human factors, largely derived from decades of endemic corruption, misrule and poverty.[8]

A striking demonstration of the ability to build earthquake-proof build-ings in the most seismically active place in the world is the massive mag-nitude 9.1 earthquake near Japan in March 2011. It released 1,500 times as much energy as the Haiti earthquake, yet only a handful of people died in the earthquake shaking. This was due almost entirely to the building codes in place in Japan. In addition, automated systems from over one thousand seismometers gave more than sixty seconds warning in Tokyo of the im-pending arrival of seismic waves. They also triggered automatic emergency braking on over thirty high-speed bullet trains travelling across the Sendai Plain at up to three hundred kilometres per hour before the seismic waves arrived. This prevented derailing and almost certain large loss of life.

If we return to the St Pierre volcanic disaster, that too should have been avoided. For two weeks prior to the eruption there had been earthquakes, ash falls, fires, sulphurous fumes, and mud flows that had already killed over six hundred people. Yet despite the self-evident danger from the ongoing eruption of Mont Pelée, barely six kilometres (3.7 miles) from St Pierre, there was no widespread evacuation. Indeed the mayor and the governor first discouraged and later prevented people leaving, using soldiers to block the trails.[9]

Why were the governor, the mayor, and the other authorities so keen to prevent people evacuating St Pierre, against all common sense? It seems clear that the reason was that elections were due, and the governor wanted to keep St Pierre's voters in town until the election was over because the de-mographics of those voters favoured his party.[10] It was an avoidable tragedy. The governor, his family, the rest of the inhabitants of St Pierre paid for it with their lives. We can hardly blame God for that.

Where floods are concerned, it is nowadays frequently possible to predict them well in advance.[11] Yet still people die. A striking example is Hurricane Katrina which hit New Orleans in 2005. Despite it occurring in the most technologically advanced nation in the world, and having been tracked in its approach for several days prior to landfall, over 1,800 people lost their lives. They were disproportionately the infirm, the elderly, and the poor who had no cars and could not evacuate the city as the storm ap-proached. A report by the University of Louisiana into the causes of more than fifty breaches of the levees concluded that 'failure of the NOFDS [New Orleans Flood Defense System] was a predictable, predicted, and prevent-able catastrophe'. It went on to say that 'this catastrophe did not result from an act of "God". It resulted from acts of "People."'[12]

Famines caused an estimated seventy million deaths during the twen-tieth century alone. They are one of the disasters most readily averted by intervention from others who have food and resources available. Indeed famines, at least in the modern age, are often caused by the direct actions and decisions of autocratic rulers and by warfare. These famines are almost entirely attributable to human agency.

It is sobering to realize that even today famine is a factor in over six million deaths annually of children under five years old. There were nearly 800 million people, or 11 percent of the world's population, undernourished in 2014–16.[13] Shockingly, there are also an estimated six hundred million people in high-income countries who are damaging their health by being obese.

There are many examples of avoidable famines that caused enormous numbers of deaths. The Irish potato famine of 1846–51 is one such. About one million people died, one eighth of the population. Two million Irish were forced to emigrate to seek livelihoods elsewhere, many landlords using the famine as a pretext to evict tenants. Though initially in 1846 the potato crop failure caused shortage of food, after 1847 there was sufficient food available which would have prevented mass starvation if it had been properly distributed to reach the smallholders and labourers in the south and west of Ireland. The Irish famine occurred on the doorstep of Britain, then the richest nation in the world. But there wasn't the political incentive amongst the ruling Whig politicians and middle class of Britain to prevent mass starvation of the Irish poor.[14]

Another example comes from China, which has always been subject to famines, either as a consequence of frequent massive floods, which were common in the south of the country, or as a result of droughts, most often in the north. A particularly bad famine, following prolonged droughts, occurred in the north of China during 1876–79. An estimated nine to thirteen million people died, more than 10 percent of the population of that area. In the hardest hit province of Shanxi, one third of the people died in the famine. News of the Chinese famine led to one of the first major international aid appeals. It included the woodcut pictures illustrated in Figure 2. The accompanying text reads:

> The glowing sun is in the sky and the locusts cover the ground. There is no green grass in the fields and no smoke of cooking from the houses. They caught rats, or spread their nets for birds, or ground the wheat-stalks into powder, or kneaded the dry grass into cakes. Alas! What food was this for men! They were at last reduced to the straits seen in the picture. Ye who spend large sums every day on your food, will you not give these sufferers a cup of soup?[15]

Much of the relief effort in the field was administered by foreign Christians, including over seventy Protestant and Catholic missionaries. One of those missionaries, Timothy Richard, subsequently wrote that

> at the close of the famine it occurred to me, that if I could show to the authorities the causes of their famines and the way to remove them, I would really be rendering them a far greater service than we did during the famine relief. The

remedies I suggested were—the Christian religion, Education, Science and invention and investigation, new manufactures, new industries, engineering and better means of communication and distribution.

Figure 2: Woodcut from appeal for funds for the 1876–79 Chinese famine. The caption was 'They strip off the bark of trees and dig up the grass roots for food'.[16]

This, he suggested would lead to 'the relief of the poor from starvation'.[17] Although Timothy Richard was perhaps a little too optimistic in his views, he was correct in pointing out that preparation for such events was better than waiting until they happened, and then sending relief. Famines were a frequent and recurrent occurrence in China prior to the particularly bad one in which he was caught up, yet the authorities did little to prepare for them or to put in place measures to mitigate their worst effects.

An example of a government causing the deaths of its own citizens occurred in China during 1958–62 as a result of Mao Zedong's policies of the *Great Leap Forward*.[18] At least forty-five million unnecessary deaths resulted from his aggressive agricultural policies. They were often accompanied by coercion, terror, and systematic violence largely against the poorest segments of the population. Even while his own people starved, Mao Zedong attempted to maintain his international reputation by putting exports above local needs. In 1959 China doubled its grain exports compared to the previous year. Culpability was compounded by continual failure to take remedial action even when the consequences of the Great Leap Forward were evident to all.

Another example of blatantly human-caused famine is the three to five million fatalities in the Ukraine famine of 1932–33, which it has been argued resulted from Stalin's rural collectivization policies.

The famines caused by *natural* processes such as droughts or floods are relatively easy to deal with in our globalized world. Those due to warfare—and particularly civil wars or local insurrections—are far harder for outside agencies to reach. Indeed, denial of food and starvation is often consciously used as a tactic in warfare. This has been the case for millennia with, for example, the Egyptian Pharaoh Thutmose III spending seven months starving into submission a Canaanite coalition in Megiddo in *circa* 1475 BC.[19] In addition, the Bible reports (in 2 Kings 6:24–29) a famine resulting from a siege of Samaria which was so severe that some Israelites in the city resorted to cannibalism.

The common factor in all these disasters is that it is the poor and the voiceless who suffer most. That is also true for one of the most pervasive causes of disasters that humans are wreaking on the earth—that of global climate change. Many disasters are related directly or indirectly to climate change, including heat waves, floods, droughts, landslides, and changes in weather patterns that impact agriculture and may lead to famines. Those of us in the high-income countries who have benefitted from burning cheap fossil fuels, thereby causing global climate change, have a moral duty to help those in low-income countries, who largely are the people who suffer from climate change. At the very least, they deserve our assistance to help them adapt to the inevitable changes that result.[20]

A Christian perspective

The problem of suffering is one which has exercised humanity from the earliest times. For example, the book of Job, one of the oldest parts of the Bible, grapples with the question of why a righteous person should suffer. There are no easy or trite answers, and we should not expect to find them. But there are some things we can usefully say about disasters that may help us to respond to them.

The first is that *nature* is not a force separate from God. As John Wesley wrote when he reflected on the 1755 Lisbon earthquake: 'What is nature itself, but the art of God, or God's method of acting in the material world?'[21] A similar idea was expressed nearly two millennia ago by Augustine (AD 354–430) when he wrote that 'nature is what God has made'.[22] Natural processes occur under the overarching sovereignty of God, and so too must natural disasters. This should underpin our thinking.

Some Christians have tried to get around the apparent problem of natural disasters by saying that processes such as earthquakes, volcanic eruptions, and floods did not occur before the Fall, when humans chose to disobey their creator God.[23] But this is simply not borne out by the evidence. There is no doubt from geological evidence that all those events were present on the earth long before humans first walked on it. Indeed, as we have already discussed, it is those very processes that have made the earth habitable and continue to do so.

What did happen at the Fall was that humans chose to put themselves first, rather than God. It is as if in a parody of the Lord's Prayer, they said to God 'not your will, but mine be done on earth'. The result was that humans put themselves out of relationship with God. They broke that intimacy that had prevailed before the Fall when God walked and talked with them 'in the cool of the evening'. And they spoilt the relationship not only between themselves and God, but also between themselves and the rest of creation. It now became toil to wrest food from the land, rather than a pleasure to work in the Garden, and there was an increase of pain in childbirth.

This was a failure to observe the very first commandment God gave humans in Genesis 1:28, which was to have dominion over all the living things on earth. It is fashionable to think of this command in terms of stewardship, and indeed this was part of what God wanted humans to do: to be good stewards of his earth. But it was an even stronger command than that—we were told to have dominion over the earth. That means taking positive steps to keep it in good order; for example, to keep wild animals away from where they can do harm, actively to make use of the resources of the world for the good of both the human and the non-human inhabitants, to actively manage and develop the world. To have dominion over the earth has overtones of ruling it. The sense is that God set humans to rule over the earth on his behalf. Our misrule is not hard to see in this age of environmental degradation, of species annihilation by humans, of widespread pollution of the sea, the land and the air, of all the changes wrought by unprecedented rapid global climate change. The result is that all creation is groaning, as the Apostle Paul put it in Romans 8:22.

God's creation is very good. That is made clear in Genesis 1:31: 'God saw everything that he had made, and behold, it was very good' (ESV). That must include earthquakes, fires and floods. Although we are tempted to think that this world was made just for us, it is clear in the Bible that God's delight in his creation extends to everything. In Job 38:26–27 the writer portrays God as watering 'a land *where no one lives*, a desert with no one in it, to satisfy a desolate wasteland and make it sprout with grass'. As Psalm 104:27 proclaims, all creatures, including both predator and prey, 'look to [God], to give them their food at the proper time'. 'The lions roar for their prey and seek their food from God', says the psalmist approvingly (Ps 104:21). God provides food 'for the young ravens when they call' (Ps 147:9). God is sovereign over inanimate matter as well as living things. For example, he is portrayed in Psalm 104:32 as the one 'who looks at the earth, and it trembles, who touches the mountains, and they smoke'. God desires all of his creation to flourish, both human and non-human, animate and inanimate alike.

As we contemplate disasters, it is helpful to see God's response to the trials suffered by Job. We know from the back-story that Job was a righteous man who never once lost that righteousness. Yet he suffered grievously at the hands of Satan, losing all that was most dear to him, including his possessions, flocks, family and even his own health. Some, at least, of the disasters were due to natural processes, such as the wind that blew down his eldest son's house and killed all his ten children (Job 1:18–19).

Job's so-called friends tried to rationalise the disasters that had befallen Job as being the result of some sin or failing on his part. Job rightly rejected those suggestions, but still he wanted an explanation from God. He wanted his day in court. When that day finally came, and God spoke to Job 'out of the storm', he did not give any tidy explanations. Instead he spoke majestically of his power over all his creation, from the stars through the weather to all the animals, and in particular all the wild animals, which were far from the domesticated environment in which Job lived. Perhaps most tellingly, God showed himself to be sovereign over the most fearsome of animals, the Leviathan. It is terrifying beyond anything with which humans can deal: 'When it rises up, the mighty are terrified' (Job 41:25). It is likely, indeed, that the Leviathan represents Satan himself.[24] Yet God had complete control over it. God's power is unsurpassably greater than that of Leviathan. We can be reassured from the story of Job that God knows all there is to know about evil, that he constrains its reach and is ultimately sovereign over it.

Though God vindicates Job and indeed praises him, Job finally understands both that God's purposes cannot be thwarted and that God's knowledge and wisdom are far beyond anything to which Job could aspire. The lesson for us is that we should not and cannot expect to understand all of God's dealings this side of heaven. 'Now I know in part; then I shall know fully' (1 Cor 13:12). But we can, and should, hold on to God's faithfulness and goodness as Job did, however dire our circumstances seem to be.

Another biblical story which hinges around a prolonged natural disaster is that of Joseph (Gen 37–45). Ultimately it was a seven-year famine which brought Joseph to the fore in Egypt. But Joseph was only on hand to oversee the storage of grain during the good years and its distribution during the bad, because of a series of evil actions by others. Initially his brothers had intended to kill him, but then sold him to some traders on their way to Egypt who providentially happened along.

From the perspective of natural disasters, there is never the slightest hint that the famine is a punishment from God for particular wrongdoing or sin. The scriptural account just takes the famine as a given, as part of the fabric of life, although it does make clear that in his sovereignty 'the matter has been firmly decided by God, and God will do it soon ' (Gen 41:32). It is a warning to us not to rush to blame the latest natural disaster on punishment by God of some particular sinful behaviour that we choose to identify.

Even more strikingly, Joseph also makes a point of saying that the whole sorry episode of human sinfulness shown by his brothers' sale of himself into slavery was used in God's providence for God's purposes. Joseph tells his brothers after they had been forced by the famine to come begging for food and eventually to move to Egypt that 'you meant evil against me, but God meant it for good, to bring it about that many people should be kept alive, as they are today' (Gen 50:20, ESV). The preservation of the Israelites became part of God's redemptive history of his people down through the ages.

Hope for the future

Though we may not understand fully why disasters happen, or what God's plans in them might be, we can hold on to the certainty of God's sovereignty over this present world and that in the fullness of time this creation will be renewed.

Nothing that happens is outside God's knowledge. So it is not meaningful to talk about natural disasters as things that happen outside his will. This sovereignty does not mean that the suffering a person experiences is necessarily God's direct punishment for their own sin. But we do need to recognise that even causes of suffering do not happen outside God's control. As the writer of Lamentations recognised, 'Although [the Lord] brings grief, he will show compassion, so great is his unfailing love' (Lam 3:32) and 'Is it not from the mouth of the Most High that both calamities and good things come?' (Lam 3:38)

It is worth recalling that God's ways are not our ways, his thoughts are not our thoughts—see, for example, Job 37:5 and Isaiah 55:9. Even when we can discern his purposes, we can do so only indistinctly, like seeing in a mirror dimly (1 Cor 13:12). Although Scripture maintains that God has revealed to us everything necessary for our salvation, and all we need to know to live lives that please him, it also makes it clear that humans, being created beings, cannot second-guess the motives of the creator. For example, Isaiah 29:16 draws the analogy that it is ridiculous for a pot to claim that the potter who made it did not in fact do so, or did not know what he was doing:

> You turn things upside down,
> as if the potter were thought to be like the clay!
> Shall what is formed say to the one who formed it,
> 'You did not make me'?
> Can the pot say of the potter,
> 'You know nothing'?

The apostle Paul makes the same point in the New Testament: 'Shall what is formed say to the one who formed it, "Why did you make me like this?"' (Rom 9:20). Yet this is precisely what we are often tempted to do, saying things such as 'If I were God, I wouldn't allow any suffering in this world'. We often prefer to make God in our own image rather than the reality which is, of course, exactly the opposite.

We cannot make sense of the suffering and death in this world, and of the evil that is often its cause, without the perspective of the new creation to come, and of the kingdom of God that Christ proclaims has already been inaugurated in this world with his coming.[25] The certainty of the new creation is the cornerstone of Christian hope.

The kingdom of God to which Christians look forward is not just a hypothetical construct, a psychological prop, a wishful 'pie in the sky, by and by'. It is a reality which ought to inform everything about the way we live in this world now. That includes our attitude to the natural environment and to the disasters which plague this world. We live in the in-between times, the 'now but not yet' between the first coming of God to earth as the man Jesus, and his return to judge the world, when all things will be renewed in the new creation. That is when he will make this world the place he intended it to be, free from all death and mourning, free from all that has been made twisted and out of order by the rebellion of humans against their creator. The death and, crucially, the resurrection of Jesus are the seal and the proof of this reality. The kingdom of heaven is here now, albeit in a highly attenuated, veiled way, but will be fulfilled in all its glory when Jesus returns.[26]

The new creation will be the fulfilment of all that God intended for the earth and for his people—where God will come down to live with his people, where all things will be renewed. This is the ultimate destiny God has promised. He promises to renew all of creation. We do not know whether or not there will be volcanic eruptions, earthquakes and the like in the new creation, and the Bible does not tell us, so we should not speculate.

But if there are volcanic eruptions, then it is clear that they will not hurt anyone. Presumably they will be beautiful spectator events, showing forth God's glory.

The new creation will be a place where God's people will feel perfectly at home. So our work in this creation should prefigure the new creation. It is part of our worship of God to use our various skills and understanding, our talents, our financial and natural resources to help reduce the effect of disasters in the future and to help those affected when they do strike. That is what will please God.

Hope for the present

Of course we wish that disasters would not happen. The very fact that we now have the capability to construct buildings that do not collapse in earthquakes, that we can see storms, typhoons, and hurricanes developing and can track them long before they hit land, that we can monitor and predict volcanic eruptions, means that we should be able to prevent the great majority of casualties from these natural processes. I take it to be a sign of God's goodness to us that he has given us a stable, understandable world where we can use the fruits of science and technology for the good of others; that we have the capability to prevent disasters and to alleviate or mitigate the harmful effects on others of some of our actions, such as causing global climate change by burning large quantities of fossil fuels. The fact that we do not do so as much as we could or should is a sign of our selfishness—of what the Bible calls our sinfulness.

This story of Joseph gives a strong message that a right and proper way to honour God and to work within his purposes is for Christians to use their gifts and abilities to seek to ameliorate the harmful consequences of occurrences such as famines. Joseph clearly was insightful, resourceful, energetic, trustworthy, and an extremely good administrator and organizer. Although at many times he wielded great power, he never failed to acknowledge that God was sovereign over both him and his circumstances. He spent his life serving others, rather than being self-serving.

This is certainly an encouragement to believers in whatever sphere they work: to scientists or engineers who seek to understand the natural world and to use that knowledge for the good of humankind; to administrators, secretaries and government officials who enable society to function even when under stress; to aid workers and politicians who try to implement practical policies to ameliorate suffering; and indeed to everyone to be good stewards of resources. The story of Joseph reminds us that there is nothing unspiritual about working hard at such mundane things, provided always that, like Joseph, we remind ourselves that both we and our circumstances are firmly under God's providence if we are faithful to him.

The Christian perspective sees the reality of the brokenness of this world, but also the truth of God's sovereignty over it and of his ultimate plans for a new creation. That does not mean that we need not strive to improve things now. Rather it points in the opposite direction, that we should work for better scientific understanding of disasters, that we should enable communities to build resilience against them, that we should strive to remove the unjust disparities in wealth and resources that mean it is so often the poor who are most vulnerable and who suffer most. Even though we may not be able to prevent every last casualty of the next disaster, there is an enormous amount we can do even from our present understanding of natural processes to hugely reduce the impact of disasters. This is surely what Jesus would want us to do, using our understanding of his creation for the good of others, and working to enable his creation to reflect his glory as he intended it to do.

Meanwhile, as we struggle in this beautiful, yet suffering world, we have the assurance from Jesus himself that those blessings we shall experience permanently in the new creation can sustain us now: 'Come to me, all you who are weary and are burdened, and I will give you rest', says Jesus (Matt 11:28).

CAN THE DESERT BE GREEN? ASIAN JOURNEYS' GREEN DESERT PROJECT IN INNER MONGOLIA

A Chinese proverb encourages one to plant a tree and to cultivate a life. Planting a tree takes an hour or so while cultivating a character takes a lifetime. The legacy of sowing into a life can have impact for a century. Such ideas lie behind the vision of the Green Desert Project, in which young people from Singapore and across Asia visit desertified areas of Inner Mongolia, and participate in afforestation projects.

The project was initiated in the autumn of 2002 after the mayor of Duolun County in Inner Mongolia invited Lawrence Ko, Asian Journeys' founder and director, to visit his region. Sandstorms have plagued northern China over the past twenty years. Overgrazing and climate change have caused formerly-pristine green pastures to turn to sand dunes; and the increasing incidence of *yellow dragons* (as these sandstorms are called, whirling through the wind tunnels across the Mongolian grassland) during the spring seasons each year has been destructive.

These sandstorms also affected the cities in northern China, bringing life in the cities of Beijing and Tianjin to a halt, and impacting the economy. Concerns over the climatic and environmental issues were raised especially after the 2008 Olympics Games were awarded to Beijing in July 2001. Strategic plans were laid out to green the grassland, including planting shrubs and trees and fencing the planted lands to curb overgrazing. A host of policies from reducing herding to developing greenhouse agricultural activities was introduced to relocate and usher the herders into new productive economic activities.

Over the last ten years, Asian Journeys has worked in partnership with these programmes, and sent hundreds of university students on short-term placements to help plant trees: over 10,000 to date. As well as this practical work, it has been a great opportunity for Singaporean youths living in an island state to visit this vast and diverse land—from the range of low mountains in the south to the prairie in the north—where these young people could glimpse the wide horizon between the earth and sky. There are many geographic landforms to explore too, ranging from

Asia's largest elm forest to rivers and blue lakes, from ancient volcanic craters to vast potato and carrot farms.

Such landscapes have often been places of spiritual renewal: each Lent we are reminded that Jesus began his earthly ministry by spending forty days in the wilderness. Perhaps that is why the desert appeals to visual artists and photographers, and captivates visionaries and dreamers, young and old.

Volunteers who have been on the programme have also organized and delivered Green Desert Kids Club programmes for children to student centres, Cub Scout troops, and church Sunday schools. It is an expressed intention to recruit and mobilize more Christian youths to become aware of the holistic nature of the gospel and how environmental steward-ship is an important part of Christian discipleship as we care for God's creation. The Green Desert Project has become in Singapore an avenue for Christian participation in creation care—a prophetic act of God's gracious restorative and redemptive work on earth.

Through the ongoing efforts of leading and organizing teams of environmental volunteers, these young people put their dreams into action and live out a vision of restoring the Mongolian grasslands and redeeming the wastelands from desertification. Through the Green Desert Project, they declare their faith in the future hope that God can make a way in the wastelands, that life can flourish in dry places, that the deserts of Inner Mongolia can become green again.

Lawrence Ko, Founder and Director of Asian Journeys Ltd

CHAPTER 13

Biodiversity Loss: A Christian Concern?

Martin J Hodson

' "Biological diversity" means the variability among living organisms
from all sources including, *inter alia*, terrestrial, marine and other
aquatic ecosystems and the ecological complexes of which they
are part; this includes diversity within species, between species
and of ecosystems.'

United Nations Convention on Biological Diversity[1]

The above definition of *biological diversity* (or *biodiversity* for short) is taken
from the Convention on Biological Diversity which was opened for signa-
ture at the United Nations Conference on Environment and Development
(popularly known as the Earth Summit) in Rio de Janeiro on 5 June 1992
and which entered into force on 29 December 1993. It is quite a complex
definition and it includes 'diversity within species, between species and of
ecosystems', although most emphasis is often given to diversity between
species, and particularly to the number of different species. Biodiversity is
essentially a measure of the variety of living organisms, including animals,
plants, fungi, and microorganisms. Despite intensive investigations for at
least 250 years, we are still not certain how many organisms share our planet
with us, but a recent estimate suggests that there are about 8.7 million eu-
karyotic (where the cells of the organism have nuclei) species globally.[2]
Roughly 1.2 million of these species have been named and classified, but
about 86 percent remain to be discovered.

Biodiversity is not evenly distributed around the planet, and is greater
in tropical areas than temperate zones, with the Arctic and Antarctic having the lowest biodiversity. Similarly, some habitats have greater biodiversity than others. For example, in temperate zones the coniferous forests
will nearly always have lower biodiversity and species numbers than chalk
grasslands.

So we can conclude that our planet is teeming with biodiversity. Unfortunately, the scientific evidence collected over the last one hundred years or
more suggests that this biodiversity is being lost at an alarming rate, and that
humanity is largely to blame. Recognition of the seriousness of the situation

has led to the recent establishment of the Intergovernmental Platform on Biodiversity and Ecosystem Services (IPBES) which will assess the state of the Earth's biodiversity and its ecosystems.[3] In September 2015 the United Nations agreed new Sustainable Development Goals (SDGs) which replaced the Millennium Development Goals (MDGs) and came into effect on 1st January 2016. From a biodiversity perspective the SDGs are an improvement on the MDGs and include two goals (14 and 15) which make specific recommendations concerning biodiversity loss.[4]

The aims of this chapter will be first to look at the reasons for loss of biodiversity and then to consider why humanity should be worried. Finally, why should people of faith, and most particularly Christians, be concerned?

Loss of biodiversity

In 2005, the Millennium Ecosystem Assessment stated that 'Over the past few hundred years, humans have increased the species extinction rate by as much as three orders of magnitude.'[5] It went on to point out that many species are currently threatened with extinction, for example: birds 12 percent; mammals 23 percent; conifers 25 percent; amphibians 32 percent; and cycads 52 percent. More recently, WWF and their collaborators produced their Living Planet Report 2012, in which they assessed current trends in biodiversity decline.[6] To do this, they calculated a Living Planet Index as a measure of biodiversity. This uses trends in population size for vertebrate species to determine average changes in abundance over time. Their key finding was that the global Living Planet Index had decreased by almost 30 percent between 1970 and 2008. This figure hid an even more worrying trend as the global tropical index decreased by 60 percent during that period. The Living Planet Index actually increased for temperate zones by 30 percent over the time period investigated, indicating a partial reversal of the trend seen prior to 1970.

There has been much discussion recently in both the scientific and general literature concerning *planetary boundaries*.[7] (See Chapter 15, 'Planetary Boundaries and the Green Economy'.) If crossed, these biophysical thresholds could have catastrophic significance for both humanity and the other organisms living on our planet. It is thought that the three planetary boundaries that have already been exceeded are biodiversity loss, climate change (see Chapter 8, 'Global Warming, Climate Change, and Sustainability'), and human interference with the nitrogen cycle.

So it is clear that global biodiversity loss is happening, and at a very rapid rate. Now we must turn to the reasons for biodiversity loss and to the acronym HIPPO. This was first coined by ecologist Edward O Wilson to denote the major factors causing biodiversity loss, and HIPPO stands for habitat loss, invasive species, pollution, overpopulation, and overharvesting of wild species.[8] We will now briefly look at each of these in turn.

Habitat Loss

Almost all authorities agree that loss of habitat has been the major cause of the decline in biodiversity that has already happened. Some figures will illustrate the scale of the problem. Andrew Balmford estimated that since the Industrial Revolution, wild habitats and populations of wild species have been reduced by about half, and that in the last 30–40 years we have been losing 0.5 percent to 1.5 percent of the remainder every year.[9] Most habitat loss has been caused by conversion to agriculture. The Millennium Ecosystem Assessment reported that over half of the world's 14 biomes (the major ecological communities of the world categorized according to the main vegetation type) showed 20–50 percent conversion to human use.[10] In temperate and Mediterranean forests and temperate grasslands, about three quarters of the natural habitat has been turned over to agricultural land. More recently, conversion rates have been highest in tropical and sub-tropical dry forests. Here deforestation has caused very serious problems, especially soil erosion. Cultivated systems were stated to account for 24 percent of the Earth's terrestrial surface. Often the change to agriculture involves going from a very rich diverse environment to a monoculture of a crop species, with maybe a few shrubs in the boundaries between fields. Following on behind conversion of wild habitats to agriculture is the conversion of agricultural land to urban use. At present, about 1 percent of the Earth's land surface is under cities and is urbanized, but this is rapidly growing.

Finally, not only is wild land lost, but that which remains undergoes fragmentation. So we often see a pattern where small islands of natural vegetation remain within a sea of agricultural fields and human settlements. If these islands are not connected, then the remaining biodiversity is extremely vulnerable.

Invasive species

Human mobility has increased markedly in the last century. We travel far more than we did, and we transport materials around the world in much bigger quantities. Sometimes we accidentally bring species from one part of the world to another, and sometimes this is deliberate. So our gardens are often full of plant species that have been introduced. In most cases, these alien species do not thrive in the wild in their new environments, but in a few they do and the species becomes an *invasive*. These invasive plant and animal species are often now free of their natural competitors from their original environment. The plants may outcompete the native species, and the animals may be major predators.

The environments that have been particularly badly affected by invasive species are freshwater ecosystems and islands. Here we will give just two examples. In the opening paragraphs of his recent *Anvil* article, Archbishop Thabo Makgoba discussed morning glory, an important invasive plant species in Southern Africa.[11] The plant had been introduced because of its pretty flowers, but was now a major problem along water courses and was very expensive to deal with.

Secondly, the neighbouring Scottish islands of North Uist, Benbecula, and South Uist are important breeding sites for sea birds. In 1974, an islander introduced hedgehogs, which are not native to the islands, with the idea of controlling slugs and snails in their garden. The hedgehogs rapidly established themselves on the islands and became invasive and problematic, eating bird eggs. In 2002, the Uist Wader Research Project, a consortium of organizations managed by Scottish Natural Heritage, decided that the problem had become so great that they needed to cull the hedgehogs, and 700 of the estimated population of 5,000 were killed.[12] This culling was very unpopular with some, and it led to the formation of Uist Hedgehog Rescue, who began capturing the hedgehogs and moving them to the mainland.[13] In 2007, the Uist Wader Project abandoned the cull and agreed to continue the translocation of hedgehogs away from the islands.

Pollution

Humans have accidentally or deliberately introduced numerous chemical substances into the environment, and many of those are toxic or have deleterious effects on biodiversity. The classic example is still DDT (dichlorodiphenyltrichloroethane), an organochlorine insecticide. In 1939, DDT's insecticidal properties were discovered, and in World War II it was used to control malaria and typhus. After the war it became a commonly used chemical in agriculture. In 1962, however, the publication of Rachel Carson's *Silent Spring* suggested that there were major problems with DDT.[14] The chemical passed up the food chain and accumulated in the fat of bird species. One of the effects was that the birds laid eggs with thin shells which easily broke. The chemical had a particularly bad effect on birds of prey such as the bald eagle and the peregrine falcon, but was also suspected of toxic effects in humans. These discoveries eventually led to a worldwide ban on the use of DDT in agriculture.

The second example we will cover is acid rain.[15] The issue rose to prominence in the late 1970s when trees in western Europe and North America died in large numbers. It was found that the major reason was air pollution with sulphur and nitrogen oxides. Once the source of the problem was

recognized, governments took prompt action, and international cooperation led to the reduction of pollution by these chemicals. Forest health improved as a result. The problem of acid rain is not completely solved, and
nitrogen pollution, in particular, remains an issue. Both DDT and acid rain
suggest that it is possible for international action on pollution problems to
be effective.

Population

The issue of human population increase and its impact on the environment is covered in Chapter 11, 'Population and Ecological Sustainability';
here we will focus only on biodiversity impacts. The Population and Sustainability Network has produced a briefing looking specifically at the interaction between human population and biodiversity loss, and we will highlight
a few of the main points.[16] Since the Industrial Revolution, and particularly
since 1950, we have seen very large increases in world population and now
humanity is the dominant force affecting planetary processes. This period
of human dominance is often termed *the Anthropocene*. Population growth,
with increased demands for natural resources (for example, food, water, land,
timber, and fossil fuels), is putting ecosystems under considerable stress, and
is an important underlying cause of biodiversity loss. The most biodiversity
rich regions of the world, where loss is greatest, generally coincide with areas
where population growth is greatest and the people are poorest.

Overexploitation

The overexploitation of biodiversity includes a number of phenomena:
hunting of animals; overfishing; collection for the pet trade; and overharvesting of plants, whether for food, wood or flowers. One of the best known
examples of an animal where hunting contributed in a major way to its extinction was the dodo. This flightless bird was first recorded on Mauritius
in 1598, and the last known sighting was in 1662. The bird was hunted by
sailors, but also by their domestic animals and the invasive species that they
introduced. It is often the case that more than one of the HIPPO factors contributes to a decline in biodiversity or extinction. Another example of over-
exploitation is overfishing (see Chapter 14, 'Creation Care of the Other 71%').

Climate Change

In 2001, when Wilson coined the HIPPO acronym, he did not include
climate change within the factors that were contributing to biodiversity
loss. However, since then, the interaction between climate change and biodiversity has been intensively studied. Warming of the Earth's land surface
since 1950 has been a little over 1°C, and further rises are anticipated this

century (see Chapter 8, 'Global Warming, Climate Change, and Sustainability'). The rate of change so far has been rapid, and it is anticipated that this change will continue or even be accelerated. Under such conditions, terrestrial organisms move towards the poles and up mountain slopes in search of cooler environments. In the United Kingdom, plants are flowering and leafing earlier in the spring, birds are laying eggs sooner, and insect emergence has advanced.[17] In the autumn, the fruiting of rowan trees has advanced by one month. There have also been some changes in plant and animal distributions, with butterflies especially showing the effects.

It is difficult to be certain whether climate change has yet directly caused species extinction. However, in future decades, the rapidity of climate change may not permit time for organisms to adjust to shifting environments. In 2014, the Intergovernmental Panel on Climate Change (IPCC) estimated that the risks of impacts on biodiversity would be moderate for additional warming of 1–2°C (relative to 1986–2005), but that extensive biodiversity loss would be likely with additional warming of around 3°C.[18]

There are other, less obvious, interactions concerning climate change and biodiversity. For example, the push for increased production of biofuels worldwide was partly driven by declining availability of fossil fuels, and partly by a desire to produce greener fuels that were not contributing as much to climate change. Unfortunately, the first generation of biofuels have proved to be problematic, and palm oil plantations, in particular, have had very bad effects on biodiversity.[19] Generally, monoculture plantations are able to support far fewer species than the forests which they replaced.

It is clear from the above that we are losing biodiversity at an alarming rate, and that there are a number of reasons for this. But why is all this important? First, we will investigate secular motives for conserving biodiversity, before we move on to consider religious and Christian reasons.

Secular reasons for conserving biodiversity

Within the discipline of environmental ethics, it is common to divide human responses to the environment into three categories: *anthropocentric* where humankind is central; *biocentric* where all organisms have equal value; and *ecocentric* where the whole environment is the focus.[20] We will now look at each of these in turn from the perspective of biodiversity conservation.

Anthropocentric

An anthropocentric view of biodiversity concentrates on the human uses of plants and animals and what is beneficial for humanity. At its simplest, we might decide to conserve biodiversity because species may yield new medicines or genetic resources. Many medicines are derived from compounds originally discovered in extracts from plants. At the moment, humans only tend to use a small number of plant species as crops, and there may be more potential crops or genetic material to enhance existing crops to be found. We are almost certainly losing species to extinction before they have even been classified, and thus we are losing potentially useful resources.

The Millennium Ecosystem Assessment would consider the above as examples of *ecosystem services*—'the benefits people obtain from ecosystems.'[21] Their full list of ecosystem services is as follows:

1. Provisioning Services: food, water, timber, and fibre

2. Regulating Services: regulation of climate, floods, disease, wastes, and water quality

3. Cultural Services: recreation, aesthetic enjoyment, and spiritual fulfilment

4. Supporting Services: soil formation, photosynthesis, and nutrient cycling

It is noteworthy that this list does include spiritual fulfilment, but even that is seen in terms of what is of benefit to humanity. There is nothing wrong with this list, and all of the factors mentioned are important, but it is framed in anthropocentric terms.

Biodiversity clearly has huge benefits to humanity, and it is obvious that we would be extremely foolish to damage it. So why are we causing biodiversity loss and other environmental problems? It is here that we need to introduce a concept from environmental economics known as *externalities*. These are defined as situations 'where the actions of some firm or individual have consequences for someone else who has no say in the matter.'[22] To illustrate this, let us return to the example of acid rain mentioned above. Major contributors to this problem were coal-fired power stations, which burned coal containing high levels of sulphur that then led to the production of sulphur dioxide. The sulphur dioxide was consequently responsible for the damage to trees, sometimes hundreds of miles away from the power stations. The difficulty arises because a decrease in the profits of the forest owner does not factor in the calculation of the power station owner's profits or in their business plan. So, in an unregulated market economy, it would not make sense for the power station to install scrubbers to decrease the pollution as it would cost money with no benefit for the business. As we saw above, governments did bring in regulations which forced the power stations to take action. However, much biodiversity loss is happening where there are no concerned forest owners to complain or governments with enough power to bring in regulations to combat the problem. In much of the Global South, companies can make huge profits and ignore the externality of biodiversity loss.

Because biodiversity loss is an externality, it is often seen as having no monetary value. Not surprisingly, perhaps, this has led to attempts to place monetary value on biodiversity and ecosystems. Tony Juniper took this approach in his book *What Has Nature Ever Done For Us?* and we will recount just a few of his examples.[23] If we were to halve the rate of deforestation, that would give carbon capture services valued at $3.7 trillion. The value of pollinators, such as bees, per annum is about $190 billion globally. The whole of nature is worth about $100 trillion annually. A fuller academic equivalent is the United Nations-sponsored The Economics of Ecosystems and Biodiversity (TEEB).[24] TEEB's starting point is that 'the failure to account for the full economic values of ecosystems and biodiversity has been a significant factor in their continuing loss and degradation.'[25] So far the project has concentrated on forests, cities, and mining. Their aim is to put an economic value on the environment and biodiversity, essentially removing the externality status. TEEB has been criticized, as humans decide what aspects of the environment they consider to be valuable. Thus small, not very pretty, not apparently *useful* organisms can be neglected, and we could easily get it wrong. We seem faced with a choice: leave biodiversity as an externality in an unregulated market economy and take the consequences of huge biodiversity loss; bring in environmental regulations which are often unpopular and difficult to enforce; or give biodiversity economic value as in TEEB.

All of the above ideas are anthropocentric, with humanity very much taking a central place. This has certainly been the dominant ethic both in secular society and in the church, but it is not the only secular approach, as we will see below.

Biocentric

A biocentric approach places a high value on individual species—or even individual organisms—and, in its extreme versions, humans are no different to other species, being one among many. As Devall and Sessions put it, 'The intuition of biocentric equality is that all things in the biosphere have an equal right to live and blossom and to reach their own individual forms of unfolding and self-realization.'[26] This is the ethic behind Deep Ecology as proposed by Arne Naess (1912–2009). Often, campaigns to save certain iconic species (for example, whales, pandas) are underpinned by biocentric ethics. Sometimes conservation organizations deliberately publicize the plight of what are known as *flagship species* with the idea that the general public will be more attracted to give financial support. Their underlying ethic may be more ecocentric (see below), but they appeal to the partly biocentric nature of the public. Flagship species are usually large mammals. The weakness of the approach is that the preservation of certain iconic species may mean that others are neglected, and that conservation efforts may be skewed. Biocentric ethics can be held in moderate or extreme forms, but tend not to fit well with the Christian idea that humans are made in the image of God, and are special.

An idea which is in some ways related to biocentric thinking is that of intrinsic value. This came originally from religious thinking and is particularly associated with the Jewish rabbi Moses Maimonides (1135–1204). He expressed it in this way: 'The universe does not exist for man's sake but each being exists for its own sake, and not because of some other thing.'[27] In other words, all plants and animals are valuable in their own right, and do not depend on humans to give them value. This contrasts very starkly with TEEB as seen above. It is interesting that the idea can now found in secular literature, including the Millennium Ecosystem Assessment.[28] It was recognized that more biodiversity would be saved if intrinsic value was taken into account in addition to that covered by human utilitarian thinking.

Ecocentric

While biocentric approaches focus on the individual organism or species, an ecocentric view will consider the conservation of whole ecosystems. George Perkins Marsh (1801–1882) was an American conservationist who was among the first to recognize environmental degradation, to see reasons for it, and to suggest possible reforms. He famously said, 'The great question, whether man is of nature or above her.'[29] Clearly, Marsh was considering ideas that were not entirely anthropocentric. Other influential early American thinkers in this area included Henry David Thoreau (1817–1862), who worried about the loss of species and called for a simple lifestyle; John Muir (1838–1914), the preservationist who established Yosemite National Park; and Gifford Pinchot (1865–1946), a forester and conservationist who advocated the wise use of resources. A key figure in the later development of ecocentric thinking was Aldo Leopold (1887–1948), who wrote in A Sand County Almanac, 'We abuse land because we see it as a commodity belonging to us. When we see land as a community to which we belong, we may begin to use it with love and respect.'[30] The Almanac was fiercely critical of anthropocentric thinking, and Leopold formulated the Land Ethic in which he extended the concept of community to the Land, and included within the Land were the soils, waters, plants, and animals. Leopold's Almanac, together with Rachel Carson's Silent Spring, had a huge influence on the development of the environmental movement in the latter half of the twentieth century. Ecocentric thinking was also very much behind James Lovelock's Gaia hypothesis. This suggests that organisms interrelate with the inorganic environment on Earth, forming a self-regulating system that maintains suitable conditions for life. Gaia is, at root, a scientific hypothesis, and has led to the development of earth system science. However, it has also been appropriated by the New Age movement and others and given various religious expressions.

It is not uncommon for those with biocentric viewpoints to have strong disagreements with ecocentric thinkers. The hedgehogs on Uist, mentioned above, are a good example. Those wishing to eradicate the invasive, non-native, hedgehogs to re-establish the ecological balance on the islands and protect the nesting birds have ecocentric thinking. On the other hand, those wishing to rescue each hedgehog had biocentric ethics. Another area of potential argument over ethical standpoints concerns non-governmental development agencies (which tend to be anthropocentric) and environmental agencies (which often show biocentric or ecocentric ethics). The development agencies will usually put human wellbeing ahead of the environment whilst the environmental agencies may downplay concern for humans. This can cause real tensions when these agencies tackle a disaster or try to work together on a project.

The weakness of ecocentric thinking from a Christian viewpoint is that, like biocentric thinking, all organisms including humans are on the same level.

Religious reasons for conserving biodiversity

Almost all religions have some type of conservation ethos, and some principles and practices which help preserve biodiversity. The Forum on Religion and Ecology at Yale covers all of the world's major religions and their attitudes to the environment and biodiversity.[31] Many religions place special significance on biodiversity, and particularly animals. So both Judaism and Islam have strict food laws, not eating certain animals because of kosher and halal regulations. In Hinduism, many animals are considered sacred, including cows and elephants. Belief in the reincarnation of a human as an animal is common in a number of religions and traditions.

It has often been considered that beliefs such as food laws, holding some animals to be sacred, and reincarnation as an animal may have a role to play in conservation, as they would deter hunting and eating. This idea was investigated by Fiona Jones in the specific case of *fady* in Madagascar, one of the biggest biodiversity hotspots in the world.[32] Fady is a type of taboo that is part of the religious practice of the various people groups on the island. In some cases, the fady involves the idea that the animal is a founding ancestor and part of the extended family, while in others the animal is simply seen as 'dirty'. Fady varies in strength from *sandrana* which cannot be altered or broken under any circumstances, through *fadin-drazana* ('fady of the ancestors') which is more flexible and negotiable, to the weakest, *fadim-piarahamonina* ('fady of the community'), founded on acceptance within a society. There is a considerable body of literature documenting fady in Madagascar, but when Jones visited the country in 2012, it became apparent that these traditions were rapidly dying out. For a variety of reasons, including migration, population increase, deforestation, education and exposure to Western ideas, fady was nowhere near as strong as it was even fifty years ago. Consequently, the suggestion that fady might have a role to play in future conservation efforts was questioned, and probably education schemes focusing on the value of biodiversity will be a more fruitful way forward.

Christianity and biodiversity

The present book has much to say about Christian environmental theology, and I do not want to repeat this material here. Rather, I will concentrate specifically on biodiversity. The Bible is full of biodiversity. It is first mentioned in Genesis 1:11: 'Then God said, "Let the land produce vegetation: seed-bearing plants and trees on the land that bear fruit with seed in it, according to their various kinds." And it was so.' The last verse that features biodiversity is in the last chapter of Revelation, and also concerns trees and fruit: 'On each side of the river stood the tree of life, bearing twelve crops of fruit, yielding its fruit every month. And the leaves of the tree are for the healing of the nations' (Rev 22:2). There are about 100 species of animal mentioned in the Bible, but the exact number is difficult to determine as we are uncertain what animals are described by certain Hebrew words, and some animals may have several words. Around 130 plant species are named in the Bible. Biodiversity is not evenly spread within the Bible, and some books contain more references to plants and animals than others. Certain biblical books are particularly rich, for example Isaiah, where the plants and animals are often used to develop theological themes.[33] The fact that animals and plants appear so frequently in the Bible suggests that they were important to the biblical writers and are important to God.

There are many publications looking at aspects of biodiversity in the Bible, and we will just highlight a few here to give some pointers to further reading. Nigel Hepper provides an excellent, scholarly, but accessible introduction to the plants of the Bible, while Peter France does the same for animals.[34] Biblical reflections have been provided by John Stott on birds and recently by Sir Ghillean Prance on biodiversity in general.[35]

In contrast to most other religions, modern Christianity does not have biodiversity as an explicit focus: there are no food laws, no holy animals, and no beliefs in the possibility of being reincarnated as an animal. So, for modern Christians, a theology of biodiversity is likely to be implicit. This may help explain why some Christians have been slow to take creation care as a serious faith issue. The Bible, however, frequently mentions plants and animals, God's value for them, and his concern that humans take care of them. This has led to a focus on stewardship, which is still the concept that most Christians would first think of when asked about biodiversity conservation (see Chapter 1, 'Ruling God's World God's Way').

Probably the best place to start in the search for a theology of biodiversity is Richard Bauckham's *Living with Other Creatures*.[36] All of the chapters in his book are useful in this regard, but the last, 'Biodiversity—a Biblical-Theological Perspective', is particularly so. After a brief survey of the problems biodiversity is facing this century, Bauckham moves on to consider the Old Testament. I will draw out just a few of the key points.

God is seen to delight in creation recognizing it as 'good'. A theme Bauckham feels has been neglected is the idea that the whole creation worships God. He sees that 'humans are distinctive among creatures', but we also have kinship with them, and we form a community with them. We are to subdue the Earth (Gen 1:28), but not at the expense of other organisms, and we have dominion within creation, not over it. Often we tend to see dominion as involving activity, but Bauckham suggests that we often need to let creation be. In his final section on preserving biodiversity, he is highly critical of TEEB, and concludes his chapter: 'Destroying any more of the biosphere than we have done already will not just cost us a lot, as though it were just a matter of financial profit and loss. We shall impoverish human life in the process of impoverishing the planet.'[37]

For some insights from the New Testament, David Clough has recently published the first volume of his theology of animals.[38] He considers three key passages to give some understanding of Jesus' thinking on animals. In the Sermon on the Mount, Jesus says, 'Look at the birds of the air; they do not sow or reap or store away in barns, and yet your heavenly Father feeds them. Are you not much more valuable than they?' (Matt 6:26). Later in Matthew we read, 'Are not two sparrows sold for a penny? Yet not one of them will fall to the ground outside your Father's care. And even the very hairs of your head are all numbered. So don't be afraid; you are worth more than many sparrows' (Matt 10:29–31). Finally, during his debate with the Pharisees over healing on the Sabbath, Jesus says to them, 'If any of you has a sheep and it falls into a pit on the Sabbath, will you not take hold of it and lift it out? How much more valuable is a person than a sheep! Therefore it is lawful to do good on the Sabbath' (Matt 12:11–12). Clough states that the 'passages provide a clear and consistent basis in the teaching of Jesus both for an emphasis on God's universal providential care for every animal but also for believing that God values human life more highly than that of birds and that humans should value human life more highly than that of sheep.'[39] So Christians should care for animals, but human life is more valuable than animal life. The same is almost certainly the case for biodiversity in the wider sense. I conclude that anthropocentric, biocentric and ecocentric views all have their strengths, but that they need to be held in balance, and to come under God—a theocentric view.

Worldwide there are many Christian environmental organizations. Most of these have a wide coverage, and do not specialize in biodiversity conservation. So, for example, the John Ray Initiative (JRI) in the United Kingdom and the Evangelical Environmental Network (EEN) in the United States both have a concern for biodiversity, but tend to concentrate more on climate change and broader environmental issues. Of the Christian environmental organizations that specialize mainly in biodiversity conservation A Rocha is by far the largest, and has worked in many countries. Their web site states that 'A Rocha is an international Christian organization which, inspired by God's love, engages in scientific research, environmental education and community-based conservation projects.'[40] Although A Rocha is the biggest Christian organization working in this area, it is tiny in comparison with the big international secular agencies. Loss of biodiversity is a major concern, and Christians need to play their part in addressing the problem.

RESTORING A MOUNTAIN, RECONCILING COMMUNITIES: A ROCHA IN AOTEAROA NEW ZEALAND

Many of the three million plus annual visitors who make the journey to Aotearoa New Zealand are attracted by the allure of *untouched* islands in the South Pacific.[1] And indeed, there are both natural wonders and scenic highlights in these far-flung islands. Aotearoa New Zealand was the last major landmass to be colonised by humans (1,000–1,200 years ago). It had no mammalian predators before human habitation; it was a wildlife paradise, and a place of unique flora and fauna. In view of the exceptionally high degree of endemism, ecological historian Jared Diamond has suggested that 'New Zealand is as close as we will get to the opportunity to study life on another planet.'[2]

And yet, the postcard images and the '100% Pure' tourist branding of the country give a somewhat misleading picture. A millennium of human habitation has been catastrophic for ecosystems—through habitat destruction (forest clearance, wetland drainage, land modification) and the introduction of mammalian predators. These pressures have driven the extinctions of 32 percent of indigenous land and freshwater birds, 18 percent of endemic sea birds, three of seven frogs species, at least twelve invertebrate species, one fish, one bat and perhaps three reptiles and possibly eleven plants species. These cataclysmic changes have been widely documented and lamented, and during the last forty years there has been an ecological awakening within the general population of New Zealand. The desire to protect the country's natural heritage is evident in the multitude of conservation projects occurring on both publically-owned land managed by the government Department of Conservation (which constitutes close to one third of the country's landmass) and on privately-owned land.

The ecological awakening has been matched during the last four decades with a cultural renaissance among Maori and a growing awareness and appreciation within broader society of Maori culture—in particular, the significance they accord to *whenua* (land).[3] A century and a half of injustices and the ruinous effects of colonization are slowly giving way to new forms of genuine bi-cultural partnership between Maori and Pakeha.[4]

With this background, what does it mean for the church to proclaim and enact 'care for creation'? Are there particular distinctive characteristics of Christians involved in practical conservation? The story of A Rocha in Aotearoa New Zealand offers some insights.

Since 2009, A Rocha Aotearoa New Zealand (ARANZ) has led a community conservation project: *Karioi—Maunga ki te Moana* (Karioi— Mountain to the Sea).[5] Mount Karioi is a volcanic cone located on the west coast of the North Island, near the internationally renowned surfing town of Whaingaroa/Raglan. Standing sentinel-like, looking out to the Tasman Sea, its peak draped in dense forest, the mountain drops from podocarp-montane forest to dramatic sea-cliffs and is the home of numerous bird species, including a remnant population of seabirds—Oi or grey-faced petrels (*Pterodroma macroptera gouldi*). Yet, despite its geographical prominence and cultural significance for local Maori, for many years little practical conservation had taken place on the mountain. A particular issue was that the community had become bitterly divided over the use of 1080 poison to control mammalian pests.[6]

Against this background, ARANZ was invited to lead a community-based project aimed at improving biodiversity on the mountain. The resulting project has the long-term vision of re-establishing Karioi Maunga as a seabird mountain by protecting and enhancing the existing Oi population, re-introducing other seabird species, and promoting the recovery of forest birds. Employing an alternative method of pest control— trapping—in contrast to aerial drops of 1080 poison which is anathema to many local residents, it was hoped to rebuild the local community's sense of care for the mountain's long-term ecological health. There were other additional beneficial outcomes—such as opportunities for environmental education, work experience, and local employment.

First and foremost, community-based conservation requires gifted community organizers. Kristel van Houte—A Rocha National Co-director and Karioi Maunga project coordinator and also a Raglan resident—has been instrumental in overcoming historical barriers and obstacles, building trust, forming partnerships, and developing a shared community vision for the mountain.

A second notable characteristic of the project has been the focus on encouraging all-age involvement. In contrast to *specialization* where conservation becomes the preserve of professional applied ecologists, or the *segregating* tendencies of many church activities which separate different age groups, work on the project (building rat trap tunnels, checking traps, monitoring birds and pest species), community events, and camps are inclusive of all ages. One example of this *whanau* (whole family) approach is a camp for children aged ten to thirteen years. The camp, incorporating a role-modelling concept, uses older teenagers and adults to help run the camp, thereby developing leadership skills and encouraging a deeper sense of commitment to the project.

A third feature of the project has been the involvement of Maori—both the local *hapu* (sub-tribe) of Whaingaroa and urban Maori. The mountain has special cultural, environmental and historical significance to Whaingaroa *tangata whenua* (people of the land) who regard themselves as the *kaitiaki* (guardians and conservers) of the *maunga* and its *taonga* (resources, treasures) for future generations. Local Maori have been working alongside A Rocha trapping for possums on 500 hectares of Maori land on the northern slopes of Karioi, and the partnership has provided funding to increase trapping of stoats and rats on Maori land. Likewise, a partnership with Desert Springs Community Centre in the nearby city of Hamilton which revolves around *Te Kaakano*—a community garden—has also fostered cross-cultural relationships and provided a stepping stone for urban dwellers (including urban Maori) to reconnect with the land and thus begin a journey towards deeper involvement in conservation.

The garden itself offers a foretaste of the kingdom. To paraphrase Galatians 3:28, 'there is no distinction between Maori and Pakeha, urban professional and the unemployed, the academic achiever and struggling solo-mother, or the frail and fragile and the young brimming with energy . . . all are one working in the garden.' Gatherings at *Te Kaakano* are composed of a range of people from diverse socio-economic and cultural backgrounds; a wide age range; and of strong, struggling, or 'no faith'; and are centred on the essential human task of tilling the soil (Gen 2:15). The manual work takes place against a backdrop of conversations, the exchanging of personal stories, garden knowledge and recipes, and after a joint *karakia* (prayer)—acknowledging the ever-present grace of God—participants join in the sacramental sharing of the bounty of collective labour and the earth's provision.

Seven years on, the development of both the Te Kaakano Garden and the Karioi Project have been exciting. Over four hundred regular and occasional volunteers have contributed over ten thousand hours to the projects. The projects have drawn together a wide range of people and organizations including local community groups, land owners and businesses, local *hapu* representatives, national and regional authorities, local schools and tertiary institutes, recreational clubs, churches, and youth groups—groups that previously may have had no shared agenda. A divided community has united to work towards achieving agreed biodiversity goals for Karioi Mountain. Attitudinal changes and the gradual transformation of people's lives through their involvement in the projects have been matched by a degree of ecological improvement on Karioi. Both the mountain and the garden are expressions of A Rocha's values of *hands-on* conservation, community, cooperation, and cross-cultural partnership, and offer glimpses of God's power to bring transformation to individual lives, communities and ecosystems.

Andrew Shepherd, National Co-Director,
A Rocha Aotearoa New Zealand

CHAPTER 14

Creation Care of the Other 71%

Meric Srokosz and Robert D Sluka

'This subject is as vast as the sea itself.'

Philippe Reymond, 1958[1]

The importance of the oceans

As the ocean covers approximately 71 percent of the surface of the Earth, it is arguable that we live on a water planet that should be called the Ocean. The so-called 'blue marble' picture taken by astronauts from space reinforces the ubiquity of the ocean. The presence of water on Earth and the existence of the ocean, from which life emerged, are critical to life on Earth. The water cycle—in simple terms, water evaporates from the ocean, is transported by the atmosphere over land, falls as rain and returns to the oceans via rivers—sustains life on land. However, the ocean also sustains life more directly, being the habitat for an amazing range of living organisms, from microscopic bacteria, phytoplankton (miniscule plants) and zooplankton (miniscule animals), through to the largest mammal on Earth, the blue whale, which can be up to thirty metres in length and weigh up to 180 tonnes. There is an amazing diversity of life in the oceans, with peculiar creatures such as sea cucumbers living on the seabed at depths of four or more kilometres, and under tremendous pressure due to the weight of water above them, through to the more familiar fish, such as cod.

Human beings have used the ocean as a resource for thousands of years. For example, seaweed, shellfish, shrimps, and fish of many kinds have been harvested from the ocean and used for food. What started out as a small-scale local enterprise—and is still such in many parts of the world—has also become big business with factory ships, which process and freeze the fish caught by fishing vessels out at sea, turning fishing into an industrial scale enterprise. Fishing provides a significant fraction, about 16 percent, of the total animal protein eaten by humans globally, with this percentage being higher in some nations, often the poorer less developed ones.

The oceans are also a crucial part of the climate system with the large-scale ocean circulation (currents) re-distributing vast amounts of heat across the globe. For example, in the North Atlantic at 26°N, the ocean currents are transporting northwards approximately 1.3 petawatts (10^{15} watts) roughly 100 times the world's present installed power generating capacity (which is about 10^{13} watts). This heat is transferred to the weather systems crossing the Atlantic and provides the United Kingdom and northwest Europe with its milder and wetter weather.[2] The presence of phytoplankton in the oceans is important for the carbon cycle. Just like plants on land, they use the carbon dioxide (CO_2) absorbed by the ocean from the atmosphere to grow. About a third of the CO_2 being emitted into the atmosphere due to the burning of fossil fuels (oil, coal, gas) is absorbed by the ocean.[3] Part is simply dissolved in the oceanic waters, leading to ocean acidification, and part is utilised by phytoplankton for growth, with the ultimate fate of some of the carbon being burial in deep-sea sediments.[4]

The ocean is also important culturally. For example, this can be seen in novels such as *Moby Dick* by Herman Melville, and the works of Joseph Conrad, who spent time at sea as a sailor.[5] Certain cultures were or are closely linked to the sea, such as the ancient Phoenicians in Old Testament times, and the Polynesians in the Pacific. The Polynesians made amazing voyages across the Pacific in very simple seagoing craft. As a result, the ocean (*Moana*) is heavily embedded in Polynesian culture and even in theology.[6] Globally, the interaction between humans and the ocean has influenced many cultures, even those that were not that involved in seafaring, such as the ancient Israelites (see next section).

In this chapter we will examine what the Bible says about the ocean as part of God's creation; consider how we should care for the other 71 percent of the Earth; give some examples of such care; and end with a reflection on the ocean and God's glory.

The ocean and the Bible

Surprisingly little has been written on the ocean from a biblical perspective, either as part of the wealth of writing on creation care, the environment and ecology, and sustainability, or as a topic in its own right.[7] While some Bible dictionaries include articles on the sea[8] and Reymond has written a fuller chapter,[9] there is a need for a more extensive treatment of the subject, which Reymond describes as 'as vast as the sea itself'[10]—an echo of Psalm 104:25—and which covers almost the whole Bible, from Genesis 1:10 to Revelation 21:1.

At the beginning of Genesis, the Bible affirms the goodness of the ocean and the creatures living in it (1:9–10, 20–21). The Psalms reiterate God's

Figure 1: The diversity of underwater life. (Photograph: Robert D Sluka)

creation and ownership of the sea and all that is in it (95:5, 146:6). God blesses the ocean creatures and tells them to be fruitful and multiply (Gen 1:22). The Genesis language of the ocean teeming with creatures is picked up in Psalm 104:25 and echoed in Ezekiel 47:10. Following the Flood, God makes a covenant with all his creatures, including those in the ocean (Gen 9:8–17). God uses creation, including the ocean, to reveal himself and his character to Job (Job 38:1–42:6). The ocean is a place where human trade and travel take place (Ps 107:23, Jonah 1:3, Acts 27:38). In the process, people see the wonders of God's creation (Ps 107:23–24). That God values his creation, and specifically the ocean, is shown in his blessing (in terms of abundance of life) and his care for his creatures (Ps 104:27–28). It is part of God's mandate to humanity that we should care for his creation as he does (Gen 1:26–28).[11]

Associated with the ocean in the Bible is the imagery of chaos and danger as, for example, in the storms experienced by Jonah, Jesus (Mark 4:35–41), and Paul (for instance, Acts 27–28).[12] However, God is seen as being in control of the waves and the sea and the creatures in it (see, for example, Ps 65:5–7, 74:13, 93:3–4, 107:29; Prov 8:29; Jer 5:22), and 'treads on the waves of the sea' (Job 9:8), echoed in Jesus' walking on the water (Mark 6:48). There is also a *mythical* element associated with the sea and some of the creatures living in it, such as Leviathan. Leviathan at times seems to be a creature of the sea, as in Psalm 104:26 where it might simply be something large like a whale frolicking in the waves.[13] In other scriptures, it appears to be more like a mythical monster in enmity and conflict with God, as in Job 41 or Isaiah 27:1—though, even here, it is clear that it is subject to God. Similarly, the ocean itself seems sometimes to be symbolic of chaos and evil in opposition to God (Job 38:8; Isa 17:12–13; Mark 4:35–41).[14] In light of this, it is probably best not to take 'and there was no longer any sea' in Revelation 21:1 as saying that there will be no ocean in the new creation. Rather, the lack of sea is more likely to be symbolic of the removal of chaos and evil from the new creation.[15]

Note that Revelation 5:13 speaks of 'every creature . . . on the sea, and all that is in them' singing praise to the Lamb (Jesus). This leads into the final aspect of the ocean to be considered here, namely that the ocean and the creatures in it were created for God's praise. In fact, they are commanded to praise him (Ps 69:34, 96:11, 98:7, 148:7). They were not created simply as a resource for humanity to use and exploit; therefore their value is not instrumental (or extrinsic). Actually, oceanic creatures, like those on land and in the air, and humanity itself, are all part of what Bauckham aptly describes as the community of creation.[16] This is well captured in Psalm 104, which reveals God's generosity to and blessing of his creation, with the world as his gift to all living creatures who share it with one another.[17] Together the whole of creation is called to worship God and bring him glory (Ps 96:11–12, 148:1–14; Isa 4:23, 49:13). Ultimately, 'the earth will be filled with the knowledge of the glory of the LORD as the waters cover the sea' (Hab 2:14).

What can be concluded from this brief biblical overview of the ocean, and the creatures in it? First, the ocean is part of God's good creation and has intrinsic value for that reason. Humans are to value the ocean and all therein, just as God does. Second, humanity's calling to care for God's creation includes caring for the ocean and the creatures in it (the other 71 percent). So, two questions arise: what are the present day problems relating to the ocean; and how is humanity to exercise its care of this part of God's creation?

Creation care and the oceans

Major problems in the oceans

As we have seen, the oceans are meant to glorify God and point us, in our awe and wonder at its beauty and majesty, to him. A trip to the beach reveals tide pools full of interesting creatures that inspire exclamations of wonder. A storm rolls in and we see the power of the waves pounding the beach. Perhaps you are a diver and save up so that you can take that once in a lifetime trip to the Great Barrier Reef or the Maldives to see *pristine* coral reefs. There are still many places in the world where we can revel in God's beauty, majesty, and creative power in, at, or around the ocean.

However, the ocean is in many aspects a shadow of its former self. Research suggests that fish are less abundant, waters are polluted, ecosystems are lost or changed beyond recognition, islands of trash float around our seas, and physical and chemical changes threaten some species' survival. There is now clear evidence of marine extinctions.[18] While we want to focus later in this chapter on the ways in which we can serve God through taking care of the ocean, we do need to spend a short time on some of the major problems that face the sea. An exhaustive list would be overwhelming, so we focus here on three major problems: overfishing, climate change, and ocean pollution.

One of the most significant issues impacting the health of the ocean is *overfishing*. Most of the major fisheries of the world are in decline: tuna, shark, cod—the list goes on. There are, of course, some notable exceptions, but the recently paid price of $1,700,000 for one bluefin tuna at a Japanese market indicates that rarity confers value in many cultures and that there can be economic incentive to hunt down the last remaining individuals.[19]

Much of this is due to simply taking more fish from the ocean than are replaced through breeding, but certain fishing practices make this worse. Fishing tends to target the larger individuals of a species, which are also the ones that produce the most offspring. For example, catching one large grouper (a fish used for food) of about a metre in size could be the same as removing hundreds of individuals half that size in terms of how many eggs they might produce.[20] Many species of fish gather in what used to be very large numbers at very specific places and times of the year to spawn. Fishermen have naturally targeted these aggregations, and it does not take a research scientist to understand that this has huge impacts on the population.

Small coastal communities can find that they are damaging the basis of their livelihood through the methods they use to fish. This can be as destructive as homemade bombs thrown into the sea destroying corals while that night's meal floats to the top for collection, or using nets that catch fish too young to have reproduced even once.

There is also a matter of justice at work here, as industrial fleets from wealthier nations ply the waters off the coast of Africa scooping up the fish that poor, coastal fishermen need to feed their families. Often governments sell fisheries contracts to other countries: the money pocketed in some distant capital never reaches the coastal fishing communities and the sea is overfished, leaving the poor without their daily bread.

These issues in poorer, developing countries are not simple. One of us (RS) lived for over a year in a fishing village in the Maldives. I spent many an hour sitting with my neighbour who was a fisherman, listening to his woes and gaining a better understanding of what it took for him to feed his family each day. He had the same dreams and desires as I did, but very few alternatives and little access to knowledge about the ocean. At a particularly low point in my time there, I poignantly remember being out on a fishing vessel and thinking his case hopeless, and wondering why I was spending my time with them anyway as they were 'only fishermen.' I had a revelatory moment shortly after as the Holy Spirit chastened me by reminding me that a huge proportion of Jesus' disciples were fishermen!

A second major problem is *climate change and its impact on the seas and coasts*. There is no doubt that climate change, driven by human use of fossil fuels, is already affecting the oceans.[21] Firstly, much of our increasing emissions of CO_2 into the atmosphere is absorbed by the ocean, changing its chemistry and in particular making it more acidic.[22] The effect has been clearly documented.[23] Secondly, the oceans are warming.[24]

These two effects are having an increasing impact on the ocean, from the tropics to the poles. Acidification changes the seawater carbonate chemistry, which in turn impacts those species that use calcium carbonate in building shells. These include some species of plankton, molluscs, and corals. Coral-algal symbiosis is particularly sensitive to fairly small changes in temperature and acidity, which will affect the long-term survival of coral ecosystems and loss of biodiversity. As about a quarter of marine species are associated with coral reefs such changes would have a severe impact.[25] Polar ocean ecosystems are affected by the unexpectedly rapid loss of sea ice in the Arctic; the polar regions are known to be more sensitive to the effects of global warming.[26]

Other biological processes and ecosystems are also being affected.[27] One example is that the warming of the ocean's surface waters is leading to changes in how phytoplankton species are distributed; warmer water species are migrating into the warmer areas and colder water species are migrating away from them. As phytoplankton are the base of the oceanic food chain, this in turn has an impact on the whole ecosystem.[28] Changes in ocean currents and mixing as the oceans warm may affect the dispersal of plankton and fish larvae. How well marine species can adapt to these changes and all the other impacts discussed is unclear, as are the long-term effects on ocean ecosystems.

Finally, sea level rise, due both to thermal expansion of the oceans and the melting of ice sheets, is well documented and will affect many of the poorer communities on the planet.[29] For example, the projected rise of approximately one metre over the next one hundred years would displace about ten million people who currently live near the coast in Bangladesh. It would also negatively affect many communities on low-lying islands, such as the Maldives in the Indian Ocean. In addition, increasing sea level, when combined with other effects such as storm surges, will also lead to increased flooding risk in low-lying coastal regions such as Bangladesh and the Netherlands.[30]

The third major problem in the world's oceans is that of *ocean pollution*. We often see the ocean as a vast and spacious resource, which we could not possibly damage. 'There is the sea, vast and spacious, teeming with creatures beyond number—living things both large and small' (Ps 104:25). Our perception of the immensity of the sea is, of course, on one level correct. Yet many still look out on the ocean and only see it two dimensionally; the vast plane of the sea hiding a three dimensional world. Yet beneath the surface the oceans are being damaged due to human activity, both directly and indirectly from the land.

Perhaps the most dramatic example of direct ocean pollution caused by human beings is the Deepwater Horizon drilling platform oil spill in the Gulf of Mexico in 2010—the largest marine oil spill ever.[31] This is just the latest of a series of major oil spills that span the last fifty years, going back to such incidents as the Torrey Canyon oil tanker spill in 1967.[32] Ironically, not only is the burning of fossil fuels affecting the ocean negatively, but the extraction and transport of the fuels themselves also leads to negative impacts. On a smaller scale, ships that clean out their tanks at sea and dispose of rubbish overboard contribute to the problem, as do containers of goods washed overboard (most famously perhaps the one full of rubber ducks washed overboard in the Pacific, of which some have made it into the Atlantic after many years, via the Arctic Ocean).[33]

What we do on land can also dramatically impact the ocean. As the saying goes, all drains lead to the sea. We build a golf course next to the ocean that needs fertilizers to keep the greens green. With the next rain it is washed off into the sea where algae are able to use it to outcompete corals—in some cases, shifting the systems from coral reefs to algal forests. Similarly, fertilizer and chemical run-off from land can cause eutrophication—the ecosystem response to the run-off—leading to harmful algal blooms (HABs), which are poisonous and can affect both marine life and humans, if we eat shellfish or fish affected by them.[34] A plastic bag is washed into the sea at a beach picnic in California and ends up circulating in the middle of the Pacific Ocean (the so-called *Great Pacific Garbage Patch*) or washes up on a beach in a South Pacific island or perhaps worse, is mistaken for a jellyfish by a sea turtle, ingested, and causes injury or death to the animal.[35]

As we have seen with our greenhouse gas emissions, what we do on the land impacts the sea. Through ocean currents what we do to the sea in one place can be transported to other far distant places where these problems did not originate. Ultimately, we are not loving our neighbours, but doing to them as we would not want them to do to us.

Practical solutions

Overfishing, climate change, and pollution: Is there hope? We believe so. While we have to exercise appropriate humility in our dealing with the ocean, we do know some things that we can do to glorify God through caring for the ocean.[36] Fisheries are managed by limiting the amount of the target species caught or their size, allowing individuals to reproduce before capture. Management can also take the form of limiting effort—for example, allowing only certain sized boats or regulating net mesh size so that small fish pass through. There is important work here for fisheries scientists, mathematicians, biologists, and ecologists who can study the target species and the fishing techniques and determine the appropriate quantities to harvest with sustainable techniques. The world needs Christians in these fields who can, as Psalm 111:1–2 exhorts, delight in and study the works of God, and guide the rest of us in our relationships with the sea.

Some familiar landbased environmental practices have parallels in the ocean. For instance, like natural parks, there is a growing network of marine protected areas which have regulations that seek to limit the damage to the ecosystems under protection.[37] In some cases this limits fishing or other extractive activities and in other cases limited levels of fishing are allowed. As on land, they cannot exist as islands of biodiversity but interact with neighbouring uncontrolled areas. Generally, and perhaps counter-intuitively, within several years, fishermen near the reserve see their catches increase. This is due to the biology of most sea creatures as noted above—the abundance of the park overflows into the surrounding areas reminiscent of the teeming and swarming and original blessing of the sea (Gen 1:22).

As discussed elsewhere in this book (Chapter 8, 'Global Warming, Climate Change, and Sustainability'), preserving and planting forests helps remove CO_2 from the atmosphere and lessen the drivers of climate change. The same is possible in the sea: mangrove forests and sea grass beds do the same, as well as providing habitats for many species, thus preserving diversity, and also lessening damage from floods.

Pollution is an area where we can have a huge impact. A beach or coast clean-up is a great activity to enjoy the outdoors. Gather a group of friends or have your church picnic at the coast and spend even thirty minutes with a rubbish bag picking up what shouldn't be there. Your neighbours will thank you. Even better is to try and avoid polluting in the first place. What human activities might need lessening or modifying, and can we as a church promote positive change?

Perhaps our biggest role is as consumers. What are we buying and where does it comes from? How was that beautiful shell caught? Which fish in your supermarket come from a sustainable source? There are a number of programmes online that document and certify which species of sea creature have been caught in a way that is not damaging to the ocean and which have populations that are not overfished.[38] The herbal and 'Chinese' medicine trade is decimating large areas of the sea by collecting things in such a way as to degrade the ocean and cause overfishing. Don't participate!

The role of aquaculture, restoration, reconciliation and disaster relief: In many places in the world, aquaculture (the cultivation of fish and shellfish for food) is becoming a much needed source of protein, especially for the poor. Family-level ponds in the back garden can be hugely important. However, large, industrial aquaculture facilities can cause more problems than they solve. In some cases, mangrove forests are cut down to create shrimp or other seafood aquaculture facilities for foreign markets. This destroys important habitats for fish that local fishermen depend upon and reduces, in different ways, the ability of the coast to absorb both waves and carbon.[39] There is also an ethical question: why do usually poor, often protein malnourished, areas export luxury protein to countries that already have so much?[40] Additionally, culturing species at higher levels in the food chain, such as salmon, can require larger inputs of protein from lower levels on the food chain. It may take several kilograms of other fish to make one kilogram of salmon, for example. These fish may come from countries where there is a protein deficit. Is this a Christian way to act? The 'market' is usually invoked as an explanation and justification. Perhaps the economic benefit is greater than the injustice, but this needs to be examined critically.

One of us (RS) recently visited an area of Borneo that has been severely degraded by fishermen using homemade bombs to fish. Snorkelling over large areas of coral rubble was disturbing, especially when compared to the un-impacted sites, which were amazing, causing wonderment and praise to God from all in our party. Yet there was hope. Local and UK conservation groups were beginning the long process of restoring these habitats. Using wire frames with live coral attached to provide suitable substrate for growth, gives the ecosystem a hand up in restoration. There are times when habitats are so degraded that without this type of help, they are unlikely to recover. Many other examples could be given, but these projects all seek to restore that which we have destroyed.

What could Christian marine creation care look like?

One element of all Christian practice is reflection and worship, and marine issues are no different. Following our earlier biblical summary, we should learn to appreciate more the beauty and wonder of the ocean. Perhaps we could take that church picnic by the sea, or explore how many of the hymns and songs we sing utilise ocean and sea imagery. Exploring this helps us to reflect on what we and our churches can do practically.

As well as caring for marine creation in the ways already noted, there are specific things that can be done which relate to our biblical mandate to bring blessing to the nations. For instance, most of the coastal fishing communities in the Indian Ocean are predominantly Muslim. This represents an important opportunity for Christians to show love to these people groups through projects related to marine conservation. Also, how does it represent Jesus well when our supposedly Christian countries come in big ships and take a poor fisherman's dinner from his family? That may seem simplistic, yes, but often it is the way the fisherman thinks.

Figure 2: Studying a tropical rockpool on the Kenyan coast.
(Photograph: Robert D Sluka)

One group working in this area is A Rocha Kenya (ARK).[41] The ARK field study centre is located on the shore of Watamu Marine National Park. This is a marine protected area with globally rare or threatened marine biodiversity. Additionally, the surrounding area is predominantly Muslim traditional fishing villages. Researchers are studying biodiversity, the impact of tourism on coral reefs, climate change issues, and beginning community outreach and education among fishermen. This is done in partnership with government management of the park and community organizations. A training programme has been set up for local and international volunteers and interns so that they can learn important marine research methods and concepts, living in a Christian community that invites people of all faith backgrounds to come and see.

There are numerous possible sources of conflict related to different uses of the same space. You go to the beach and jet skiers ruin your swimming experience. You want to fish, but find out that your favourite fishing spot has been turned into a marine park. This second area of conflict resolution is covered in Chapter 18, 'Creation Care as a Ministry of Reconciliation'.

Thirdly, Christians can support disaster relief and disaster prevention, but in an informed way (see also Chapter 12, 'Un-natural Disasters'). While the global Christian church responded generously to the recent tsunamis, there appeared to be very little attention paid to marine conservation issues.[42] In some cases many small boats were purchased and donated to people in areas where there was once a diversity of sizes of boats. This tended to concentrate fishing inshore where there were already significant overfishing problems. Few, if any, Christian groups were involved in restoration of coral reef habitats or fisheries issues, and few objected to the loss of coastal habitats, which afford the land a measure of protection from storms and erosion.[43] When we destroy these natural protective barriers it can cause great misery for coastal dwellers. Often it is the big business in a distant inland capital that is doling out land for large sums of money for hotels or other ventures and so causing difficulties for the poor. Finally, should Christians be supporting the international effort to develop tsunami warning systems? Wouldn't investing in these warning systems be a more effective use of money than responding after the damage and death has occurred? This, would, though, take a whole new way of thinking about how to utilise money, respond proactively, and partner with scientific and government agencies globally.

Reflection

As we reflect on what we have written, things can seem hopeless, but as Christians we know that there is always hope in Jesus Christ, however bleak things look, because he is faithful (Hebrews 3:6) and all things were created by him, through him and for him, and reconciled through him, too (Colossians 1:15–20). Perhaps a well-known story can help here:

A man was walking along a beach immediately after a storm that had thrown a large number of fish up onto the shore. As he walked along he was picking up fish and throwing them back into the ocean. Another person on the beach saw him and seeing the thousands of stranded fish said, 'This is hopeless, you aren't making any difference.' In response the man stooped down, picked up another fish and threw it into the ocean, saying, 'I made a difference to that one.'

Perhaps we are doing a small thing that may seem insignificant and lacking impact in the grand scheme of things but God says to us, 'your labour in the Lord is not in vain' (1 Cor 15:58). All this, all that we have written about, needs to be seen and set in the context of the seventh confession of faith from the *Cape Town Commitment*:

> We share God's passion for his world, loving all that God has made, rejoicing in God's providence and justice throughout his creation, proclaiming the good news to all creation and all nations, and longing for the day when the earth will be filled with the knowledge of the glory of God as the waters cover the sea.[44]

CHAPTER 15

Planetary Boundaries and the Green Economy

Paul Cook

'It was the best of times, it was the worst of times, it was the age of wisdom, it was the age of foolishness, it was the epoch of belief, it was the epoch of incredulity, it was the season of Light, it was the season of Darkness, it was the spring of hope, it was the winter of despair, we had everything before us, we had nothing before us, we were all going direct to Heaven, we were all going direct the other way . . .'

Charles Dickens, *A Tale of Two Cities*

One of the most positive trends in the world over the last twenty years has been the struggle to tackle poverty. We have seen tremendous improvements in many areas, and the fight looks as though it should be winnable. However, there is a big threat to this progress continuing: climate change and related issues of environmental damage. Ironically, it is economic development which largely lies behind both trends: improving people's wellbeing in one way, but pushing us beyond planetary limits in another.

In this chapter we will look at what progress has been made in reducing poverty, then summarize ways in which we are putting pressure on our planet—some looked at in previous chapters, others not—and how this risks damage both to the planet and to the fight against poverty. Finally, we discuss the role of the church as a global body and how it can take action.

Measures of poverty

Following much clear biblical teaching on the subject, the Christian church has seen addressing poverty as a major part of its mission over many centuries—both in local areas and, more recently, on a worldwide scale, with numerous agencies set up to aid the poor and help them to develop better lives.

Governments and international bodies have also taken on this role. The United Nations has been involved in development work since its foundation.[1] In 2000, the UN set some explicit targets for the alleviation of poverty: the Millennium Development Goals.[2] These goals, to be met by the end of 2015, were listed under eight headings, including the eradication of extreme poverty and hunger; universal primary education; improvements in maternal health and child mortality; lower prevalence of HIV/AIDS, malaria, and other diseases; as well as development which is environmentally sustainable. Another set of targets, broadly similar in scope but with more emphasis on sustainability, have now been agreed on for 2030, the Sustainability Development Goals.[3]

When the final statistics are compiled for the Millennium Development Goals, some of the targets will have been met. For instance, halving the proportion of people living on less than $1.25 a day from 1990 levels had already been met by 2010. Rates of new HIV infections and deaths from malaria, where the target was to halt further increases, were both nearly halved between 2000 and 2012. Others will probably be missed: it is unlikely that all children will yet have the opportunity to go to school, but 90 percent had the opportunity to by 2012.[4]

Almost every indicator of poverty, whether one of the explicit goals or not, is showing similarly positive trends. But there is still plenty left to do: getting the number living in extreme poverty to near zero, getting clean water and sanitation to the 2.5 billion who currently lack it, and so on.

One of the major factors behind these improvements in poverty has been economic development, combined with what national governments have chosen to do with the money generated by their economies. These sums are far bigger than could be supplied by aid from abroad. In some cases, the money has been spread around and many millions brought out of poverty. In other countries economic development has tended to benefit a small elite—and perhaps the capital city—at the expense of rural areas: here the number coming out of poverty is far smaller. A combination of economic development and the provision of basic services for the 'poorest' is hence needed for the continued alleviation of poverty.

Climate change and agriculture

But climate change and other forms of environmental damage pose a real threat to these positive trends. Communities around the world are discovering that weather is becoming more unstable and threatening both their crops and their livelihood. Seasons are shifting, so people no longer know when to plant their crops. Even when planted, crops are destroyed by flooding from extreme rains—alternatively, drought prevents crops growing. In some areas, deserts are growing; in others, soil productivity is dropping.

Tearfund's *Dried Up, Drowned Out* report interviewed people from many countries to find their responses.[5] This view, from Malawi, is typical: '"Those who have lived here for a long time say they are living in a different world", says Victor Mughogho from Tearfund partner Eagles in Malawi . . . Communities report feeling frustration and uncertainty about the changes they're experiencing. There is a profound lack of confidence about the future.'[6]

We tell similar stories from elsewhere in Part 3 of this book.

Unfortunately, what we can have reasonable confidence in, is that both shifts in weather and more extreme weather will be increasingly common as the effects of climate change increase. They will also not be restricted to the poorer areas of the world. For instance, an unprecedented heat wave and drought in 2010 in Russia devastated the wheat harvest and led to food shortages worldwide. While climate change may not necessarily be culpable for this particular event, it is predicted that climate change will result in similar extreme weather situations becoming more common as the century progresses, with consequent damage to agriculture and human life.[7] If people cannot survive or cannot eat, all other attempts to alleviate their poverty become futile.

Planetary boundaries and global footprint

Climate change is, however, only one of a number of interlocking ways in which we are stretching our planet. Earth scientists have provided various methods of classifying and measuring these factors. We will consider two particular models—*planetary boundaries* and *global footprint*.

The planetary boundaries model

This model was devised by a group of earth scientists led by Johan Rockström and Will Steffen and has been subsequently refined.[8] They identified and quantified a set of nine ways in which we are changing the planet. For each, the scientists specified a *boundary*—a specific quantity which, if exceeded, risks causing damage to the planet. For instance, for climate change, the boundary was set at 350 parts per million (ppm) of CO_2 in the atmosphere, compared to the 280 ppm present before the Industrial Revolution and the approximately 400 ppm present now. This boundary has thus been exceeded. The model also attempts to monitor progress (or deterioration) with respect to the nine boundaries:

1. Climate change

2. Ocean acidification

3. Stratospheric ozone depletion

4. Nitrogen and phosphorus cycles (biochemical flows)

5. Global freshwater use

6. Change in land use

7. Biodiversity loss

8. Atmospheric aerosol loading

9. Chemical pollution (or *novel entities*)

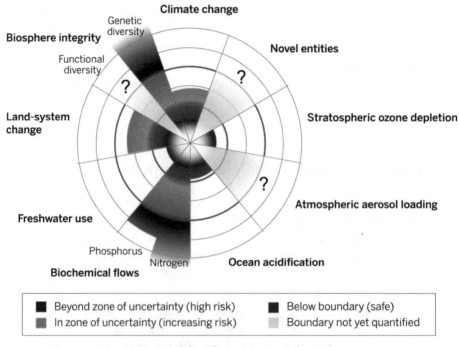

Figure 1: The Planetary Boundaries.[9]

In two areas already discussed—*climate change* (Chapter 8, 'Global Warming, Climate Change, and Sustainability') and the genetic aspect of *biodiversity loss* (Chapter 13, 'Biodiversity Loss: A Christian Concern')—we have already exceeded the boundaries, as can be seen from Figure 1.

Three further boundaries relate directly to our ability to provide food and water to our growing population. One is *fresh water use* (although a large proportion is used in industrial processes rather than being used for farming or drunk directly). In terms of *land use*, the specified limit is on the amount of forest cover lost. This land is normally converted for either growing crops or grazing domestic animals.

The third issue that relates to the provision of food and water is the *nitrogen and phosphorus cycles*. The two boundaries here, both of which have been exceeded, specify how much of those two elements can be used by humanity if human and other life is to continue to flourish. The major use of both is in chemical fertilisers, on which much of the world's agriculture depends.

The remaining four boundaries all relate to pollution. *Ocean acidification* is another effect of increased CO_2 emissions and is having a detrimental effect on sea life, as discussed in Chapter 14, 'Creation Care of the Other 71%'. We also risk damaging our atmosphere and oceans through *chemical pollution*, *excessive aerosol use* (emitting small liquid or solid particles such as smoke), and *damage to the ozone layer*. These last three have many negative effects on human and other life. Millions, particularly in cities, suffer ill health from pollution. Ocean pollution kills marine life, and other species such as sea birds which feed on them. Many sources of sea-based food are now too toxic for humans to eat.

The global footprint model

A second measure—the *global footprint* or *ecological footprint*—compares human demands on the world's resources (our footprint) with the planet's *biocapacity*, its ability to provide those resources and regenerate. Biocapacity represents earth's biologically productive areas, including forests, cropland, fisheries, together with its ability to absorb our waste, including carbon emissions. The amount of each is converted into units called *global hectares,* by calculations devised by the Global Footprint Network to give the total biocapacity of the world or a region.[10]

Our footprint is measured similarly, by computing the total number of global hectares required to provide the renewable resources humanity is using and to absorb its waste. Productive area currently occupied by human infrastructure (cities, roads, and so on) is included in this calculation by reducing the amount of biocapacity: this land could be biologically producing but is not.

According to their calculations, our global footprint has exceeded biocapacity since the 1970s. We now use the equivalent of 1.5 Earths a year.[11] Put simply, we not only use all the resources planet Earth can provide—we are also drawing down the reserves as well (for instance, by cutting down forests and degrading agricultural soils). This clearly cannot be continued indefinitely.

The richer nations consume a disporportionately high percentage of earth's resources; a typical European will use nearly twice the global average, a typical American nearly three times. If every person in the world lived like someone from the USA, we would need about four Earths.[12]

Economics and possible collapse

We are pushing against the limits of the finite planet we live in. But what is the prime driver? Ironically, it is the same economic system which has brought millions out of poverty. At the same time as driving up living standards for the poorest in the world, that economic system has done the same for the world's richest—fostering a culture of materialism, overconsumption, and the relentless pursuit of profit at the expense of everything else. This even includes sustaining the supply of raw materials it ultimately depends upon.

A number of historians and academics have looked at the problem of when societies outconsume their natural resources. Joseph Tainter and Jared Diamond, among others, have looked at various societies which have collapsed, sometimes suddenly, and found that many of them shared a common trigger: they had outconsumed their natural resource bases, and had often mismanaged them.[13]

An example of one such society is that of the Norse colony on Greenland, founded in AD 984 but which went extinct in the early fifteenth century.[14] Founded at a time when the regional climate was favourable, the colony initially flourished, but gradually the residents of that colony damaged their environment through deforestation, overgrazing, and soil erosion. As a consequence, they ran short of lumber, and—particularly as the climate cooled from about 1200 onwards—they ran short of food as well. They survived for a while through support and trade with Norway and other colonies, but, as those groups were also hit by a poorer climate, they were gradually forced to abandon their Greenland colony. Parallel Inuit settlements in Greenland, which continue to the present day, show that life is possible even in such a harsh climate—but only by managing resources in ways which are both sustainable and appropriate to the surroundings.

A more dramatic example of collapse is that of the last years of the Roman province of Britannia (roughly modern-day England and Wales). Although there was already some instability by the late fourth century AD, a typical Briton born then would probably have lived in a town, had a reasonable education and standard of living, and be part of an international economy in a relatively stable and peaceful society. However, their grandchild—born around AD 450—would be incredibly poor, have no education, and live in a village where (they hoped) the local warlord could provide some protection from the general tension and conflict following the collapse of Roman civic rule.

Of course, the problem we have now is that we have a global society, one global economy, and if we are outconsuming—not just locally but globally—our decline or collapse is going to be at a global level too. Like the Norse Greenlanders, we will be forced to live with the consequences of previous environmental damage. Today, rich nations of the world can step in to assist poorer areas following a natural disaster—but, if the whole world were struggling, resources to help others would be limited.

Our choice

The inhabitants of planet Earth are at an incredible point in our history. We are at a fork in the path—and there are two ways we can go. We can continue on the path we are taking, in which we can expect a massive increase in poverty. On that path, all the indicators that have been so positive in the past run in reverse—with an increase in conflict, mass migration, massive economic collapse, and the probable death of millions.

To travel on the other path, we need to figure out how to transform our economy into one that is both greener and fairer. It must be an economy that continues to provide the good things we want, that alleviates poverty, and provides employment—but one that does so without the environmental destruction and excessive depletion of resources. In particular, it is immoral for those of us living in rich countries to kick the ladder away from behind us. We cannot say to those elsewhere in the world that it is fine for us to have an affluent and comfortable lifestyle—but that they must forego it.

Discussing how to achieve this is the defining issue of our generation. The way in which we have addressed these challenges will be a major feature when the history books of the twenty-first century are written. The choices we make underlie all the other issues—conflicts, poverty issues, other environmental issues, economics, and so on. They are being discussed in many disciplines and in many organizations, by politicians, business leaders, economists, scientists, environmentalists, NGOs, think tanks and, informally, by concerned people everywhere.

The question for Christians is how we and the church as a whole can participate in this debate. We surely cannot sit on the sidelines and ignore it. I would argue not only that the church should be involved—but that it has an almost unique role to play. Industry leaders frequently say that it is often difficult to make the right decisions: if one company makes decisions which are more ethical but not as profitable, but others do not follow and indeed undercut them, then shareholders will seek to sack the leadership within a week. To get businesses to move, government needs to make appropriate legislation, and to set emissions targets, pollution targets, and the like. Then all business will move together. However, the government says that, while it would love to make such laws, it risks being voted out at the next election if it does so, because such actions are likely to undermine people's income or standard of living.

Ultimately, then, power lies neither with captains of industry nor in the political corridors of power. Change starts with ordinary members of the public like you and me engaging with our political representatives, telling them what we believe. We also need to speak out publicly, demonstrating and getting the right message in the media. Finally, we need to choose which products and services we purchase or avoid—to send the right economic signals that can guide political and business progress in the right directions.

The church is probably the world's largest civic society organization—present in virtually every nation and every community, and having an immense impact on how people think. If the church can harness this influence to inspire people to care more for creation and to act upon this care, then the world will be a very different place.

The church has acted like this in the past—for instance, in campaigning against slavery—although not unanimously. We now look back at Christians who owned slaves, or who opposed emancipation, and wonder how they could ever have behaved like that. Those coming after us will make similar judgements about us and how we look after our environment.

EVOLVING CHURCH ACTION ON DEFORESTATION IN ARGENTINA

My grandfather served with the Anglican Church among the hunter-gatherer tribes of northern Argentina. When he arrived in 1926, the country's native forests covered an area equivalent to France and Spain (one million square kilometres). Ministry focused on Bible translation, evangelism, and the provision of health care and schooling within their communities. There was no apparent need at that time to protect the seemingly-endless forests.

My father followed in my grandfather's footsteps in 1963. By then, some forests were being lost to lumber and tannin extraction, agriculture, and cattle. Because there was so much forest, this process initially had little effect on the indigenous peoples. They faced other problems, derived from the fact that they were not recognized as citizens. Much of my father's ministry was, therefore, given over to advocacy work, helping people to get out of problems with the police, obtain documents, and receive proper attention from government authorities.[1]

I joined the Anglican Church's work in 1999, by which time Argentina's native forests had been reduced to an area the size of Italy (three hundred thousand square kilometres).[2] In 2007, the country recorded the highest rate of deforestation in the world, and the process was having a devastating effect on forest dwelling indigenous communities.[3] For them, the process was akin to present-day urban dwellers having their supermarkets and shops destroyed. It also meant moving to insalubrious townships, with a consequent loss of traditional cultural and family values.

Concern for the wellbeing of indigenous people nudged the church towards addressing the issue of forest loss. Today, alongside its pastoral work, it plays a leading role in a campaign to stop deforestation. Through research and strategic legal actions, it has contributed to a two-year moratorium on deforestation and the introduction of new legislation aimed at protecting native forests.

Andrew Leake, Anglican Communion Environmental Network (ACEN) representative for the Southern Cone and director of Land for Life, a Christian conservation initiative

PART 3—GOD'S WORK

CHAPTER 16

Holistic Environmental Stewardship in East Africa

Serah Wambua

The training ... equips church leaders with simple tools that enable them ... to begin the transformation process in their own communities with existing resources—no matter how poor they may be ... Christians are challenged to be engaged in healing relationships with others and to better steward the creation.

Breakthrough Partners[1]

East Africa has changed much in recent years. I clearly remember my childhood experiences in the eastern part of Kenya. We used to *harvest* and not *cut* trees for firewood. In this regard, we went out to collect dry wood for firewood—in fact, it was culturally offensive to bring home firewood that was not dry. I remember the predictable pattern of the long and short rains. During those days, rivers and streams were clean; fruit grew in the forests and we just helped ourselves on our way to school.

Today's children have a very different experience. Calamities common today—such as severe droughts, floods, and landslides—were barely known then. Levels of forestation have dropped as trees have been felled to provide charcoal.

What have we done to God's creation as passed on by our fathers and forefathers? Why can we no longer co-exist with nature? As I have seen things change, I have tried to answer these questions and help concerned Christians work out how to respond to our failure to care for creation—and how to act to help put things right. In this region, the church has immense influence—over 80 percent profess Christian faith—and it is belatedly catching up with its mandate to care for what God has bequeathed to us.

There is good news in some areas. For example, villagers in Kithangatini, Kenya are being helped by church organizations in a number of ways: cooking using biogas rather than firewood and charcoal; planting trees rather than cutting them down; and improving relationships between local areas in Kenya and Uganda. But there is a great need to take this and other initiatives to many more people.

In this chapter, we will examine some of the environmental problems facing creation in East Africa—in particular, problems associated with population growth and the rise of capitalism. We consider how they might be addressed both at the large and small scale, and then reflect on how the good news of Christ includes redemption for the entire world. Finally, we will look at a case study exploring how the church might bring this about in practice.

Environmental problems due to population growth

A major challenge for East Africa is simply the increasing number of people. Even with no change in living standards, the needs of a larger population put more stress on the environment, as explained further in Chapter 11, 'Population and Ecological Sustainability'. Rates of fertility and population increase are tending to slow in other areas of the world—but this is not yet the case in East Africa.

One of the main challenges associated with population growth is the *problem of energy supply*. For example, since the amount of dead branches is now insufficient to meet the energy needs of the population, people cut down living trees and bushes—to use the wood either directly or in the form of charcoal. Inevitably, there has been a rapid loss of forest cover as a result.

Charcoal meets an estimated 80 percent of urban household energy needs in Eastern Africa, mainly due to its availability and low cost.[2] However, it is often produced poorly using methods such as earth-mould kilns where only 10 percent of the wood used in charcoal production is converted into charcoal, with the rest going to waste. Legislation and better control of the production, transportation, and distribution of charcoal in East Africa could make charcoal much more sustainable. However, no country in this region has yet formulated policies or enacted laws covering this, with the exception of Sudan. Meanwhile, industry continues this booming business that mainly benefits the middle men—at the expense of the poor, who are the main producers and users of charcoal.

Increase in population leads to urbanization, as populations migrate to establish towns and cities.[3] In common with most of the Global South, rapid urbanization as witnessed in East Africa has given rise to informal settlements and slums, further complicating the supply and demand of energy. For example, the Ngong Forest adjacent to the Kibera slums in Nairobi faces acute destruction as people seek alternatives to expensive sources of energy such as kerosene, liquefied petroleum gas (LPG), and electricity, and cut down trees for fuel.

A second challenge associated with population growth is the *problem of poor agricultural practices*. Economies in sub-Saharan Africa and particularly East Africa are still largely dependent on rain-fed agriculture, even though manufacturing and service industries are sluggishly gaining momentum. However, land holdings have shrunk in size because of population increase, resulting in overuse of land by farmers who are unable to implement good farming practices such as rotational farming.[4] This has led to a host of problems: land degradation, low or no yields, drought and famine, food insecurity, pollution, diminishing water supplies, diseases, and a threatening poverty cycle. Soils have been overused and toxified through use of fertilisers because no rest is given to the farms—resulting in reduced crop yields and food insecurity. Moreover, land degradation and soil erosion has caused desertification.

In traditional African societies, crop and land rotation was practised to recharge and rest the soils in readiness for future planting season. This traditional African way of managing land agreed with the Old Testament communities' instructions on renewal and regeneration of land (Exodus 23:11). Land was communal, which ensured equity and a clear demonstration of love towards one's neighbour. However, the ultimate goal was to ensure that the land rested, as the environment benefitted from this rest. Highly mechanised agriculture both takes away from this rest, and requires the bringing in of different energy sources—both directly for operating machinery and equipment on the farm, and indirectly for the production of pesticides and fertilisers produced off farm.

In some parts of East Africa, overstocking of livestock is common for reasons of prestige and power—or purely on economic grounds. Cattle rustling and conflicts have become commonplace among and between the Pokot and Turkana communities in Kenya, and Karamoja in Uganda. This has been largely due to competition over scarce and receding pastures, though destructive cultural practices are also on display. Failed rains, reduced forest and green cover, rising population, and desertification exacerbate the situation, resulting in limited and reduced pastures.

Population growth also contributes to *other forms of environmental degradation*—such as inappropriate waste disposal, devalued quantity and quality of water, as well as a strain on the land's carrying capacity.

Environmental problems associated with capitalism

African communities have generally been praised for the practice of communal living and community-based support systems. However, this good practice is apparently dying fast and affecting many sectors including the environment sector. The focus is on survival for the moment and there is a failure to factor in the survival of future generations. Increased self-centeredness and individual survival replace the communal good of everyone. This attitude is widely spread and affects the young and the old, the educated as well as the illiterate. Capitalism is at the centre of this scenario because it champions the individual and shuns the common good.

Today's world defines development by liberalization and globalization. This gives room for investments in industries while promoting the widening of consumer choices through capitalism. As countries try to industrialise and compete favourably in global markets, the environment and water has suffered.

First, setting up of commercial centres and industries has meant *loss of green cover*. This green cover, which has been removed to make way for construction, has been replaced with paved and cemented grounds, reducing infiltration and percolation. Land that is covered with plant growth allows water to go into the soil and underground reservoirs, and thus promotes plant growth. Where the land is paved, water runs off and is lost. Flooding disasters also increase as most of the water is not retained on land but released to the oceans. Moreover, competition between domestic and industrial use for environmental resources is often heightened by the development and growth of industries in a specific area.

A second problem associated with capitalism is *industrial air pollution*. Chemicals emitted from these industries contaminate the atmosphere, often leading to acid rains and hence poor quality of water. Fossil fuels such as coal and petroleum used by most industries emit carbon dioxide and other greenhouse gases harmful to the environment. In addition, emissions of greenhouse gases from vehicles and household appliances also contribute to climate change. Waste water consisting of hard metals and other chemicals is usually released back into watercourses, leading to brown, polluted water.

Thirdly, many countries in Africa have seen huge *exploitation of natural resources* by countries elsewhere—for example, oil in the Niger Delta of Nigeria and Abyei in the Sudan, copper in Zambia, rubber in Liberia, gold and timber in the Democratic Republic of Congo. Large-scale oil explorations in Kenya and Uganda have contributed to the depletion of green cover. Similarly, poor regulation of mining has also led to destruction of the environment. Some companies in the logging business have been aggressively involved in felling trees for self gain; and other businesses—especially tea companies—make excessive use of wood fuels in their production process.

It is worth noting that these large corporations also make particular use of energy from hydro sources which are highly dependent on rainfall. Since the water catchment areas are receding at a fast rate, this source of energy becomes unsustainable and costly; as a result, rationing is often witnessed within the countries in the east African region.

The solution: whose responsibility is it?

I recently travelled across South Sudan, the newest nation in the world, and was delighted to see stretches of that old, rich, green ecosystem decorated with indigenous trees and large tracts of teak plantations. This reminded me of those early years of my life. Teak is an endangered species in Kenya and protected under the Convention on International Trade in Endangered Species (CITES). CITES and similar treaties are partial solutions to protecting the environment and securing the livelihoods of the future generations, but more efforts need to be made to consolidate the gains already achieved. All countries of the world should formulate and adhere to international policies and treaties that protect and replenish the environment as well as the use of safe energy sources.

Several international agencies including the United Nations work closely with the government in addressing these important subjects. Some of these agencies are research-based while others focus more on advocacy. A number of community-based organizations have moved in and are also helping create environmental awareness in communities. These efforts are commendable but they are rather limited in impact as there is a lack of coordination and collaboration.

It is essential to review ecological policy in Africa and rethink the national laws upon which we will build the foundation for a new ecological and moral norm. The lasting solutions to environmental protection in Africa lie in the active recovery and utilization of Africa's previously immobilized cultural sensibilities, resource management skills, practices, moral values, and knowledge systems in connection with ecological matters.[5] This implies that both traditional as well as modern ways need to be adopted in the provision of sustainable energy, but also in the protection of the environment.

National governments are the main stakeholders in addressing issues of the environment. In Kenya, for example, the Ministry of Environment and Mineral Resources records that the country has less than 2 percent forest cover as opposed to the recommended 10 percent. It is also reported that Kenya is already witnessing the disappearance of the glaciers on Mount Kenya. Yet the country's hydropower potential is on the water system fed by glacial melts from this famous mountain. This phenomenon is already affecting agricultural activities and water availability and is presenting serious economic challenges. In a country where 80 percent of the land mass is arid to semi-arid, these effects on the remaining productive land have far-reaching implications—on livelihoods, health, water resources, agricultural production, and food security, as well as nature-based tourism. Clan and tribal conflicts have been witnessed in drought-stricken areas where communities are fighting for water and food for their own survival and that of their animals.

Countries need to implement their own policies on the environment but also strengthen the legislation. In Kenya, this has been done through the revised Environmental Policy Draft 2012. Champions such as the late Noble Laureate Prof Wangari Maathai—and her movement, the Green Belt movement—started this work of restoration through her passion and actions.[6] Her efforts were also seen in the desire to save all the water towers in Kenya, including those in Mau Forest, since these affect the whole East African region. Mau Forest stores rain during the wet seasons and pumps it out during the dry months. But during the last fifteen years, more than one hundred thousand hectares of the protected forest reserve have been settled and cleared. It is estimated that ten million people depend on the rivers from this forest. These rivers drain into six major lakes including the famous Lake Victoria which is source of the River Nile and serves the world's famous Masai Mara, Serengeti, and Lake Nakuru game reserves.

Figure 1: The Mau Forest in 2011. (Photograph courtesy of Mau Complex Zone CBO.)

The Nairobi-based UN Environmental Programme reports that when the rains in Kenya stop falling, the twelve rivers which stem from the Mau Forest become the lifeline for about ten million people.[7] The invasion of the Mau Forest has affected food production in the Narok area, one of Kenya's breadbasket districts, causing serious suffering. It has resulted in the death of millions of livestock in the arid and semi-arid areas. It has also affected tea production in the western Kenya region—not to mention the negative impact it has had on tourism. The revised Environmental Policy Draft 2012 has gone some way to addressing this problem. It was recently reported on the BBC that over three hundred schools in central and eastern regions of Kenya are converting latrine waste into biogas for cooking and other uses. This is a new adaptation, as traditional sources of energy get depleted.

The Kenyan government has also enacted other policies that aim at better management of the environment and mitigate against environmental degradation. It declared 2012 as the Green Year, an initiative aiming to promote environment-friendly practices, including the reducion of carbon dependency by individuals and corporate bodies. In line with the Millennium development goals, the government came up with extensive tree-planting campaigns—targeting schools, youth, and women's groups across the country with great effect. The main challenge, however, remains that of implementation.

Theological reflection

I grew up in a mission compound which had a church, a school, a health centre, and a mission farm which served as a demonstration farm teaching good farming practices. This farm served both Christians and non-Christians alike and was indeed a good Christian witness to the community. This concept of a mission station was a common feature in many African countries. It should have made huge impact in communities except that it imported a dualistic worldview which separated the spiritual realm as holy from the physical and essentially worldly realm. This approach seems to have lost the important component of growing disciples of Jesus by factoring in the whole counsel of God's word. As a result, many Christians in Africa to this day are not practising what they say they believe. Nigerian theologian Tokunboh Adeyemo wrote that 'Africa has been evangelized but the African mind has not been captured for Christ.'

We know that many Christians in Africa embraced the faith only as it was present in the mission station and did not carry it along with them to impact their lives throughout the week. This perhaps explains the Sunday-Christianity concept so prevalent in Africa—and, consequently, our relationship to the environment which is largely viewed as irrelevant to the church.

With the annual growth of the church in Africa estimated at 3 percent, there is incredible potential for the healing of the continent. Yet, all too often, the church is disengaged from the crying needs of the community, focusing exclusively on spiritual concerns. Despite Christians being a majority in many African communities, poverty, disease, conflict, and environmental degradation abound, making the church seem irrelevant to non-believing community members. The church holds the key to the challenges facing communities in Africa. It is God's principally ordained agency for social and cultural transformation. It is perhaps the single most indigenous, sustainable institution in any community, with members drawn from virtually every sphere of society—the arts, business, governance, education, including the environment sector. This is particularly true of Africa with an estimated 50 percent of the population (about four hundred million people) going to church. Africans are traditionally known to be a worshipping society—yet there is need for programs that ground that faith.

God's redemption

The whole of creation is under the authority of God—and all that he has created is interdependent. Genesis 1 exhorts humanity to take care of creation and, in turn, creation shall provide for humanity's food (Genesis 1:28–31). Our covenant with God requires us to be stewards, protectors, and defenders of all creation—and the creation will indeed serve us. God created order in the environment and intended that his creation should live in perfect harmony.

However, the Fall distorted this harmony. Greed and self-centeredness entered the world and broken relations started to be witnessed. Bryant Myers observes that 'poverty is the absence of shalom in all its meaning'.[8] This poverty is defined by the absence of peace or *shalom*, and it leads to relationships that do not work, that are not just, not for life, not harmonious, and not enjoyable. This can be witnessed through exploitation of the environment for personal gain at the expense of one's neighbour who suffers.

However, the good news is that Christ came so that all these could be corrected. Reconciliation of everything in creation, including the environment, is critical to harmonious and peaceful relations (Colossians 1:19–20). This peace was achieved through the shedding of blood on the cross. The Samaritan Strategy—an initiative of CMS Africa which is being practised in thirty-four countries in both English and French-speaking Africa—adopts a biblical view that earth is the Lord's and everything in it. As such, reconciliation can only be achieved if individuals consider others as better than themselves—hence loving their neighbours more than themselves. The initiative encourages participants to reach out to neighbours, especially those in need, using local resources.

This is because individuals do not *own* the earth—they are just stewards who need to harness it on behalf of God. God has provided the resources necessary for everyone to experience *shalom* or peace in all their relations including with the environment, so all humanity must learn to redeem and make prudent use of their locally available resources, even in their limited state. In God's relational economy, there is no waste. This is what different churches have recognized as they seek to facilitate *shalom* through sustainable stewarding of the environment.

The only institution charged with facilitation of reconciliation and attainment of *shalom* is the church (2 Corinthians 5:17–20). Since the environment transcends geographical boundaries, it was intended to benefit everyone in the present—as well as the future generations who need the same resources. A number of churches have recognized that the care of creation is a God-given mandate and are responding to the environmental agenda in Kenya and elsewhere in East Africa, which is bearing fruit as the church engages communities at the grassroots level.

Notable examples of these initiatives in Kenya include these.

1. One of Kenya's champions, Margaret Oluoch, is working in partnership with the Anglican Church in the western region of Kenya to empower communities to demonstrate evergreen agriculture by planting trees whose droppings form fertilizer.

2. Mount Kenya South Diocese encourages every member to plant a tree at every birthday or funeral. This simple act has gone a long way in communicating the importance of the environment.

3. Care of Creation Kenya (CCK), an international NGO, has done commendable work in awakening and mobilizing pastors and leaders in Kenya and within East Africa to a God-centred vision for creation stewardship. CCK works in partnership with CMS Africa with many farmers going through Farming God's Way training.

The church is slowly beginning to respond to environmental concerns— some practical examples of how they are seeking to serve their communities are given here. All these processes started because of CMS Africa's Samaritan Strategy training that encouraged churches to seek ways of using the locally available resources to demonstrate love to the communities.

Case study—community transformation in Machakos, Kenya

CMS Africa came up with the holistic community transformation model. This encourages churches across Africa to discover and effectively advance God's intentions by rediscovering the church as God's principal agent of social and cultural transformation. It aims to reorient individuals from a worldly view to a biblical view of their environment, their communities, and their nation.

The training equips pastors and leaders of local churches to proclaim and demonstrate the whole gospel while using the local available resources. Part of the church in Africa has looked to others for resources because she believed she was poor; the training allows the church to realize her own resources and potential. As well as teaching this vision, the training provides the church with the tools necessary for holistic transformation. Small is beautiful—the churches learn to demonstrate love in the community through small ministries. These *seed projects* use local resources and ideas to initiate and sustain positive change. One example of this is the biogas initiatives in Machakos, Kenya.

The pilot phase of this initiative in the Anglican Diocese of Machakos aimed to demonstrate environmental stewardship of God's creation using local resources to meet the local needs. Several Vision Conferences helped to lay a solid foundation for holistic transformation. As part of the preparation for the farmers, Farming God's Way training (offered by Care of Creation in Kenya) emphasized the biblical perspective on farming and environmental stewardship that connects faith with farming.

The biogas initiative encourages the use of cooking using the gas derived from animal excrement, rather than using firewood or charcoal. The old system used up scarce trees, and produced smoky kitchens which were bad for health and less environmentally-friendly than the new stoves. Through the use of farm waste to produce natural energy, farms have found they can reduce the use of conventional energy sources harmful to the environment.

Figure 2a (left): BEFORE—cooking on traditional stoves which
are fuelled by increasingly scarce firewood or charcoal and
result in smoky kitchens and damage to the environment.
Figure 2b (right): AFTER—cooking on the new, clean, biogas stoves using
the gas derived from animal excrement. (Photographs: CMS Africa.)

Figure 3: Rachel Karanja of Greenspan Bio-Technologies and two masons working on a biogas unit area in Kenya. Greenspan is fully-owned by CMS Africa and manages the biogas project following the success of the biogas initiative earlier launched in Machakos in 2010. (Photograph: CMS Africa.)

Case study: Evangelism and partnership in Uganda

This biogas project also bore fruit in partnership between Kenya's Machakos Diocese and the Ugandan Diocese of Mukono. A group of forty from Machakos toured Mukono; the main purpose of the visit was to share the vision of care for creation and some of the practical ideas developed in Kenya. Many in Uganda are now adopting these practices, adapted to local circumstances and conditions.

But the visit also had some unexpected consequences. Rev Patrick Munuve was preaching in a service that happened to be attended by many controversial political figures, as well as the local Uganda media. Furthermore, there was an existing conflict within the church of which Rev Munuve knew very little, yet God used him to deliver a sermon packed with messages of healing and reconciliation. It was widely reported locally that a Kenyan had been sent to reconcile a warring church.

The Kenyan visitors were able to experience different evangelistic methods, and to witness to Christ in places new to them—hospitals, police stations, a sugar factory. They too had much food for thought from the visit and took plenty of ideas back home with them.

The visit produced a partnership and mission going way beyond creation care. CMS Africa International Director Dennis Tongoi summed it up by saying: 'This is the kind of Christian witness that we would love to see the church in Africa engaging in. When one community witnesses Christ to another, then mission has occurred, hence true transformation and mindset change.'

The potential for greater change

In this and the many other examples we have looked at, we have seen how both lives and the environment can be changed for the better when the church, or the government, adopts a mindset which prioritises creation. So far what has been achieved is relatively limited, but there is hope: ideas and practices can spread from one area and group to another; more can share that vision and help to ensure that care for creation is a truly integral part of the church's mission. Then the church can use its numerical strength to influence governments and businesses as well.

In this way, we will be fulfilling our call to be both stewards and redeemers of a damaged and hurting land; we can act to protect against the worst effects of climate change; and we can do our best to restore East Africa to the fertile and harmonious region it once was.

A CASE STUDY FROM UGANDA

A Rocha Uganda works to restore degraded environments, conserve nature, and encourage local communities to use natural resources in a sustainable way. Projects include working in communities to restore natural spring wells thus improving access to clean water; constructing and installing biosand water filters, undertaking various environmental education activities in schools, and carrying out research in wetlands.

The journey which has led me to engagement with creation care started as I looked at my faith, my education, and the environmental degradation which was visible then, but has worsened since. It is clear that my desire to combine these three was, and still is, a prophetic call. In simple obedience and with no resources, let alone experience, I got started passionately in 2006. As I launched out, I remember being urged to first do something practical that would demonstrate my commitment and show what was possible. This would help to persuade other Christians that we all urgently need to engage our spiritual mandate to care for creation in the current ecological crisis and encourage them to start taking appropriate action. A few years into this role, I am continually encouraged by the increasing number of people looking to the infallible word of God—for hope for both the present and the future of the earth.

One of our projects is aimed at restoring and conserving a degraded wetland in the city of Kampala which has lost 40 percent of its area since 2003 and has shown the kinds of opportunities and challenges our work includes. For instance, after a few months of investigation into what we could do, we were shocked to find a huge chunk of our site suddenly backfilled with earth to make way for a government sewage treatment plant. Not long after that, a group of local people literally invaded another portion of the same wetland and set up market stalls. Their argument was that if the government took one part, they thought they could take another. However, their invasion lasted only a few days as they were chased off the wetland by a government agency. This left us an opportunity to protect the remaining fragment, with benefits for the future.

A Rocha Uganda is a small organization, struggling to remain in operation due to limited financial resources. How can it convince the powerful to desist from selfish ambitions that block future benefits for people now and in future generations? Looking after our natural environment glorifies God, but most of the church is yet to awaken to such a vision. The struggle is not yet over.

Sara Kaweesa, National Director of A Rocha Uganda

CHAPTER 17

The Church and Sustainable Cities in East Asia

David Gould

Some wandered in desert wastelands,
finding no way to a city where they could settle.
They were hungry and thirsty,
and their lives ebbed away.
Then they cried out to the LORD in their trouble,
and he delivered them from their distress.
He led them by a straight way
to a city where they could settle.

Psalm 107:4–7

The cities of the future will face many challenges. Here are four of them—rapid growth, food insecurity, unsustainable consumption, and greater impacts from hazards. First, *rapid growth*: it is estimated that by 2050, some 70 percent of the world's population, about 6.3 billion people, will be living in cities—an increase of 2.6 billion from 2011. Asia's urban population is projected to increase by 1.4 billion.[1] China alone is planning and building new and enlarged cities for the 350 million migrants expected to move from rural areas in the period 2005–25.[2] Second, *food insecurity*: farming and fishing yields are declining because of unsustainable practices and climate change, and the resulting degradation of soils, oceans, and fresh water systems.[3] Third, *unsustainable consumption*: the current worldwide rate of *per capita* consumption will have to be halved by mid-century so as to achieve a sustainable global economy.[4] To quote the London *graffito* attributed to the artist Banksy: 'Sorry! The lifestyle you ordered is currently out of stock.' And fourth, *greater impacts from hazards*: many cities of the future will be in areas of high risk of natural hazard: flooding, drought, cyclones, earthquakes, landslides, and volcanic eruptions; other hazards will include severe atmospheric and water pollution, and toxic waste. These hazards and their likely impacts will be particularly severe in many of East Asia's large cities.[5]

In 1968, Francis Schaeffer wrote *Death in the City*, a seminal critique of urban cultures that attempt to solve their problems without reference to God.[6] Since then, these problems have multiplied—yet the nature of our predicament has not changed. We still live in a broken world, alienated by our sin from God, from each other, from ourselves, and from the rest of creation. We are still dependent on the gospel, which is 'the power of God that brings salvation to everyone who believes' (Romans 1:16); and we still look for *substantial healing* through faith in Christ for all four kinds of alienation, while we await the renewal of all things at Christ's return.[7] In the light of the challenges that are now confronting us, we must heed the call to 'urgent and prophetic ecological responsibility' that was addressed to the church by the Lausanne Movement in 2010.[8] This chapter explores some aspects of what this might mean for missional churches in the cities of East Asia.

A welcoming city

Some wandered in desert wastelands, finding no way to a city where they could settle. (Ps 107:4)

Figure 1: A typical scene from the Greater Jakarta Metropolitan Area. (Photograph: David Gould)

Cities attract newcomers from their hinterlands and from abroad with the prospect of good jobs, further education, better services, and more interesting lifestyles. Many of the early immigrants to Singapore came from coastal provinces in China affected by famine; their successors come from many parts of East and South Asia and beyond—to provide labour for the service, construction, and manufacturing industries, and talents for the high-end business, education, research, and service sectors. It has become one of a number of global cities that compete internationally for a limited pool of such talents.

However, migrants have housing, food, sanitation, and other needs—and put pressure on cities which are often already overcrowded. There is frequently tension between them and existing residents. Some cities have found ways to control the numbers of immigrants and often make clear distinctions between short-term migrant workers and longer-term settlers. Others—such as the rapidly growing cities of Jakarta, Manila, Bangkok, Shanghai, Yangon, and Ho Chi Minh City—find such control problematic, not least because they are in larger nations where much of the immigration is internal. It is these cities that can be expected to attract many of the *ecological migrants* who will be displaced from rural areas by flooding, drought, soil degradation, and so on.[9] In 2010–11 alone, 42 million people in Asia were displaced by extreme weather events.[10]

Whether as a result of government policy, cultural differences, or their overwhelming numbers, migrants may receive a very limited welcome in the cities. They are often separated from their immediate and extended families—and many of them come and go, following short-term employment opportunities. Such transience and the attrition of public places discourage new community life in the city. So there is a significant opportunity for the churches to be missional by welcoming the stranger and making the city a place of *radical hospitality*.[11] A missional church is one where the whole membership is involved in some aspect of mission, so that mission is not a *function* of the church but its *essential nature*.[12] Even in jurisdictions that do not tolerate public expressions of faith, there can be tacit acceptance of community initiatives by non-government groups and agencies, including churches. This may result from pragmatic considerations such as the lack of funding for investment and welfare provision, but also from the search for the *harmonious society*, which encourages initiatives at a local level.[13] Christianity is being welcomed in some jurisdictions as a source of beneficial morality.[14]

Examples of a missional approach to welcoming the stranger include churches in Singapore and Hong Kong with a ministry to migrants, often based on common ethnicity. They minister through evangelism and discipleship, help-lines, skills training, soup kitchens, counselling, legal and medical assistance, and social and cultural activities. In Manila, Bukang Liwayway (Dawn for the Poor) seeks to foster a holistic church movement among the urban poor; its work includes developing cooperatives and businesses for self-sufficiency, and planting churches within the urban poor squatter areas.

A sustainable city

They founded a city where they could settle. They sowed fields and planted vineyards that yielded a fruitful harvest. (Psalm 107:36–37)

In cities with effective controls on immigration, migrants may be trained in their home communities to provide the skilled labour required by the cities' businesses etc—for instance, some Singapore construction companies have training camps for tradesmen in Bangladesh. In other cities, migrants often come to compete in the urban job market without such training. In both situations, there is scope for migrants to find new applications in the city for their agricultural and related craft-based skills, to help cities become more sustainable in food production. They can also be trained to help develop low-cost reproducible solutions to the chronic lack of affordable power, clean water, and waste management in many of Asia's large cities.

Half of Shanghai's pork and poultry, 60 percent of its vegetables, and 90 percent of its milk and eggs come from the city and its outskirts. Elsewhere in Asia, 80 percent of Hanoi's fresh vegetables come from farms within and around the city.[15] In more densely developed cities, *vertical farming* can produce up to a five-fold increase in output compared with *soil-based farming*, given the same land area.[16] Even in city areas with high land values, there can be significant amounts of fallow land reserved for future development. As concerns for food security grow, it may be possible to negotiate short-term leases with municipal or state owners of such land, as part of a strategy for increasing urban food production.

Many large cities face huge infrastructure and public health challenges. In Manila, for example, electric power is more expensive than in many first world cities; bottled water is a necessity in the absence of potable water mains; the drainage infrastructure is often blocked with plastic and other waste; and there is severe atmospheric pollution. As a result, unsafe power connections are made, so that death by electrocution is common during the frequent severe flooding, and water-borne and respiratory diseases are widespread.

These and other concerns were explored in a prize-winning entry for the 2012 Singapore railway corridor ideas competition.[17] This entry proposed the following new uses for the state-owned land and derelict buildings adjacent to the northern end of the railway corridor in a rather neglected part of the city well away from the vibrant city centre at its southern end:

- an urban farmers' market and food co-op, selling food from local farms, and educating city dwellers in urban food production techniques;

- a forum for urban sustainability: a place for invention, experimentation, failure, and breakthrough where start-up businesses, students from nearby colleges, and others can explore and share solutions for sustainable urban living, remedies for different forms of pollution, and recycling and up-cycling of industrial, building, organic, and electronic waste;

- a gateway to the nearby north coast, where visitors can be introduced to the significant mangrove ecology and contribute as volunteers to its conservation.

These uses will encourage regeneration and fuller community life in a relatively undeveloped part of the island, and help to generate cost-effective and transferable solutions for other cities in East Asia.

One important aspect of community life is the passing on of wisdom from one generation to the next—a strong tradition in the cultures of East Asia. For example, on one of our walks, we met a man who told us about the medicinal and nutritional benefits of what to us looked like weeds springing up along the railway corridor. His delight in simple things was infectious. Such knowledge used to be handed down in the villages (*kampongs*) of pre-urban Singapore, and could be shared again among community gardeners in the modern housing estates.

Combining a farmers' market and food co-op with a forum for urban sustainability will encourage exploration of radical solutions for food production and alternative technology for sustainable urban living. These are urgent needs: for instance, in many parts of East Asia, the reduction of fish yields and the difficulties in meeting the demand for meat necessitate the further exploration of vegetable protein sources. In addition, the growing inadequacy and unpredictability of water supplies require the development of aquaculture, hydroponics, and similar techniques to reduce water consumption while increasing the recycling of nutrients. The use of contaminated water for irrigation has raised food safety concerns, and has created the need for cheap and efficient methods of water testing and filtration.[18] Showcasing sustainable local food production and alternative technology will encourage community and home-based initiatives throughout Singapore and beyond.

It is hoped that the inclusion of a gateway to the north coast mangrove will help ensure its survival. Singapore has long prided itself in being a *garden city*. This idea has matured into a *city in a garden*, and recently it has been proposed that Singapore should be seen as a *city in a wilderness*, in which greater emphasis is given to conserving and celebrating the remaining forests, wetlands, mangroves, and coral reefs.[19] This recognises the importance of giving city dwellers opportunities to stay connected with such natural ecologies and so mitigate their *ecological homelessness*.[20]

The success of this proposal will depend on its low-cost base, careful negotiations, and trust building with the authorities—and its ability and willingness to move and adapt to other sites, as and when required. There are precedents in highly regulated cities for temporary, low-cost facilities on fallow land, such as the well-managed housing camps for migrant workers in Singapore.

In addition to exploring new uses for neglected land in highly regulated cities, much creativity is being brought to unofficial land use in large areas of the cities of East Asia. One example is the Code River Settlement in Jogjakarta, where a priest working with architectural students helped a squatter community to transform its settlement.[21] Houses were repaired and decorated with abstract patterns derived from local culture, and a *third space* was created for pre-school and other community uses.[22] A *de facto* settlement became an officially accepted part of the city, attracting grants from the municipal authority for further improvements such as flood defences and tree planting. Large areas of squatter settlements in the cities are on land marginalized by flooding and other risks, simply because other land is unavailable. As the number of urban immigrants increases, so too will the impacts on them of natural disasters. These present huge challenges in providing adequate housing on marginal land in Asian cities, so that hope-based responses—such as the transformation of the Code River Settlement—become all the more significant and inspiring.

Another example is Gawad Kalinga—a movement committed to building integrated, holistic, and sustainable communities in slum areas—first in the Philippines and now in Indonesia, Cambodia, and Papua New Guinea. Its construction projects seek to ensure security of tenure for community members, and to use their *sweat equity*, as well as volunteers from outside the community, to construct low-cost housing and community buildings that comply with national building codes.[23] Some cities struggle to develop adequate infrastructure to service their rapid expansion. It is therefore necessary for such local initiatives to include this in their projects, at least to the extent of providing safe water, power, waste management, and recycling systems.

Elsewhere in East Asia governments are now concerned to develop green technologies and industries. In South Korea, for instance, the development of chemical, ship-building, and other heavy industries over the last forty years has resulted in severe ecological degradation.

Since 2008 the government of South Korea has responded to this by developing a *low-carbon, green growth* strategy.[24] There is a growing desire within the churches to contribute to this movement toward a sustainable economy. This has led to protests on ecological grounds against the Four Rivers Restoration Project, and to positive action such as the Green Church 21 program.[25] This encourages churches to adopt practices that foster a more sustainable way of life, such as trading cars for bicycles, planting trees and vegetable gardens, and installing solar panels. Bible studies emphasize the scriptural basis for taking better care of the planet.[26]

In Malaysia, some church groups, such as the Gereja Presbyterian Malaysia, are exploring the theology and practice of creation care, and encourage the appointment of creation care champions in local churches. Much can be learned from traditions such as *satoyama*—the use of marginal land in Japan; from the zero-waste economy of pre-industrial China; and from more recent initiatives such as the Mottainai Movement in Japan, the Transition Town Movement and Edible Landscapes in the United Kingdom, and Edible Estates in United States and elsewhere.[27] Co-benefits can include the transformation of work: for instance, some at least of the many grass-trimmers who maintain the fallow land in Asian cities could be re-trained as urban gardeners. And, in the spirit of Jeremiah's call to the exiles in Babylon (Jeremiah 29:5), enabling migrants to plant gardens can encourage them to identify with their new, and usually temporary, home.

A hopeful city

Let them exalt him in the assembly of the people. (Psalm 107:32)

Transience and pressures of space in the cities also impact church life, making it more difficult to build and maintain church centres. Those who succeed can find that the costs outweigh the benefits in terms of funding, personnel, and distraction from core ministry objectives. So, instead of building church centres, it may often be more appropriate to rent spaces, including fallow and marginal land and buildings that can be used for a variety of events throughout the week. These church spaces can be shared with other organizations such as vocational training schools. Recently in Singapore, the government relaxed zoning controls to allow for 'limited and non-exclusive' religious use of industrial facilities.[28] By embracing such short-term, low-cost approaches to resourcing ministry, combining community services, food production, disciple-making, training, and worship, the church can practise an incarnational presence within the city, and model a life based on grace, hope, and simplicity. This is one example of what a *creative future* might look like for the church in the city, as opposed to *conventional* and *counter* futures, which tend to lead to irrelevance or unfruitful confrontation.[29] Behind these alternative futures is a spiritual battle within the church, a battle for our imaginations. This battle is at least as old as the Babylonian exile: 'Babylon had a deep grip—a death grip—on the imaginations of the Jews. They could not imagine outside the purview of empire.'[30] So, what does it mean for us to reject the values and priorities of our dominant, consumerist culture, to 'come out of Babylon', the city of 'excessive luxuries' (Revelation 18:3, 4), and to live kingdom-based lives in the city?

All cities have *ecological footprints* that extend well beyond their built-up areas.[31] City dwellers often have little feeling for their dependence on their city's hinterland, and so find it difficult to understand and welcome the newcomers who flood into the city from rural areas. Creative responses to these challenges could include urban church communities quantifying, monitoring, and moving towards sustainable and equitable ecological footprints; and extending urban mission to *welcome the stranger* from outside the city, for gospel witness, discipleship, fellowship, and shared learning about sustainable living in the city and beyond.

Paul's missional practice in Ephesus has much to teach us about reaching out to visitors from outside the city: Paul 'had discussions daily in the lecture hall of Tyrannus. This went on for two years, so that all the Jews and Greeks who lived in the province of Asia heard the word of the Lord' (Acts 19:9–10). Paul based himself in a provincial capital where he could meet many visitors from the towns and rural districts in that province; he chose a public hall in the heart of the city (next to the fish market!) that was rented, not bought; and the hall was a relatively small and intimate space, enabling interaction between the speaker and all those attending. Of course, Paul's methods were suited to a predominantly Greek culture where public debate was an important part of daily life (as described in Acts 17:16–34). In many parts of Asia, it is not customary to engage a speaker in debate in a large group—so instead, plenary sessions for teaching can be followed by meetings and workshops in small groups. In these group meetings, particular needs and opportunities can be discussed, leading to the development of ongoing mentoring and prayer-partner relationships. Such meetings can be run by cell groups in homes and, where permitted, in cafés and karaoke bars, for example. Some of these cell groups can grow into *cell churches*, with the resources to engage in significant ways in initiatives such as the railway corridor proposal described above, without being tied to a fixed church centre.[32]

Here is a tentative model for how missional churches with a heart for hopeful, sustainable life in the city might work in practice.

- Migrants to the cities and others are welcomed into the fellowship of believers and come to faith in Christ; they are discipled to grow to maturity.

- Training options provided by the city churches could include plenary classes and group workshops in topics such as:

  - biblical exposition, doctrine, spirituality, ethics, and values

  - church planting, preaching, youth work, etc

  - sustainable agriculture, aquaculture, animal husbandry, and forestry

  - recycling and up-cycling, waste and water management, and renewable energy solutions

  - alternative technology

  - missional business practice

  - training of trainers, and so on

- Those who return to their rural home communities will be encouraged and trained to share their new faith and skills. Some will seek to build relationships of trust with *people of peace* in local government and other organizations; to establish or develop local businesses; and to contribute to sustainable local food production and training. These initiatives will reduce the need for others to migrate to the cities.[33]

- Where possible, friends from the city churches will visit the home communities of the migrants to learn from and about local needs and opportunities, and to foster links between the city and rural church communities.

- Some migrant workers will return regularly to work in the cities. They will be encouraged to renew and deepen their fellowship with the city church, take part in further training, and contribute to the training of others.[34]

- This approach to training will foster a two-way learning process that will help to combine the best of traditional wisdom and practice and new, appropriate technology in both rural areas and the cities. This will affirm and celebrate the complementary gifting and experience of those who come from different rural and urban backgrounds.

- The city churches could also provide support services such as caring for urban migrant children, children's educational advice and training, microfinance advice and loans, marriage courses, and so on.

This model for a missional church will require the continuing development and teaching of a more distinctively Asian biblical theology of integral mission, including creation care. This could explore such themes as the reverence for all forms of life, the significance of place, and the primacy of good relationships, in many Asian cultures; as well as critiquing the dualism of much Western theology. Recent events that have contributed to this exploration have included the forum held in 2009 at the Asian Theological Seminary (ATS) in Manila on *The Earth is the Lord's and Everything in it*.[35] Themes covered included a biblical theology of land and its application in Mindanao; tree planting as part of a strategy for holistic development; and '*theology for the garbage bin*'. ATS is now including creation care in its curriculum, including a course on *transformational theology*. In 2012, the Asia Theological Association held a consultation on Scripture at which a paper was presented on 'Evangelicals and the Environment'. This made a plea to 'go beyond stewardship' in developing an *eco-justice* response to the ecological crisis, in which 'caring for the earth and caring for humanity, particularly for the poor and marginalized, are inextricably linked together'.[36]

Can any of this make a significant difference? The early church grew from a few hundred believers in a remote province to become the dominant faith movement in the Roman Empire. It did this with little or no secular power, and without dedicated church buildings. Rather it was made up of individuals gathering in small communities who lived hopefully as Christians in their world as salt, light, and yeast. They did not 'despise the day of small things' (Zechariah 4:10). Their trust in their Lord's goodness, their love for each other and for their neighbours, and their courage in the face of persecution, famine, and enforced migration, gradually transformed the dominant values of the societies in which they lived.[37]

Psalm 107 is full of a hope based on the Lord's goodness. Because 'he sent out his word and healed them', we can 'give thanks to the LORD for his unfailing love' (Psalm 107:20–21). Our hope is based on 'God's good news, through the cross and resurrection of Jesus Christ, for individual persons, for society, and for creation. All three are broken and suffering because of sin; all three are included in the redeeming love and mission of God; all three must be part of the comprehensive mission of God.'[38] The model for city churches that I have described should be motivated, in the words of Richard Bauckham, both by 'ultimate hope' in the 'final achievement of all God's purposes for his creation' and by 'proximate hopes for the temporal future, because God honours what we do by making of it more than we can make of it ourselves.'[39] In our busyness we must continue to consider the great love of the Lord (Ps 107:43) and make it the foundation for all we do, seeking to share it with others, and so bring glory to his name.

A ROCHA LIVING WATERWAYS

More than 50 percent of the world's population lives in cities, so urban sustainability is key to our planet's future. As a church minister in multiracial Southall, London, I noticed the damaging effect of a poor and polluted urban environment. A local government report from 1998 spoke of 'a lack of greenery, open space, clean air and environmental awareness—all of which contribute to a lack of confidence and pride in the area'.

Nearby was a ninety-acre area of open space known as 'the Minet tip'. It was an eyesore, with illegal fly-tipping, motorbike scrambling, and an unregulated car-boot sale. The resultant tons of rubbish and quagmire of mud did nothing to inspire local pride. Walking around Minet, I sensed God asking, 'How do you think I feel about this place?' I sensed creation's groaning to be set free (Rom 8:21), and felt a desire to seek the healing of the land (2 Chron 7:14).

My wife and I had been inspired by A Rocha, whose projects care both for wildlife habitats and local communities. So, we sought the transformation of the Minet site to launch A Rocha UK's first project: A Rocha Living Waterways, envisioning 'a greener, cleaner, Southall and Hayes'. From initial plans in 1998, through the project launch in 2001, to the eventual opening of a transformed Minet Country Park in 2003, the project took five years of prayer, sacrifice, and hard work.

The land belonged to the London Borough of Hillingdon, and there was pressure for commercial development. However, a community consultation showed overwhelming support for an accessible, green open space. A Rocha UK provided vision, ecological consultancy, and the link between council and community, involving locals in clearing rubbish and planting trees. Since work was completed, A Rocha's involvement has continued in conservation, environmental education, and community engagement. Thousands of schoolchildren visit each year, and the park is used daily by hundreds of local people. Wildlife enjoys it too, with breeding kingfishers and woodpeckers, newts, dragonflies, foxes and butterflies. A Rocha's local community projects include a successful urban food-growing initiative which attracts many people from diverse refugee backgrounds. Most significantly, Minet has become a sign of hope for local people. Change is possible for even the most damaged and polluted areas, and for hopeless and hurting lives. A Rocha Living Waterways is a story of *good news*, perhaps even a small sign of God's kingdom: 'your will be done, *on earth* as it is in heaven' (Matt 6:10, emphasis added).

Dave Bookless, Director of Theology, A Rocha International

CHAPTER 18

Creation Care as a Ministry of Reconciliation: A Framework for Environmental Missions

Susan D Emmerich

For God was pleased to have all his fullness dwell in him,
and through him to reconcile to himself all things,
whether things on earth or things in heaven,
by making peace through his blood, shed on the cross.
Colossians 1:19–20

Many parts of Christendom have woken up to the biblical mandate to care for creation. However, they have not always fully worked out—nor communicated to the church, its institutions and missionaries—how creation care forms a part of the broader gospel mandate. This discussion is critical, since conflicts over use of natural resources, the negative impact of unsustainable economies, and the increasingly visible effects of climate change are fostering conditions that can quickly escalate into violence. Communities and peoples are left divided; trails of long-lasting and far-reaching alienation, bitterness, and brokenness are also common.

It is this world in which Christian missions must make their way. Andy Crouch, writer on Christianity and culture, comments, 'There is no other resource for dealing with brokenness that's as powerful as the gospel lived out creatively and effectively in the context of local culture. The gospel gives us enough hope to enter into these very difficult, seemingly hopeless situations.'[1] The relationship of creation care to the gospel stems from God's plan for the reconciliation of *all things* in Christ—including not only the reconciliation of individual persons to God, but also of people towards each other, and the reconciliation of the whole creation with God. Our human ministry of reconciliation flows out of God's work and includes each of these three dimensions—the spiritual, the social, and the ecological. This in turn enables effective healing for all manner of brokenness.

Missionaries are uniquely poised to live out the gospel and provide hope in seemingly hopeless situations. They are able to address conflicts over resources in a way that reconciles individuals to God, to one another, and to the creation through Christ. This three-fold ministry of reconciliation is rooted in 2 Corinthians 5:19 and Colossians 1:19–20. Creation care as a ministry of reconciliation should seek to 'address the world of sin, suffering, injustice and creation disorder in a way that transforms the totality of people's personal and social responsibilities', thereby positively transforming society and the creation.[2] This broader concept of reconciliation is becoming increasingly clear in terms of biblical studies and theology, but the question remains: what does the broadened concept of reconciliation mean and what does it look like in practice? Moreover, how can the practice of creation care as a three-fold ministry of reconciliation contribute to the concept of *environmental missions*?

To answer these questions we take up the story of the decades-long battle over crab fishery regulations and pollution in the Chesapeake Bay— and particularly on Tangier Island, Virginia—on the east coast of the United States of America. The battle eventually began to ease through a process of reconciliation, which I helped facilitate, between God, the watermen of Tangier, and their perceived enemy, the Chesapeake Bay Foundation (CBF)—an environmental group concerned about the destruction of the bay and its fisheries.

Background: Tangier Island, the environmental conflict and the need for reconciliation

Tangier Island, located in the Virginia waters of the Chesapeake Bay, is a marshy island only 3.4 miles long and 1.5 miles wide. It is an hour by boat from the mainland of Maryland, and about three hours by car from Washington, DC. It is considered to be 'an island out of time' by author and former *Baltimore Sun Times* columnist, Tom Horton. The islanders are known to cling tenaciously to cherished traditions, conventional folk wisdom, and their motto, *semper eadem*—'always the same'. Tangier's economy is almost entirely centred on the harvesting of blue crabs—hence the term *watermen* rather than *fishermen*—as they earn their livelihood out on the water, but not necessarily from fishing. The two churches on the island are the centre of community life—as they were 200 years ago. Of the 700 inhabitants, 84 percent consider themselves conservative evangelical Christians.

Conflict over the fisheries has been a part of Tangier's history since the oyster wars in the mid-1800s, and the islanders have suffered environmental, social, and spiritual brokenness and alienation as a result. Today, fishery conflicts erupt over the oyster and blue crab regulations that are promulgated by state boards of fisheries. In Virginia, regulations are issued by the Virginia Marine Resources Commission, and influenced by proposals from environmental groups such as the Chesapeake Bay Foundation (CBF) whose motto is: Save the Bay!

Figure 1: A display of faith on a Tangier fishing hut. (Photograph: Jeffrey Pohorski, Skunkfilm Productions, used with permission)

In 1995, conflict erupted over a blue crab regulation proposed by CBF that would have created a crab sanctuary—and put watermen out of work for the winter. Irate watermen placed signs against CBF on their crab shanties and along the island's channels. The regulation also led to violence on a neighbouring island when a CBF shed was burned to the ground. After these events, I went to Tangier to gain a better understanding of the causes of the conflict between CBF and the Tangier islanders, and to see if a faith-based approach to stewardship could provide a bridge to the two groups working together to help save the fishery and the culture of the watermen.

I attempted to build close relationships with the people of Tangier, living at the same economic level as the majority on the island; respected their cultural mores and taboos; and listened to and served the people of Tangier. Through this and my studies I discovered that the women, pastors, and lay church leaders were important change agents, and that the church was the most powerful institution for change. It also showed that the biblical ethic of caring for God's creation provided the Tangier islanders with the basis for *living right* with the environment. CBF, a secular group, had overlooked the truth that the Tangier islanders' faith was an important part of the way they viewed the world. They had thereby disrespected the cultural mores and taboos of the community and had failed to earn the right to be heard by the islanders. These factors, along with CBF's support for crab regulations, led the islanders to fear and mistrust them. It also led to feelings of apathy and despair about the situation.

Following this ethnographic study, I returned to Tangier Island to help the community develop a faith-based stewardship effort that addressed their felt need of maintaining the watermen's livelihoods and culture in the context of their biblical faith. I adopted the position of a *paracletic change agent*, exhorting, encouraging, comforting, helping, and advocating—sometimes on their behalf, sometimes on the behalf of the environmentalists.[3] I thus shared the biblical message of faith and hope related to caring for God's creation; better stewarding their fishery and island; and loving, reconciling and working with their neighbours, the environmentalists. This was communicated through pulpit messages, Bible studies, one-on-one discussions, and community meetings. The message, however, was not readily received by all, and some islanders ostracized the Tangier stewardship leaders, as well threatening me, as I sought to facilitate and mediate.

In just three months, however, I witnessed a dramatic transformation of the Tangier islanders' minds and hearts toward God, toward their neighbours and environmentalists, and towards creation. Some of the islanders committed to covenants with God to be better stewards of the fishery and island, to exhibit the virtue of contentment, and to implement the three Rs—reducing, reusing, and recycling—in their homes and island. Some watermen also reconciled with Chesapeake Bay environmentalists and began to work together with them to save the bay. Lastly, the islanders created a Vision Plan for their community, based on their biblical understanding of stewardship, and two new organizations—The Tangier Watermen's Stewardship for the Chesapeake (TaSC) to implement the vision, and Families Actively Involved in Improving Tangier's Heritage (FAIITH) to engage in fishery policy.

The ministry of reconciliation and the Cape Town Commitment

The events that occurred among the Tangier islanders during the faith-based stewardship effort are an example of the transforming 'ministry of reconciliation' (2 Cor 5:18). For three decades, a series of environmental groups and individuals had promoted environmental stewardship on Tangier Island. However, these views had little effect on the Tangiermen's worldview and behaviour toward the fishery because they failed to take into account that *faith* was the lens through which the Tangiermen viewed the world. When the future of the watermen's culture and their conflict with environmentalists were addressed in the context of the good news of the *gospel*, then hearts and minds were transformed; fear, anger, and apathy were replaced by hope and action.

The *Cape Town Commitment* similarly offers a lens through which creation care advocates can consider their efforts. It is a lens of faith, of invoking the Lord Jesus Christ as 'the creator, owner, sustainer, redeemer and heir of all creation.'[4] The *Cape Town Commitment* brings creation care into particularly sharp focus when it speaks in terms of reconciliation: 'In his death on the cross, Jesus took our sin upon himself in our place, bearing its full cost, penalty and shame, defeated death and the powers of evil, and accomplished the reconciliation and redemption of all creation.'[5] If we consider our faith in Christ as a set of binoculars through which we view creation care conflicts, then reconciliation can be seen as the eyepiece adjustor by which we bring the problem and solutions into clear resolution.[6]

'We love the story the gospel tells', the *Cape Town Commitment* declares.[7] It concludes with a reference to reconciliation in not one, but three, dimensions:

> God accomplished the reconciliation of believers with himself and with one another across all boundaries and enmities. God also accomplished his purpose of the ultimate reconciliation of all creation, and in the bodily resurrection of Jesus has given us the first fruits of the new creation. 'God was in Christ reconciling the world [*kosmos*] to himself' [a reference to 2 Corinthians 5:19].[8]

Hence, the three-fold ministry of reconciliation is with God, with our neighbours, and also with creation. 'We love the mission of God', the *Commitment* also declares.[9] Under this heading, it states:

> The whole Bible reveals the mission of God to bring all things in heaven and earth into unity under Christ, reconciling them through the blood of his cross. In fulfilling his mission, God will transform the creation broken by sin and evil into the new creation in which there is no more sin or curse.

In two statements about the core values of the Lausanne Movement—the gospel and the mission of God—creation care is included and reconciliation is the framework. As Colossians 1:19–20 declares, 'For God was pleased to have all his fullness dwell in him, and through him to reconcile to himself all things, whether things on earth or things in heaven, by making peace through his blood, shed on the cross.' This verse, so important to John Stott in his thinking about Christian missions, carries an essential message in this era of personal, social, and environmental disruption—that *integral missions* today should seek not only to reconcile or restore individuals' relationship to God, but also to one another and to the creation 'as all three are broken and suffering because of sin ... and must be part of the comprehensive mission of God's people.'[10]

Creation care is, therefore, part of the ministry of reconciliation. It stems, first and foremost, from realizing *all* the dimensions of God's saving work in Christ—our relationship with the Lord, with others (Matthew 19:19; Jeremiah 9:23–24), and with creation. With this proposition in mind, we will now explore the results of the Tangier stewardship initiative where creation care was implemented as a ministry of reconciliation.

The Tangier Island case: results from a three-fold ministry of reconciliation

Although we saw many fruits of reconciliation on Tangier, it was not a complete success. Perhaps the most significant setback was our inability to obtain the support of the President of the Tangier Watermen's Association. A professed non-Christian, he made it clear from the start that he would not support any effort connected with the church. This led to a power struggle between the president's followers and those in the stewardship initiative about who should represent the Tangier watermen before the state board of fisheries. Many were harassed, ostracized, and threatened, and one of the stewardship leaders was wrongly led to believe that CBF had lied to the FAIITH and TaSC groups regarding their stand on a particular fishery regulation. The stewardship leader responded by sending a letter to the newspaper condemning CBF. This escalated the tension in the already fragile relationship between CBF and the FAIITH and TaSCs group—although the tensions eased years later.

After the initiative, I hoped that CBF would bring in changes based on the lessons they learned from the stewardship initiative—such as the importance of communicating their message in a culturally sensitive manner, obtaining feedback from an adequate number of watermen before deciding on fishery regulations, and developing long-lasting relationships with people in the communities in which they reside. Instead, CBF's immediate response was to reject any close ties with the watermen because that might have prevented them from recommending the tough regulations needed to save the fishery. However, they continued to work with the FAIITH and TaSC groups and, a few years later, hired more watermen from Tangier and other islands. They also aimed to be more culturally sensitive while working among watermen communities.

Some good will was shown by both Christian and non-Christian islanders— abiding by the laws, actively engaging the public on fishery regulations, and reconciling and working with environmentalists. However, several factors beyond the control of Tangier watermen significantly affected their ability to make a living over the following fourteen years. These factors included fertilizer and manure runoff, illegal harvesting, reduction in crabbing permits, tighter fishery regulations in 2008, and crab imports from Louisiana and Asia. Many Tangier watermen had to find other work on tug boats down the bay, or move to the mainland. However, the blue crab population began to turn in 2012 with a 66 percent increase in population—the highest level since 1993.[11] It appears that the fishery regulations instituted in 2008 are working to bring back the crab populations. In addition, as a result of TaSC's effort to get watermen hired by the state of Virginia and Maryland to place *spat*, or baby oyster seedlings, in the right environment within the Chesapeake Bay, the oyster fishery has come back enough to provide some oystering during the winter months. Moreover, according to James 'Ooker' Eskridge, 'most of the crab processing plants now only buy crabs from Chesapeake Bay watermen, rather than from Louisiana or Asia.' This has helped create more markets for the Tangier watermen and, although still a struggle, times are a bit better for them.[12]

The initiative was ultimately successful in that most, if not all, of the personal relationships were mended from the divisions that arose during the stewardship initiative. The majority of the 2020 Vision Plan's provisions were implemented, and, according to Susan Parks, Director of TaSC, and Carlene Shores, Director of FAIITH, 'both groups ceased to continue after five years because they had fulfilled their main purposes—to instil a stewardship ethic among the community and to create a better working relationship with the CBF and the Virginia Marine Resources Commission (state board of fisheries).'[13] Some of the islanders are still hesitant to use the term *stewardship* in public on the island for fear of creating dissension; however, most of the covenanters still maintain their pledge and support further efforts. If one judges the success of the stewardship's effort solely on the basis of whether watermen were able to get crab permits or whether the stewardship organizations continued, then it could be viewed only as a qualified success. While there were repeated setbacks and breakdown in relationships, the overall Tangier initiative succeeded if one uses the appropriate *missional* definition of success. I am proposing that the practice of creation care as a *three-fold ministry of reconciliation* can not only define environmental missions—but can also be a valuable measure of its effectiveness.

Reconciliation: a measure of success for environmental missions

The Tangier initiative provides several examples of a broadened concept of reconciliation. Perhaps even more importantly, the initiative provides a biblically-based measure of effectiveness for environmental missions.

Reconciliation with God

As I came alongside the community for this time, my aim was to communicate the truth of God's revelation and the biblical principles related to caring for creation, loving one's neighbour (especially the CBF environmentalists), and submitting to the civil authorities and civil laws. This was achieved through Bible studies and a missionary message given at a combined service of both churches on the island. People were called to repentance for their unlawfulness and unloving behaviour toward the environmentalists, and encouraged to submit every part of their life to Christ as loving and obedient disciples. Both men and women repented and recovenanted with God. For some, reconciling their broken relationship with God fostered environmental, economic, and social responsibility. For others, it was a matter of renewal or deepening their relationship with God. One thing is certain: reconciliation with God through Christ opened their minds to new ideas—such as their relationship with creation and their responsibility for it, diversifying their economy, engaging in the political process, and relating well to environmentalists and other neighbours.

Reconciliation with creation

During the combined service of the two churches, many watermen committed to a Watermen's Stewardship Covenant in which they agreed to be better stewards of God's creation, to obey civil laws including fishery and pollution regulations, and to commit to brotherly accountability. The morning after the service, many citizens cleaned up their yards and streets, as well as the island's creeks and docks. To signify their change of heart, the watermen covenanters flew a red ribbon on their boats symbolizing Christ's shed blood on the cross. As a result, these watermen no longer threw their trash on the island or overboard into the Chesapeake Bay, and no longer overharvested the fishery—taking undersized crabs or crabbing before the allotted time. One of the longstanding spiritual strongholds among the watermen, according to the pastors, was the inability to trust God for their income. By taking the covenant, the watermen and their families took a step of faith, placing their work life under Christ's lordship and trusting him to provide the crab harvest to meet their income needs. This change of heart led to many things—one of which was that some watermen were willing to diversifying their income base by farming eels and clams, as well as self-imposing certain regulations that would ensure a sustainable crabbing fishery. The overnight transformation among many of the people was amazing, and the visible results in creation were undeniable.

In addition to the changes among the watermen, some Tangier women acknowledged some unlawful practices and harmful habits. Some repented of illegal crabmeat processing in their homes; others rejected excessive

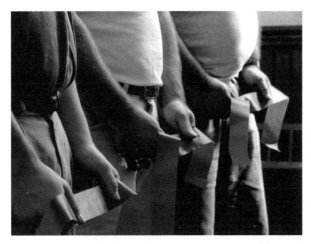

Figure 2: Tangier fishermen receiving the red ribbons they promised to display on their boats. (Photograph: Jeffrey Pohorski, Skunkfilm Productions, used with permission.)

consumption habits and discontent with what material things they had. They agreed to the Women's Stewardship Commitment, and began to reuse and recycle materials, to change consumption patterns by placing less demands on their husbands, and to teach stewardship principles such as contentment and simple living to their children.[14] Several women began planning to ensure they could stay on the island. Some created businesses that are still thriving today; others developed crafts to sell; and still others went to college in order to obtain degrees in healthcare. Those families that heeded the stewardship message prepared for the future and, therefore, fared much better than during the period of crab shortage.

Reconciliation with environmentalists and other neighbours

Some took to heart the admonition to 'love your neighbour' amidst the conflict with CBF environmentalists and those islanders who worked for CBF. The Tangier islanders also learned that the Bible term *neighbour* applied to everyone whom they affected, as well as all those who affected them. It led to a meeting between the Tangiermen and CBF officials where each repented for their actions toward the other, asked for the others' forgiveness, forgave and reconciled with the understanding that they would begin to trust one another in order to save the fishery. Their *neighbours* now encompassed people who existed beyond their island community, including farmers who lived up the bay, mainlanders, and environmentalists. As a result of this paradigm shift, the idea of working for the common good became more at the forefront of their thinking. This led to other fruitful results.

*Figure 3: Bay farmers being shown the way of life of the
fishermen. (Photograph: Jeffrey Pohorski, Skunkfilm
Productions, used with permission.)*

Public engagement for the common good

Inspired by a renewed sense of hope based on their Christian faith, Tangier residents became more politically, economically, and socially active on behalf of their community and the entire bay's watershed. With help, they developed a strategic plan for their community called the Tangier 2020 Vision—a unique plan premised on biblical principles of stewardship. Environmentalists from the CBF and other organizations, as well as state officials, were moved by the testimonies of the covenanters given at the final conference, where islanders proudly presented the 2020 Vision plan for their community. The environmentalists, scientists, and state officials were also enlightened that faith is an important lens through which people see the world, and that it is not—as they had assumed—the main hindrance to people accepting an environmental ethic. As a result, CBF hired other Christians to work for them on several island communities. The Tangier islanders' activism also led to the creation of the two grassroots organizations introduced above—Families Actively Involved in Improving Tangier's Heritage (FAIITH) and the Tangier Watermen's Stewardship for the Chesapeake (TaSC). These organizations provided a voice at the policy table to help ensure the passage of just and fair fishery regulations. They also fostered peaceful working relationships with all stakeholders in the bay such that everyone benefitted.

Through TaSC, the Tangiermen reached out to farmers in three states in the Chesapeake Bay and gave their testimonies of what God had revealed to them about creation care, loving your neighbour, and living as obedient disciples of Christ. This, in turn, inspired farmers eight hours north of Tangier to take their own stewardship covenant with God in order to honour Christ and protect their neighbours at the other end of the bay.[15]

The role of the missionary

The role of the missionary or change agent is explained in great detail in other accounts of the Tangier stewardship effort.[16] What deserves emphasis is that achieving the reconciliations and subsequent transformation on Tangier Island entailed great personal sacrifice. At one of my seminars where I teach the methods and approaches used in the Tangier initiative, a professor asked the question, 'Given how difficult this ministry is and the personal sacrifices on the part of the change agent or missionary that are required, why would anyone want to do it?' Scripture provides the answer. First, the entire church is called to the ministry of reconciliation, not just environmental missionaries. Second, as Paul states in Romans 8:19, 'The creation waits in eager expectation for the children of God to be revealed.' Who are these 'children of God?' In the Sermon on the Mount (Matthew 5:9), Jesus declared, 'Blessed are the peacemakers, for they will be called children of God.' In other words, believers who are actively intervening to create peace through the ministry of *reconciliation,* including the creation care mandate, will be acknowledged as the children of God.

My experience with the Tangier initiative, and subsequent outreaches, point to a more biblically grounded definition of success. The true measure of success in environmental missions is relational—building healthy relationships in accordance with the three-fold framework of reconciliation in this world. In addition, we have the hope of our calling which is the final reconciliation of all things—of all creation—when Jesus returns.

Recommendations

What would happen if the mission community established a three-fold ministry of reconciliation as an overarching framework for environmental missions? The answer, in my opinion, is that environmental missions would be based on fostering closer relationships with the Lord, a loving and serving relationship with neighbours, and a caring relationship toward creation. Not only does the ministry of reconciliation describe the dynamics of creation care, it also relates naturally to the way in which Christian missions organizations do their work in the areas of relief and development. At least six recommendations flow from the adoption of this framework for environmental missions.

Relationships

First, environmental missions should be defined in a more holistic, biblical way in light of the three-fold framework, the eschatological hope culminating in Christ's return, and the final reconciliation of all things including the created order. As a result, the measure of effectiveness would be based primarily on building God-honouring relationships. This, in turn, would help guard against discouragement in the creation care movement and maintain an eschatological attitude of hopefulness.

Creation care terminology

Second, *environmental missions* should be adopted as an additional term in creation care ministry (see Chapter 4, 'Environmental Missions: An Introduction'). Environmental missions would be the broader umbrella terminology incorporating references such as creation care or environmental stewardship. This fits better with the accepted approaches used by other mission organizations, particularly those in North America that have *medical missions*.

Training and education

Based on my experience implementing the Tangier initiative, those called to environmental missions as a ministry of reconciliation will need intensive training and education. This will include: 1) formulating a biblically-based worldview that includes an awareness of spiritual strongholds and the power of prayer; 2) cultivating a commitment to civics, citizenship, and the common good; 3) training in conflict management and resolution; 4) educating in participatory action research and community organizing; 5) raising awareness of the problems involved with intercultural communication; and 6) implementing instruction about environmental science, social psychology, and economic and business sustainability.

Spiritual gifts, virtues, and skills

It is important to determine the Christian spiritual gifts, virtues, and skills needed for an environmental missionary and how they could be cultivated. Some examples include the fruits of the spirit: love, joy, peace, patience, kindness, goodness, and, especially for a peacemaker, self control. Moreover, the spiritual gifts of wisdom and knowledge are necessary along with the gift of teaching and pastoring (Ephesians 4:11–13). An environmental missionary must know how to use the word of God for teaching, rebuking, correcting and training in righteousness (2 Timothy 3:16).

Ongoing support for missionaries

Attention should be given to the problems involved in encouraging and sustaining those called to environmental missions as a ministry of reconciliation. Environmental missionaries must have a clear understanding of the hope for the created order, a hope based on the biblical truth that all of creation will be redeemed when Jesus returns. Knowing this truth will help prevent despair among environmental missionaries, given the difficulty of saving many parts of creation that are exploited or under duress. Other important components are: 1) organizing prayer teams; 2) retreating from their battlefront to be spiritually, emotionally and physically renewed; and 3) studying the lives of prominent leaders (Christian and non-Christian) who have made significant contributions to creation care.

Need for exemplars and mentors

The mission community needs to find exemplars and mentors for those who are aspiring to or doing this kind of work. More case studies like the Tangier stewardship initiative need to be found and undertaken to serve as examples of the approach advocated in this chapter. Mentors are critically important in this arena because of the often overwhelming challenges involved and the risk of discouragement, cynicism, and burnout.

Summary

Christians are uniquely poised in this century to live out the gospel and provide hope in seemingly hopeless situations by addressing conflicts over resources in a way that more fully reconciles individuals to God, to one another, and to the creation through Christ. This three-fold ministry of reconciliation is rooted in Scripture, particularly in passages such as 2 Corinthians 5:19 and Colossians 1:19–20. Creation care as a ministry of reconciliation should seek to 'address the world of sin, suffering, injustice and creation disorder in a way that transforms the totality of people's personal and social responsibilities', thereby transforming society and the creation for the better.[17]

The knowledge gained from the Tangier initiative—and from subsequent similar outreaches—supports the idea that the three-fold ministry of reconciliation can act as a valuable framework for future environmental missions, as well as for creation care ministry generally. This proposal offers a holistic approach that fosters new and closer relationships with God, with neighbours, and with the creation. Creation care carried out as a ministry of reconciliation also provides a firm biblical foundation for assessing the effectiveness of environmental missions. In other words, the true measure of environmental mission is in building relationships in light of the three-fold framework of reconciliation, and in the hope of our calling grounded in the final reconciliation of all things—of all creation—when Jesus returns.

The Lausanne Consultation on Creation Care asked how creation care should be regarded in terms of the gospel. My answer is that creation care is a vital part of the ministry of reconciliation that flows directly from working out, in full, the implications of one's relationships with the Lord, with others, and with creation.[18]

Towards a Robust Theology of the Environment

Ken Gnanakan

'[Creation care] is not only biblically justified, but an integral part of our mission and an expression of our worship to God for his wonderful plan of redemption through Jesus Christ.'

Jamaica Call to Action[1]

This book represents considerable diversity, in content and authorship, spanning six continents. Yet all writers focus on one question: What does it mean to say, 'Creation Care is a "gospel issue within the Lordship of Christ"'?[2]

The answer combines faith and action, Scripture's teaching and the need to face pressing ecological issues. The study of the Bible—the original intent, plan, and command to care for creation, the resurrection narratives, and the profound truth that in Christ all things have been reconciled to God—provides the foundation. The *Call to Action* carries a firm conviction: 'We are faced with a crisis that is pressing, urgent, and that must be resolved in our generation.' The 2012 gathering resolved that these together compel us to 'urgent and prophetic ecological responsibility.'[3]

The unanimity to move forward was clear. We reminded ourselves of various areas for adequate preparation, many covered in this work. We focus here on the urgent need for continued 'new and robust theological work'. Jonathan Moo has rightly reminded us in Chapter 2—'In the biblical hope of new creation, we are in fact given the gift of seeing this world with new eyes. We are freed to love and find joy in *nature* as God's good creation—just as the psalmists did; and we are enabled to join alongside all of creation in its praise of God in Christ.' As Las Newman in the Foreword, appropriately states, 'The Christian gospel is a gospel of hope for the life of *the world to come*—a hope that should inform our present reality. The brokenness of our world is set against the background of the truth of God's sovereignty over it and his ultimate plans for redeeming the world.'

So our theologies are written from the perspective of a 'new creation', seeing it through 'new eyes' with a concrete hope of what God will do in the future. This book examines aspects of our current creation and how to move closer to this new creation. We need to combine our approach into a more 'integrated theology of creation care', in which creation itself is an integrated whole.

Creation is a whole, the gospel is a whole, and everything in which we live, move, and have our being is an integrated whole. Creation is all about such intricate interconnections that make up God's glorious handiwork. As we bring together various theological themes, we discover more of the magnificent mosaic God has already orchestrated as a masterpiece. We see the Bible's unmistakable holism. Such a theology—we will discover—is more than merely 'a gospel issue'. It is thoroughly integral to the whole gospel. Our creation-based mission, our creation care, and all else we do in the name of God must display this strong, integrated, holistic foundation.

Holism and dualism

The Bible is essentially holistic. Creation itself, the Hebrew concept of *shalom* and all that is revealed, implies an integrated, interconnected synergy of the whole that God himself epitomises. A systematic understanding of the whole and parts became popular through the Greek philosopher Aristotle, who pointed out that 'The whole is more than the sum of its parts.'[4] Aristotle's basic definition of the whole and the parts summarized what was generally believed to be the essence of holism, and the concept has emerged more influentially in recent decades in certain fields of study and practice. With the ecological movement gaining momentum and with the impact of quantum physics and systems thinking in management, holism has become a compelling concept, re-emerging to undergird our grasp of various areas of life.

Why did we depart from this integrated, holistic view of life? To answer this, we need to point bluntly to modern Western dualistic thinking. The problem escalated with Enlightenment philosophy. Brute facts were called for; the Bible and even the historicity of Jesus Christ were questioned. Simply put, matters of faith were to be separated from matters of fact.

The influence haunts us even today. In church we Christians sing, 'God is Lord of all'—but outside we believe the world is in the clutches of Satan. We have separated the church from the world. We need to break from such dualistic perspectives and return to biblical holism.

Dualism in various forms has been around for centuries with influential Greek and Hindu teachings. We need to be careful in understanding correctly the New Testament references to body, mind, spirit, and soul. Dualism describes a system of two distinct but related parts, sometimes referring to opposites at work in incongruity. But there is also a sense in which they work complementarily. When it comes to creation, the split is between the material and spiritual. So dualistic creation theology sees either an opposition between God/faith and science/facts, in its extreme, or in complementarity, something that was separated yet not in conflict.

Many theologies have been written in lofty terms about creation and God, hardly reflecting the realities we live amidst. Even Christian philosophers have sometimes seen mind and matter as ontologically separate categories. But such thinking is being more and more challenged with integrated approaches. For instance, Alister McGrath says 'belief in a creator God—however that notion is understood—offers a powerful incentive to the investigation and appreciation of the natural world. To study nature is to study God indirectly.'[5]

Wholes and parts in creation

Evangelicals have begun moving forward with a wider understanding of God's work and an integrated approach, bringing together various aspects of God's mission. The Lausanne Movement has served as a catalyst in such thinking. What we need is not just holistic mission, but a holistic theology. For this we need a whole gospel. Holism is neither a new invention, nor something we as Christians have just discovered. While the philosophy has been around for centuries in our traditional cultures, it has taken time to enter our discussions. A version of it gained popularity more recently through the New Age Movement, and perhaps this is why Christians have hesitated to embrace it.

As we delve deeper into God-made wholes in the natural world, we find they illustrate all that God has designed for us as a whole. Sadly, we have been guilty of reducing the world to almost irreconcilable parts. Historically, primitive and traditional societies held holistic worldviews. Traditional societies, it is established by anthropologists, existed in intricate holistic networks. For most times, even Christian communities saw strong interconnections between their existence and the natural world. Their integrated life, their deeply (and widely) networked families, their societal as well as environmental interconnections were what made them complete. Our forefathers lived their lives in this kind of an interconnected integrated setting—the world and all its varied aspects belonged to one great whole, rather than the disjointed fragmented pieces modern life has seemed to become.

The church, and our theology, needs to return to such integrated patterns of life. One of the significant voices to help make holistic mission acceptable is that of René Padilla. When evangelicals were struggling to grasp a fuller understanding of evangelism, Padilla at the 1974 International Congress on World Evangelization, along with a group of young radicals, made an

indelible impact. Writing later, he questioned our narrow 'evangelism' perspective: 'Should mission be [limited to a narrow view of evangelism] as "the
proclamation of the historical, biblical Christ as Saviour and Lord, with a
view to persuading people to come to him personally and so be reconciled
to God?" '[6] It had to be broader. In India, there were those like Vinay Samuel
who promoted mission among the poor and, in doing so, gradually grew
towards thinking holistically: 'the relation between evangelism and social
responsibility is not a matter of either/or, but one of inseparability.'[7]

This book takes the discussion one step further. There is synergy as the
countless parts of the environment all work together; the ecological crisis
is seen more and more as primarily the disruption of these interconnections. We need a theology of holistic networks, not just within nature, but
in all of life—a theology which bears on everything we write or act upon as
Christians. That is what holism must lead us towards.

Ecology and wholes

Scientific studies have drawn attention to the need to understand intricate aspects of our perception of humans and nature. But scientific reduc-
tionism looked at minute components rather than the whole. This is when
science and faith began to be seen as separate domains—science seeking
evidence through minute facts, with faith as a broader, inner inspiration
through revelation. In its extreme, science and faith were also seen by some
people to contradict one another. However, as we have noted, there is now
a more healthy relationship of mutuality.

Science has been a boon to humanity, but also posed problems. Let
us start with environmental science and see how strongly the emphasis
on wholes is being restored. Over the latter part of the last century, the
environmental movement has brought us closer to holism. Eyes have been
opened to the strong scientific and intricate interconnections within nature.
We are beginning to perceive nature or creation as one great whole where
the parts are integrally linked.

In 1926, the South African statesman Jan Smuts published *Holism and
Evolution*. For Smuts, holism was referring to the 'the tendency in nature
to form wholes that are greater than the sum of the parts through creative
evolution.'[8] Although mainly addressing the biological world, its influence
grew wider, and now the concept has become accepted as addressing interconnections within the entire environment.

My own convictions about holism and the interrelated web within
creation started with popular studies on ecology. In 1970, Francis Schaeffer argued in *Pollution and the Death of Man* that while Christians had

neglected caring for the environment, there was in Scripture a profound and radical understanding of God's relationship to the earth.[9] Schaeffer was responding to various movements of the 1960s, and reflected on the biblical mandate for mankind to care for the earth. His call to Christians to a more biblical view of ecology was an eye-opener for evangelicals.

Rachel Carson (1907–1964), a scientist and a leading light in the early days of environmentalism, brought a refreshing view. Carson was a tireless opponent of ecological manhandling and its damaging influences, and in a large way precipitated the environmental movement. She is often referred to as 'the mother of the age of ecology' and she played a prominent part as an inspiration to large sections of the younger generation—for instance, the hippies and similar groups.

Rachel Carson was mainly concerned with problems of pesticides, evident in technical literature that was appearing from the 1950s onwards. Carson began her crusade in the early 1960s, focusing on the alarming increase in the production and use of these chemicals. Her masterpiece, *Silent Spring*, was a book underlining how pesticides were not only harmful, but gave rise to other interconnected problems—pests soon developed resistance and survived while beneficial insects and animals were being harmed.[10] The earth's capacity to support human life was being destroyed, and Carson was calling for careful management of our interconnected ecosystems towards the sustainability of the human future.

Creation Care and the Gospel provides an engagement with related concerns, while coming from a different, Christian tradition. And it calls for both action and a holistic theology. As our *Call to Action* states: 'Many of the world's poorest people, ecosystems, and species of flora and fauna are being devastated by violence against the environment in multiple ways, of which global climate change, deforestation, biodiversity loss, water stress, and pollution are but a part. We can no longer afford complacency and endless debate.' It also identifies the need for 'A theology that examines humanity's identity as both embedded in creation and yet possessing a special role toward creation.' A holistic theology.

God as creator and redeemer

For a robust and integrated theology, we must delve deeper into an understanding of God—not only as creator, but also as redeemer. Here we see our theological foundation. For God not only created, but also redeemed us. In him, these acts are interconnected. We are concerned not only with what God has done in the past or is doing at present, but what he will do in the future, for us humans and for the created world.

Whatever has been destroyed through human sin in our present created order will be restored through God's new-creation activities, as we
read in Revelation 21:1–5. Everything we see and do now must anticipate
the consummation of God's creative acts in the future. This is where we see
the gospel of God in its fullest scope. The Bible compels us to note the many
references to God's creative handiwork, and its implications for humans, a
God who is not just a creator but a redeemer.

Our attitude to creation is misguided and thus questionable. We may
seek to be spiritually separated from the world, yet we exploit and selfishly
enjoy its physical bounties. Such conflicting views have hindered us from
appreciating God as Lord of all. We must keep reminding ourselves to recover a positive view of creation in whatever state it is today, and widen the
horizons we have set for the gospel and mission.

If God is creator, there should be an ongoing relationship between God
and his redeemed people, through whom mission to the world flows. Accepting God as redeemer must include acceptance of him as creator and *vice
versa*. Isaiah 48 underlines this strongly—the God who says 'My own hand
laid the foundations of the earth' (v 13) is the one who is 'Redeemer, the Holy
One of Israel' (v 17). God calls his people to declare his saving message 'with
shouts of joy and proclaim it. Send it out to the ends of the earth' (v 20).

Creation is a powerful starting point for mission: the church's redemptive
mission is built on the foundation of God's creative handiwork. God has given
us charge of all he has created. From here we see our mandate for mission, a
mandate which incorporates socio-political, environmental, and every other
kind of engagement in his world. If we exercise God's mission, bringing the
whole gospel to the whole world, we must not hesitate to grasp the total scope
of redemptive activity, which impacts everything that God has created.

The role of the Holy Spirit

There was recognition of the role of the Holy Spirit in our *Call to Action*,
and this is foundational to any theological exploration. The Holy Spirit's role
in creation, as one of the Trinity, is indispensable to the wholeness of mission. There are several themes that could be pursued to underline this. Let
us look at the theme of Pentecost, recorded in Acts 2. We find it implicitly
addressing the wholeness that connects us to creation.

The word 'Pentecost' is derived from the Greek word for 'the fiftieth day'
and is one of the great Jewish national festivals, instituted in Deuteronomy
16:9–12. It is also called the Feast of Weeks or the day of firstfruits (Numbers
28:26) which fell on the fiftieth day after the feast of the Passover. Like all
Jewish feasts, Jewish Pentecost had two significances. It had an agricultural

significance, clearly to do with God's creation. It marked the beginning of the wheat harvest, and one of its great dramatic ceremonies was the offering of two loaves made from the flour of the new wheat (Leviticus 23:17). But, perhaps not so much emphasized is that it also had a historical significance, as Pentecost commemorated the giving of the law on Mount Sinai.

God chooses this significant day for the fulfilment of the promise of the Holy Spirit, and the manifestation of his total power. It was both the fulfilment of Old Testament prophesies (Joel 2:28–32) and Jesus' own promise. The festival, symbolising fullness, was an ideal time for the proclamation of the gospel, as the Jews had gathered in Jerusalem from all over the world. It was the day of thanksgiving for a successful harvest. Here is a spiritually symbolic harvest of redemption brought to completion in Jesus Christ. This is the *fullness* of time in which Jesus comes to fulfil the plans of God. God's creative work continues through the activity of the Spirit. This is when creation and redemption merge together into one large whole.

Pentecost is, according to Peter, the fulfilment of Joel's prophecy and directly relates to the power of the gospel of Jesus Christ, now available through his disciples (Acts 1:8). God is in the business of recreating, and says, as recorded in Joel 2:25, 'I will repay you for the years that the locusts have eaten—the great locust and the young locust, the other locusts and the locust swarm—my great army that I sent among you.' There will be newness. The Holy Spirit's coming upon the church is in direct fulfilment of the promise of God for the coming of wholeness into the church. Its impact and experience are available for the whole church. But the Spirit also binds creation in the past with our redemption today, and the ultimately redeemed creation into one integral whole.

The coming of the Holy Spirit empowered the disciples of Jesus to embark boldly on their mission in all its fullness. Over recent history, the whole has been sacrificed for just one central part. William Carey, often called the father of modern mission, brought singular emphasis to preaching in his *An Enquiry into the Obligations of Christians to Use Means for the Conversion of the Heathens*, written in 1792. He argued rightly that Jesus' teaching recorded in Matthew 28:18–20 is an obligation on Christians today and not just for the Apostles. From this, the preaching of the gospel became the one compelling passion for the church and its mission.

Recent centuries have witnessed the ministries of those like D L Moody and Billy Graham, for whom proclamation evangelism was their sole passion. There is enough in the Bible to continue to justify this, but we have learned that mission must be fleshed out into wholeness by the total Godhead in the fullness of Pentecost. The Holy Spirit makes us see our link with all of God's creation, and therefore we accept the need for care for all creation as an essential aspect of the gospel for today.

In our arguments for holistic mission, we have taken account of God's revelation from creation through to the incarnation of Jesus Christ and on into the final consummation. In the embodiment of such holism, the Holy Spirit makes the things of Christ known, and empowers God's people for mission. It is the Trinity in action, working together. There could be no better demonstration of holism for us as we develop a theological foundation on this synergy for our creational mission.

Our commitment to care for creation then becomes far more than merely a *gospel issue*. It is an essential part of the gospel that God revealed through the Lord Jesus Christ. The gospel impacts creation as directly as it does human beings. This is very obvious in Paul's message to the Romans in 8:20–22:

> For the creation was subjected to frustration, not by its own choice, but by the will of the one who subjected it, in hope that the creation itself will be liberated from its bondage to decay and brought into the freedom and glory of the children of God. We know that the whole creation has been groaning as in the pains of childbirth right up to the present time.

Disasters, climate change, ecological disruptions

The early chapters of Genesis make a clear connection between the sin of Adam and Eve and all the disruptions in God's good creation. Genesis 3:17–19 records:

> To Adam he said, 'Because you listened to your wife and ate fruit from the tree about which I commanded you, "You must not eat from it,"
>
> 'Cursed is the ground because of you;
>   through painful toil you will eat food from it
>   all the days of your life.
> It will produce thorns and thistles for you,
>   and you will eat the plants of the field.
> By the sweat of your brow
>   you will eat your food
> until you return to the ground,
>   since from it you were taken;
> for dust you are
>   and to dust you will return.'

Disruptions and disasters are not what God intended, but the consequence of human sin. And the Apostle Paul writes of the groaning of creation for its redemption, as we have seen in Romans 8. The implication of this is powerful. Redemption, made possible through Jesus Christ, was not just for humans. Through the Second Adam, the blessings of redemption now extend to creation.

Over the past centuries, sin in the form of human greed has caused havoc and the intricate ecological chains and cycles have carelessly been disturbed. Unbridled human activity has increased in its intensity and caused destruction all over the world. We need to bring about corrective measures. Rapid increases in the use of natural resources and the phenomenal growth in human population have put extreme pressures on the sensitive interconnections. And as a result ecosystems are being distressed and made ineffective to perform their God-created functions.[11]

This book contains practical, down-to-earth actions that could bring change. Our mission as *stewards* is to raise awareness of problems, bring new attitudes, work to correct our actions and rectify the wrongs that have caused the disaster. We have been urged to 'respond radically and faithfully to care for God's creation, demonstrating our belief and hope in the transforming power of Christ.'[12] Redeemed human beings must be God's agents in bringing this redemption to creation. God's wounded creation cries out for concerned Christians to act urgently and reverse the downward trend.

We must bring about corrective action. In his oft-quoted lecture *The Historical Roots of Our Ecologic Crisis*, Lynn White Jr accused Christians and too narrow a view of the biblical doctrine of creation for being responsible for the present day environmental complications. He summed up: 'Especially in its Western form, Christianity is the most anthropocentric religion the world has seen.'[13] What we make of White's accusations is not here the point. We must accept that human beings who were created to be theocentric (God-centred) have largely become anthropocentric (human-centred). If we see the strong link between human sin and the ecological crisis, we are bound to accept that Christians share in that responsibility.

Sin has its ongoing control on human life. God's good creation is continually being drawn back to chaos by continuing exploitative and sinful human interventions. We must recognize that we are redeemed to serve God as stewards in the Garden. Our human-centred lifestyles must be transformed, so we exercise God-centred actions that glorify our creator. We must see how God's mission to the world will extend to benefit all creation. Echoing this, Dave Bookless writes in Chapter 6: '[it is] a major shift in thinking for many evangelicals—to extend the work of the cross from individuals to a cosmic scale—yet it is entirely biblical.'

Bookless speaks of five biblical acts: creation; fall; Israel; Jesus; the present; and the future age. Examining them through the lens of God's purposes for the whole creation he writes, no Christian who takes Scripture seriously and reads it with an open mind can honestly ignore the implication that we have got it wrong in terms of our definition of mission. From Genesis to Revelation, God's purposes are far wider than human salvation or human welfare—although the place of humanity within those purposes is critical.

Responsible stewardship for today

Our mission is to care for creation as God would care for it, calling people to responsible action. But, how do we respond? Stewardship is the most appropriate way to define our mission in relation to our role and responsibilities towards creation, even as we 'respond radically and faithfully to care for God's creation' as stated in the *Call to Action*. We spelled out various practical ways in which we engage as stewards in God's world.

In his reflections on Psalm 8 in Chapter 1, Edward Brown speaks of three goals—name, kingdom, people—which 'offer us a framework on which to build a dominion based on God's goals for us and his creation, rather than on our own goals for ourselves'. These are worthy of note. Proclaiming God's name, he states, has implications for how we practise our faith. Evangelism, worship, prayer all have to do with proclaiming God's name in one way or another. 'But God reveals himself through creation as well as through the Bible, and so there are implications for how we care for creation as well'. And

> establishing God's kingdom follows directly from proclaiming his name: God's kingdom is established where his influence—his values—are visible and operative. Establishing God's kingdom means creating a society that is based on what we have already called *kingdom values*. Today's social justice movement fits into this category, and it is wise to remember that no matter how much we want God's kingdom, we cannot achieve it without God himself. We proclaim his name, *then* we can establish his kingdom.

Finally, in the Lord's Prayer, we pray for God's kingdom to come and say 'Give us this day our daily bread.' So the kingdom ought to be where our needs are met. Edward Brown concludes: 'If God's name is proclaimed, if his kingdom is established, it will follow quite naturally that people will be provided for.' Our stewardship of God's resources must meet the needs of all in our community, particularly the hungry and the needy.

Stewardship, then, must become part of our God-given mission. John Hall, in an excellent book entitled *The Steward*, stresses the stewardship metaphor 'because it encapsulates the two sides of human relatedness, the relation to God on the one hand and to nonhuman creatures of God on the other.'[14] Our responsibility is both ways. We look to God for direction for our mission, and then to God's creation to fulfil this mission. The steward metaphor provides the corrective for the anthropocentric and arrogant attitudes that have caused the ecological crisis. 'The human being is, as God's steward, accountable to God and responsible for his fellow creatures.'[15]

The Old Testament depicts a steward as a person who is 'over a house' (Gen 43:19; 44:4; Isa 22:15). In the New Testament, there are two words translated as steward. The first is *epitropos* found, for instance, in Matthew 20:8 and Galatians 4:2—one to whom care or honour one has been entrusted, a curator or a guardian—and this could appropriately describe our creational mission in the world. We have a responsibility entrusted to us and it is in fulfilling it that we are engaging in God's work in the world. The other word is *oikonomos* (Luke 16:2–3; 1 Corinthians 4:1–2; Titus 1:7; 1 Peter 4:10)—which means a manager, a superintendent. It is also where our term *economy* comes from. Taken from the word *oikos* (house) and *nemo* (to 'dispense or manage) there is reference to the relationship within the home, an ownership with which this responsibility must be performed.

An important fact, however, is that the words imply a delegated responsibility, as in the oft-quoted parables of the talents (Matthew 25:14–30) and the unjust steward (Luke 16:1–14). God has placed us in the world on his mission to be his representatives, acting on his behalf. Responsible stewardship serving in God's love will result in God's work that will not only help in fulfilling our mission, but in developing right attitudes for living today. This must lead us 'to live within the proper boundaries of God's good gift in creation, to engage further in its restoration and conservation, and to equitably share its bounty with each other.'[16]

And how? First, we Christians who are called to care for creation will see the need for care for creation that will elicit a respect for the rights of creation. Our care for creation will show in our love to protect, conserve, and bring healing to a wounded world. Ecology, we have seen, implies interrelatedness, and this will show in our own feeling of hurt empathetically for a creation that has been hurt. We become healers. Sara Kaweesa writes that it is her goal to contribute to the transformation and rebuilding of Uganda's natural resources by demonstrating creation care.

Second, we are called to conserve creation's resources sustainably. Conserving calls for protecting in the present for future use. Sustainability in conservation calls us to make careful use of resources for our present needs, but protect them for responsible use for future generations. God's mission entrusted to us must include a major dimension of sustainability. Regardless of how much devastation has been caused we could bring major change that is sustainable. It is appropriate that Lawrence Ko's work involves the restoration of deserts. He writes: 'Deserts have always been associated with wastelands and pictures of dryness, dead bones and death. Interestingly, the spiritual life appears to begin with the desert places. The voice booms forth in the wilderness, preparing the way for a new season of salvation.'[17]

Finally, we have a responsibility towards God to honour him for the way in which he has honoured us with responsibility over all of creation. All that we have said above will fall into its right perspective when we see God as the one who invests integrity, dignity, and responsibility to us humans. As the *Call to Action* reminds us, this will lead us to becoming better stewards, caring for creation 'having tasted of the grace and mercies of God in Christ Jesus and through the Holy Spirit, and with hope in the fullness of our redemption' and serving responsibly.

Living Out Our Care for Creation

When it comes to readying ourselves to act on God's call to care for creation, we are blessed to be 'standing on the shoulders of giants', to use Isaac Newton's phrase. Many organizations have provided resources for a small group or fellowship to engage meaningfully in creation care. This Appendix is a toolbox for you and your fellowship to choose the tools you need and put them to good use. While the ambitions and capacities of your church may not match them perfectly, they are helpful starting points. We also chose to include helpful hints for those with a passion to practise creation care, who might feel alone in caring about this subject or do not know how to direct their energies.

New organizations are being founded and new resources published all the time: an up-to-date list can be found on the Lausanne Creation Care Network website (www.lwccn.com). We welcome feedback on what is there and information on new material—perhaps something you have done inspired by this book! Someday, others may stand on your shoulders. Our prayer is that our ceiling, the highest we can reach, will be the floor for those coming after us.

Helpful hints for moving forward

For the individual

1. Don't be shy—make a public declaration of your beliefs by signing the *Jamaica Call to Action* and telling your family, friends, small group, pastor, and so on. It can be signed at: http://www.lausanne .org/creationcare.

2. Make creation care an integral part of your personal Bible study, prayer life, and discipleship—and think about how to share this with others.

3. Be enthusiastically teachable—look into some of the books, organizations, and programmes listed below. Learn new ways of doing things—like composting, vegetarian cooking, biking to work, sharing cars and other implements, or shopping second-hand.

4. Find local and national environmental groups you can join, learn from, and share with. If possible, contribute financially to their work.

5. Actively seek ways of living 'more lightly', either finding more environmentally friendly alternatives, or by living a more simple life and doing without what is unnecessary. Be aware how much the world encourages us to engage in consumerism.

6. Use things for longer before replacing them, repairing them if possible. Recycle materials rather than throw things away.

7. See what you can do to save energy in the home—for instance, by heating or cooling a little less, turning things off when not in use, and buying more efficient appliances. Also, use less water (in showers, toilets, washing, etc), which includes reusing water for watering gardens, flushing toilets, etc.

8. Consider your diet: eat food grown locally—perhaps buying direct from a local farmer. Try to waste less. Eat less dairy and meat (which have a high environmental footprint).

9. Try to drive less and fly less.

10. Contact your elected representatives, encouraging them to take action on issues like climate change and funding adaptation measures for low-income countries. Talk to businesses encouraging them to adopt more environmentally-friendly practices.

With others

1. Share with Christians and others what you are doing to care for creation personally, and why you are doing it. This is a good way of sharing the gospel with environmentalists!

2. Encourage your church to include creation care in its activities: to teach on it, to display and share resources, to organize book reading and discussion groups, and to include it in mission. Ask them to sign the *Jamaica Call to Action*.

3. Make your church buildings and surroundings as environmentally-friendly as possible, using the space both to demonstrate the beauty of creation and to enhance biodiversity.

4. Call for social action, strong political will, and church dedication to creation care. Try to get your denomination and wider church groupings to take creation care more seriously.

5. Learn about threats to the environment in your area and take action to address them, either joining existing groups or starting your own. For instance, support efforts to conserve threatened animal or plant species, clean up areas affected by pollution or rubbish, campaign against projects which would threaten the environment, support reforestation projects.

6. Develop a vision for sustainable agriculture and for ministering to communities facing chronic food shortages by learning about (and supporting) effective interventions such as Farming God's Way.

7. Encourage others to cook economically and efficiently. For example, in areas where electricity is easily accessible, perhaps promote the use of economical methods such as slow-cookers. Alternatively, for those in areas where there is a struggle to find enough firewood, charcoal, or other cooking fuels, encourage the use of methods such as fireless cookers. (This is a simple insulated basket, like a homemade crock pot, which can slow-cook many kinds of food and provide significant savings in the usage of fuel at the same time.)

8. Identify new skills to practise as a group—for example, lift-sharing or ride sharing, starting or joining a community garden, reducing wasteful habits.

9. Identify a passion, and create a pledge to reach that certain creation care goal—for instance, 'Blackhawk Church life groups pledge to eat and drink only fair-trade, organic snacks and teas for the health of our bodies, for the sake of our neighbours across the planet, and to protect God's world.'

List of books and resources

Bookless, Dave, *Planetwise: Dare to Care for God's World* (Nottingham: IVP, 2008). Also available in other languages.

Bookless, Dave, *God Doesn't Do Waste: Redeeming the Whole of Life* (Nottingham: IVP, 2010).

Brown, Edward R., *Our Father's World: Mobilizing the Church to Care for Creation* (Downers Grove, IL: IVP, 2008).

Brown, Edward R., *When Heaven and Nature Sing: Exploring God's Goals for His People and His World* (South Hadley, MA: Doorlight Publications, 2012).

Dedel, Daffodil C., *Creation Care Sunday School Curriculum: Every Christian is a Steward* (Philippines: Parañaque City, CSM Publishing, 2013).

Available in English and Tagalog: order online at http://csm-publishing
.org/creation-care/.

Hayhoe, Katharine, and Andrew Farley, *A Climate for Change: Global Warming Facts for Faith-based Decisions* (New York: FaithWords, 2009).

LeQuire, Stan L., and Chantelle Du Plessis, *Wild and Wonderful: Tourism, Faith, and Communities* (San Jose, CA: Resource Publications, 2013).

Lowe, Ben, *Green Revolution: Coming Together to Care for Creation* (Downers Grove, IL: IVP, 2009).

Mellen, Andy, and Neil Hollow, *No Oil in the Lamp: Fuel, Faith and the Energy Crisis* (London: Darton, Longman & Todd, 2012).

Moo, Jonathan A., and Robert S. White, *Hope in an Age of Despair: The Gospel and the Future of Life on Earth* (Leicester: IVP, 2013), published in the USA as *Let Creation Rejoice: Biblical Hope and Ecological Crisis* (Downers Grove, IL: IVP, 2014).

Sleeth, Nancy, *Go Green, Save Green: A Simple Guide to Saving Time, Money, and God's Green Earth* (Carol Stream, IL: Tyndale House, 2009).

Sojourners, *Christians and the Environment*, http://sojo.net/resources /christians-and-environment-ebook.

Spencer, Nick, and Robert S. White, *Christianity, Climate Change and Sustainable Living* (London: SPCK, 2007). The USA edition has additional material written by Virginia Vroblesky (Ada, MI: Brazos, 2009).

Stott, John R. W., *The Radical Disciple: Some Neglected Aspects of Our Calling* (Nottingham and Downers Grove, IL: IVP, 2010).

Valerio, Ruth, *L Is for Lifestyle: Christian Living that Doesn't Cost the Earth* (Nottingham: IVP, 2004).

White, Robert S., *Who Is to Blame? Nature, Disasters and Acts of God* (Oxford: Lion Hudson, 2014).

Resources for fellowships

At Your Service (A Rocha)

Full of poems and songs, materials for use in church services, Bible studies in several languages: www.atyourservice.arocha.org.

Blessed Earth

Tips for honouring God's creation in the church:
http://www.blessedearth.org/wp-content/uploads/2011/09/Church.pdf.

Cool Congregations (Interfaith Power and Light)

Focused on reducing carbon footprint: http://www.coolcongregations.org/. Plus Cool Congregations Challenge: http://www.coolcongregations.org/wp -content/uploads/2013/06/CoolCongregations2013Complete.pdf.

Creation Time/Seasons of Creation

Runs from 1 September to the feast of St Francis on 4 October. Resources are available for many countries including:
https://www.ctbi.org.uk/creation-time-2015 (UK),
http://seasonofcreation.com/calendar/ (Australia),
http://www.letallcreationpraise.org/season-of-creation (USA),
http://www.united-church.ca/worship-liturgical-season/creation-time-4 (Canada).

Earth Care Congregations

http://www.presbyterianmission.org/ministries/environment/earth-care -congregations/.

Eco-Church (A Rocha UK)

http://www.ecochurch.arocha.org.uk/.

Eco-Management of Church Facilities (Blessed Earth)

http://wp.blessedearth.org/wp-content/uploads/2010/08/facilities_eco -management.pdf.

Green Congregations (Web of Creation)

http://www.webofcreation.org.

Greening Your Church (Eco-Justice Ministries)

http://www.eco-justice.org/Greening-Overview.asp.

Sustainable Sanctuary Coalition

Partners with, encourages, and assists faith groups to preach, teach, model and advocate for sustainable living and ecological justice for all creation: http://ssckc.org/.

Organizations

A Rocha

An international Christian organization which, inspired by God's love, engages in scientific research, environmental education, and community-based conservation projects, www.arocha.org.

CAFOD

CAFOD is the official Catholic aid agency for England and Wales. It works for a safe, sustainable, and peaceful world with people of all faiths and none, including more than 500 partners overseas. It is inspired by Scripture and Catholic social teaching, and the experiences and hopes of people living in poverty: www.cafod.org.uk.

Care of Creation

Care of Creation's core objectives are about pursuing a God-centred response to the environmental crisis. They think that the people who believe God made the world should be passionate about taking care of it, www.careofcreation.net.

Christian Aid

Christian Aid has a vision—an end to poverty—and they believe that vision can become a reality: www.christianaid.org.uk.

Christians in Conservation Philippines

The goal of CCP is to teach Christian individuals and communities about creation care—and how to practise it. They currently work in the field at Deaf Evangelical Alliance Inc on a 10-hectare plot of land, where they minister to and teach the students at the school: http://christiansinconservation.org.ph/tag/creation-care/.

Climate Stewards

A useful website for calculating how much carbon you produce—for example, in flying or driving—and then enabling you to donate an appropriate sum to offset that carbon production. The proceeds are spent on Christian work assisting people in low-income countries to adapt to the consequences of climate change: www.climatestewards.net.

ECHO

ECHO exists to reduce hunger and improve the lives of small-scale farmers worldwide. They work to identify, validate, document, and disseminate best practices in sustainable agriculture and appropriate technology. They provide agricultural and appropriate technology training to development workers in more than 165 countries: http://echonet.org/.

Evangelical Environmental Network

EEN is a ministry dedicated to the care of God's creation. They seek to equip, inspire, disciple, and mobilize God's people in their effort to care for God's creation. On their website you will find podcasts, videos, Bible studies, and other resources for acting on creation care: www.creationcare.org.

The Faraday Institute for Science and Religion

The Faraday Institute is an interdisciplinary enterprise researching and engaging in the public understanding of the relationship between science and religion. Its website contains many papers and lectures on science and religion, all free to download, including a number on Christianity and the environment: http://www.faraday.st-edmunds.cam.ac.uk/.

John Ray Initiative

The John Ray Initiative is an educational charity that provides resources for those seeking to connect science, the environment, and Christianity: http://www.jri.org.uk/.

Lausanne Creation Care Network

A partnership of Care of Creation and A Rocha International, the Lausanne Creation Care network can be your gateway to global involvement in creation care: www.lwccn.com.

Plant With Purpose

Plant With Purpose, based in San Diego, California, is a Christian development organization that transforms lives in rural areas around the world where poverty and environmental degradation intersect. They equip impoverished farming families to change their circumstances, provide for their children, and live with God-given hope and dignity. They do this through sustainable agriculture training, land restoration, savings-led microfinance, church mobilization, and local leadership development. Currently they are active in 350 communities worldwide: www.plantwithpurpose.org.

Southern African Faith Communities' Environment Institute

SAFCEI is an institute of people of many faiths, united in diversity through their common commitment to *Earth keeping*. They seek to raise environmental awareness, engage in formulating policy and ethical guidelines within faith communities, facilitate environmental responsibility and action, confront environmental and socio-economic injustices, and support environmental training and learning: http://safcei.org/.

TEAR Australia

TEAR Australia is a movement of Christians in Australia responding to the needs of poor communities around the world. They work in partnership with other Christian groups, including churches, relief and development agencies, and community-based organizations, which are working with the poor in their communities. They work in the category of environmental sustainability in several countries, www.tear.org.au.

Tearfund

Tearfund is a relief and development charity, working in partnership with Christian agencies and churches worldwide to tackle the causes and effects of poverty. This includes addressing climate change and other environmental challenges, such as reducing vulnerability to natural disasters: www.tearfund.org.

Upland Holistic Development Project

UHDP seeks to provide an appropriate Christian response related to rural development among increasingly marginalized hill-tribe people in the Golden Triangle region of Southeast Asia: www.uhdp.org.

World Renew

Compelled by God's deep passion for justice & mercy, World Renew joins communities around the world to renew hope, reconcile lives, and restore creation. They work in over three thousand communities and forty countries: http://worldrenew.net/.

World Vision

World Vision works alongside communities in close to one hundred countries to bring about long-term change. They respond quickly to the emergencies that affect more than 250 million people around the world each year. As they do this, they focus on three key areas: child protection, child health, and emergency relief. Their vision is of a world in which every child is loved, protected, and cared for, and can enjoy good health and an education: http://www.wvi.org/.

Young Evangelicals for Climate Action

YECA is an organization of young evangelicals in the United States who are coming together and taking action to overcome the climate crisis as part of Christian discipleship and witness. They work closely with students and run a Climate Leadership Fellows program, open to a limited number of applicants each year: www.yecaction.org.

Author Profiles

Seth Appiah-Kubi is the National Director and a founding member of A Rocha Ghana. Though his background is in finance, he has been involved in formulating the conservation models used by A Rocha Ghana. He lives in Accra with his wife Josephine and their two children. He spends part of his time lecturing in Banking and Finance at the University of Ghana.

Richard Bauckham is a biblical scholar and theologian. Until 2007, he was Professor of New Testament Studies at the University of St Andrews, Scotland. Richard retired early to concentrate on research and writing, and moved to Cambridge. His academic work and publications are wide ranging, and mostly within New Testament studies and theology. He has a keen interest in biblical and theological approaches to environmental issues, and has published several books and articles in the area including *Bible and Ecology: Rediscovering the Community of Creation* (Darton, Longman & Todd, 2010) and *Living with Other Creatures: Green Exegesis and Theology* (Paternoster, 2011).

R J (Sam) Berry was Professor of Genetics at University College London (1978–2000). He is a former President of the Linnean Society, British Ecological Society, European Ecological Federation, and Christians in Science; and was Moderator of the Environmental Issues Network of Churches Together in Britain and Ireland (1992–2008). He chaired the Environmental Issues Reference Panel of the General Synod of the Church of England for ten years, chairing the groups which produced *Our Responsibility for the Living Environment* (Church House Publishing, 1986) and *Christians and the Environment* (Board for Social Responsibility, 1991); and has served on the Ethics Working Group of the International Union for Conservation of Nature (IUCN). His publications include *Inheritance and Natural History* (New Naturalist, 1977), *God and the Biologist* (Apollos, 1996), and *Ecology and the Environment* (Templeton, 2011). In addition, he edited *Environmental Dilemmas* (Chapman and Hall, 1992), *Care of Creation* (IVP, 2000)—a commentary on the Evangelical Declaration on the Care of Creation, *Environmental Stewardship* (T&T Clark, 2006), *When Enough is Enough* (IVP, 2007), and (with Tom Noble) *Darwin, Creation and the Fall* (IVP, 2009).

Lowell Bliss is Director of Eden Vigil, an environmental missions organization. Before that, he was a church-planting missionary for 14 years with Christar in India and Pakistan. He served on the writing team of the

Jamaica Call to Action and is the author of *Environmental Missions: Planting Churches and Trees* (William Carey Library, 2013). Lowell and his wife live in the tallgrass prairie ecosystem of Kansas, USA, with their three children.

Dave Bookless is Director of Theology for A Rocha International, and also studying for a part-time PhD in Theology and Biodiversity Conservation at the University of Cambridge. With a background in teaching and church ministry, he co-founded A Rocha UK in 2001. His passion is communicating biblical teaching to contemporary cultures, and he speaks and writes widely in the UK and beyond, at conferences, colleges and churches. Dave has contributed to several books and authored two—*Planetwise* (IVP, 2008) and *God Doesn't Do Waste* (IVP, 2010)—and his monthly blog can be found at www.blog.arocha.org. He was born in India to a missionary family. He now lives in multicultural Southall, London, with his wife Anne and their four daughters. He is an ordained Anglican and assists in the leadership of a local, multiracial church; he has also served on or led several national Christian environmental committees.

Dorothy Boorse is a Professor of Biology at Gordon College, Wenham, Massachusetts, USA. She holds a BS in Biology (Gordon College), an MS in Entomology (Cornell University) and a PhD in Oceanography and Limnology (University of Wisconsin-Madison). Her research with students is in wetland ecology and invasive species. She also spends a great deal of time studying the integration of faith and science, particularly in the realm of environmental ethics. Dorothy was lead author of *Loving the Least of These, Addressing a Changing Environment*, a report on poverty and climate change (National Association of Evangelicals, 2011), and is a co-author of an environmental science textbook. She is interested in helping the Christian community understand and become leaders in solving problems associated with environmental degradation, especially climate change. She lives in Beverly, Massachusetts, with her husband and their two children.

Edward R Brown is the Director and CEO of Care of Creation, and serves as the Lausanne Movement's Senior Associate for Creation Care, based in Madison, Wisconsin, USA. He directs the work of Care of Creation in the USA, Kenya, and Tanzania. As Senior Associate, he is responsible for developing a global creation care network under the Lausanne Movement's umbrella. His current project is the Lausanne *Creation Care and the Gospel* global campaign. Ed has been involved in the creation care movement for 15 years; he speaks throughout the USA and internationally. He is author of two books: *Our Father's World: Mobilizing the Church to Care for Creation* (IVP, 2008), and *When Heaven and Nature Sing: Exploring God's Goals for His People and His World* (Doorlight Publications, 2012).

Paul Cook is Advocacy Director for Tearfund. Based in the UK, he oversees Tearfund's two major advocacy programmes: the first, building a global movement among Christians for a green and fair global economic system; and the other, fostering the development of national church-based advocacy movements in the Global South. Paul has over 20 years of experience in working in NGOs on human rights, conflict, and interfaith dialogue as well as development and environment. He studied Theology at Nottingham University. He is married with three children.

Stan Doerr was appointed President/CEO of ECHO in 2006. ECHO is a global Christian organization equipping people with agricultural resources and skills to reduce hunger and improve the lives of the poor. Since 1981, Stan has worked in many parts of the world—particularly Africa—in education, community development, administration, and agricultural consultancy. ECHO has grown internationally during his eight years as President/CEO—with offices in Thailand, Tanzania, Burkina Faso, and South Africa. It works with organizations and individuals in 177 countries, providing tropical agricultural technical support and training along with seeds for tropical plants and networking opportunities with a particular focus on small-scale farmers. ECHO also conducts research in South Africa on ways to build the capacity of soils to produce better crops.

Susan D Emmerich is a nationally known writer and speaker on community-based environmental stewardship and conflict resolution from a faith perspective. She earned her PhD in Land and Water Resources from the University of Wisconsin-Madison, USA, and is currently a part-time director of Special Programs at the Economic Alliance of Kankakee County, near Chicago. She is the CEO of Emmerich Environmental Consulting, and Director of the Creation Care Program for the Center for Law and Culture, housed at Olivet Nazarene University, Illinois. Through these positions, she implements her innovative stewardship, sustainability, and reconciliation approach to benefit communities in conflict over environmental, social, and economic issues. She is the co-producer of two award winning films about this stewardship approach. Susan served as a US Delegate to the United Nations on environmental affairs and was a former Harvey and Presidential Fellow and Assistant Professor of Biology at Trinity Christian College in Palos Heights, IL.

Ken Gnanakan is an Indian educator, environmentalist, social activist, and theologian with a background in chemical engineering and a PhD in philosophy. His environmental work spans teaching and writing, a programme of environmental awareness across schools in India, and practical work including reuse of waste plastics and a holistic approach to socio-economic development starting with the recycling of urban waste. He also founded

ACTS, a network of education, health and environmental projects in India. He is President of the International Council for Higher Education and promotes the concept of Integrated Learning in numerous contexts. His books include *God's Word: A Theology of the Environment* (SPCK, 1999), *Responsible Stewardship of God's Creation* (Theological Commission of the World Evangelical Alliance, 2004), and *Integrated Learning* (Oxford University Press, 2011).

David Gould is an architect, and for many years was a partner of an architectural practice in the UK. He studied environmental science at London University, and ever since has had a concern for different aspects of sustainability. Since 2002, David and his wife Ruth have been members of OMF International, the mission agency based in Singapore with a vision for indigenous biblical church movements among the peoples of East Asia. David is OMF's International Facilitator for Creation Care; he is tasked with exploring the growing ecological challenges, their impacts on the peoples of East Asia, and appropriate missional responses. David was program director for the first Lausanne regional conference on creation care and the gospel, held in Manila in March 2014. The conference encouraged the formation of creation care movements in the countries of SE Asia.

Martin J Hodson is a plant scientist and environmental biologist, and a former Principal Lecturer and now Visiting Researcher at Oxford Brookes University, UK. He teaches Biological Conservation in the Institute of Human Sciences, University of Oxford, where he is an Associate Member. Martin is also Operations Manager for the John Ray Initiative—a charity connecting the environment, science and Christianity. Tour scientist for the Hope for Planet Earth tours, Martin speaks and writes widely on environmental issues. He has over ninety publications, mostly in international science journals. His recent books are *Cherishing the Earth* (Monarch, 2008), *A Christian Guide to Environmental Issues* (BRF, 2015), both with Margot R Hodson, and *Functional Biology of Plants* (Wiley, 2012), with John Bryant. Further information at www.hodsons.org/MartinHodson/.

John Houghton has had a long career as a research scientist and government advisor, particularly in the fields of meteorology and climate science. Sir John is an Honorary Scientist of the Hadley Centre for Climate Prediction and Research at the UK Meteorological Office, and President of the John Ray Initiative. Previously he was Chairman or Co-Chairman of the Scientific Assessment Working Group, Intergovernmental Panel on Climate Change (1988–2002), Director General of the UK Meteorological Office (1983–91), and a Trustee of the Shell Foundation. Among his books are *The Search for God: Can Science Help?* (John Ray Institute, UK, and Regent College Bookstore, Vancouver, 1995), *Global Warming: The Complete Briefing*, 5th edition (Cambridge University Press, 2015), and his autobiography, *In the Eye of the Storm* (Lion, 2013).

Sara Kaweesa is currently working as director at A Rocha Uganda, a conservation organization that engages in research, environmental education, and community-based conservation projects. She was previously a secondary school teacher before moving on to her Master's in Forestry. She also holds training certificates in environmental conservation from agencies such as Tearfund UK, the United Nations Environment Program, Oxfam GB, International Institute for Environment and Development, and the International People's College Denmark, among a host of others. Sara continues to play an important role with church and community initiatives, environmental themes in multicultural settings at international audiences, student bodies, colleges, church congregations, and local communities. She has had influence in several environmental, faith, and science alliances at national and global levels—a task closely knit with her passion.

Lawrence Ko is Founder-director of Asian Journeys Ltd, a Singapore-based social enterprise dedicated to working with youths from Singapore and elsewhere in Asia. He is a writer, cultural researcher, and consultant who has extensive experience in human resources development and spiritual formation, having served as pastor, human resources manager, media director, events organizer, and training consultant over the past twenty-five years. He enjoys networking and nurturing young leaders towards the vision of a creative and responsible community rooted in a love for God, humans, and creation. He is author of *Can the Desert be Green? Planting Hope in the Wilderness* (Singapore Centre for Global Missions, 2014).

Andrew Leake is the Anglican Communion Environmental Network (ACEN) representative for the Southern Cone and Director of Land for Life, a Christian conservation initiative aimed at establishing protected areas in northern Argentina. Dr Leake holds degrees in environmental sciences and rural development.

John P McKeown worked for five years as a Module Leader for Church History and Theology at the University of Gloucestershire, UK. He was also an Associate Lecturer in History for the Open University. Before that, he was a Research Associate with Teaching and Learning Technology Program (TLTP) Geography with Leicester University for six years. He then worked for the Christian creation-care ministry John Ray Initiative for fourteen years until recently moving to the Cornwall campus of the University of Exeter where he currently works in IT at the College of Life and Environmental Sciences. John is married to Lynda and they have two teenage children. His

PhD on historical and modern interpretation of Bible verses relating to fecundity was published as *God's Babies: Natalism and Bible Interpretation in Modern America* (Open Book Publishing, 2014). John occasionally tweets on environment and population: @jpmckeown.

Jonathan A Moo is an associate professor of New Testament and environmental studies in the theology department at Whitworth University in Spokane, Washington, USA. He holds master's degrees in wildlife ecology and theology, and a PhD in biblical studies from the University of Cambridge; and he researches and teaches in the areas of New Testament, early Judaism, environmental ethics, and science and faith. His recent books include *Let Creation Rejoice: Biblical Hope and Ecological Crisis*, co-authored with Robert White (IVP-USA, 2014) and *As Long as the Earth Endures: The Bible, Creation and the Environment*, co-edited with Robin Routledge (Apollos, 2014). He also recently collaborated with an artist to produce a guide to the natural history and tree species of Whitworth's Verbrugge Environmental Studies Center. Jonathan and his wife Stacey live in Spokane.

Juliana Morillo Horne is Colombian. She has a BSc in Chemistry from Messiah College, Pennsylvania, USA, and a Masters in Development and Environmental Management from the Javeriana University, Bogota, Colombia. She also did post-graduate studies in Risk Management and Disaster Prevention, with the Andes University of Colombia. Juliana worked for government and non-government sectors in Colombia in the area of environment and disaster management and prevention, and also has experience in environmental education. During the last 12 years, she has been working with the mission Latin Link, and is presently living in Cusco, Peru, with her husband Ian and two sons. She is involved in training and awareness-raising on environmental issues, in church and secular contexts, both locally and further afield.

Las G Newman is President of the Caribbean Graduate School of Theology (CGST) in Kingston, Jamaica. Among his many ministry engagements, he currently serves as the Honorary International Deputy Director (Caribbean) for the Lausanne Movement for World Evangelization. Dr Newman is a former Associate General Secretary of the International Fellowship of Evangelical Students (IFES). A graduate of Tyndale University College, Toronto, and the University of Waterloo, Ontario, Canada, he holds a PhD in Mission Studies from the Oxford Centre for Mission Studies/University of Wales. He is a member of the Anglican Diocese of Jamaica and the Cayman Islands and attends St Andrew Parish Church, Half Way Tree, Kingston, where he serves as a lay preacher and Vice Chairman of the St Andrew Parish Foundation.

James Pender is currently Programmes and Advocacy Officer/Environmental Advisor for Asia, for The Leprosy Mission England and Wales, which includes making sure new projects are environmentally sustainable and climate resilient. Before this, he worked for 10 years as a Mission Partner with the Church of Bangladesh Social Development Programme with a particular focus on community-based adaptation to climate change, as well as promoting creation care in Asia through workshops in Bangkok (Thailand), Dhaka (Bangladesh), Chennai (India) and Pokhara (Nepal). He has always had a passion for conservation, ornithology, and social justice, becoming involved in various projects around the world, such as involvement in A Rocha, including helping to found A Rocha Ghana. He is also an associate of The John Ray Initiative, UK.

Mick Pope has a PhD in meteorology from Monash University, Melbourne, Australia, and is involved in forecast meteorologist training. He also has degrees in mathematics, physics, and theology. Mick speaks and writes on climate change and ecotheology for a variety of organizations including Ethos: Evangelical Alliance (Australia)'s Centre for Christianity and Society, TEAR Australia, and Hope for Creation. He is also involved with Friends of A Rocha Australia. Mick is co-author with Claire Dawson of *A Climate of Hope: Church and Mission in a Warming World* (Urban Neighbours Of Hope, 2014). Further information at: http://about.me/mick.pope.

Sally Shaw trained as a nurse/midwife in the UK and then spent three years working in the Cambodian refugee camps in Thailand. After that she moved to Cambodia to work with World Vision. There she was involved in maternal and child health and community development programs with Doug, her Australian husband. Later, she established Chrysalis, a local non-governmental organization which used improvisational drama to develop the self-esteem of people from very disadvantaged backgrounds. In 2007, they moved to live in South Australia with their three children. Sally received a Graduate Diploma in Creative Writing, followed by a Master of Education at Tabor Adelaide. She is on the steering group of Friends of A Rocha Australia and active in a Transition Towns group in the Adelaide Hills.

Andrew Shepherd is the National Co-Director (Education and Advocacy) of A Rocha Aotearoa New Zealand. He teaches in the areas of theology and ethics for a range of tertiary institutions. Much of Dr Shepherd's writing is concerned with themes of Christian living in response to ecological issues. His most recent publication is The *Gift of the Other: Levinas, Derrida, and a Theology of Hospitality* (Pickwick, 2014).

Robert D Sluka grew up loving the ocean, despite living far from it. Starting diving at thirteen and then earning the PhD in marine biology from the University of Miami, he became convinced that a life lived studying the ocean was for him. Only recently did he discover how his faith relates to his love of the ocean. He is working towards a life that integrates his beliefs and love of the ocean in a way that brings blessing to people, nations, and the planet. He consults with a number of organizations on marine conservation and research and holds various roles, official and not official. He is Lead Scientist of A Rocha International's Marine and Coastal Conservation Programme and also works with A Rocha Kenya's Marine Conservation and Research Programme. He is an associate of the Faraday Institute for Science and Religion. His academic work and writings can be accessed at http://robertdsluka.blogspot.co.uk/.

Craig Sorley grew up in three different countries of East Africa as the son of medical missionaries, where he developed his own calling to foreign missions and his keen interest in creation stewardship. Holding a degree in Environmental Science and a Master's in Forestry and Education, Craig is a co-founder of Care of Creation USA, a mission organization dedicated to awakening and mobilizing evangelicals to lead the world by example in developing a God-centred response to the environmental issues of our day. Since 2003, Craig has served as the director of Care of Creation Kenya, a branch of the USA office, where he and his team of Kenyan counterparts train pastors, Christian leaders, farmers and local communities in a biblically-based approach to environmental and agricultural stewardship. Craig and his wife Tracy live and work in Kijabe, a rural town about an hour's drive from Kenya's capital city of Nairobi. They have two boys.

Meric Srokosz is Professor of Physical Oceanography at the National Oceanography Centre (NOC), Southampton, UK, and was formerly the Associate Director of the Faraday Institute for Science and Religion, Cambridge, UK. Following a PhD on the theoretical modelling of wave power devices, he worked on remote sensing of the oceans and breaking waves. Since 1997, he has been at NOC and works additionally on biological-physical interactions in the upper ocean (observations and modelling). In 2001, he became the Science Coordinator for the Natural Environment Research Council Rapid Climate Change programme, studying the role of the North Atlantic in future changes in the climate. Meric is a member and trustee of Christians in Science, and has a BA in theology.

Serah Wambua holds a Master's degree in Sociology from the University of Nairobi. She has been working with a variety of church groups in the area of sustainable development and training since the early 1980s. A focus has been the question of poverty in Africa: she believes that *mindset* poverty is more of a problem than *real* poverty, and that Africans, particularly

Christians, need to be liberated in the mind first—then they will begin to appreciate and tap into resources that God has placed in their midst. Serah currently works with CMS Africa, an African mission agency equipping the church in Africa with the vision to see every church committed and engaged in evangelistic and transforming mission at every level of society. She serves as the Mission Network Manager for CMS Africa and spends many days visiting churches in Africa to share this transforming truth of the gospel. She is married to Henry and they have three grown up children.

Robert S White is Professor of Geophysics in the Department of Earth Sciences at the University of Cambridge (since 1989) and Director of the Faraday Institute for Science and Religion. Bob was elected a Fellow of the Royal Society in 1994. He leads a research group investigating the Earth's dynamic crust: in particular, the way in which enormous volumes of volcanic rock are produced when continents and oceans rift apart, and the movement of molten rock under active volcanoes. He has organised many overseas fieldwork projects and supervised fifty PhD students at Cambridge, many of whom are now prominent in academia, industry, government, and education. His work at sea has taken him to the Atlantic, Indian, and Pacific Oceans and his research group is currently investigating the internal structure of volcanoes in Iceland. His scientific work is published in over 350 papers and articles, and he has written or edited eight books on aspects of science and Christianity—most recently (with Jonathan Moo), *Hope in an Age of Despair* (IVP-UK, 2014) and *Who is to Blame? Nature, Disasters and Acts of God* (Lion Hudson, 2014).

Lausanne Movement

Connecting influencers and ideas for global mission

The Lausanne Movement takes its name from the International Congress on World Evangelization, convened in 1974 in Lausanne, Switzerland, by the US evangelist Billy Graham. His long-time friend John Stott, the UK pastor-theologian, was chief architect of *The Lausanne Covenant*, which issued from this gathering.

Two further global Congresses followed—the second in Manila, Philippines (1989) and the third in Cape Town, South Africa (2010). From the Third Lausanne Congress came *The Cape Town Commitment: A Confession of Faith and a Call to Action*. Its Call to Action was the fruit of a careful process conducted over four years to discern what we believe the Holy Spirit is saying to the global church in our times. In the words of the *Commitment's* chief architect, Chris Wright, it expresses 'the conviction of a Movement and the voice of a multitude.'

The Lausanne Movement connects evangelical influencers across regions and across generations: in the church, in ministries and in the workplace. Under God, Lausanne events have often acted as a powerful catalyst; as a result, strategic ideas such as Unreached People Groups, the 10/40 Window, and holistic/integral mission have been introduced to missional thinking. Over thirty specialist Issue Networks now focus on the outworking of the priorities outlined in *The Cape Town Commitment*.

The movement makes available online over forty years of missional content. Sign up to receive *Lausanne Global Analysis* to your inbox. Watch videos from Lausanne's gatherings. On the website you will also find a complete list of titles in the Lausanne Library.

www.lausanne.org

Notes

Notes to Foreword

1. The Third Lausanne Congress on World Evangelization, *The Cape Town Commitment: A Confession of Faith and a Call to Action* (Lausanne Movement, 2010; Hendrickson Publishers, 2011), I-7-A.

Notes to Introduction

1. Lausanne Movement, 'Lausanne Global Consultation on Creation Care and the Gospel: Call to Action' (St Ann, Jamaica: Lausanne Movement, 2012).

Notes to Call to Action

1. The Third Lausanne Congress on World Evangelization, *The Cape Town Commitment: A Confession of Faith and a Call to Action* (Lausanne Movement, 2010; Hendrickson Publishers, 2011), I-7-A.
2. The full text and a list of participants and signatories to the *Jamaica Call to Action* is available at: 'Lausanne Global Consultation on Creation Care and the Gospel: Call to Action' (St Ann, Jamaica: Lausanne Movement, 2012), accessed 1 March 2016, http://www.lausanne.org/content/statement/creation-care-call-to-action.
3. Second Lausanne Congress on World Evangelization, *The Manila Manifesto* (Lausanne Movement, 1989), A-1.

Notes to Chapter 2

1. Wendell Berry, 'Manifesto: The Mad Farmer Liberation Front', in *The Country of Marriage* (New York: Harcourt, 1973), 14–15.
2. Martin Rees, *Anniversary Address 2006* (London: Royal Society, 2006).
3. Berry, 'Manifesto: The Mad Farmer Liberation Front'.
4. Christopher J. H. Wright, *The Mission of God: Unlocking the Bible's Grand Narrative* (Downers Grove, IL: IVP Academic, 2006), 395.
5. These observations are taken from Jonathan A. Moo and Robert S. White, *Hope in an Age of Despair: The Gospel and the Future of Life on Earth* (Nottingham: IVP, 2014), 108–27, where the connections between Romans 8 and Isaiah 24 are developed at greater length; see too Jonathan A. Moo, 'Romans 8.19–22 and Isaiah's Cosmic Covenant', *New Testament Studies* 54 (2008), 74–89.
6. See Howard Snyder and Joel Scandrett, *Salvation Means Creation Healed: The Ecology of Sin and Grace; Overcoming the Divorce between Earth and Heaven* (Eugene, OR: Cascade, 2011).

7. For the textual details, see Jonathan A. Moo, 'New Testament Hope and a Christian Environmental Ethos', in *As Long as the Earth Endures: The Bible, Creation and the Environment*, ed. Jonathan A. Moo and Robin Routledge (Nottingham: Apollos, 2014), 155, n. 18 and Richard J. Bauckham, *Word Biblical Commentary, Volume 50: Jude, 2 Peter* (Waco, TX: Word Books, 1983), 303, 316–21.

8. On this point, see Edward Adams, *The Stars Will Fall from Heaven: Cosmic Catastrophe in the New Testament and Its World*, Library of New Testament Studies 347 (London: T & T Clark, 2007), 226.

9. See Jonathan A. Moo, 'The Sea that is No More: Rev 21.1 and the Function of Sea Imagery in the Apocalypse of John', *Novum Testamentum* 51 (2009), 148–67.

10. In John R. W. Stott's final book, *The Radical Disciple: Some Neglected Aspects of Our Calling* (Downers Grove, IL: IVP, 2010), he called attention—as he often had in his ministry—to creation care as a necessary and neglected aspect of what it is to be a radical disciple of Christ.

11. These observations are developed further in Moo and White, *Hope in an Age of Despair*, 182–92. See also Chapter 3 of this volume, Richard Bauckham, 'Ecological Hope in Crisis'.

12. The Third Lausanne Congress on World Evangelization, *The Cape Town Commitment: A Confession of Faith and a Call to Action* (Lausanne Movement, 2010; Hendrickson Publishers, 2011).

13. Aldo Leopold, *Round River* (New York: Oxford University Press, 1972), 165.

14. I am indebted for this observation to Dr Ajith Fernando (from a discussion at Whitworth University, Spokane, WA, 3 October 2012).

Notes to Chapter 3

This chapter was previously published as Richard Bauckham, 'Ecological Hope in Crisis?' *Anvil* 29, no. 1 (2013), 43–54.

1. Jared Diamond, *Collapse: How Societies Choose to Fail or Survive* (London: Allen Lane, 2005).

2. Bill McKibben, *Eaarth: Making a Life on a Tough New Planet*, 2nd ed. (with new Afterword) (New York: St. Martin's Griffin, 2011).

3. McKibben, *Eaarth*, xiv.

4. McKibben, *Eaarth*, xiv.

5. Rob Hopkins, *The Transition Companion: Making Your Community More Resilient in Uncertain Times* (Totnes: Transition Books, 2011).

6. McKibben, *Eaarth*, 204.

7. McKibben, *Eaarth*, 151.

8. eg Rom 5:3–4; James 1:3; Rev 13:10.

Notes to Chapter 4

1. Amy Carmichael, *If: What Do I Know of Calvary Love? The Dohnavur Fellowship, 1938* (Fort Washington, PA: CLC Publications, 2011), 27.

2. G. Hansson and A. Nilsson, 'Ground-Water Dams for Rural Water Supplies in Developing Countries', *Ground Water* 24, no. 4 (July–August 1986), 497–506.

3. Eric Bernard, interview with author, Department of Landscape Architecture, Kansas State University, 1 March 2010.

4. The Third Lausanne Congress on World Evangelization, *The Cape Town Commitment: A Confession of Faith and a Call to Action* (Lausanne Movement, 2010), I-7-A.

5. Stuart K. Hine, *Not You, But God: A Testimony to God's Faithfulness*, 1st ed. (SK Hine, 1953).

6. Lausanne Movement, 'Lausanne Global Consultation on Creation Care and the Gospel: Call to Action' (St Ann, Jamaica: Lausanne Movement, 2012), accessed 1 March 2016. https://www.lausanne.org/content/statement/creation-care-call-to -action.

7. Dana L. Robert, 'Historical Trends in Missions and Earth Care', *International Bulletin of Missionary Research* 35, no. 3 (2011), 123–28.

8. William Carey, quoted in George Smith, *The Life of William Carey: Shoemaker and Missionary* (Middlesex: Echo, 2006), 301.

9. James Culross, *William Carey* (London: Hodder & Stoughton, 1881), 191.

10. Lowell Bliss, *Environmental Missions: Planting Churches and Trees* (Pasadena, CA: William Carey Library, 2013), xiii.

11. Christopher J. H. Wright, *The Mission of God's People* (Grand Rapids, MI: Zondervan, 2010), 60.

12. Bliss, *Environmental Missions*, 48.

13. Paul Brand, 'A Handful of Mud', *Christianity Today*, 16 April 1985, accessed 1 March 2016, http://www.christianitytoday.com/ct/2003/julyweb-only/7-7-47.0.html.

14. 'American Nun Murdered in Brazil', *Wikinews*, 15 February 2005, accessed 1 March 2016, http://en.wikinews.org/wiki/American_nun_murdered_in_Brazil.

15. Bliss, *Environmental Missions*, 127–28.

16. William Carey, quoted in Smith, *Life of William Carey*, 204.

17. Michelle Vu, 'Prominent Missiologist Identifies Biggest Trend in Global Mission', *Christian Post*, 30 July 2008, accessed 1 March 2016, http://www.christianpost.com/news/prominent-missiologist-identifies-biggest-trend-in-global-mission -33570/.

18. Stuart McAllister, 'The Power of Beauty', *Just Thinking* 21, no. 1 (2013), 27.

19. Jeffrey D. Pomerantz, 'The Practice of Medicine & The First Commandment: General Considerations', *Journal of Biblical Ethics in Medicine* 1, no. 1 (2003), 21.

20. John Thomas, 'An Account of the Hindoos, and of the Possibility of Spreading the Gospel Among Them: Correspondence to the Rev. Mr Rippon, London, August 25th, 1792', in *The Baptist Annual Register for 1790, 1791, 1792 and Part of 1793*, ed. John Rippon (London, 1973), 353.

21. Thomas, 'An Account', 353.

22. Shree Parbotee Brahman, in Thomas, 'An Account', 369.

23. John Thomas quoted in Arthur C. Chute, *John Thomas, First Missionary to Bengal, 1757–1801* (Halifax, Nova Scotia: Baptist Book and Tract Society, 1893), 52.

24. Chute, *John Thomas*, 55.

25. Courtesy of Center for the Study of the Life and Work of William Carey, D.D. (1761–1834), William Carey University, Hattiesburg, Mississippi.

26. Joshua Ward quoted in Chute, *John Thomas*, 63.

27. *Cape Town Commitment*, II-D-1-53.

28. Bill McKibben, *The End of Nature* (New York: Random House LLC, 1989).

29. Bill McKibben, 'The Most Important Number in the World' (presented at the Center for Applied Christian Ethics, Wheaton College, Wheaton, IL, 14 April 2009).

30. Bill McKibben. *Oil and Honey* (New York: Times Books, 2013), 208.

31. McKibben. 'The Most Important Number'.

32. Henry David Thoreau, *Walden,* vol. 1, Riverside Aldine series (New York: Houghton Mifflin, 1882), 120.

33. *Cape Town Commitment,* I-7-A-19.

34. *Cape Town Commitment,* II-B-6-46.

35. *Cape Town Commitment,* I-7-A-19.

36. *Cape Town Commitment,* II-B-3-C-43.

37. 'The Nature of Evangelism', in *The Lausanne Covenant* (Lausanne Movement, 1974; Hendrickson Publishers, 2011).

Notes to Case Study 1

1. *The Cape Town Commitment: A Confession of Faith and a Call to Action* (Lausanne Movement, 2010; Hendrickson Publishers, 2011), I-7-A.

Notes to Chapter 5

1. John Calvin, *Genesis* (1554), trans. John King [Commentary on Genesis 2:15] (The Banner of Truth Trust, 1965), 125, accessed 1 March 2016, http://www.ccel.org /ccel/calvin/calcom01.viii.i.html.

2. For a useful explanation, see 'Energy Access: Fireless Cooker', *Practical Action,* accessed 1 March 2016, http://practicalaction.org/fireless-cooker.

3. National Environment Management Authority (NEMA), *State of the Environment Report for Kenya 2003* (Nairobi: NEMA, 2004), 10.

4. Roland Bunch, *Restoring the Soil* (Winnipeg, MB, Canada: Canadian Food Grains Bank, 2012), 84.

5. See Food & Agriculture Organization of the United Nations, *FAO Country Programming Framework for Kenya 2013–2017,* accessed 1 March 2016, ftp://ftp.fao .org/TC/CPF/Countries/Kenya/CPF_KEN_2013-2017.pdf. Also World Bank, 'Life Expectancy at Birth, Total (years)', accessed 1 March 2016, http://data.worldbank .org/indicator/SP.DYN.LE00.IN.

6. Joseph A. Sittler, *Gravity and Grace: Reflections and Provocations* (Minneapolis, MN: Augsburg, 1986), 15.

7. Paul W. Brand, '"A Handful of Mud": A Personal History of My Love for the Soil', in *Tending the Garden: Essays on the Gospel and the Earth,* ed. Wesley Granberg-Michaelson (Grand Rapids, MI: W. B. Eerdmans, 1987), 147.

8. For information on Farming God's Way, see http://www.farming-gods-way .org/ (accessed 1 March 2016) or contact Care of Creation Kenya at www.kenya.careof creation.net (accessed 1 March 2016).

Notes to Chapter 6

Some of the ideas explored here appeared in an earlier paper: Dave Bookless, 'Christian Mission and Environmental Issues: An Evangelical Reflection', *Mission Studies* 25 (2008), 37–52.

1. *The Cape Town Commitment: A Confession of Faith and a Call to Action* (Lausanne Movement, 2010; Hendrickson Publishers, 2011), I-7-A.

2. Francis A. Schaeffer, *Pollution and the Death of Man: The Christian View of Ecology* (Carol Stream, IL: Tyndale House Publishers, 1970). Schaeffer particularly sought to answer the critique of Lynn White which blamed mainstream Christian interpretations of humanity as the image of God for allowing the exploitation and destruction of the natural environment: Lynn White, 'The Historical Roots of Our Ecologic Crisis', *Science* 155, no. 3767 (10 March 1967), 1203–7.

3. Au Sable Institute of Environmental Studies, www.ausable.org (accessed 1 March 2016); A Rocha, www.arocha.org (accessed 1 March 2016).

4. David W. Bebbington, *Evangelicalism in Modern Britain: A History from the 1730s to the 1980s* (London: Unwin Hyman, 1989), 2–17.

5. John R. W. Stott, *Christian Mission in the Modern World* (London: Falcon Books, 1975).

6. John R. W. Stott, *The Radical Disciple* (Nottingham: IVP, 2010), 65.

7. Tom Wright, 'Jerusalem in the New Testament', in *Jerusalem Past and Present in the Purposes of God*, ed. P. W. L. Walker, 2nd ed. (Carlisle: Paternoster, 1994), 70.

8. Dave Bookless, *Planetwise: Dare to Care for God's World* (Nottingham: IVP, 2008).

9. Anglican Consultative Council, *Mission: The Five Marks of Mission* (1984), accessed 1 March 2016, www.anglicancommunion.org/ministry/mission/fivemarks.cfm.

10. Cal Thomas, 'The Agenda Driven Life', *Washington Times*, 15 February 2006.

11. Ronald Sider, *Rich Christians in an Age of Hunger* (London: Hodder & Stoughton, 1978).

12. Third Lausanne Congress, *Cape Town Commitment*, I-7-A.

13. Richard Bauckham, *Bible and Ecology: Recovering the Community of Creation* (London: Darton, Longman & Todd, 2010); Richard Bauckham, *Living with Other Creatures: Green Exegesis and Theology* (Waco, TX: Baylor University Press, 2011).

14. N. T. Wright, *New Heavens, New Earth: The Biblical Picture of Christian Hope* (Cambridge: Grove Publishing, 1999); N. T. Wright, *Surprised by Hope* (London: SPCK, 2007).

15. Howard Peskett and Vinoth Ramachandra, *The Message of Mission* (Leicester: IVP, 2007).

16. Christopher J. H. Wright, *God's People in God's Land: Family, Land, and Property in the Old Testament* (Grand Rapids, MI: W. B. Eerdmans, 1990); Christopher J. H. Wright, *Old Testament Ethics for the People of God* (Leicester: IVP, 1994); Christopher J. H. Wright, *The Mission of God: Unlocking the Bible's Grand Narrative* (Nottingham: IVP, 2006).

17. Ken Gnanakan, *God's World: A Theology of the Environment* (London: SPCK, 1999).

18. Loren Wilkinson, ed., *Earthkeeping in the Nineties: Stewardship of Creation* (Grand Rapids, MI: W. B. Eerdmans, 1991).

19. Zac Niringiye, 'In the Garden of Eden: Creation and Community; Creation-Community Distorted, Torn Apart', *Journal of Latin American Theology: Christian Reflections from the Latino South* 5, no. 1 (2010), 18–42.

20. James Jones, *Jesus and the Earth* (London: SPCK, 2003).

21. Robert S. White and Jonathan A. Moo, *Hope in an Age of Despair: The Gospel and the Future of Life on Earth* (Nottingham: IVP, 2013).

22. Steven Bouma-Prediger, *For the Beauty of the Earth: A Christian Vision for Creation Care* (Grand Rapids, MI: Baker Academic, 2001).

23. Ruth Padilla DeBorst, 'God's Earth and God's People: Relationships Restored', *Journal of Latin American Theology: Christian Reflections from the Latino South* 5, no. 1 (2010), 6–17.

24. Walter Brueggemann, *The Land* (Philadelphia: Fortress Press, 1977).

25. Christopher J. H. Wright, *Living as the People of God* (Leicester: IVP, 1983), 59.

26. Jones, *Jesus and the Earth*.

27. Jones, *Jesus and the Earth*, 12.

28. Robert D. Woodberry, 'The Missionary Roots of Liberal Democracy', *American Political Science Review* 106, no. 2 (2010), 244–74.

29. Wright, *Surprised by Hope*.

30. Richard Bauckham and Trevor Hart, *Hope Against Hope: Christian Eschatology at the Turn of the Millennium* (London: Darton, Longman & Todd, 1999).

31. Calvin DeWitt, ed., *Missionary Earthkeeping* (Macon, GA: Mercer University Press, 2002).

32. Rev. Dr. Rob Frost, quoted on A Rocha UK Video (2005).

33. Peter Harris, *Under the Bright Wings* (London: Hodder & Stoughton, 2003); Peter Harris, *Kingfisher's Fire* (Oxford: Monarch, 2008).

34. Leah Kostamo, *Planted: A Story of Creation, Calling, and Community* (Eugene, OR: Cascade, 2013).

35. Chris Naylor, *Postcards from the Middle East* (Oxford: Lion, 2015).

36. Dave Bookless, *God Doesn't Do Waste: Redeeming the Whole of Life* (Nottingham: IVP, 2010).

37. Black Environmental Network, *Ethnic Communities & Green Spaces: Guidance for Green Space Managers*, 2005, accessed 1 March 2016, http://www.ben-network.org.uk/pdfs_publications/Green%20Spaces%20Part%202.pdf.

38. Restoring Eden, http://restoringeden.org/connect/CreationVoice/2007/July 2007/letstendthegarden (accessed 1 March 2016).

39. Environment Agency, 'The 50 Things That Will Save the Planet: Results from a Poll of 25 Experts', *Your Environment Extra*, no. 17 (November 2007–January 2008), accessed 1 March 2016 http://image.guardian.co.uk/sys-files/Environment/documents/2007/10/31/50top.pdf.

40. WWF-UK and Sustainable Development Commission, *Sustainable Development & UK Faith Groups: Two Sides of the Same Coin?* (2005), accessed 1 March 2016, http://www.sd-commission.org.uk/data/files/publications/SDandUKFaith Groupsv2_1.pdf.

41. Michael Shellenberger and Ted Nordhaus, *The Death of Environmentalism: Global Warming Politics in a Post-Environmental World*, 2004, accessed 1 March 2016, http://www.thebreakthrough.org/images/Death_of_Environmentalism.pdf.

42. Peter Harris, quoted verbatim in Bookless, 'Christian Mission and Environmental Issues', 50.

43. Sider, *Rich Christians in an Age of Hunger*; Lausanne Movement, *Lausanne Occasional Paper 20: An Evangelical Commitment to Simple Life-style* (Lausanne Movement, 1980), accessed 1 March 2016, http://www.lausanne.org/content/lop/lop-20.

44. Ronald Terchek, *Gandhi: Struggling for Autonomy* (Lanham, MD: Rowman & Littlefield, 1998), 117.

45. Generous, http://generous.org.uk (accessed 1 March 2016); Breathe, www
.breathenetwork.org (accessed 1 March 2016); A Rocha UK, http://arocha.org.uk
/our-activities/living-lightly (accessed 1 March 2016).

46. World Evangelical Alliance, www.worldea.org/whoweare/introduction (accessed 1 March 2016).

Notes to Chapter 7

1. John R. W. Stott, Foreword to *The Care of Creation: Focusing Concern and Action*, ed. R. J. Berry (Leicester: IVP, 2000), 7.

2. Clarence J. Glacken, *Traces on the Rhodian Shore* (Berkeley, CA: University of California Press, 1967); H. Paul Santmire, *The Travail of Nature* (Philadelphia, PA: Fortress Press, 1985); Clive Ponting, *A Green History of the World* (London: Sinclair-Stevenson, 1991); Ken Gnanakan, *God's World* (London: SPCK, 1999); Steven Bouma-Prediger, *For the Beauty of the Earth* (Grand Rapids, MI: Baker Academic, 2001); Richard Bauckham, *Bible and Ecology* (London: Darton, Longman & Todd, 2010).

3. Richard Bauckham, *Living with Other Creatures* (Waco, TX: Baylor University Press, 2011), 20.

4. 'Scientists' should, more strictly, be 'proto-scientists'; the word 'scientist' was only coined in 1883.

5. Cited by Bauckham, *Living with Other Creatures*, 22.

6. Peter Harrison, *The Fall of Man and the Foundations of Science* (Cambridge: Cambridge University Press, 2007).

7. Francis Bacon, *Instauratio Magna* (1620).

8. Quoted by Peter Medawar, *The Limits of Science* (New York: Harper & Row, 1964), 66.

9. John Calvin, *Genesis* (1554), trans. John King [Commentary on Genesis 2:15] (The Banner of Truth Trust, 1965), 125, accessed 1 March 2016, http://www.ccel.org /ccel/calvin/calcom01.viii.i.html.

10. Matthew Hale, *The Primitive Origination of Mankind* (London, 1677), 370.

11. John Ray, *Wisdom of God Manifested in the Works of Creation* (London, 1691), 167.

12. Francis Willughby, *The Ornithology of Francis Willughby* (London, 1678).

13. Peter Harrison, *The Bible, Protestantism and Natural Science* (Cambridge: Cambridge University Press, 1998).

14. Gilbert White, *The History and Antiquities of Selborne* (London, 1789), 180.

15. John Wesley, *A Survey of the Wisdom of God in the Creation*, 3rd ed. (London, 1777), 242.

16. Glacken, *Traces on the Rhodian Shore*, 168.

17. Robin Attfield, *The Ethics of Environmental Concern* (Oxford: Blackwell, 1983), 28.

18. Chris Patten et al., *Respect for the Earth: Sustainable Development* (London: Profile, 2000), 81.

19. Joseph Sittler, 'A Theology for Earth', Reprinted in Steven Bouma-Prediger and Peter W. Bakken, eds., *Evocations of Grace* (Grand Rapids, MI: W. B. Eerdmans, 2000), 20–37.

20. Lynn White, 'The Historical Roots of Our Ecologic Crisis', *Science* 155, no. 3767 (10 March 1967), 1203–7.

21. Joseph K. Sheldon, 'Twenty-One Years After "The Historical Roots of Our Ecologic Crisis": How Has The Church Responded?' *Perspectives on Science and Christian Faith* 41 (September 1989), 152–58; Joseph K. Sheldon, *Rediscovery of Creation. A Bibliographic Response of the Church's Response to the Environmental Crisis* (Metuchen, NJ: Scarecrow Press, 1992); Elspeth Whitney, 'Lynn White, Eco-theology, and History', *Environmental Ethics* 15, no. 2 (1993), 151–69.

22. Francis Schaeffer, *Pollution and the Death of Man* (London: Hodder & Stoughton, 1970).

23. Max Oeschlaeger, *Caring for Creation* (New York: Yale University Press, 1994), 1–2.

24. Jonathan A. Moo and Robin Routledge, eds., *As Long as the Earth Endures* (Nottingham: IVP, 2014).

25. Cornwall Alliance, *Cornwall Declaration on Environmental Stewardship* (2000), accessed 1 March 2016, http://www.cornwallalliance.org/docs/the-cornwall-declaration-on-environmental-stewardship.pdf.

26. Naomi Oreskes and Erik Conway, *Merchants of Doubt* (New York: Bloomsbury, 2010); Katharine Wilkinson, *Between God and Green* (New York: Oxford University Press, 2012).

27. Calvin Beisner, *Where Garden Meets Wilderness* (Grand Rapids, MI: W. B. Eerdmans, 1997).

28. Church of England, *Man in His Living Environment: An Ethical Assessment*, ed. G. W. Dimbleby (London: Church Information Office [for] the Church Assembly Board for Social Responsibility, 1970).

29. Hugh Montefiore, *Question Mark. The End of Homo Sapiens?* (London: Collins, 1969).

30. John Cobb, *Is It Too Late?* (Beverly Hills, CA: Bruce, 1972).

31. Charles Birch, William Eakin and Jay McDaniel, eds., *Liberating Life: Contemporary Approaches to Ecological Theology* (New York: Orbis, 1990); Philip Clayton, *God and Contemporary Science* (Edinburgh: Edinburgh University Press, 1997).

32. Rachel Carson, *Silent Spring* (Boston, MA: Houghton Mifflin, 1962); Crispin Gill, Frank Booker and Tony Soper, *The Wreck of the Torrey Canyon* (New York: Tapllinger, 1967).

33. Donella H. Meadows et al., foreword to *The Limits to Growth* (New York: Universe Books, 1972), 10.

34. Meadows et al., *The Limits to Growth*.

35. Edward Goldsmith et al., 'A Blueprint for Survival', *The Ecologist*, no. 2 (1972), 1–43.

36. T. R. E. Southwood et al., letter to the editor, *The Times of London*, January 25, 1972.

37. Barbara Ward and René Dubos, *Only One Earth: The Care and Maintenance of a Small Planet* (London: André Deutsch, 1972).

38. Patricia W. Birnie and Alan Boyle, *Basic Documents on International Law and the Environment* (Oxford: Oxford University Press, 1995), 3. See also, http://www.unep.org/Documents.Multilingual/Default.asp?documentid=97&articleid=1503 (accessed 1 March 2016).

39. International Union for Conservation of Nature and Natural Resources, United Nations Environment Programme and World Wildlife Fund, *World Conservation Strategy* (Gland, Switzerland: UNEP, IUCN, WWF, 1980), para. 1.3.

40. Richard Mabey, *The Common Ground* (London: Hutchinson, 1980), 27.

41. Peter Jacobs and David A. Munro, eds., *Strategies for Sustainable Development* (Gland, Switzerland: IUCN, 1987); J. Ronald Engel and Joan Engel, eds., *Ethics of Environment and Development* (London: Belhaven, 1990); *Caring for the Earth: A Strategy for Sustainable Living* (Gland, Switzerland: IUCN, UNEP, WWF, 1991).

42. United Nations World Commission on Environment and Development, *Our Common Future* (Oxford: OUP, 1987), accessed 1 March 2016, http://www.un-documents.net/our-common-future.pdf.

43. Caring for the Earth: *A Strategy for Sustainable Living*, 10.

44. The Secretaries of State, *This Common Inheritance: Britain's Environmental Strategy (Cm 1200)* (London: Her Majesty's Stationery Office, 1990), para. 1.14.

45. R. J. Berry, ed., *Environmental Dilemmas: Ethics and Decisions* (London: Chapman and Hall, 1993), 262–63.

46. R. J. Berry et al., *Christians and the Environment* (London: Board for Social Responsibility, 1991), GS Misc. 367.

47. Wesley Granberg-Michaelson, *Redeeming the Creation* (Geneva: World Council of Churches, 1992).

48. United Nations, *Convention on Biological Diversity.* (New York: United Nations, 1992), accessed 1 March 2016, http://www.cbd.int/, published as Grubb, M. et al., *The Earth Summit Agreements* (London: Earthscan, 1993).

49. Robert T. Watson et al., eds., *Protecting Our Planet, Securing Our Future* (Nairobi, Kenya and Washington DC: UNEP, NASA and the World Bank, 1998), accessed 1 March 2016, http://siteresources.worldbank.org/INTRANETENVIRON MENT/Resources/ProtectingOurPlanet.pdf.

50. Millennium Ecosystem Assessment, *Ecosystems and Human Well-being* (Washington, DC: Island Press, 2005).

51. https://sustainabledevelopment.un.org/topics (accessed1 March 2016)

52. Peter W. Bakken, Joan Gibb Engel and J. Ronald Engel, eds., *Ecology, Justice, and Christian Faith: A Critical Guide to the Literature* (Westport, CT: Greenwood Publishing Group, 1995).

53. Hans Küng, ed., *Yes to a Global Ethic* (London: SCM, 1996).

54. The World Evangelical Fellowship is now the World Evangelical Alliance.

55. Mark J. Thomas, 'Evangelicals and the Environment: Theological Foundations for Christian Environmental Stewardship', *Evangelical Review of Theology* 17, no. 2 (1993), 119–286;

56. Robert Carling and Marie Carling, eds., *A Christian Approach to the Environment* (Cheltenham: John Ray Initiative, 1995); R. J. Berry, ed., *The Care of Creation* (Leicester: IVP, 2000); Richard Wright, 'The *Declaration* Under Siege', in *The Care of Creation*, by R. J. Berry, 74–79; Richard Bauckham, 'Reading the Bible in the Context of the Ecological Threats of Our Time', Lecture to the Evangelical Theology Society, November 2012.

57. E. Calvin Beisner, *Where Garden Meets Wilderness* (Grand Rapids, MI: W. B. Eerdmans, 1997).

58. 'Preserving and Conserving the Earth: An Appeal for Joint Commitment in Science and Religion', accessed 1 March 2016, http://earthrenewal.org/Open_letter _to_the_religious_.htm.

59. John Paul II, 'Peace with God the Creator, Peace with all of Creation' (1 January 1990), accessed 1 March 2016, https://w2.vatican.va/content/john-paul-ii/en /messages/peace/documents/hf_jp-ii_mes_19891208_xxiii-world-day-for-peace .html.

60. 'Renewing the Earth: A Invitation to Reflection and Action on Environment in Light of Catholic Social Teaching', 14 November 1991, accessed 1 March 2016, http://www.usccb.org/issues-and-action/human-life-and-dignity/environment/renewing-the-earth.cfm.

61. Marlise Simons, 'Bartholomew I of Constantinople's Bold Green Stance', *The New York Times*, December 3, 2012.

62. Draft International Covenant on Environment and Development (Gland, Switzerland: IUCN, ICEL), xvii.

63. Pope Francis, *Laudato Si—Praise Be to You; On Care for Our Common Home* (Catholic Truth Society, 2015), or online at http://w2.vatican.va/content/francesco/en/encyclicals/documents/papa-francesco_20150524_enciclica-laudato-si.html.

64. See also the Lambeth Declaaration on Climate Change "recognizing the demands of justice as well as creation." Originally issued by Archbishop Rowan Williams in 2009 "as representative of the vast numbers of people of faith across the globe" and reissued in June 2015 by Archbishop Justin Welby and other British faith leaders: http://www.churchcare.co.uk/images/Lambeth_Declaration_2015_on_Climate_Change_website.pdf (accessed 1 March 2016).

65. For instance Peter Forster and Bernard Donoughue, 'The Papal Encylical: A critical Christian response' (The Global Warming Policy Foundation, 2015), 2–3, http://www.thegwpf.org/content/uploads/2015/07/Forster-Donoughue1.pdf.

66. R. J. Berry, 'A Worldwide Ethic for Sustainable Living', *Ethics, Place and Environment* 2 (1999), 97–107; R. J. Berry, *Ecology and the Environment* (West Conshohocken, PA: Templeton, 2011).

Notes to Chapter 8

1. Kenneth Boulding was Professor of Economics at The University of Colorado. See Kenneth E. Boulding, 'The Economics of the Coming Spaceship Earth', in *Environmental Quality in a Growing Economy*, ed. H Jarrett (Baltimore, MD: John Hopkins University Press, 1966), 3–14.

2. United Nations World Commission on Environment and Development, *Our Common Future* (1987), accessed 1 March 2016, http://www.un-documents.net/our-common-future.pdf.

3. Adapted from D. Raynaud, J. Jouzel, J. M. Barnola et al., 'The Ice Record of Greenhouse Gases', *Science* 259 (1993), 926–34.

4. Nick Spencer, Robert White, and Virginia Vroblesky, *Christianity, Climate Change, and Sustainable Living* (Peabody, MA: Hendrickson Publishers, 2009), p. 23.

5. *El Niño* events occur in the Pacific Ocean at intervals of about three to five years, when a large area of warm water appears off the coast of South America and persists for a year or more. Floods, droughts, and unusual weather events in the American, Asian, Australian, and even African continents can be associated with these events.

6. Years 500–1860: Northern Hemisphere from proxy data (shading indicates uncertainty in the reconstructed temperatures). Years 1861–2010: global instrumental observed. Years 2010–2100: a range of projections using various assumptions about emissions of greenhouses gases; the lowest projection is aiming at the desired temperature target of no more than 2°C increase from 1850. Ian Allison et al., *The*

Copenhagen Diagnosis: Updating the World on the Latest Climate Science (Elsevier, 2011), accessed 1 March 2016, www.copenhagendiagnosis.com.

7. Adapted from Intergovernmental Panel on Climate Change, ed., 'Technical Summary', in *Climate Change 2013*, 49.

8. Adapted from J. D. Milliman, J. M. Broadus and F. Gable, 'Environmental and Economic Implications of Rising Sea Level And Subsiding Deltas: The Nile and Bengal Examples', *Ambio* 18 (1989), 340–45.

9. Intergovernmental Panel on Climate Change, ed., 'Summary for Policymakers', *Climate Change 2007—The Physical Science Basis: Working Group I Contribution to the Fourth Assessment Report of the IPCC* vol. 4 (Cambridge: Cambridge University Press, 2007).

10. S. N. Jonkman, 'Global Perspectives on Loss of Human Life Caused by Floods', *Natural Hazards* 34, no. 2 (2005), 151–75.

11. For example, Norman Myers, Jennifer Kent, et al., *Environmental Exodus: An Emergent Crisis in the Global Arena* (Washington DC: Climate Institute, 1995).

12. Reports can be downloaded from: Intergovernmental Panel on Climate Change, www.ipcc.ch (accessed 1 March 2016).

13. John Houghton, *In the Eye of the Storm: The Autobiography of Sir John Houghton* (Oxford: Lion Books, 2013).

14. The Exxon Company and other energy companies in the USA were in the forefront of this campaign. See Naomi Oreskes and Erik M. Conway, *Merchants of Doubt: How a Handful of Scientists Obscured the Truth on Issues from Tobacco Smoke to Global Warming* (New York: Bloomsbury, 2010).

15. H. M. Treasury, *Stern Review: The Economics of Climate Change* (Cambridge: CUP, 2007), accessed 1 March 2016, http://webarchive.nationalarchives.gov.uk /+/http:/www.hm-treasury.gov.uk/independent_reviews/stern_review_economics _climate_change/stern_review_report.cfm.

16. United Nations, *Framework Convention on Climate Change* (1992), Article 3, accessed 1 March 2016, http://unfccc.int/files/essential_background/background _publications_htmlpdf/application/pdf/conveng.pdf.

17. J. T. Houghton, *Global Warming: The Complete Briefing*, 4th ed. (Cambridge: Cambridge University Press, 2009).

18. Although agreed upon in 1997, it did not come into force until 2005. The USA has not ratified the protocol; Australia ratified it in March 2008.

19. James Hansen et al., 'Target Atmospheric CO_2: Where Should Humanity Aim?' *Open Atmospheric Science Journal* 2 (2008), 217–31, accessed 1 March 2016, doi:10.2174/1874282300802010217.

20. International Energy Agency (IEA), Energy Technology Perspectives 2012 (Paris: IEA, 2012), accessed 1 March 2016, www.iea.org/publications/freepublications /publication/ETP2012_free.pdf. International Energy Agency, World Energy Outlook Special Report 2013: Redrawing the Energy Climate Map, 10 June 2013, 126, accessed 1 March 2016, www.iea.org.

21. See, for example, N. T. Wright, *New Heavens, New Earth: The Biblical Picture of Christian Hope* (Cambridge: Grove Books, 1999).

22. This policy is known as *Contraction and Convergence*. For more details, see Contraction and Convergence: Climate Truth and Reconciliation, http://www.gci .org.uk/ (accessed 1 March 2016).

Notes to Chapter 9

1. Most Rev. William S. Skylstad, Public Address, Regis University, February 2008.

2. Source: YouTube/OneWorldTV, 'Philippines Negotiator Makes Emotional Plea at Doha Climate Talks—Video', *The Guardian*, 6 December 2012, accessed 1 March 2016, http://www.theguardian.com/environment/video/2012/dec/06/philippines-negotiator-emotional-plea-doha-climate-talks-video.

3. John Vidal, 'Will Philippines Negotiator's Tears Change Our Course on Climate Change?', *The Guardian*, 6 December 2012, accessed 1 March 2016, http://www.theguardian.com/global-development/poverty-matters/2012/dec/06/philippines-delegator-tears-climate-change.

4. Jessica Shankleman, 'COP 19: Filipino Diplomat Goes on Hunger Strike to Demand Climate Progress', *businessGreen*, 11 November 2013, accessed 1 March 2016, http://www.businessgreen.com/bg/news/2306196/cop-19-filipino-diplomat-goes-on-hunger-strike-to-demand-climate-progress.

5. Ria Voorhaar, 'Civil Society to Announce They Will Fast in Solidarity with the Philippines' Yeb Saño', *Climate Action Network International*, 12 November 2013, accessed 1 March 2016, http://www.climatenetwork.org/node/3828.

6. Dorothy Boorse, *Loving the Least of These: Addressing a Changing Environment*, National Association of Evangelicals, 2011.

7. Millennium Project, 'Fast Facts: The Faces of Poverty', accessed 1 March 2016, http://www.unmillenniumproject.org/resources/fastfacts_e.htm.

8. Dale W. Jamieson and Marcello Di Paola, 'Climate Change and Global Justice: New Problem, Old Paradigm?' *Global Policy* 5, no. 1 (February 2014), 105–11.

9. Anwar Ali, 'Climate Change Impacts and Adaptation Assessment in Bangladesh', *Climate Research* 12, no. 2–3 (1999), 109–16.

10. Kiribati Climate Change, 'Climate', http://www.climate.gov.ki/climate/ (accessed 1 March 2016).

11. Arthur P. Webb and Paul S. Kench, 'The Dynamic Response of Reef Islands to Sea-Level Rise: Evidence from Multi-Decadal Analysis of Island Change in the Central Pacific', *Global and Planetary Change* 72, no. 3 (June 2010), 234–46, accessed 1 March 2016, doi:10.1016/j.gloplacha.2010.05.003.

12. A. Fedec and A. Sousa, 'CO_2 Emissions (metric Tons per Capita) in Kiribati', Trading Economics, accessed 1 March 2016, http://www.tradingeconomics.com/kiribati/co2-emissions-metric-tons-per-capita-wb-data.html.

13. Shoibal Chakravarty et al., 'Sharing Global CO_2 Emission Reductions among One Billion High Emitters', *Proceedings of the National Academy of Sciences* 106, no. 29 (21 July 2009), 11884–88, accessed 1 March 2016, doi:10.1073/pnas.0905232106.

14. Rachel Massey, 'Environmental Justice: Income, Race, and Health', *Global Development and Environment Institute*, 2004, accessed 1 March 2016, http://environmental-economists.net/teaching/Massey_Environmental_Justice.pdf.

15. Manuel Pastor et al., 'Minding the Climate Gap: What's at Stake If California's Climate Law Isn't Done Right and Right Away', USC Program for Environmental & Regional Equity, Los Angeles, 2010.

16. Simon Caney, 'Human Rights, Climate Change, and Discounting', *Environmental Politics* 17, no. 4 (2008), 536–55.

17. Lucy Stone and Katherine Lofts, 'Climate Change, Child Rights and Intergenerational Justice', *Institute of Development Studies*, 13 (November 2009), accessed 1 March 2016, http://www.ids.ac.uk/files/dmfile/IF13.2.pdf.

18. John Calvin, *Genesis* (1554), trans. John King [Commentary on Genesis 2:15] (The Banner of Truth Trust, 1965), 125, accessed 1 March 2016, http://www.ccel.org/ccel/calvin/calcom01.viii.i.html.

19. Philippine Atmospheric, Geophysical and Astronomical Services Administration, 'Climate Change in the Philippines', accessed 1 March 2016, https://web.pagasa.dost.gov.ph/index.php/climate-change-in-the-philippines.

20. National Research Council (U.S.), *Advancing the Science of Climate Change: America's Climate Choices* (Washington, DC: National Academies Press, 2010). Also, Intergovernmental Panel on Climate Change ed., *Climate Change 2013—The Physical Science Basis: Working Group I Contribution to the Fifth Assessment Report of the IPCC* (Cambridge: Cambridge University Press, 2014).

21. Martin Vermeer and Stefan Rahmstorf, 'Global Sea Level Linked to Global Temperature', *Proceedings of the National Academy of Sciences* 106, no. 51 (2009), 21527–32.

22. Ali, 'Climate Change Impacts and Adaptation Assessment in Bangladesh'.

23. Center for Integrative Environmental Research, *The US Economic Impacts of Climate Change and the Costs of Inaction: A Review and Assessment* (University of Maryland, October 2007), 33–37, accessed 1 March 2016, http://cier.umd.edu/documents/US%20Economic%20Impacts%20of%20Climate%20Change%20and%20the%20Costs%20of%20Inaction.pdf.

24. Anthony J. McMichael et al., 'Global Climate Change and Health: An Old Story Writ Large', in *Climate Change and Human Health: Risks and Responses*, ed. Anthony J. McMichael et al. (Geneva: World Health Organization, 2003), 1–17.

25. G. Nichols, 'Water and Disease and Climate Change', in *Health Effects of Climate Change in the UK 2008: An Update of the Department of Health Report 2001/2002*, ed. Sari Kovats (Department of Health and Health Protection Agency, 2008), 76–80. Also, David A. Relman et al., 'Global Climate Change and Extreme Weather Events: Understanding the Contributions to Infectious Disease Emergence, Workshop Summary', in *Global Climate Change and Extreme Weather Events: Understanding the Contributions to Infectious Disease Emergence, Workshop Summary* (Washington, DC: National Academies Press, 2008).

26. Nichols, 'Water and Disease and Climate Change'.

27. Centers for Disease Control and Prevention, 'Climate and Health: Climate Effects on Health—Air Pollution', accessed 1 March 2016, http://www.cdc.gov/climateandhealth/effects/air_pollution.htm.

28. Intergovernmental Panel on Climate Change ed., *Climate Change 2013—The Physical Science Basis: Working Group I Contribution to the Fifth Assessment Report of the IPCC* (Cambridge: Cambridge University Press, 2014).

29. Sari Kovats, Tanja Wolf, and Bettina Menne, 'Heatwave of August 2003 in Europe: Provisional Estimates of the Impact on Mortality' (November 3, 2004), accessed 1 March 2016, http://www.eurosurveillance.org/ViewArticle.aspx?ArticleId=2409. Also, Jean-Marie Robine et al., 'Death Toll Exceeded 70,000 in Europe during the Summer of 2003', *Comptes Rendus Biologies* 331, no. 2 (February 2008), 171–78, accessed 1 March 2016, doi:10.1016/j.crvi.2007.12.001. And, Peter A. Stott, Dáithí A. Stone, and Myles R. Allen, 'Human Contribution to the European Heatwave of 2003', *Nature* 432, no. 7017 (2004), 610–14.

30. Thomas Kleinen and Gerhard Petschel-Held, 'Integrated Assessment of Changes in Flooding Probabilities due to Climate Change', *Climatic Change* 81, no. 3–4 (2007), 283–312.

31. Jinwon Kim, 'A Projection of the Effects of the Climate Change Induced by Increased CO_2 on Extreme Hydrologic Events in the Western US', *Climatic Change* 68, no. 1–2 (2005), 153–68.

32. Jonathan A. Patz et al., 'Impact of Regional Climate Change on Human Health', *Nature* 438, no. 7066 (2005), 310–17.

33. P. C. D. Milly et al., 'Increasing Risk of Great Floods in a Changing Climate', *Nature* 415, no. 6871 (2002), 514–17. Also, N. S. Diffenbaugh, M. Scherer, and R. J. Trapp, 'Robust Increases in Severe Thunderstorm Environments in Response to Greenhouse Forcing', *Proceedings of the National Academy of Sciences* 110, no. 41 (October 8, 2013), 16361–66, accessed 1 March 2016, doi:10.1073/pnas.1307758110.

34. A. Grinsted, J. C. Moore, and S. Jevrejeva, 'Homogeneous Record of Atlantic Hurricane Surge Threat since 1923', *Proceedings of the National Academy of Sciences* 109, no. 48 (November 27, 2012), 19601–5, accessed 1 March 2016, doi:10.1073/pnas.1209542109.

35. Relman et al., 'Global Climate Change and Extreme Weather Events'.

36. Taikan Oki and Shinjiro Kanae, 'Global Hydrological Cycles and World Water Resources', *Science* 313, no. 5790 (2006), 1068–72.

37. J. L. Hatfield, 'Agriculture-Chapter 2', in *The Effects of Climate Change on Agriculture, Land Resources, Water Resources, and Biodiversity in the United States*, ed. Margaret Walsh et al., 2008, accessed 1 March 2016, http://www.cabdirect.org/abstracts/20083180112.html. Also, Paul C. D. Milly, Kathryn A. Dunne, and Aldo V. Vecchia, 'Global Pattern of Trends in Streamflow and Water Availability in a Changing Climate', *Nature* 438, no. 7066 (2005), 347–50.

38. A. Rabatel et al., 'Current State of Glaciers in the Tropical Andes: A Multi-Century Perspective on Glacier Evolution and Climate Change', *The Cryosphere* 7, no. 1 (2013), 81–102. Also, National Academy of Sciences. 'Himalayan Glaciers Retreating at Accelerated Rate in Some Regions: Consequences for Water Supply Remain Unclear', *ScienceDaily*, accessed 1 March 2016, www.sciencedaily.com/releases/2012/09/120912125826.htm.

39. Elsevier, 'One Billion Are Hungry: Can We Reduce Hunger Now and By 2050?' *ScienceDaily*, 1 February 2010, accessed 1 March 2016, www.sciencedaily.com/releases/2010/02/100201101901.htm.

40. Hatfield, 'Agriculture-Chapter 2', in *The Effects of Climate Change*. See also John Upton, 'At Least There's One Positive Thing Happening because of Climate Change', *Grist*, 2 January 2014, accessed 1 March 2016, http://grist.org/news/at-least-theres-one-positive-thing-happening-because-of-climate-change/.

41. Stanford University, 'Global Warming May Hurt Some Poor Populations, Benefit Others', *ScienceDaily*, 1 March 2010, accessed 1 March 2016, http://www.sciencedaily.com/releases/2010/02/100220184329.htm.

42. Purdue University, 'Climate Change Could Deepen Poverty in Developing Countries, Study Finds', *ScienceDaily*, 21 August 2009, accessed 1 March 2016, http://www.sciencedaily.com/releases/2009/08/090820082101.htm.

43. Anita Swarup, 'Haiti: A Gathering Storm: Climate Change and Poverty' (Oxford: Oxfam International, 2009). Also, Michelle D. Staudinger et al., *Impacts of Climate Change on Biodiversity, Ecosystems, and Ecosystem Services: Technical*

Input to the 2013 National Climate Assessment (Washington, DC: US Global Change Research Program, 2013).

44. Pavan Sukhdev et al., *The Economics of Ecosystems and Biodiversity: Interim Report* (Cambridge: Branson, 2008).

45. U. Thara Srinivasan et al., 'Food Security Implications of Global Marine Catch Losses due to Overfishing', *Journal of Bioeconomics* 12, no. 3 (2010), 183–200, accessed 1 March 2016, doi:10.1007/s10818-010-9090-9.

46. National Oceanic and Atmospheric Administration, 'Ocean Acidification: The Other Carbon Dioxide Problem', accessed 1 March 2016, http://www.pmel .noaa.gov/co2/story/Ocean+Acidification.

47. NOAA, 'Ocean Acidification'.

48. Maplecroft, 'Climate Change and Environmental Risk Atlas 2015', 29 October 2014, accessed 1 March 2016, http://maplecroft.com/portfolio/new-analysis /2014/10/29/climate-change-and-lack-food-security-multiply-risks-conflict-and -civil-unrest-32-countries-maplecroft/.

49. 'Data: Country and Lending Groups', 22 October 2013.

50. Sven Harmeling and David Eckstein, 'Global Climate Risk Index 2013: Who Suffers Most from Extreme Weather Events? Weather Related Loss Events in 2011 and 1992–2011' (Bonn: Germanwatch, 2012), accessed 1 March 2016, http://german watch.org/fr/download/7170.pdf.

51. Maplecroft, 'Climate Change and Environmental Risk Atlas 2014'.

52. Syud A. Ahmed, Noah S. Diffenbaugh, and Thomas W. Hertel, 'Climate Volatility Deepens Poverty Vulnerability in Developing Countries', *Environmental Research Letters* 4, no. 3 (2009), 8. Also, Karen O'Brien et al., 'Mapping Vulnerability to Multiple Stressors: Climate Change and Globalization in India', *Global Environmental Change* 14, no. 4 (2004), 303–13.

53. K. Warner, K. van der Geest, and S. Kreft, *Pushed to the Limit: Evidence of Climate Change-Related Loss and Damage when People Face Constraints and Limits to Adaptation* (Bonn: United Nations University Institute of Environment and Human Security, 2013, accessed 1 March 2016, http://collections.unu.edu/view /UNU:1849. Also, Paragraph 9 of the Doha Climate Gateway decision reads: 'Decides to establish, at its nineteenth session, institutional arrangements, such as an international mechanism, including functions and modalities, elaborated in accordance with the role of the Convention as defined in paragraph 5 above, to address loss and damage associated with the impacts of climate change in developing countries that are particularly vulnerable to the adverse effects of climate change', cited in Warner, van der Geest, and Kreft, *Pushed to the Limit*, 19.

54. Ahmed, Diffenbaugh, and Hertel, 'Climate Volatility Deepens Poverty Vulnerability in Developing Countries', 8.

55. R. Morello-Frosch et al., *The Climate Gap: Inequalities in How Climate Change Hurts Americans and How to Close the Gap*. Los Angeles, CA: Program for Environmental and Regional Equity, the University of Southern California, 2009, accessed 1 March 2016, http://dornsife.usc.edu/assets/sites/242/docs/Climate GapReport_full_report_web.pdf.

56. Fabian Scholtes and Anna-Katharina Hornidge, *Waiting for the Water to Come: Poverty Reduction in Times of Global Climate Change* (Bonn: Center for Development Research, University of Bonn and Care, 2009), accessed 1 March 2016, http:// www.zef.de/uploads/tx_zefportal/Publications/care_study_scholteshornidge _2009_en.pdf.

57. National Adaptation Programs of Action, 'NAPAs Received by the Secretariat', United Nations Framework Convention on Climate Change, 2013, accessed 1 March 2016, http://unfccc.int/adaptation/workstreams/national_adaptation_programmes _of_action/items/4585.php.

58. Martin L. Parry et al., *Assessing the Costs of Adaptation to Climate Change: A Review of the UNFCCC and Other Recent Estimates* (London: International Institute for Environment and Development and Grantham Institute for Climate Change, 2009).

59. Desmond Tutu, 'We Do Not Need Climate Change Apartheid in Adaptation', *Human Development Report 2007/2008: Fighting Climate Change*, 2007, 166–86.

60. Claudio Guler, 'The Climate Refugee Challenge', *International Relations and Security Network*, 14 April 2009, accessed 1 March 2016, http://www.isn.ethz.ch /Digital-Library/Articles/Detail//?ots591=4888CAA0-B3DB-1461-98B9-E20E7 B9C13D4&lng=en&id=98861.

61. United Nations Office for the Coordination of Humanitarian Affairs and the Internal Displacement Monitoring Centre, *Monitoring Disaster Displacement in the Context of Climate Change* (Geneva: UN-OCHA, IDMC, 2009).

62. Clark L. Gray and Valerie Mueller, 'Natural Disasters and Population Mobility in Bangladesh', *Proceedings of the National Academy of Sciences* 109, no. 16 (2012), 6000–05.

63. K. Warner et al., 'Climate Change, Environmental Degradation and Migration', *Natural Hazards* 55, no. 3 (2010), 689–715.

64. Joshua W. Busby, 'The Climate Security Connection: What It Means for the Poor', in *Climate Change and Global Poverty: A Billion Lives in the Balance?* ed. Lael Brainard, Abigail Jones, and Nigel Purvis (Washington, DC: Brookings Institution Press, 2009), 155–80.

65. J. Kloos et al., 'Climate Change, Water Conflicts and Human Security: Regional Assessment and Policy Guidelines for the Mediterranean, Middle East and Sahel', United Nations University Institute for Environment and Human Security, 2013, 6, accessed 1 March 2016, http://collections.unu.edu/view/UNU:1848.

66. Kloos et al. 'Climate Change, Water Conflicts and Human Security'.

67. United States Department of Defense, *Quadrennial Defense Review Report* (Washington, DC, February 2010), 104.

68. T. Kabanda and C. Munyati, 'Anthropogenic-Induced Climate Change and the Resultant Tendency to Land Conflict', in *Climate Change and Natural Resources Conflicts in Africa*, ed. Donald Anthony Mwiturubani and Jo-Ansie Van Wyk (Pretoria: ISS, 2010), 139–59.

69. Marshall B. Burke et al., 'Warming Increases the Risk of Civil War in Africa', *Proceedings of the National Academy of Sciences* 106, no. 49 (2009), 20670–74.

70. Lloyd Timberlake, foreword to *Dictionary of Environment and Development: People, Places, Ideas, and Organizations*, ed. Andy Crump (London: Earthscan Publications, 1991), cited in Celia Deane-Drummond, 'Development and Environment: In Dialogue with Liberation Theology', *New Blackfriars* 78, no. 916 (1997), 279–89.

71. Hans-Martin Füssel, 'How Inequitable Is the Global Distribution of Responsibility, Capability, and Vulnerability to Climate Change: A Comprehensive Indicator-Based Assessment', *Global Environmental Change* 20, no. 4 (2010), 597–611.

72. Diana Ürge-Vorsatz and Sergio Tirado Herrero, 'Building Synergies between Climate Change Mitigation and Energy Poverty Alleviation', *Energy Policy* 49 (2012), 83–90.

73. José A. Puppim de Oliveira, Christopher N. H. Doll, and Aki Suwa, *Urban Development with Climate Co-Benefits: Aligning Climate, Environmental and Other Development Goals in Cities* (Yokohama, Japan: United Nations University and Institute of Advanced Studies, 2013).

74. Kendra McSweeney and Oliver T. Coomes, 'Climate-Related Disaster Opens a Window of Opportunity for Rural Poor in Northeastern Honduras', *Proceedings of the National Academy of Sciences* 108, no. 13 (2011), 5203–8.

75. Mark E. Keim, 'Building Human Resilience: The Role of Public Health Preparedness and Response as an Adaptation to Climate Change', *American Journal of Preventive Medicine* 35, no. 5 (2008), 508–16.

Notes to Chapter 10

1. Cusco *campesina* or 'woman farmer' cited in Asociación para la Conservación de la Cuenca Amazónica (ACCA), *El Clima De Mi Tierra Está Cambiando: Cambio Climático En Las Zonas Altoandinas*, DVD (Peru: Inca Digital, 2011).

2. UNFCCC, *Climate Change: Impacts, Vulnerabilities and Adaptation in Developing Countries* (Bonn, Germany: 2007). See also J. Marengo et al., 'Climate Change: Evidence and Future Scenarios for the Andean Region' in *Climate Change and Biodiversity in the Tropical Andes,* eds. Sebastian Herzog et al. (Brazil: Inter-American Institute for Global Change Research [IAI] and Scientific Committee on Problems of the Environment [SCOPE], 2011).

3. G. Valdivia and M. Málaga, 'Desafíos, Estrategias Y Arreglos Institucionales De Las Comunidades Campesinas De Espinar Para Enfrentar Los Efectos Del Cambio Climático Sobre Los Medios De Vida' in *Los Desafíos De La Adaptación Al Cambio Climático En Comunidades Rurales Altoandinas*, by G. Valdivia et al. (Lima: Soluciones Prácticas, 2012).

4. The latest National Census reveals figures of over 55 percent extreme poverty and 20 percent illiteracy rate in provinces most affected by climate change impacts.

5. M. Bazán et al. (2008) reports a growth of 8 percent a year in the Cusco region. See M. Bazán et al., 'La Exclusión e Iniciativas de Crecimiento con Inclusión en el Cusco—Una Aproximación' (Lima: Foro Nacional Internacional, 2012).

6. Source: Ecoticias, www.ecoticias.com (accessed 1 March 2016).

7. PACC Perú, Senhami and COSUDE, 'Caracterización Climática de las Regiones Cusco y Apurimac' (Peru: PACC Perú, 2012), available at: http://www.siar .regioncusco.gob.pe/ (accessed 1 March 2016).

8. Intergovenmental Panel on Climate Change ed., *Climate Change 2013—The Physical Science Basis: Working Group I Contribution to the Fifth Assessment Report of the IPCC* (Cambridge: Cambridge University Press, 2014).

9. Gobierno Regional del Cusco and PACC, 'Diagnóstico Situacional Regional Y Estrategia Regional Frente Al Cambio Climático' (Cusco, 2011).

10. The queuña tree (*Polylepis spp*), native to Cusco highlands and an endangered species, withstands extreme weather conditions at altitudes up to 5,000 metres.

11. Jaime Llosa L. et al., *Cambio Climático, Crisis Del Agua Y Adaptación En Las Montañas Andinas* (Lima: Red Ambiental Peruana-DESCO, 2010).

12. The Climate Change Adaptation Programme (PACC, in Spanish) has conducted studies on this phenomenon in Cusco since 2009. See PACC Perú, http:// www.paccperu.org.pe (accessed 1 March 2016).

13. Cusco *campesina*, cited in ACCA, *El Clima De Mi Tierra Está Cambiando*.

14. Raymundo Paniera, quoted in A. Flores and G. Valdivia, 'Impactos De La Variabilidad Y Cambio Climático En Los Sistemas Productivos Rurales Y En Las Condiciones De Vida Y Desarrollo Campesinos', informe final, Microcuenca Huacrahuacho (Cusco: CBC-Colegio Andino, 2010).

15. ACCA, *El Clima De Mi Tierra Está Cambiando*.

16. PACC Perú, *La Vida Ya No Es Como Antes: Percepciones Sobre Los Cambios De Clima En Dos Microcuencas De Los Andes Del Sur Del Perú*, video (Cusco, 2011).

17. CBC and PREDES, 'Impactos De La Variabilidad Y Cambio Climático En Los Sistemas Productivos Rurales Y En Las Condiciones De Vida Y Desarrollo Campesinos: Una Visión Desde La Población Rural De Cusco', informe final (Lima, Cusco: 2011).

18. Quoted in Karin Kancha, 'Interview with Agronomist Karin Kancha' (Peru: PREDES, 2011).

19. PACC Perú, http://www.paccperu.org.pe (accessed 1 March 2016).

20. Marina Imata cited in Flores and Valdivia, 'Impactos De La Variabilidad'.

21. *Kañiwa* is a dark reddish-brown seed from the Andes Mountains in Peru, similar in character and uses to the closely related quinoa, and rich in protein, fibre, iron, calcium, and zinc.

22. Testimony quoted in Flores and Valdivia, 'Impactos De La Variabilidad'.

23. Gobierno Regional del Cusco-PACC, *Diagnóstico Situacional*.

24. Kancha, 'Interview'.

25. PACC Perú, *La Vida Ya No Es Como Antes*.

26. PACC Perú, *La Vida Ya No Es Como Antes*.

27. PACC Perú, *La Vida Ya No Es Como Antes*.

28. Quoted in CBC and PREDES, 'Impactos De La Variabilidad'.

29. PACC Perú, 'Estudio De Demanda Hídrica Actual En Las Regiones De Cusco Y Apurimac' (Cusco: IMA-PACC, 2010).

30. In Cusco, growth is especially due to tourism, extractive industries, and construction. See Bazán et al., 'La Exclusión E Iniciativas De Crecimiento Con Inclusión En El Cusco' (Lima: 2008), 2.

31. Gilberto Romero et al., 'Estudio De Impactos De La Variabilidad' (Cusco: PREDES, 2011).

32. Residents of Huarcachapi, quoted in Romero et al., 'Estudio De Impactos De La Variabilidad'.

33. Flores and Valdivia, Impactos De La Variabilidad (emphasis added).

34. CBC and PREDES, Impactos De La Variabilidad.

35. This shift to more commercial, improved-variety crops has also been promoted by the government and certain NGOs.

36. Gobierno Regional del Cusco, *Estrategia Regional Frente al Cambio Climático: ERFCC Cusco* (Cusco, Peru: 2012).

37. Conversation with missionary Ian Horne, Cusco, October 2011.

38. Regions Beyond Missionary Union and Evangelical Union of South America, now merged to form the mission Latin Link.

39. Kancha, 'Interview'.

40. Kancha, 'Interview'.

41. Flores and Valdivia, 'Impactos De La Variabilidad'.

42. Flores and Valdivia, 'Impactos De La Variabilidad' and Kancha, 'Interview'.

43. Juan Condori, Chuquira Community, quoted in PACC Perú, *La Vida Ya No Es Como Antes*.

44. Gobierno Regional del Cusco, *Estrategia Regional Frente al Cambio Climático*.
45. Agronomist Kancha, from PREDES organisation, participated in the PACC study on climate change.

Notes to Chapter 11

1. Rob Dietz and Dan O'Neill, *Enough is Enough: Building a Sustainable Economy in a World of Finite Resources* (Abingdon: Earthscan, 2013), 78.
2. Mathis Wackernagel et al., 'Tracking the Ecological Overshoot of the Human Economy', *Proceedings of the National Academy of Sciences* 99, no. 14 (2002), 9266–71.
3. The global biocapacity of 12 billion gha (global hectares), if shared equally between 7.2 billion people, would allow 1.67 gha each. Mali's per-person footprint in 2010 was around 1.7 gha, see WWF International, Zoological Society of London, Global Footprint Network, and Water Footprint Network, *Living Planet Report* 2014 (Gland, Switzerland: WWF International, 2014).
4. The Third Lausanne Congress on World Evangelization, *The Cape Town Commitment: A Confession of Faith and a Call to Action* (Lausanne Movement, 2010), II-B-3-C, accessed 1 March 2016, http://www.lausanne.org/content/ctc /ctcommitment.
5. United Nations Department for Economic and Social Affairs (UN DESA), *World Population Prospects: The 2015 Revision* (New York: United Nations, 2015), accessed 1 March 2016, http://esa.un.org/wpp/.
6. R. C. Sproul Jr., *Believing God* (Lake Mary, FL: Reformation Trust, 2009), 41–52. And see John McKeown, 'Receptions of Israelite Nation-Building: Modern Protestant Natalism and Martin Luther', *Dialog: A Journal of Theology* 49, no. 2 (2010), 133–40.
7. Carol Meyers, 'Procreation, Production, and Protection: Male-Female Balance in Early Israel', *Journal of the American Academy of Religion* 51 (1983), 581.
8. Hans-Joachim Kraus, *Psalms 60–150* (Minneapolis: Augsburg, 1989), 455; Daniel Fleming, 'Psalm 127: Sleep for the Fearful, and Security in Sons', *Zeitschrift für die alttestamentliche Wissenschaft* 107 (1995), 435–44; Robert Davidson, *The Vitality of Worship* (Edinburgh: Handsel, 1998), 419.
9. Christopher Hays, *Death in the Iron Age II and in First Isaiah* (Tübingen: Mohr Siebeck, 2011).
10. Eusebius of Caesarea, *The Proof of the Gospel*, trans. W. Ferrar (London: SPCK, 1920), 157.
11. Matthew Sleeth, *Serve God and Save the Planet* (Grand Rapids: Zondervan, 2007), 187.
12. Roman Catholic support for 'artificial birth control' was 91 percent in Latin America (polling Argentina, Brazil, Colombia, and Mexico), 40 percent in Africa (Uganda and Congo), and 31 percent in the Philippines, www.univision.com/inter activos/openpage/2014-02-06/la-voz-del-pueblo-matriz-1 (accessed 1 March 2016).
13. Kathy Gaca, *The Making of Fornication: Eros, Ethics, and Political Reform in Greek Philosophy and Early Christianity* (Berkeley: University of California Press, 2003).
14. Keith Grüneberg, *Abraham, Blessing, and the Nations: A Philological and Exegetical Study of Genesis 12:3 in its Narrative Context* (Berlin: Walter de Gruyter, 2003), 102; Gordon Wenham, *Genesis 1–15* (Waco, TX: Word, 1987), 24.

15. Royal Society, *People and the Planet* (London: Royal Society, 2012).

16. Norman Borlaug, 'The Green Revolution, Peace, and Humanity' (Nobel Lecture, 1970), accessed 1 March 2016, http://www.nobelprize.org/nobel_prizes/peace/laureates/1970/borlaug-lecture.html.

17. George H. W. Bush, foreword to *World Population Crisis: The United States Response*, by Phyllis Piotrow (New York: Praeger, 1973).

18. United Nations World Commission on Environment and Development, *Our Common Future* (1987), accessed 23 February 2015, http://www.un-documents.net/our-common-future.pdf.

19. United Nations Population Information Network, Report of the IPCD (International Conference on Population and Development), 1994, accessed 1 March 2016, http://www.un.org/popin/icpd/conference/offeng/poa.html.

20. An insider account of the 1990s loss of concern about population, including the shift of funders' attention from family planning to HIV, and the ambiguous role of feminists and some religious groups, appears in a talk by Catherine Budgett-Meakin, 'Population: Making Connections and Avoiding Heffalump Traps', 2011, accessed 1 March 2016, http://populationandsustainability.org/psn-debates-population-issues-with-mensa/. A recent academic analysis is given by Diana Coole, 'Too Many Bodies? The Return and Disavowal of the Population Question', *Environmental Politics* 22, no. 2 (2013), 195–215.

21. John Guillebaud and Pete Moore, 'Population Matters: Voluntary Contraception for Environmental Sustainability', in *Creation in Crisis: Christian Perspectives on Sustainability*, ed. Robert S. White (London: SPCK, 2009), 84–100.

22. UN population data uses the categories 'more developed countries' and 'less developed countries'. A subset (currently 48) of the latter are identified as the 'least developed countries'. So, for summaries of that data, and throughout to avoid confusion, I have used that classification and terminology.

23. WWF International et al., *Living Planet Report 2014*, 33.

24. Using annual birth records that begin from 1909, the cumulative number of births in the USA from 1909 to 2012 was 359.5 million, Center for Disease Control and Prevention, www.cdc.gov (accessed 1 March 2016). Over the same period the cumulative number of legal immigrants was 52.4 million, Department of Homeland Security, www.dhs.gov (accessed 1 March 2016). Therefore, more people were added by birth than by legal immigration in a ratio of more than 6 to 1.

25. Data source: Center for Disease Control and Prevention, www.cdc.gov (accessed 1 March 2016), with thanks to Amy M. Branum and Robert N. Anderson.

26. Royal Society, *People and the Planet*, 54.

27. United Nations, *World Population Policies 2011* (United Nations, 2013).

28. Mike Brewer, Anita Ratcliffe, and Sarah Smith, 'Does Welfare Reform Affect Fertility? Evidence from the UK', *Journal of Population Economics* 25, no. 1 (2012), 245–66.

29. Adair Turner, 'Population Ageing: What Should We Worry About?' *Philosophical Transactions of the Royal Society B: Biological Sciences* 364, no. 1532 (2009), 3009–21.

30. Sarah Harper, *Ageing Societies: Myths, Challenges and Opportunities* (London: Hodder Arnold, 2006), 21.

31. Jeroen Spijker and John MacInnes, 'Population Ageing: The Timebomb That Isn't?' *British Medical Journal* 347 (2013), http://www.bmj.com/content/347/bmj.f6598. If 'elderly' is defined as 'less than 15 years remaining life expectancy', the pro-

portion of elderly has declined since 1980 in England and Wales, The Conversation, 'Forget the Ageing Population, We're Actually Getting "Younger"', https://theconver sation.com/forget-the-ageing-population-were-actually-getting-younger-21249 (both accessed 1 March 2016).

32. Harper, *Ageing Societies*, 24.

33. UN DESA, *World Population Prospects: 2012 Revision*.

34. UN DESA, *World Population Prospects: The 2012 Revision, Highlights*, 31.

35. Ashok Khosla in Global Humanitarian Forum*: 2009 Forum—Human Impact of Climate Change* (Geneva: Global Humanitarian Forum, 2009), 141, accessed 1 March 2016, http://www.gci.org.uk/Documents/GHF_2009_.pdf.

36. R. Hussain, F. F. Fikree, and H. W. Berendes, 'The Role of Son Preference in Reproductive Behaviour in Pakistan', *Bulletin of the World Health Organization* 78, no. 3 (2000), 379–88.

37. Leontine Alkema et al., 'National, Regional, and Global Rates and Trends in Contraceptive Prevalence and Unmet Need for Family Planning between 1990 and 2015: A Systematic and Comprehensive Analysis', *The Lancet* 381, no. 9878 (2013), 1642–52.

38. Royal Society, *People and the Planet*, 38.

39. Population Media Centre, https://www.populationmedia.org/ (accessed 1 March 2016), highlights examples of broadcast media.

40. Guillebaud and Moore, 'Population Matters'.

41. Karan Singh, *Autobiography* (Delhi: Oxford University Press, 1994), xv.

42. United Nations Department of Economic and Social Affairs, *Completing the Fertility Transition* (New York: United Nations, 2009), 175.

43. Paul Demeny, 'European Parliament on the Need for Promoting Population Growth', *Population and Development Review* 10 (1984), 569–70.

44. UN DESA, *World Population Prospects: 2015 Revision*, 132.

45. Eurostat, http://ec.europa.eu/eurostat (accessed 1 March 2016).

46. Data source: U.S. Census Bureau. National Population Projections 2015–2060.

47. CCIH (Christian Connections for International Health), 'Family Planning and Reproductive Health', http://www.ccih.org/family-planning-a-reproductive-health .html (accessed 1 March 2016).

48. CCIH and the Institute for Reproductive Health, Georgetown University (2013), http://www.ccih.org/Love-Children-Family-Planning.pdf (accessed 1 March 2016).

49. Including an interview with Dr. Tonny Tumwesigye, Uganda Protestant Medical Bureau (UPMB) Executive Director, http://upmb.co.ug/family-planning-interview -executive-director-upmb/ (accessed 1 March 2016).

50. CCIH, Faith and International Family Planning, http://www.ccih.org /activities/information-sharing/news/47-general/549-launch-of-faith-and-family -planning-report.html (accessed 1 March 2016).

51. CHASE Africa, http://www.chaseafrica.org.uk/. An interview with one of the founders of CHASE Africa is at http://www.jri.org.uk/associates/caroline -pomeroy/ (both accessed 1 March 2016).

52. Blue Ventures, http://blueventures.org/ (accessed 1 March 2016).

53. Ecological Christian Organisation, http://www.ecouganda.org/ (accessed 1 March 2016).

54. See note 21 and John Guillebaud, 'Population Growth, Global Warming and Sustainability of the Environment', *The Bible in Transmission* (Bible Society, 2006).

55. Susan Power Bratton, *Six Billion and More: Human Population Regulation and Christian Ethics* (Louisville: Westminster John Knox Press, 1992).

56. James Martin-Schramm, *Population Perils and the Churches' Response* (Geneva: WCC Publications, 1997).

57. Jim Ball, 'Evangelicals, Population, and the Ecological Crisis', *Christian Scholars Review* 28, no. 2 (1998), 226–53.

58. Christine E. Gudorf, 'Resymbolizing Life: Religion on Population and Environment', *Horizons* 28, no. 2 (2001), 183–210.

59. J. Matthew Sleeth, '6.5 Billion and Counting: A Christian Case for Small Families', *Books and Culture: A Christian Review* 36, no. 8 (2007).

60. Olly Mesach, 'The Role of the Christian Community in the Family Planning Movement in Indonesia: A Case Study', *Transformation* 13, no. 2 (1996), 31–33.

61. Daisy N. Nwachuku, 'The Gender Factor in Family Size and Health Issues in Modern Nigerian Homes', *Transformation* 13, no. 3 (1996), 13.

62. J. Kwabena Asamoah-Gyadu, ' "Broken Calabashes and Covenants of Fruitfulness": Cursing Barrenness in Contemporary African Christianity', *Journal of Religion in Africa* 37 (2007), 437–60.

63. Bill McKibben, *Maybe One? A Personal and Environmental Argument for Single Child Families* (New York: Simon & Schuster, 1998).

64. John McKeown, *God's Babies: Natalism and Bible Interpretation in Modern America* (Cambridge: Open Book Publishers, 2014).

65. UN DESA, *World Population Prospects: 2015 Revision*.

66. UNICEF, *Annual Report* (New York: UNICEF, 1992).

Notes to Chapter 12

1. Jim Wallis, editor of *Sojourners*, in Michael A. Fletcher, 'Katrina Pushes Issues of Race and Poverty at Bush', *The Washington Post*, 12 September 2005, sec. Nation, accessed 29 February 2016, http://www.washingtonpost.com/wp-dyn/content/article/2005/09/11/AR2005091101131.html.

2. Team Louisiana, *The Failure of the New Orleans Levee System Following Hurricane Katrina and the Pathway Forward* (Baton Rouge: Louisiana Department of Transportation and Development, 2006), Appendix VI.

3. Original in Museu da Cidade, Lisbon. From New Collection Kozak, Prague, reprinted with permission.

4. R. M. W. Musson, *The Million Death Quake* (New York: Palgrave Macmillan, 2012).

5. J. Polkinghorne, 'The Anthropic Principle and the Science and Religion Debate', *Faraday Paper* No. 4 (2007), free download from the Faraday Institute, www.faraday.stedmunds.cam.ac.uk/ (accessed 29 February 2016).

6. The average surface temperature in the absence of greenhouse gases in the atmosphere would be about -6°C or lower. John T. Houghton, *Global Warming: The Complete Briefing, Third Edition* (Cambridge: Cambridge University Press, 2004).

7. C.-F. Volney, 'Travels through Syria and Egypt: In the Years 1783, 1784, and 1785. Containing the Present Natural and Political State of Those Countries', translated from French (London: printed for G. G. J. and J. Robinson), 1787.

8. P. Farmer, *Haiti After the Earthquake* (New York: PublicAffairs, 2011).

9. G. Thomas and M. Morgan-Witts, *The Day Their World Ended* (London: Souvenir Press, 1969).

10. S. Contour, *Saint-Pierre, Martinique, Vol. 2: La Catastrophe et Ses Suites* (Paris: Ed. Caribéennes, 1989).

11. Even in remote areas, satellites can be used to monitor and forecast floods. See, for example, the real-time Global Flood Monitoring System at University of Maryland, 'Global Flood Monitoring System', http://flood.umd.edu/ (accessed 29 February 2016).

12. Team Louisiana, *The Failure of the New Orleans Levee System*. See also R. Solnit, *A Paradise Built in Hell* (London: Viking, 2009), 239–240.

13. UN Food and Agriculture Organization, *The State of Food Insecurity in the World 2015*, available free from www.fao.org/hunger/en (accessed 29 February 2016).

14. J. Donnelly, *The Great Irish Potato Famine* (Stroud: Sutton Publishing, 2002).

15. From Committee of the China Famine Relief Fund, *The Famine in China* (London: C. Kegan Paul & Co., London, 1878).

16. Committee of the China Famine Relief Fund, *Famine in China*.

17. Timothy Richard letter to the Baptist Missionary Society, 17 October 1888. The underlines are his.

18. Frank Dikotter, *Mao's Great Famine: The History of China's Most Devastating Catastrophe, 1958–62* (London: Bloomsbury Publishing, 2010).

19. James B. Pritchard, ed., *Ancient Near Eastern Texts Relating to the Old Testament with Supplement*, 3rd rev. ed. (Princeton, NJ: Princeton University Press, 1969), 238.

20. Nick Spencer, Robert White, and Virginia Vroblesky, *Christianity, Climate Change, and Sustainable Living* (Peabody, MA: Hendrickson Publishers, 2009).

21. John Wesley, 'Serious Thoughts Occasioned by the Late Earthquake in Lisbon', in *The Works of John Wesley*, ed. Thomas Jackson, 3rd ed., 14 vols. (London: Wesleyan Methodist Book Room, 1755); reprint ed. (Grand Rapids, MI: Baker, 1979), vol. 11, 4.

22. Augustine of Hippo, *De Genesi Ad Litteram*.

23. See, for example, Roger Carswell, *Where Is God in a Messed-up World?* (Nottingham: IVP, 2006), 37; and John Blanchard, *Where Was God on September 11?* (Darlington: Evangelical Press, 2002), 17.

24. Robert S. Fyall, *Now My Eyes Have Seen You: Images of Creation and Evil in the Book of Job* (Downers Grove, IL: IVP, 2002); see also a helpful book by Christopher Ash, *Out of the Storm: Grappling with God in the Book of Job* (Leicester: IVP, 2004).

25. N. T. Wright, *Evil and the Justice of God* (London: SPCK, 2006).

26. Jonathan A. Moo and Robert S. White, *Let Creation Rejoice: Biblical Hope and Ecological Crisis* (Downers Grove, IL: IVP, 2014).

Notes to Chapter 13

1. United Nations, *Convention on Biological Diversity* (New York: United Nations, 1992), http://www.cbd.int/ (accessed 1 March 2016).

2. Camilo Mora et al., 'How Many Species Are There on Earth and in the Ocean?' *PLoS Biology* 9, no. 8 (August 23, 2011), e1001127, accessed 1 March 2016, doi:10.1371/journal.pbio.1001127.

3. The Intergovernmental Platform on Biodiversity and Ecosystem Services (IPBES), http://www.ipbes.net/ (accessed 1 March 2016).

4. United Nations, 'Sustainable Development Knowledge Platform: Sustainable Development Goals', https://sustainabledevelopment.un.org/topics (last accessed 1 March 2016).

5. Millennium Ecosystem Assessment, *Ecosystems and Human Well-being: Biodiversity Synthesis* (Washington, DC: World Resources Institute, 2005), 43.

6. World Wide Fund International, *Living Planet Report 2012: Biodiversity, Biocapacity and Better Choices* (Gland, Switzerland: WWF International, 2012).

7. Johan Rockström et al., 'A Safe Operating Space for Humanity', *Nature* 461, no. 7263 (September 24, 2009), 472–75, accessed 1 March 2016, doi:10.1038/461472a.

8. Josie Glausiusz, 'Biologist Edward O. Wilson: The Bard of Biodiversity', *Discover Magazine*, 1 December 2001, accessed 1 March 2016, http://discovermagazine.com/2001/dec/breakdialogue.

9. Andrew Balmford, *Wild Hope: On the Front Lines of Conservation Success* (Chicago: University of Chicago Press, 2012), 4.

10. Millennium Ecosystem Assessment, *Ecosystems and Human Well-being*, 2.

11. Thabo Makgoba, 'Hope and the Environment: A Perspective from the Majority World', *Anvil* 29, no. 1 (1 January 2013), 55–70, accessed 1 March 2016, doi:10.2478/anv-2013-0005.

12. Uist Wader Research, http://www.snh.gov.uk/land-and-sea/managing-wild life/uist-wader-research/ (accessed 1 March 2016).

13. Uist Hedgehog Rescue, http://www.uhr.org.uk/ (accessed 1 March 2016).

14. Rachel Carson, *Silent Spring* (Boston, MA: Houghton Mifflin, 1962).

15. Martin J. Hodson and Margot R. Hodson, *Cherishing the Earth* (Oxford: Monarch, 2008), 48–52.

16. Sarah Fisher, *Population Dynamics and Biodiversity: A PSN Briefing Paper* (London: Population and Sustainability Network, 2012).

17. Geordie Torr, 'Unnatural Acts', *The Geographical Magazine* 86, no. 3 (2014), 30–38.

18. Intergovernmental Panel on Climate Change, ed., *Climate Change 2014— Impacts, Adaptation, and Vulnerability: The Summary for Policymakers of the Working Group II Contribution to the Fifth Assessment Report*, 30 March 2014, accessed 1 March 2016, http://ipcc-wg2.gov/AR5/images/uploads/IPCC_WG2AR5_SPM _Approved.pdf.

19. Martin J. Hodson and John A. Bryant, *Functional Biology of Plants* (Chichester: Wiley-Blackwell, 2012), 291–97.

20. Hodson and Hodson, *Cherishing the Earth*, 15–18.

21. Millennium Ecosystem Assessment, *Ecosystems and Human Well-being*, 1.

22. Stephen Smith, *Environmental Economics: A Very Short Introduction* (Oxford: Oxford University Press, 2011), 11–13.

23. Tony Juniper, *What Has Nature Ever Done for Us? How Money Really Does Grow on Trees* (London: Profile Books, 2013).

24. The Economics of Ecosystems & Biodiversity (TEEB), *Mainstreaming the Economics of Nature: A Synthesis of the Approach, Conclusions and Recommendations of TEEB* (October 2010), accessed 1 March 2016, http://www.teebweb.org/our -publications/teeb-study-reports/synthesis-report/.

25. TEEB, *Mainstreaming the Economics of Nature*, 9.

26. Bill Devall and George Sessions, 'Deep Ecology', in *Environmental Ethics: Readings in Theory and Practice*, 4th ed. ed. Louis P. Pojman (Belmont: Wadsworth/ Thomson Learning, 2005), 202.

27. Moses Maimonides, *The Guide for the Perplexed*, trans. from the original [1190] Arabic text by M. Friedländer [1881], with an introduction by D. Taffel (New York: Barnes and Noble, 2004), 461.

28. Millennium Ecosystem Assessment, *Ecosystems and Human Well-being*, 7.

29. George Perkins Marsh, *Man and Nature: or, Physical Geography as Modified by Human Action* (New York and London, 1864), 549.

30. Aldo Leopold, foreword to *A Sand County Almanac* (New York, Ballantine Books, 1949).

31. Mary Evelyn Tucker and John Grim, *Overview of World Religions and Ecology*, The Forum on Religion and Ecology at Yale (Yale University, 2009), accessed 1 March 2016, http://fore.research.yale.edu/religion/.

32. Fiona Jones, *Fading Fady: The Biological and Cultural Cost to Madagascar* (Final Honour School of Human Sciences Dissertation, Oxford University, 2013).

33. Margot R. Hodson, *Uncovering Isaiah's Environmental Ethics* (Cambridge: Grove Books, 2011).

34. F. Nigel Hepper, *Illustrated Encyclopedia of Bible Plants* (Leicester: IVP, 1992); Peter France, *An Encyclopedia of Bible Animals* (Tel Aviv: Steimatzky, 1986).

35. John R. W. Stott, *The Birds Our Teachers: Biblical Lessons from a Lifelong Bird-watcher* (Carlisle: Candle Books, 1999); Ghillean Prance, *Go to the Ant: Reflections on Biodiversity and the Bible* (Glasgow: Wild Goose Publications, 2013).

36. Richard Bauckham, *Living with Other Creatures* (Waco: Baylor University Press, 2010).

37. Bauckham, *Living with Other Creatures*, 232.

38. David L. Clough, *On Animals—Volume I: Systematic Theology* (London: T & T Clark International, 2012).

39. Clough, *On Animals*. 75.

40. A Rocha, 'About A Rocha', http://www.arocha.org/int-en/who.html (accessed 1 March 2016).

Notes to Case Study 7

1. Aotearoa is one of the indigenous Maori names for the landmass that is New Zealand.

2. Over 80 percent of the 2,500 species of native conifers, flowering plants and ferns; all six species of frog; all reptiles; 90 percent of insects; 90 percent of freshwater fish species are endemic; and, of the 245 species of birds breeding in Aotearoa New Zealand before human arrival, 71 percent were endemic. See Jared M. Diamond, 'New Zealand as an Archipelago: An International Perspective', in *Ecological Restoration of New Zealand Islands*, ed. D. R. Towns et al. (Wellington: Department of Conservation, Victoria, University of Wellington, 1990), 3–8.

3. Maori are the indigenous 'first nation' people of Aotearoa.

4. Pakeha are non-Maori New Zealanders.

5. Karioi: Maunga ki te Moana, www.karioimaunga.co.nz (accessed 1 March 2016).

6. Following common practice, the primary method employed by the Department of Conservation (DOC) to reduce predator numbers on the large area which comprises Karioi, was through the aerial application of poison (sodium monofluoroacetate/1080, a naturally occurring toxin, highly toxic to mammals).

Notes to Chapter 14

1. Philippe Reymond, 'Chapter 5: La Mer', in *L'eau, Sa Vie et Sa Signification Dans l'Ancien Testament suppl. Vetus Testamentum* (Leiden: E. J. Brill, 1958).

2. M. Srokosz et al., 'Past, Present, and Future Changes in the Atlantic Meridional Overturning Circulation', *Bulletin of the American Meteorological Society* 93, no. 11 (21 March 2012), 1663–76, accessed 1 March 2016, doi:10.1175/BAMS-D-11-00151.1.

3. Approximately half remains in the atmosphere, leading to global warming, and the rest is taken up by terrestrial vegetation. See Intergovernmental Panel on Climate Change, ed., *Climate Change 2013—The Physical Science Basis: Working Group I Contribution to the Fifth Assessment Report of the IPCC* (Cambridge: Cambridge University Press, 2014), accessed 1 March 2016, http://ebooks.cambridge .org/ref/id/CBO9781107415324.

4. Royal Society (Great Britain), *Ocean Acidification due to Increasing Atmospheric Carbon Dioxide* (London: Royal Society, 2005).

5. For example: Joseph Conrad, *Typhoon*; *The Mirror of the Sea*; and *The Rescue*. See also Bernhard Klein, ed., *Fictions of the Sea: Critical Perspectives on the Ocean in British Literature and Culture* (Aldershot: Ashgate Publishing Limited, 2002).

6. Winston Halapua, *Waves of God's Embrace: Sacred Perspectives from the Ocean* (Norwich: Canterbury Press, 2008).

7. Exceptions include S. P. Bratton, 'Sea Sabbaths for Sea Stewards', in *Environmental Stewardship, Critical Perspectives—Past and Present Series*, ed. R. J. Berry (London: T & T Clark, 2006), 208–12. See also R. D. Sluka et al., 'The Benefits of a Marine Fishery Reserve for Nassau Grouper *Epinephelus Striatus* in the Central Bahamas', *Proceedings of the 8th International Coral Reef Symposium, Panama* 2 (1997), 1961–64.

8. See, for example: *Theological Dictionary of the Old Testament*; *New International Dictionary of Old Testament Theology and Exegesis*; and *Anchor Yale Bible Dictionary*.

9. Reymond, *L'eau, Sa Vie et Sa Signification Dans l'Ancien Testament*.

10. A translation from the French of 'Le sujet est vaste comme la chose elle-même.'

11. Both Meric Srokosz and Richard Bauckham question the idea of stewardship as the appropriate model for the mandate that God gave to humanity. *The care of creation* seems more appropriate terminology as care flows out of love, primarily the love of God. See M. A. Srokosz, 'God's Story and the Earth's Story: Grounding Our Concern for the Environment in the Biblical Metanarrative', *Science & Christian Belief* 20 (2008), 163–74; and Richard Bauckham, *Bible and Ecology: Recovering the Community of Creation* (London: Darton, Longman & Todd, 2010), chap. 1.

12. On the theme of 'chaos' in the Old Testament see R. S. Watson, *Chaos Uncreated: A Reassessment of the Theme of 'Chaos' in the Hebrew Bible* (Berlin: Walter de Gruyter, 2005). There is not space to explore this further here.

13. On a personal note one of us (MS) has had the experience of being on an oceanographic research vessel in the North Atlantic in a Force 11 storm and watching a pod of pilot whales frolicking around the ship in the large breaking waves.

14. The storm that Jesus calms is both real and symbolic—the two are not mutually exclusive categories; see Bauckham, *Bible and Ecology*, 168–71.

15. Jonathan A. Moo, 'The Sea That Is No More: Rev 21:1 and the Function of Sea Imagery in the Apocalypse of John', *Novum Testamentum* 51, no. 2 (2009), 148–67.

16. Bauckham, *Bible and Ecology*, chap. 3.

17. Bauckham, *Bible and Ecology*, 64–72.

18. Nicholas K. Dulvy, Yvonne Sadovy, and John D. Reynolds, 'Extinction Vulnerability in Marine Populations', *Fish and Fisheries* 4, no. 1 (2003), 25–64.

19. 'Japan Tuna Fetches Record \$1.7m', *BBC News*, 5 January 2013, sec. Asia, accessed 1 March 2016, http://www.bbc.co.uk/news/world-asia-20919306.

20. Sluka et al., 'The Benefits of a Marine Fishery Reserve'.

21. IPCC, *Climate Change 2013*; also Chapter 8 of this volume, John Houghton, 'Global Warming, Climate Change, and Sustainability'.

22. Sarah R. Cooley et al., eds., 'Frequently Asked Questions about Ocean Acidification: U.S. Ocean Carbon and Biogeochemistry Program and the UK Ocean Acidification Research Programme, version 2', 24 September 2012, accessed 1 March 2016, www.whoi.edu/OCB-OA/FAQs.

23. Scott C. Doney et al., 'Ocean Acidification: The Other CO_2 Problem', *Annual Review of Marine Science* 1 (2009), 169–92.

24. IPCC, *Climate Change 2013*.

25. Scott C. Doney et al., 'Climate Change Impacts on Marine Ecosystems', *Annual Review of Marine Science* 4 (2012), 11–37.

26. Wieslaw Maslowski et al., 'The Future of Arctic Sea Ice', *Annual Review of Earth and Planetary Sciences* 40 (2012), 625–54; also Doney et al., 'Climate Change Impacts'.

27. Doney et al., 'Climate Change Impacts'.

28. Julia L. Blanchard et al., 'Potential Consequences of Climate Change for Primary Production and Fish Production in Large Marine Ecosystems', *Philosophical Transactions of the Royal Society B: Biological Sciences* 367, no. 1605 (2012), 2979–89.

29. See, for example, Anny Cazenave and William Llovel, 'Contemporary Sea Level Rise', *Annual Review of Marine Science* 2 (2010), 145–73.

30. Henrike Brecht et al., 'Sea-Level Rise and Storm Surges: High Stakes for a Small Number of Developing Countries', *Journal of Environment and Development* 21, no. 1 (1 March 2012), 120–38.

31. Christopher M. Reddy et al., 'Composition and Fate of Gas and Oil Released to the Water Column during the *Deepwater Horizon* Oil Spill', *Proceedings of the National Academy of Sciences* 109, no. 50 (2012), 20229–34.

32. D. J. Bellamy et al., 'Effects of Pollution from the Torrey Canyon on Littoral and Sublittoral Ecosystems', *Nature* 216 (1967), 1170–73.

33. See Geotimes, 'Voyage of the Ducks', http://www.geotimes.org/sept07/article .html?id=nn_ducks.html (accessed 1 March 2016).

34. Donald M. Anderson, Allan D. Cembella, and Gustaaf M. Hallegraeff, 'Progress in Understanding Harmful Algal Blooms: Paradigm Shifts and New Technologies for Research, Monitoring, and Management', *Annual Review of Marine Science* 4 (2012), 143–76.

35. Jocelyn Kaiser, 'The Dirt on Ocean Garbage Patches', *Science* 328, no. 5985 (2010), 1506.

36. Robert D. Sluka, *Hope for the Ocean: Marine Conservation, Poverty Alleviation and Blessing the Nations* (Cambridge: Grove Books, 2012).

37. Sarah E. Lester et al., 'Biological Effects within No-Take Marine Reserves: A Global Synthesis', *Marine Ecology Progress Series* 384, no. 2 (2009), 33–46.

38. A website to start with is Marine Conservation Society, 'Fish Online', www .fishonline.org (accessed 1 March 2016).

39. Katie K. Arkema et al., 'Coastal Habitats Shield People and Property from Sea-Level Rise and Storms', *Nature Climate Change* 3, no. 10 (14 July 2013), 913–18, accessed 1 March 2016, doi:10.1038/nclimate1944.

40. Connor Bailey, 'Ethics, Ecosystems, and Shrimp Aquaculture in the Tropics', in *Values at Sea: Ethics for the Marine Environment*, ed. Dorinda G. Dallmeyer (Athens, GA: University of Georgia Press, 2003), 75–92.

41. A Rocha, www.arocha.org (accessed 1 March 2016).

42. For a longer report on this topic written as part of a project focusing on the 2004 Asian tsunami relief and development, e-mail bob.sluka@arocha.org.

43. Arkema et al., 'Coastal Habitats'.

44. *The Cape Town Commitment: A Confession of Faith and a Call to Action* (Lausanne Movement, 2010; Hendrickson Publishers, 2011.)

Notes to Chapter 15

1. United Nations, *Charter of the United Nations*, 24 October 1945, Article 55, accessed 1 March 2016, http://www.un.org/en/sections/un-charter/chapter-ix/index.html.

2. United Nations General Assembly, 'United Nations Millennium Declaration: Resolution Adopted by the General Assembly. 55/2. September 18, 2000' (New York: United Nations, 2000), accessed 1 March 2016, http://www.un.org/millennium/declaration/ares552e.pdf.

3. 'Sustainable Development Knowledge Platform: Sustainable Development Goals', United Nations. https://sustainabledevelopment.un.org/topics (last accessed 1 March 2016).

4. United Nations, *Millennium Goals and Beyond 2015*, accessed 1 March 2016, http://www.un.org/millenniumgoals/.

5. Tearfund, *Dried Up, Drowned Out 2012 Summary Report* (Teddington: Tearfund, 2012), 6, accessed 1 March 2016, http://www.tearfund.org/en/about_you/campaign/climatechange/driedup/.

6. Tearfund, *Dried up, Drowned Out 2012 Summary Report*.

7. David Barriopedro et al., 'The Hot Summer of 2010: Redrawing the Temperature Record Map of Europe', *Science* 332, no. 6026 (8 April 2011), 220–24.

8. The original boundaries were published in Johan Rockström et al., 'Planetary Boundaries: Exploring the Safe Operating Space for Humanity', *Ecology and Society* 14, no. 2 (2009), 32, accessed 1 March 2016, http://www.ecologyandsociety.org/vol14/iss2/art32. The model was refined, taking into account newer scientific studies in Will Steffen et al., 'Planetary Boundaries: Guiding Human Development on a Changing Planet', *Science* 347, no. 6223 (2015), accessed 1 March 2016, http://www.sciencemag.org/content/347/6223/1259855, doi:10.1126/science.1259855.

9. From Steffen et al., 'Planetary Boundaries: Guiding Human Development on a Changing Planet', reprinted with permission from AAAS.

10. Global Footprint Network, http://www.footprintnetwork.org/ (accessed 1 March 2016).

11. WWF International, *Living Planet Report 2014 Summary* (Gland, Switzerland: WWF International, 2014), accessed 1 March 2016, http://assets.wwf.org.uk/downloads/living_planet_report_2014_summary.pdf?_ga=1.75807440.45955648 7.1422888956, 3.

12. WWF International, *Living Planet Report 2014 Summary*, 13.

13. Joseph A. Tainter, *The Collapse of Complex Societies* (Cambridge: Cambridge University Press, 1988); Jared Diamond, *Collapse: How Societies Choose to Fail or Survive* (London: Allen Lane, 2005).

14. Diamond, *Collapse*, 211–76.

Notes to Case Study 8

1. David Leake, *Under an Algarrobo Tree* (Worthing: Loxwood Press, 2012).

2. Adrián Gustavo Zarrilli, 'El Oro Rojo: La Industria Del Tanino En La Argentina (1890–1950)', *Silva Lusitana* 16, no. 2 (2008), 239–59.

3. Lucas Seghezzo et al., 'Native Forests and Agriculture in Salta (Argentina), Conflicting Visions of Development', *The Journal of Environment & Development* 20, no. 3 (2011), 252.

Notes to Chapter 16

1. Breakthrough Partners, *Wholistic Discipleship Training: Samaritan Strategy Africa*, accessed 1 March 2016, http://www.breakthroughpartners.org/how-to-engage /learn-more/white-papers.aspx#holisticministry, 1.

2. World Agroforestry Centre, *Eastern and Central African Policy Brief No. 3*, 2005.

3. United Nations Human Settlements Programme, *The Challenge of Slums: Global Report on Human Settlements, 2003* (London: Earthscan Publications, 2003), xxv.

4. World Agroforestry Centre, *Eastern and Central African Policy Brief*.

5. K. Mwambazambi, 'Environmental Problems in Africa: A Theological Response', *Ethiopian Journal of Environmental Studies and Management* 3, no. 2 (2010), accessed 1 March 2016, http://www.ajol.info/index.php/ejesm/article/view File/59827/48101.

6. The Green Belt Movement, http://www.greenbeltmovement.org/ (accessed 1 March 2016).

7. James Morgan, 'Kenya's Heart Stops Pumping', *BBC*, 29 September 2009, sec. Africa, accessed 1 March 2016, http://news.bbc.co.uk/1/hi/world/africa/8057316.stm.

8. Bryant L. Myers, *Walking with the Poor: Principles and Practices of Transformational Development* (Maryknoll, NY: Orbis Books, 1999).

Notes to Chapter 17

1. United Nations, 'Executive Summary', in *World Urbanization Prospects: The 2011 Revision* (New York: United Nations, 2012), 1.

2. Institute for Global Futures, *China's Population & Megacities*, December 2010.

3. Gerald C. Nelson et al., *Food Security, Farming, and Climate Change to 2050: Scenarios, Results, Policy Options*, vol. 172 (International Food Policy Research Institute, 2010).

4. See World Wide Fund International, *Living Planet Report 2012: Biodiversity, Biocapacity and Better Choices* (Gland, Switzerland: WWF International, 2012), which analyses consumption in terms of ecological footprint, or the 'area of land and productive oceans' needed 'to produce renewable resources and absorb CO_2 emissions'. Currently the global ecological footprint is about 1.6 times what the Earth can support.

5. UN, *World Urbanization Prospects*, 17–25.

6. Francis Schaeffer, *Death in the City* (London: IVP, 1969).

7. A phrase from another of Schaeffer's books, Francis A. Schaeffer, *Pollution and the Death of Man; the Christian View of Ecology* (Wheaton, IL: Tyndale House Publishers, 1970).

8. The Third Lausanne Congress on World Evangelization, *The Cape Town Commitment: A Confession of Faith and a Call to Action* (Lausanne Movement, 2010), I-7-A, accessed 1 March 2016, http://www.lausanne.org/content/ctc/ctcommitment.

9. UK Government Office for Science, 'Migration and Global Environmental Change: Final Project Report', The Government Office for Science, London, October 2011.

10. Asian Development Bank, *Addressing Climate Change and Migration in Asia and the Pacific* (Mandaluyong City, Philippines, 2012).

11. Matt 25:35; Steven Bouma-Prediger and Brian J. Walsh, *Beyond Homelessness: Christian Faith in a Culture of Displacement* (Grand Rapids, MI: W. B. Eerdmans Pub, 2008), 273.

12. Craig Van Gelder, *The Essence of the Church: A Community Created by the Spirit* (Grand Rapids, MI: Baker Books, 2000), 31.

13. The Economist, *Special Report: China's Economy—Pedalling Prosperity* (London: The Economist, 26 May 2012), accessed 1 March 2016, http://www.economist.com/sites/default/files/20120526_chinas_economy.pdf.

14. Gerda Wielander, 'Beyond Repression and Resistance—Christian Love and China's Harmonious Society', *The China Journal* 65 (January 2011), 119–39.

15. Future Agenda, 'Local Foods', http://archive.futureagenda.org/pg/cx/view#419 (accessed 1 March 2016).

16. Vertical farming is growing food in high-rise urban buildings and greenhouse stacking systems. See Dickson Despommier and Majora Carter, *The Vertical Farm: Feeding the World in the 21st Century*, reprint ed. (New York: Picador, 2011); Agri-Food & Veterinary Authority (AVA) Singapore, 'Farming Vegetables Skywards', March 2011.

17. Prepared by members of a number of Singapore churches.

18. Asian Development Bank, 'Stockholm World Water Week: The Water-Food-Energy Nexus' (24 August 2012), accessed 1 March 2016, http://www.adb.org/features/water-food-energy-nexus.

19. Dr Ho Hua Chew, 'By Invitation: Preserving Singapore's Green Heartland', *Straits Times*, 14 July 2012.

20. Bouma-Prediger and Walsh: *Beyond Homelessness*, 179–81.

21. 'Informal Settlements and Affordable Housing' (Surabaya, Indonesia, 17 November 2005), accessed 1 March 2016, http://www.cibworld.nl/site/searchn/results.html?offset=20&wtgtype=W&wtgrid=28&wtgtypef=&wtgridf=&pth=&pthf=&year=&q=.

22. *Third space* refers to places that are freely open to the public and are distinct from home and workplaces.

23. Gawad Kalinga, Community Development Foundation, 'Infrastructure'. http://gk1world.com/newInfrastructure (accessed 1 March 2016).

24. United Nations Environment Programme, *Overview of the Republic of Korea's National Strategy for Green Growth* (Geneva: UNEP, April 2010).

25. Church of England Newspaper, 30 May 2010.

26. UCA News, 'Saving the Planet in Faith and Practice', http://www.ucanews.com /news/saving-the-planet-in-faith-and-practice/52175 (accessed 1 March 2016).

27. See Franklin Hiram King, *Farmers of Forty Centuries: Or, Permanent Agriculture in China, Korea and Japan* (Mrs F. H. King, 1911). Mottainai Movement is derived from a Japanese term meaning 'a sense of regret concerning waste when the intrinsic value of a resource is not properly recognised'.

28. Urban Redevelopment Authority and Ministry of Community Development, Youth and Sports, 'New Guidelines on Allowable Spaces for Religious Activities', Ministry of Social & Family Development, Singapore, 12 June 2012.

29. Jay E. Gary, 'The Future of Business as Mission: An Inquiry into Macro-Strategy', in *Business as Mission: From Impoverished to Empowered*, ed. Tom A. Steffer and Mike Barnett, vol. 14, Evangelical Missiological Society Series (Pasadena, CA: William Carey Library, 2006), 261–64. 'Conventional future' is the future of the mainstream, dominant culture; 'counter future' opposes this by protest and rebellion; 'creative future' offers a radical alternative, growing out of and modelling kingdom values.

30. Walter Brueggemann, *Journey to the Common Good*, 1st ed. (Louisville, KY: Westminster John Knox Press, 2010), 98, discussing the Babylonian exile. This theme is explored in the context of the Roman Empire in Brian J. Walsh and Sylvia C. Keesmaat, *Colossians Remixed: Subverting the Empire* (Downers Grove, IL: IVP, 2004).

31. See Global Footprint Network website for a definition of this and case studies of ecological footprint calculations for cities, http://www.footprintnetwork .org/ (accessed 1 March 2016).

32. See Michael Green, *Church without Walls: A Global Examination of Cell Church* (Carlisle: Paternoster, 2002) with a review of cell churches in Singapore and Malaysia.

33. See Bill McKibben, *Deep Economy: Economics as If the World Mattered* (Oxford: Oneworld, 2008) for an analysis of the impacts of industrial faming on rural communities in the USA and China. This often relies on government subsidies for fertiliser etc and aims to maximise short-term productivity at the expense of soil conservation and local employment. Excessive use of fertilisers is a widespread problem in China and elsewhere, causing eutrophication in adjoining waterways and so reducing their fish yields. McKibben gives descriptions of local responses, such as 'farmer-run schools'—see McKibben, *Deep Economy*, 70.

34. This iterative approach to training is described (in the context of India) in Paul R. Gupta and Sherwood G. Lingenfelter, *Breaking Tradition to Accomplish Vision: Training Leaders for a Church-Planting Movement: A Case from India* (Winona Lake, IN: BMH Books, 2006).

35. Timoteo Gener et al., eds., *The Earth Is the Lord's: Reflections on Stewardship in the Asian Context* (Mandaluyong City, Philippines: OMF Literature, 2011).

36. Athena E. Gorospe, 'Evangelicals and the Environment: Going Beyond Stewardship', *Evangelical Review of Theology* 37, no. 3 (July 2013).

37. More recent examples are discussed by Steve Addison, *Movements that Change the World* (Smyrna, DE: Missional Press, 2009).

38. Third Lausanne Congress, *Cape Town Commitment*, I-7-A.

39. Richard Bauckham, 'Ecological Hope in Crisis?' *Anvil* 29, no. 1 (September 2013), 43–54, accessed 1 March 2016, doi:10.2478/anv-2013-0004. Reprinted as Chapter 3 in this volume.

Notes to Chapter 18

1. Andy Crouch, 'Being Culture-Makers', *InterVarsity StudentSoul*, 19 January 2007, accessed 1 March 2016, http://studentsoul.intervarsity.org/andy-crouch.

2. *Cape Town Commitment,* I-10-B (Lausanne Movement, 2010; Hendrickson Publishers, 2011).

3. The term *paracletic change agent* is derived from the related Greek words *paraklesis* and *parakletos* which have no direct equivalents in English. *Paraklesis* conveys the ideas of 'exhortation', 'encouragement', 'comfort', and 'challenge'; *parakletos* (one who engages in *paraklesis)* is an advocate, counselor or helper: this term is frequently applied to the Holy Spirit (eg John 14:16–17). For more information see Susan Emmerich, 'Fostering Environmental Responsibility on the Part of the Watermen of the Chesapeake Bay: A Faith and Action Research Approach', in *Mutual Treasure: Seeking Better Ways for Christians and Culture to Converse*, by Harold Heie and Michael King (Telford, PA: Cascadia Publishing House, 2009).

4. *Cape Town Commitment*, II-5.

5. *Cape Town Commitment*, I-4.

6. Wording came from discussion with Lowell Bliss, Director of Eden Vigil, on October 18, 2012.

7. *Cape Town Commitment*, I:8:B

8. *Cape Town Commitment*, I-8-B.

9. *Cape Town Commitment*, I-10.

10. *Cape Town Commitment,* I-7-A.

11. 'Chesapeake Bay Blue Crab Population Reaches Highest Level in 20 Years', *Chesapeake Bay News*, 19 April 2012, accessed 1 March 2016, http://www.chesapeakebay .net/S=0/blog/2012/04.

12. Interview with James 'Ooker' Eskridge, waterman and mayor of Tangier Island, November 2013.

13. Interviews with Carlene Shores and Susan Parks, December 2008.

14. One Tangier family commented that they could not wait to get to heaven because it was going to be just like Wal-Mart.

15. The story of the Pennsylvania farmers and their covenant is told in the film *When Heaven Meets Earth.* For the film's trailer and all covenants and other research materials and papers written on the subject go to http://whenheavenmeetsearth .org/ (accessed 1 March 2016).

16. For more detail, see Emmerich, 'Fostering Environmental Responsibility on the Part of the Watermen of the Chesapeake Bay'.

17. *Cape Town Commitment*, 1-10-B.

18. The author would like to thank Charles Emmerich, Lowell Bliss, and Vern Visick for insightful discussions and suggestions in the writing of this chapter.

Notes to Conclusion

1. Lausanne Movement, 'Lausanne Global Consultation on Creation Care and the Gospel: Call to Action' (St Ann, Jamaica: Lausanne Movement, 2012), accessed 1 March 2016, http://www.lausanne.org/content/statement/creation-care-call-to -action.

2. *The Cape Town Commitment: A Confession of Faith and a Call to Action* (Hendrickson Publishers, 2011; Lausanne Movement, 2010), I-7-A.

3. *Cape Town Commitment.*

4. Artistotle, *Metaphysics,* Book H, 8.6.1045a:8–10.

5. Alister McGrath, 'Breaking the Science-Atheism Bond,' *Beliefnet* August 2005, accessed 1 March 2016, http://www.beliefnet.com/News/Science-Religion /2005/08/Breaking-The-Science-Atheism-Bond.aspx.

6. C. René Padilla, 'Holistic Mission', in Lausanne Movement, *Lausanne Occasional Paper 33: Holistic Mission*, ed. Dr Evvy Hay Campbell (Lausanne Movement, 2004), 11, accessed 1 March 2016, http://www.lausanne.org/wp-content/uploads /2007/06/LOP33_IG4.pdf. Padilla is quoting John Stott here.

7. Vinay Samuel and Chris Sugden, eds., *Mission as Transformation: A Theology of the Whole Gospel* (Oxford: Regnum, 1999), 227f.

8. Jan C. Smuts, *Holism and Evolution* (London: Macmillan, 1926).

9. Francis A. Schaeffer, *Pollution and the Death of Man* (London: Hodder and Stoughton, 1970).

10. Rachel Carson, *Silent Spring* (Boston, MA: Houghton Mifflin, 1962).

11. Jonathan A. Moo and Robert S. White, *Hope in an Age of Despair: The Gospel and the Future of Life on Earth* (Leicester: IVP, 2013).

12. Lausanne Movement, *Jamaica Call to Action.*

13. Lynn White Jr., 'The Historical Roots of Our Ecologic Crisis', *Science* 155 no. 3767 (10 March 1967), 1203–07.

14. Douglas John Hall, *The Steward: A Biblical Symbol Come of Age* (Grand Rapids, MI: W. B. Eerdmans, 1990).

15. Hall, *The Steward.*

16. Lausanne Movement, *Jamaica Call to Action.*

17. Lawrence Ko, unpublished essay.